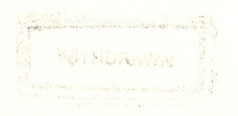

The Critical Response to Anais Nin

The Critical Response to Anais Nin

Edited by
Philip K. Jason

Critical Responses in Arts and Letters, Number 23
Cameron Northouse, Series Adviser

Greenwood Press
Westport, Connecticut • London

Library of Congress Cataloging-in-Publication Data

The critical response to Anais Nin / edited by Philip K. Jason.
     p.   cm.—(Critical responses in arts and letters, ISSN
1057-0993 ; no. 23)
   Includes bibliographical references and index.
   ISBN 0-313-29626-X (alk. paper)
   1. Nin, Anais, 1903-1977—Criticism and interpretation. 2. Women
and literature—United States—History—20th century. I. Jason,
Philip K. II. Series.
PS3527.I865Z594   1996
818'.5209—dc20   96-6344

British Library Cataloguing in Publication Data is available.

Library of Congress Catalog Card Number: 96-6344
ISBN: 0-313-29626-X
ISSN: 1057-0993

First published in 1996

Greenwood Press, 88 Post Road West, Westport, CT 06881
An imprint of Greenwood Publishing Group, Inc.

Printed in the United States of America

The paper used in this book complies with the
Permanent Paper Standard issued by the National
Information Standards Organization (Z39.48-1984).

10 9 8 7 6 5 4 3 2 1

Copyright Acknowledgments

The editor and publisher gratefully acknowledge permission for use of the following material:

Frank Baldanza, "Anais Nin." *The Minnesota Review*, Vol. 2 (Winter 1962). Published at the Department of English, East Carolina University. Copyright (c) 1962 by *The Minnesota Review*. Reprinted with permission of the Editor and Publisher. Copyright 1962.

Oliver Evans, "Anais Nin and the Discovery of Inner Space." Reprinted from *Prairie Schooner* by permission of the University of Nebraska Press. Copyright 1962 University of Nebraska Press. Copyright renewed 1990 by the University of Nebraska Press.

Stephanie A. Demetrakopoulos (Gauper), "Anais Nin and the Feminine Quest for Consciousness: The Quelling of the Devouring Mother and the Ascension of the Sophia." *Bucknell Review*, Vol. 24, No. 1 (Spring 1978). Copyright 1978 by Bucknell University Press. Reprinted by permission of the publisher and the author.

Estelle C. Jelinek, "Anais Nin: A Critical Evaluation." *Feminist Criticism*, edited by Cheryl L. Brown and Karen Olson. Copyright 1978 by Scarecrow Press. Reprinted with permission of Scarecrow Press.

Sharon Spencer, "The Music of the Womb: Anais Nin's 'Feminine Writing.'" *Breaking the Sequence: Women's Experimental Fiction*, eds. Ellen G. Friedman and Miriam Fuchs. Copyright 1989 by Princeton University Press. Reprinted by permission of Princeton University Press and the author.

Stuart Gilbert, "Passion in Parenthesis." *Reading and Collecting*, Vol. 1, No. 12 (November 1937).

Paul Rosenfeld, "Refinements on a Journal." *The Nation*, September 26, 1942. Reprinted with permission from *The Nation* magazine. (c) The Nation Company, L.P.

William Carlos Williams, " 'Men . . . Have No Tenderness': Anais Nin's *Winter of Artifice*." *New Directions No. 7*. Copyright 1941 by William Carlos Williams. Reprinted by permission of New Directions Publishing Corp.

Contents

SERIES FOREWORD by Cameron Northouse   xv

CHRONOLOGY   xvii

INTRODUCTION   1

GENERAL ASSESSMENTS

Anais Nin
Frank Baldanza   9

Anais Nin and the Discovery of Inner Space
Oliver Evans   17

Anais Nin and the Feminine Quest for Consciousness:
The Quelling of the Devouring Mother and the
Ascension of the Sophia
Stephanie A. Demetrakopolous (Gauper)   29

Anais Nin: A Critical Evaluation
Estelle C. Jelinek   45

The Music of the Womb: Anais Nin's "Feminine Writing"
Sharon Spencer   55

NIN'S SHORTER FICTION

Passion in Parenthesis
Stuart Gilbert   67

Refinements on a Journal
Paul Rosenfeld 68

"Men . . . Have No Tenderness": Anais Nin's *Winter of Artifice*
William Carlos Williams 70

Review of *Under a Glass Bell*
Edmund Wilson 75

Review of *Under a Glass Bell*
Isaac Rosenfeld 76

Review of *Under a Glass Bell*
Violet R. Lang 77

The Textual Evolution of the First Section of "Houseboat"
Benjamin Franklin V 80

Discourse and Intercourse, Design and Desire in the
Erotica of Anais Nin
Smaro Kamboureli 89

NIN'S NOVELS

Surrealist Soap Opera
Herbert Lyons 105

Freudian Noah's Ark
René Fülop-Miller 106

Temperament vs. Conscience
Maxwell Geismar 107

Humanity Is the Principle
Malcolm Mudrick 108

Nin: The Topic of Paris
James Korges 111

Contents   *xiii*

Sexuality and the Opposite Sex: Variations on a Theme
by Théophile Gautier and Anais Nin
Paul Brians   118

Lillian Beye's Labyrinth: A Freudian Exploration of
Cities of the Interior
Suzette A. Henke   133

NIN'S *DIARY*

Un Etre Etoilique
Henry Miller   147

The Charmed Circle of Anais Nin
Karl Shapiro   154

Free Women
Patricia Meyer Spacks   158

"Excuse Me, It Was All a Dream": *The Diary of Anais Nin,*
1944-1947
Evelyn J. Hinz   161

The *Diaries* of Anais Nin
Lynn Luria-Sukenick   172

Anais Nin in the *Diary*: The Creation and Development of
a Persona
Duane Schneider   178

Truth and Artistry in the *Diary of Anais Nin*
Joan Bobbit (McLaughlin)   190

Dropping Another Veil: Anais Nin's *Henry and June*
Philip K. Jason   199

A Story Never Told Before – Reading the New, Unexpurgated
Diaries of Anais Nin
Erica Jong   205

NIN HERSELF

Looking Again at Anais Nin
Maxine Molyneux and *Julia Casterton*   215

A Mirror of Her Own: Anais Nin's Autobiographical
Performances
Elyse Lamm Pineau   233

BIBLIOGRAPHY   253

INDEX   269

Series Foreword

Critical Responses in Arts and Letters is designed to present a documentary history of highlights in the critical reception to the body of work of writers and artists and to individual works that are generally considered to be of major importance. The focus of each volume in this series is basically historical. The introductions to each volume are themselves brief histories of the critical response an author, artist, or work has received. This response is then further illustrated by reprinting a strong representation of the major critical reviews and articles that have collectively produced the author's, artist's, or work's critical reputation.

The scope of *Critical Responses in Arts and Letters* knows no chronological or geographical boundaries. Volumes under preparation include studies of individuals from around the world and in both contemporary and historical periods.

Each volume is the work of an individual editor, who surveys the entire body of criticism on a single author, artist, or work. The editor then selects the best material to depict the critical response received by an author or artist of his/her entire career. Documents produced by the author or artist may also be included when the editor finds that they are necessary to a full understanding of the materials at hand. In circumstances where previous isolated volumes of criticism on a particular individual or work exist, the editor carefully selects material that better reflects the nature and directions of the critical response over time.

In addition to the introduction and the documentary section, the editor of each volume is free to solicit new essays on areas that may not have been adequately dealt with in previous criticism. Also, for volumes on living writers and artists, new interviews may be included, again at the discretion of the volume's editor. The volumes also provide a supplementary bibliography and are fully indexed.

While each volume in *Critical Responses in Arts and Letters* is unique, it is also hoped that in combination they form a useful, documentary history of the critical response to the arts, and one that can be easily and profitably employed by students and scholars.

Cameron Northouse

Chronology

1903   Born in Neuilly, France.

1914   Nin, with her mother and two brothers, arrives in New York. While on the ship, she begins keeping her diary.

1923   Marries Hugh Parker Guiler, who, as Ian Hugo, later establishes himself as an engraver and avant-gard filmmaker.

1924   Hugh and Anais set up residence in France.

1931   Meets Henry and later June Miller.

1932   Publishes her first book, *D. H. Lawrence: An Unprofessional Study*. Becomes a patient of Otto Rank.

1934   Writes "Preface" for Miller's *Tropic of Cancer*. Follows Rank to New York and works with him as a lay analyst.

1935   Returns to France.

1936   Self-publishes *House of Incest* through Siana Editions. Returns briefly to New York.

1937-39 Associated with *The Booster* and *Delta* publications of the Villa Seurat circle. Miller's essay on her diary published in *The Criterion*, *The Phoenix*, and in his collection *The Cosmological Eye*.

1939   Brings out *Winter of Artifice* with Obelisk Press. Towards end of year, relocates in New York.

1942   Founds Gemor Press with Gonzalo Moré. In the following years, publishes several of her own works as well as those of others.

1944   Entry on Nin in *Current Biography* helps spur her reputation.

1946   Enjoys first commercial publication, Dutton *Ladders to Fire*.

1946-47 Publishes her manifestos: *Realism and Reality* and *On Writing*.

1947   Meets Rupert Pole.

1948   Begins bi-coastal life with homes (and husbands) in California and New York.

1949   Her father, Joaquin Nin, dies in Cuba.

1950   Dropped by Dutton; Nin's last commercial publication for a decade is the Duell, Sloan and Pierce *The Four-Chambered Heart*.

1954   Her mother, Rosa Nin y Culmell, dies. No longer commercially vi-able, Nin returns to self-publishing with the British Book Centre edition of *A Spy in the House of Love*.

1959   Self-publishes first edition (unpaginated) of *Cities of the Interior*.

1961   Alan Swallow reissues Nin's old titles and bring out new ones.

1964   Swallow publishes *Collages*, Nin's final novel, and reissues the D. H. Lawrence study.

1965   Miller's *Letters to Anais Nin* fans the flames of legend.

1966   First volume of *Diary* appears. Acclaim on swift ascent.

1968   First book-length study of Nin's fiction appears (by Oliver Evans); also, *The Novel of the Future*.

1970   Richard Centing founds newsletter, *Under the Sign of Pisces: Anais Nin and Her Circle*.

1971   Evelyn J. Hinz publishes book-length study of Nin's criticism, fiction, and diaries.

1973   Robert Snyder produces his film *Anais Observed*; Benjamin Franklin V's *Anais Nin: A Bibliography* appears.

1974   Elected to National Institute of Arts and Letters; first complete edition of *Cities of the Interior* published.

1977   Dies, of cancer, in Los Angeles; Sharon Spencer's *Collage of Dreams* appears.

1977-80 *Delta of Venus*, *Little Birds*, and *Linotte: The Early Diary of Anais Nin, 1914-1920* begin the train of posthumous publications.

1978   Rose Marie Cutting's *Anais Nin: A Reference Guide* appears; special Nin issue of *Mosaic*.

1982-83 Richard Centing publishes *Seahorse: The Anais Nin/Henry Miller Journal*.

1983   Gunther Stuhlmann initiates *Anais: An International Journal*.

1986   *Henry and June*, first "unexpurgated" diary volume.

1987   Nin-Miller correspondence published as *A Literate Passion*.

1990   Philip Kaufman's film, *Henry & June*, released.

1992   A novel based on Nin's life, by Elisabeth Barillé, is published in France.

1993   First full-length biography of Nin by Noël Riley Fitch.

1994   Nin conference at Southampton Campus of Long Island University.

1995   Deirdre Bair's biography; first collection of Nin's interviews (edited by Wendy DuBow).

The Critical Response to Anais Nin

Introduction

The history of responses to Anais Nin's writings begins with Waverley Root's *Chicago Tribune* review (Paris edition, March 28, 1932) of her first book, *D. H. Lawrence: An Unprofessional Study*. The review, mischievously titled "The Femininity of D. H. Lawrence Emphasized by Woman Writer,"[1] was followed by a brief mention in the London *Times Literary Supplement* omnibus review called "D. H. Lawrence in Retrospect" (May 5, 1932) in which Nin's effort receives this short paragraph:

> This perceptive feeling could become, in the novels, a realization of women's states of mind which the author of the last book on our list calls androgynous writing. Miss Nin's "unprofessional study" is presented to us as the first book about Lawrence by a woman – a circumstance that, whether important or not, seems to have made it more rather than less appreciative. Indeed, its appreciativeness is so thorough-going and its manner so staccato that it appears more sketchy than perhaps it actually is. For the essay says some pertinent things about the place of dream and fantasy in Lawrence's novels, and the way one should regard his characters; and it treats him as a poet of intuitive experiences.

The theme of Nin's writing appearing to be more sketchy than perhaps it actually is runs through the critical commentary that has gathered over the last sixty-five years. The equivocating "perhaps" reminds us that many critics have found in Nin's writing somewhat less than meets the eye, and certainly no more. Another critical theme emerges from the linkage of the words "first" and "woman," for Nin made a career of her esthetic femininity or femaleness, establishing herself as a trailblazer and helping to shape the terms of critical discourse around the issue of a genre of gender.

This interest in a new feminine writing affects Nin criticism, then, almost from the beginning; it is at the heart of the early commentaries by Isaac Rosenfeld and William Carlos Williams. With the publication of Nin's *Diary* volumes, this aspect of Nin's contribution began to receive additional scrutiny. Her life-long project was judged, in part, as a unique contribution to the literature of feminine sensibility. The publication of her erotic stories (in *Delta of Venus* and *Little Birds*) provided a unique body of material and a new dimension to the inquiry into female writing, spurring major essays by Judith Roof, Cathy Schwichtenberg, and Karen Brennan. In the present volume, the contribution by Smaro Kamboureli represents this area of critical concern. The unexpurgated *Diary* volumes continue to spur comment on woman's sensual experience and its literary record; Erica Jong's appraisal celebrates the significance of these volumes.

Critical writings about Anais Nin cluster around this issue of "feminine writing" and several other issues. The first is Nin's argument with literary realism and the consequences of her esthetic position on her own creative efforts. Nin first argued her own case in *Realism and Reality* and *On Writing*, two pamphlets of the mid-forties.[2] James Korges, for one, believes that Nin is a victim of her ideas about fiction. Just what those ideas are is best covered in Evelyn J. Hinz's book, which helps readers and critics see Nin in the best light of her own intentions. Hinz interprets the importance of Nin's Lawrence study and *The Novel of the Future*. Her essay-review on *Diary IV* encapsulates this argument, while Oliver Evans's essay is an earlier, more conventional, but important step in this direction.

This debate over realism and reality includes the somewhat smaller topic of Nin's particular brand of psychological realism. Thus, discussions of Nin's intentions and affinities include those responses that view Nin's work in the light of the European Surrealist and Symbolist movements as well as the international modernist development of the "poetic novel"(just as often called the "psychological novel") in which temporal (or chronological) maps of experience give way to lyrical and spatial modes of organization. Sharon Spencer's work is important here (beginning with her 1971 *Time, Space and Structure in the Modern Novel*), as is that of her mentor, Anna Balakian.

Such explorations already bring into focus a concern with genre. Just what *kind* of art is Nin creating and by what standards should it be assessed? This concern becomes further complicated in Nin's case because of the interrelationship of her diaries and her fiction. Even while Nin's first volumes of fiction were coming into print, Henry Miller was trumpeting the diaries. Some reviewers of Nin's fiction, like Paul Rosenfeld, can not divorce their assessment of Nin's fiction from their realization that the fictions were drawn from the diaries. Frank Baldanza, a critic who has mostly negative things to say about Nin's fiction, notes the hazard of attempting to assess "the failure of the fiction without taking into account the effect of the diary-writing habit on her art." From the beginning, critical responses to Nin's stories and novels had a biographical slant.

Once the volumes of *The Diary of Anais Nin* (and later titles drawn from diary writing) finally became available, assessments of the fiction became only more complicated because of the obvious and available parallels. At the same time, Nin's *Diary* came to be viewed as her primary contribution to literature. Slowly, attention to the fiction faded. By the 1980s most Nin criticism centered on the *Diary*. Here, too, the issue of genre provides the basis of argument and assessment. Critics have put various complexions on the rewriting and editing process by which the *Diary* has come to the public. The essays by Lynn Luria-Sukenick, Duane Schneider, Joan B. McLaughlin, and myself represent a spectrum of opinion on this issue. Are we finally reading retrospective autobiography, imaginative fictions spun out of a woman obsessed with self-creation, or a new kind of writing for which we have no name?

These and other issues receive elaborate treatment in six major critical monographs: Oliver Evans's *Anais Nin* (1968); Evelyn J. Hinz's *The Mirror and the Garden: Realism and Reality in the Writings of Anais Nin* (1971, rev. 1973); Sharon Spencer's *Collage of Dreams* (1977, rev. 1981); Bettina L. Knapp's *Anais Nin* (1978); Benjamin Franklin V and Duane Schneider's *Anais Nin: An Introduction* (1979); and Nancy Scholar's *Anais Nin* (1984). The admirable biographies by Noël Riley Fitch (1993) and Deirdre Bair (1995) illuminate many of the shadowy corners of Nin's life while presenting new perspectives on the nature and role of the diaries. Elisabeth Barillé provides uncanny insights on Nin in her loosely biographical novel (1991 in French, English translation 1992). Of course, Henry Miller's several biographies must attend to his relationship with Nin. Nin's own voice is best heard in Wendy M. DuBow's *Conversations with Anais Nin* (1994). Inevitably, Nin is a subject (or target) in countless memoirs by other writers and artists. The several pages on Nin in James Broughton's *Coming Unbuttoned* (1993) are a case in point. A forthcoming collection of memoirs about Nin, prepared by Benjamin Franklin V, should tell us even more about the woman behind the artist.

Indeed, for many who have considered her career, Nin the personage, the personality, is of greater consequence than Nin the artist. Writing in *The New Yorker* (March 1, 1993), Claudia Roth Pierpont finds it impossible to assess *Henry and June* and *Incest* without examining and attacking the Nin whom she thinks is revealed in those volumes. Many critiques (like Estelle Jelinek's) seem to be more about who Nin is than what she wrote. Oliver Evans can't tell his story of coming to know Nin's works without giving some attention to the impression made by Nin herself. Duane Schneider's examination of the created persona raises questions about measurable (and unmeasurable) distances between the Anais Nin who lived and the Anais Nin who appears in books by an author of the same name. Thus, a brief section on "Nin Herself" seems in order in any gathering of critical responses. The interview by Maxine Molyneux (in "Looking Again at Anais Nin") provides an example of Nin's self-presentation, while Julia Casterton's commentary contemplates Nin's presence and her writings together. Elyse Lamm Pineau examines the ways in which Nin "presents herself as a living text" on the lecture stage, a most important forum in the last decade of her life.

The earliest reviews of Nin's fiction, as is often the case with emerging writers, were written by friends who wanted to give her career a boost. Stuart Gilbert's review of *House of Incest*, included here, is the earliest such piece. Nin notes (in *Fire* 342) that Henry Miller persuaded Gilbert to write the review.[3] Miller's friend Alfred Perlès reviewed the first edition of *Winter of Artifice*, though this review is a far less friendly effort than Gilbert's. At other critical junctures in her career, close friends or would-be friends found opportunities to praise Nin's work. In the present volume, such obvious puff pieces have been kept to a minimum. For example, I have found no good reason to reprint William Burford's essay on Nin now that Deirdre Bair, in her excellent biography, has revealed the extent to which Nin influenced that piece. And yet, because Nin assiduously cultivated friends and acquaintances who could help her find an audience, selecting a body of criticism untainted by the bias of relationship would be next to impossible. Moreover, it would discount the many sincere appraisals by critics whose fond words led to Nin's personal favor. It is no secret and certainly no sin that friends try to help each other. In Nin's case, she has left an unusually detailed trail of information about her relationships with her reviewers; thus we can discover the supportive acts of collusion and manipulation that most writers (if they don't avoid such acts) manage to keep hidden. I felt obliged to include the first of several reviews by that critical titan, Edmund Wilson, even though his brief affair with Nin complicates our assessment of his objectivity. For Henry Miller, I needn't do more than mention his name.

Several fine and seminal essays have been excluded only because they are readily available elsewhere. Foremost among these is the thrice-published "Poetic Reality of Anais Nin" by Anna Balakian. Similarly, the protective review of *This Hunger* by Edmund Wilson and the devastating one by Diana Trilling are easily available to Nin scholars as Nin herself virtually transcribed them in volume 4 of her *Diary* (84-87). Moreover, Trilling's has been reprinted in a collection of her essays, while Gore Vidal's playful, patronizing review of *Diary 4* appears in a similar collection of his work. An editor working with space (and cost) limitations needs to take advantage of such easy outs. Indeed, considerations of space have led me, regretfully, to exclude commentary on Nin's own criticism. For insights on her critical formulations, students should consult Patricia A. Deduck's book comparing the fictional theories of Nin with those of Alain Robbe-Grillet as well as the relevant chapters in the monographs by Hinz and Franklin/Schneider.

The principle of selection has been to establish a network of contrasting views while including comment from each decade from the 1930s to the present one. In this way, the undertaking differs considerably from Robert Zaller's *A Casebook on Anais Nin* (1974) which is admittedly "a book that makes a case" (xiv). Whenever feasible, I have pushed this objective to an extreme, juxtaposing reviews or essays that implicitly or explicitly argue with one another. Thus, the 1962 essays by Oliver Evans and Frank Baldanza establish the extremes of appreciation and denigration that followed Alan Swallow's courageous publication of most of Nin's extant writings. The Edmund Wilson / Isaac Rosenfeld positions on Nin form (as James Korges notes) part of an ongoing cultural debate waged in their respective forums. Maxwell Geismar and Malcolm Mudrick present sharply differing perspectives on *A Spy in the House of Love* (with Paul Brians offering an extended examination of Nin's handling of sexuality in that novel). Lynn Luria-Sukenick and Joan B. McLaughlin argue (it would seem) over the issue of honesty and authenticity in Nin's *Diary* volumes; Duane Schneider's assessment provides a middle ground. Estelle C. Jelinek and Sharon Spencer engage us in determining the nature and consequence of Nin's feminism.

A good deal of important Nin criticism has as its source Nin's own interest in psychoanalysis. Indeed, it would be possible to gather enough material on Nin related to psychoanalytic theory to fill a hefty volume. Such orientations are represented in the present collection by Stephanie A. Gauper (for Jung) and Suzette A. Henke (for Freud). For the more direct and profound influence of Otto Rank, students should consult articles by Sharon Spencer, Margaret Lee Potts, and myself listed in the bibliography.

After careful consideration, I decided to avoid reproducing excerpts from the six critical monographs. These studies should be readily available to interested scholars and are best read in their entirety. Of the six, the first three should be considered trailblazers. Evans's book, while conventional in its approach, allowed Nin to be taken seriously by academics. Hinz's study provides a much deeper understanding of Nin's critical perspective and her objectives as an artist. Sensing the ways in which Nin's fiction was all of a piece, Hinz sets aside Evans' book by book approach and builds chapters that instead examine Nin's themes and her unusual handling of the elements of fiction. Like Hinz, Spencer prefers to build chapters around issues rather than specific works. Her contributions include sketching the psychoanalytic insights that energize Nin's vision and placing her art in the context of European modernism. These three critics, along with Knapp – whose treatments of *House of Incest* and the *Cities* sequence are rich and provocative – tend to overvalue Nin's achievement. In spite of making solid contributions to our understanding of Nin's art, each suffers from the kind of thoroughgoing appreciativeness that the *TLS* author objected to in Nin's book on Lawrence. A steadier assessment of strengths and weakness is found in the volume by Franklin and Schneider, while Nancy Scholar perhaps goes too far in the direction of belittling her subject even while raising crucial questions.

A reader of the present collection may well wonder why I have not arranged the criticism under the titles of specific works by Nin, as is customary in such endeavors. The main reason is that Nin criticism has not taken such a path. While several of the monographs are so chaptered, most Nin scholarship cuts across titles to pursue issues or continuing characters. This dominant approach is in keeping with Nin's frequent assertion that her various publications are parts of a unified, ongoing work. Another reason is that

Nin's canon, if we put aside the three collections of occasional pieces, the book on Lawrence, and *The Novel of the Future*, is now comprised of fourteen diary volumes, six novels, two collections of short stories, two collections of erotica, a collection of novellas, and a prose poem. These twenty-seven volumes defeat any attempt at a representative criticism subordinated to book titles, were such a body of criticism available. Once we get beyond reviews, we most often find essays like Gauper's, which consider *Diary* materials and fiction together, or like Henke's, which discuss seminal Nin characters (or images, or themes) that appear in several works.

In making selections, I have kept in mind the critical consensus that has named *The Four-Chambered Heart* and *Seduction of the Minotaur* as Nin's most accomplished novels, while *A Spy in the House of Love* has been the most successful with readers and publishers. Thus, essays are included here that give these works extended attention. The shorter discussions of other titles (found in passages within essays I have selected) may be located by consulting the "Index," while a perusal of the "Bibliography" will lead interested students to the wide range of Nin criticism.[4]

Brief explications of specific texts can be found in the trailblazing periodical *Under the Sign of Pisces: Anais Nin and Her Circle* and its successor, *Seahorse: The Anais Nin/Henry Miller Journal* (both masterminded by Richard Centing), while somewhat longer single-work explorations appear in the indispensable annual *Anais: An International Journal*, presided over by Gunther Stuhlmann. Students will also wish to consult the *Journal of the Otto Rank Association*, issues of which contain many contributions of interest to Nin scholars. Aside from the Zaller collection cited earlier, two other volumes of Nin criticism demand attention: Evelyn J. Hinz's *The World of Anais Nin: Critical and Cultural Perspectives* (1978), and Sharon Spencer's *Anais, Art, and Artists* (1986). As I write, Suzanne Nalbantian is putting the finishing touches on a collection of new essays, many of which grew out of papers presented at a Nin conference held at the Southhampton Campus of Long Island University in May of 1994. Anne Salvatore is gathering new essays for a volume on Nin's fiction. None of these collections attempts the historical perspective of the present endeavor. Key resources for studying Nin's critical fortunes are Rose Marie Cutting's *Anais Nin: A Reference Guide* (1978) and my own *Anais Nin and Her Critics* (1993). Benjamin Franklin V's *Anais Nin: A Bibliography* (1973) is still the standard (but now seriously outdated) treatment of Nin's publications in English. Richard Centing is preparing a comprehensive bibliography of writings about Nin.

The record shows that critical interest in Anais Nin and her writings has not flagged in the almost twenty years since her death. If anything, it has increased. The contours of the critical response over her long career, as represented by the selections gathered in the present volume, leave Nin and her reputation somewhat enigmatic. Even those critics who don't take her seriously cannot bring themselves to ignore her. Her life – as rendered into art first in her diary and then distilled and transformed into her fiction and then selectively reconfigured in the first series of published *Diary* volumes and more recently revealed in the "unexpurgated" *Diary* volumes – has achieved the endless fascination and mystery of a paradigmatic creative act. It seems impossible to approach and judge her art within the covers of individual books. Her creations won't let go of her, and yet they seem to be in the service of a deep-seated and sharable drive toward liberation.

Writing in 1932, Otto Rank, Nin's mentor (and short term lover), imagined a new epoch, a new type of humanity, in which people with creative power would renounce "artistic expression in favour of the formation of personality" (430).[5] Creative energies would be put in the service of "personality-creation" (431) while the historic sacrifice of life itself to the obsessive, neurotic creation of artwork would vanish. To put it another way, creativity and living would be identical processes. To understand the career of Anais Nin is to recognize (without necessarily accepting) the power of such a proposition.

NOTES

[1]Reprinted as "Literary Sexism in Action" in *Anais: An International Journal* 6 (1988): 75-76.
[2]Collected in *The Mystic of Sex and Other Writings*, ed. Gunther Stuhlmann. Santa Barbara: Capra Press, 1995.
[3]New York: Harcourt Brace & Company, 1995.
[4]The "Bibliography" is highly selective on book reviews, fairly comprehensive on books, book chapters, and articles in periodicals.
[5]*Art and Artist*. Trans. Charles Francis Atkinson. New York, 1932; rpt. New York: W. W. Norton, 1989. This edition has a foreword by Nin. The first two volumes of Nin's *Diary* as well as the more recently published "unexpurgated" volumes are filled with references to this and other writings by Rank.

General Assessments

Anais Nin

Frank Baldanza

This is coterie writing. It must appeal to the coterie mind because it receives high praise from Henry Miller and Lawrence Durrell, two coterie writers who at one time edited a review with Miss Nin before they broke through to a wider audience. Miss Nin's characters share a pattern of experience with people like Miller (indeed, Jay, the painter who shows up repeatedly in *Cities of the Interior*, bears a very close resemblance to him); one can say with fair confidence, however, that Miss Nin is not likely to make the same literary break-through herself. She printed her own early works on a foot-powered press, and now they have reappeared under the imprint of Alan Swallow of Denver, who would very probably qualify as a coterie printer.

What makes a coterie writer is fierce intransigence against compromise of any sort with commercial or conventional values; Miss Nin herself has said "A real writer only wants his book read by those people who want to read it, and if there are one hundred of them it is enough to keep his work alive and sustain his productivity." If the writer has the power and genius of a Joyce, this intransigence is the tail that wags the dog, since it helped to displace the entire flow of the traditional novel. But if the writer remains, apart from all aims and claims, an exclusively coterie figure, then his fascination for the no-coterie reader must be largely the fascination of failure.

Current Biography informs us that Miss Nin's concert-pianist father, Joaquin Nin, walked out on her and her mother and brothers when she was eleven; she started a diary at that time out of ambivalent impulses – largely in the hope that she could share subsequent experience with her father when he returned, but also out of a baffled desire for companionship. At any rate, the diary became an obsession, and as she piled up volume after volume (it had reached 65 volumes in 1944), friends like Miller warned her that this solipsistic drive could have unfortunate effects. Whether the material for her books is drawn even indirectly from the diaries – and one wonders how it could be otherwise – is not important; it is obvious that the diary habit is one of the basic shaping influences in her work. In the act of self-communion, little attention is given to communication with outsiders; this self-perpetuating activity obviously revels in opulent quantity of production; a female fussiness over detail can easily pass for the rigor of discipline; and there is no need to bother about selection of content, since all reverie is important in this hermetically sealed world. Such incessant daily writing – without editing – would also necessarily congeal stylistic traits into a rigid mold of habit.

Miss Nin is also said to have studied and practiced Spanish dancing and psychoanalysis.

The Swallow edition of *Cities of the Interior* includes "Ladders to Fire" and "Children of the Albatross" (each of which consists of two stories), "The Four-Chambered Heart," "A Spy in the House of Love," and "Solar Barque," all bound in one volume of 789 unnumbered pages. The so-called "line engravings" in this volume (by Ian Hugo, who Miss Nin married in 1920, at the age of 17) add nothing to its appeal.

The stories are pointless, rambling explorations of erotic entanglements and neurotic fears in bohemian Paris, The Village, and Mexico in which many of the same characters recur, nearly always haunted by an organ grinder playing airs from *Carmen*. The handling of characters and incidents is so erratic and baffling that one must assume the writer simply means to spill random impressions onto the page. But where elements of traditional plot adhere to the impressions, the result is an inchoate jumble.

In "This Hunger," Lillian takes up with Gerard (the first in a series of homosexuals to whom Nin heroines turn for their gentleness and sense of fantasy), and then with Djuna, whom she abandons for Jay, who she abandons for Helen, who simply leaves town. A quick miscarriage of Jay's child and a concert close this episode. Lillian's husband, Larry, and the children dropped out of sight early in the story. At the opening of "Bread and the Wafer" Lillian and Jay are living together in Paris; when he brings Sabina home with him, Lillian's jealousy and frustration lead her to spend a night of wild passion with Sabina before the break-up, which is followed by a drunken party at which Lillian disrobes. The focus shifts to Djuna, a dancer, in "The Sealed Room," where a series of relationships with adolescent homosexuals (who typically paint their pet mice turquoise) culminates in an affair with Paul, which gets beyond the gesture usual to these relations – the boy's twining his little finger in Djuna's. "The Four-Chambered Heart" recounts Djuna's years of passion on a leaky houseboat on the Seine with Rango, a primitive Guatemalan whom Djuna raises from a tramp café singer to a minor revolutionary; Rango eventually forces Djuna, however, into nursing his insane wife Zora.

Very few of the characters in Nin fiction carry a surname – and those are all in "Solar Barque." The *cognoscenti* undoubtedly find much of their pleasure in identifying the real-life counterparts; for the outsider, at least, these characters have a history, which they habitually reveal in a sudden, long speech (" 'I was born in the most utter poverty. My mother lying in bed with consumption. . . .' " " 'Why am I not free? I ran away from my husband and my two little girls many years ago. . . .' " " 'I was about six years old when a brand-new battleship docked at the Brooklyn Navy Yard. All the boys in the neighborhood had been taken to see it but me. . . .' ") The confession inevitably concerns a childhood trauma which splintered the speaker's personality; and it is always in terms of this trauma that the speaker takes an unworthy lover, suffers great agony, or justifies a bedraggled and frayed pattern of irresponsibilities. The failure of discipline in the lives of the characters is ubiquitous; and to the degree that style ought to mirror the content, the manner is appropriate.

For one thing, there comes a point when the continued flamboyant use of sentence fragments simply must mean that the writer will not be bothered by the effort of putting meaning into mature patterns. In choice of words, awkward neologisms are more trouble than they are worth (when characters give a long speech, they "monologize" or they "dissert"). Reliance on large and lazy abstractions indicates a reluctance to render experience in fictional terms ("In watching the moon she acquired the certainty of time by depth of emotion, range and infinite multiplicity of experience"). The rhythms of expression are agglutinative, as must necessarily occur when there are few verbs:

> Golconda of the golden age, the golden aster, the golden eagle, the golden goose, the golden fleece, the golden robin, the goldenrod, the goldenseal, the golden warbler, the golden wattles, the golden wedding, and the gold fish, and the gold of pleasure, the goldstone, the gold thread, the fool's gold.

At the lowest level, there is simple inaccuracy (a French waiter asks a pair of lovers if they wish a *"cabinet particular"*), poor pronoun reference, and insensitivity to syntax and canons of usage.

On the positive side, Miss Nin strives for gaudy, opulent effects in her imagery, but most often manages a shaky structure of gilt and paste that crumbles under direct scrutiny. The figures are usually banal and cliché, and they are badly mixed; pathetic fallacy runs through it all. Take Sabina putting on a cape:

> The toreador's provocative flings, the medieval horsemen's floating flag of attack, a sail unfurled in full collision with the wind, the warrior's shield for his face in battle, all these she experienced when she place a cape around her shoulder.
> A spread out cape was the bed of nomads, a cape unfurled was the flag of adventure.
> Now she was dressed in a costume most appropriate to flights, battles, tournaments.
> The curtain of the night's defencelessness was rising to expose a personage prepared.

> Prepared, said the mirror, prepared said the shoes, prepared said the cape.

Perhaps these qualities are even better illustrated in this sentence: "Debris of stained glass wafted up by the seas, splintered by the radium shafts of the sun and the waves and tides of sensuality covered their bodies, desires folding in every lapping wave like an accordion of aurora borealis in the blood."

"A Spy in the House of Love" is not a peeping-tom in a bordello, but Sabina, who desperately needs to retain the love of her gentle husband Alan along with the "joyous epilepsies" provided on the Provincetown dunes by Philip, the blue-eyed *heldentenor* from the Black Forest who is always bursting out with a "song" from *Tristan*; by John, the frenzied young aviator who has looked into the eyes of the dying; and by Mambo, the Caribbean Negro drummer who is hurt that white women want him only for his tropic flavor. One of Sabina's most acute problems is avoiding letting Mambo see her at the movies with Alan and vice versa. It is difficult enough to remember which films each has already seen or would not want to see, but then the problem becomes incredibly complex when Sabina remembers that one of them might, conceivably, want to see the same film twice. Her motherly capacities are called forth by the chaste embraces of Donald (one of Djuna's young men), after which Sabina meets her crisis of awareness at Mambo's cafe when she re-encounters Jay, home from Paris because of the war. By the combined efforts of Djuna and the "lie detector" who has been shadowing her throughout the story, Sabina decides she has only been the spy in the house of many loves because she has never learned to love. (By another excursion into childhood, we learn that her pathological lying stems from the ambivalence of her playing a motherly and a fatherly role in love, from her enormous capacity for self-deception, and from her inability ever to believe completely in another human being.)

The cloying eroticism lets up a bit in "Solar Barque" in which Lillian has come to a southern resort city in Mexico for an engagement as a jazz pianist. Here she leaves the joyous epilepsies to others as she observes the spiritual torments of Dr. Hernandez, a humanitarian who is shot by dope addicts to whom he refused relief, and Hatcher, an American who attempts to go native, all the while requiring Woolworth napkins and canned goods. The assortment of other characters seems haphazard. Although relatively coherent in their repetition, the images of stratified cities and boats imprisoned on dry land symbolize painfully simple and banal generalizations about time and memory. The sentences are gauche and at one point even spelling is uncertain. The childhood trauma continues to explain everything. The only new elements are the increasingly obtrusive recall of philosophical scraps from Henry Miller and D. H. Lawrence, along with a charmingly boyish toreador whose blue satin trousers are ripped by the bull in a way which the author informs us is very exciting to the lady spectators.

House of Incest seems to have been the most inspiring of the author's works in her immediate circle; it was the subject of a ten-minute avant-garde movie by Ian Hugo, and it suggested many of the images for Henry Miller's *Scenario*, which is inherently a much finer work than the one that inspired it. The House of Incest is that of Jeanne, who bewails her attachment to her brother as she breaks strings on her guitar; there are also a passage about the narrator's passionate experience with Sabina (still swirling her cape), a scene involving Lot and his daughter during the destruction of the Cities of the Plain, a description of pre-natal life, and a description of the narrator's madness and proclivity toward lying. Trains of surrealist images alternate with paragraphs of abstract sentimentalizing. This is a fair sample:

> Semen dried into the silence of rock and mineral. The words we did not shout, the tears unshed, the curse we swallowed, the phrase we shortened, the love we killed, turned into magnetic iron ore, into tourmaline, into pyrate agate, blood congealed into cinnabar, blood calcinated, leadened into galena, oxidized, aluminized, sulphated, calcinated, the mineral glow of dead meteors and exhausted suns in the forest of dead trees and dead desires.

The three stories that comprise *Winter of Artifice* mark the appearance of a figure who strikingly recalls the author's father – alternately an actor and a concert-pianist, he is a great Don Juan, an impeccably dressed, cosmopolitan figure. Stella, the movie-star heroine of a story that bears her name, maintains an abortive affair with Bruno, a married man, and Philip, who may or may not be identical with Sabina's *heldentenor*, but her inability to find satisfaction in these affairs is explained by her reminiscences of the father and of her ambivalent attitude toward him. For the rest, the story is very like all the others; Stella resembles Sabina in her frenzied efforts to keep one lover from tracking down the other; and the gaucheries continue unabated: " . . . that first kiss of which she had been so frightened that at the moment of the miracle, out of panic, nerves, from her delicately shaped stomach came dark rumbling like some long-sleeping volcano becoming active." The story approaches soap opera in the scene in which Stella, in her big movie-star car, turns on the windshield wipers in a moment of high emotional transport, only to discover it is not raining outside. There are tears in her eyes!

The title story, "Winter of Artifice," reviews the unsuccessful reunion of a nameless heroine with a concert-pianist father in his old age, after she has kept a twenty-year diary to chronicle her life during their separation. Both father and daughter recount amorous adventures to each other, but under disguises and evasions so that the father will not appear too unfaithful to his wife, and so that the daughter will retain for the father the fiction that he is the emotional center of her life. The story features a long, italicized surrealist passage in which father and daughter are symbolized by instruments, melodies, and rhythms in symphonic concert.

"The Voice" is a psychiatrist with offices in Hotel Chaotica who hears a series of confessions – from Djuna who is detached from the flow of life; from Lillian, whose lesbian misadventures get a thorough airing; and from Mischa, a cellist whose immobile hand is a psychic disguise to draw attention away from his crippled leg. Then there appears a friend of Djuna's and Mischa's, Lilith, whose fear of consummating her marriage to a simple (but baffled) man is somehow connected with the lifelong ambivalent conflict of feelings for her father, an echo of the first two stories in this volume. As her interviews with The Voice continue, Lilith imagines, despite her satisfying affair with Djuna, that she is coming to love The Voice; he, conversely, finds in her a human warmth that relieves him from the empty professional role of father-seer-god. But we never know, aside from hints of Lilith's revulsion from The Voice as a perspiring human being, what is the outcome. The ending dissolves into another long italicized spate of surrealistic images, including the boat on dry land that haunted Lillian in "Solar Barque," elevators from the hotel, someone whose lungs are made of cocoon milk, and Proust's window.

These three stories can be summarized, perhaps, in a few lines from the last one: "Awareness hurts. Relationships hurt. Life hurts. But to float, to drift, to live in the dream does not hurt." As works of art, these stories refuse to face up to a coherent awareness; they do not provide even an approximation of defining relationships; and they have little to do with life in any way. They float and drift, not even with dream logic – a private, incommunicable nightmare.

Miss Nin's thirteen short pieces, *Under a Glass Bell*, consist primarily of character sketches of mad painters, a mad astrologer, and assorted eccentrics. Once cannot argue with any authors choice of subject; to that degree, once must grant Miss Nin the right to handle these violent, repulsive types. But one can question the quality of sympathy evoked for straightjacket cases. Miss Nin usually presents these persons in a manner that forces the reader to participate directly and wholeheartedly in their fantasies and hallucinations, much like Virginia Woolf's treatment of Septimus Warren Smith in *Mrs. Dalloway*. But here the interior sense of madness is not counterbalanced by the elegant discipline of Mrs. Woolf's prose, nor is there any steadying agent like the motherly Clarissa Dalloway.

"Houseboat" and "The Mouse" concern events on a vessel much like that in "The Four-Chambered Heart." The title story is a surrealist piece about Jeanne (whom we encountered in *House of Incest*) and her two brothers who live in a fantastically decadent house; Jeanne has a vision of death in a mirror, and as she kisses her brother's shadow, another guitar string breaks. Most of the other selections appear to be simply the skeletons of fleeting ideas on which are hung a gaudy and glittering display of surrealist images.

Certainly the most effective piece in this book – indeed, the single most controlled and compelling of all Miss Nin's writings – is the story "Birth," a short, first-person account of bearing a dead six-month child. The story succeeds largely because of the stark directness and economy with which this excruciating experience is related. It must be a minor classic for those who follow Miller's dicta about facing the facts of life in all their bloody detail. It is the one work in all of Miss Nin's production that rises genuinely above vulgarity.

The "brand new" *Seduction of the Minotaur* consists . . . of the text of "Solar Barque" (95 pages) which has been changed, as far as I can determine, only in a few unimportant matters of spacing between paragraphs. The addition of 41 new pages at the end consists of an airplane reverie on the part of Lillian, who is returning from Mexico to White Plains, apparently to rejoin Larry, whom we last encountered in the opening pages of *Cities of the Interior*. Lillian recalls her long affair with Jay (who now seems to resemble Henry Miller more than ever) and the side-issue of her attraction to Sabina (which reinforces the view given in *House of Incest*, that it was largely a passionate spiritual experience, punctuated by one kiss), and her early relation with Gerard. Djuna, too, appears briefly. The Minotaur of the brand new title appears to be the life of the subconscious. Lillian returns to the childhood trauma in accounting for various characteristics of her mature erotic life in terms of the ambivalent pleasure-pain she felt during her stern father's daily spankings of his daughter whom he wanted to be a son. The story closes with a long and inept effort to analyze the reticences and distances of Larry in a metaphorical extension built up around a popularized scientific treatise on the moon. Briefly, Larry's childhood trauma occurred when a Negro nurse, in whose family Larry had found pagan relief from his puritanical parents, reported to his parents that she had observed him and his brother in the bathroom, comparing their bodies. The burden of the analysis is that the shock of the nurse's betrayal has made Larry as distant and cold as the moon.

It would be hazardous to speculate on the relation of this fiction to Anais Nin's diary without the privilege of reading the diary; but it would be equally hazardous to attempt to assess the failure of the fiction without taking into account the effect of the diary-writing habit on her art. A diary is not a work of art, and the very qualities that make a diary most successful are largely antithetical to the aims of art. In "Un Etre Etoilique" (*The Cosmological Eye*) and "More About Anais Nin" (*Sunday After the War*) Henry Miller speaks of the devastating honesty and the complete lack of malice in her journal; of the gargantuan inclusiveness and the complete self-absorption of the reverie; and of the fluid, undersea sinking of the narrative personality, so that each time one thinks the personality has reached rock-bottom, it reveals deeper and darker vistas. Without the disciplined control that is synonymous with art, such honesty becomes vulgarity, the lack of malice seems a lack of standards, the inclusiveness looks flabby, and the self-absorption leaves the reader puzzled and uncertain, since he – by what must be one of the most elementary laws of epistemology – does not share the same self.

Mr. Miller has, of course, a very direct and simple answer to my objection, in the former essay: ". . . in a profound sense, [the diary] *is* the work of art which never gets written – because the artist whose task it is to create it never gets born. We have here, instead of the consciously or technically finished work (which to-day seems to us more than every empty and illusory), the unfinished symphony which achieves consummation because each line is pregnant with a soul struggle." I assume that he would extend the same judgments to her fiction. If so, thank you, but I as a reader cannot interest myself in works of art that never get written by artists who never get born.

I would, however, regret the entire loss of Anais Nin's work, although the exact reason for preserving it is a difficult one to establish. When Henry Miller wrote to a literary agent in defense of the journal, he said "I can think immediately of at least three eminent psychologists who would pounce with avidity on Miss Nin's work were they apprised of its existence. There would be little or no difficulty in securing the support of a medical publication . . . " One could also imagine that cultural historians would be delighted with this document on the folkways of Bohemia. But whatever the reason for preserving this work, it has little to do with literature.

From *The Minnesota Review* 2 (Winter 1962): 263-71.

Anais Nin and the Discovery of Inner Space

Oliver Evans

We are going to the moon. That is not very far. Man has so much farther to go within himself. – Anais Nin

In the spring of 1945, after my discharge from the Air Force, I went to live in New York. My two years of military service I considered wasted except for a few poems I had somehow managed to produce – poems that afforded a temporary escape from the appalling monotony of barracks life – and I was anxious to start living again. I chose New York because it was full of what the places I had been stationed were empty of: color, movement, variety, life; and like so many other young men there with literary leanings I found part-time jobs with book agents and publishers. Though precarious and underpaid, this work was ideal for my purpose: I did not want a full-time job; I wanted to revel in my new liberty, to live in the shining city as fully and as freely as possible.

One day as I was browsing in the Gotham Book Mart my eye fell upon an odd-looking little book entitled *Under a Glass Bell*. It was obviously the product of an amateur press, a collection of short stories with wildly fanciful engravings by an artist named Ian Hugo – but as I leafed through it, reading a paragraph here and there out of what was at first mere idle curiosity, I became increasingly absorbed and astonished. The prose was wonderfully clear and simple, the images accurate and spontaneous. I had never heard of the author, Anais Nin, but I decided I must have the book. That evening and the remainder of the week I ate a little more lightly at the Automat than I would otherwise have done, but the sacrifice was justified: I was getting something that did not come out of a slot, and though it is hard for me to say precisely what it was, it somehow involved the idea of freedom. For as I read the stories in this book I was struck, more than anything else, by their extraordinary airiness; by the impression they gave of being somehow dimensionless, and thus illimitable, unconfined, and unrestrained; and by their serene independence of the conventions of ordinary fiction. I suppose it was inevitable, reading her at that particular time in the shining city, that I should have made some sort of connection between the freedom of this author's technique and that of my own personal situation. In any case, ever since that spring, seventeen long years ago, Anais Nin has constituted for me a symbol of freedom, excitement, and discovery.

It could not have been much later than this, perhaps the following year, that I saw her name, again in the Gotham Book Mart, on the cover of a pamphlet entitled *Realism versus Reality* [sic], which turned out to be an essay defending her theory of fiction. My copy of this pamphlet (which unfortunately is out of print) disappeared at least ten years ago, but I remember that in it she accused the ordinary realistic novel of superficiality, of being concerned with only the external aspects of existence and character. It was not enough, she declared, merely to record the actions and words of a character, since much of the time people act and speak to conceal their deepest feelings, and the realists who believed they were depicting the natural man were only depicting impersonations. The novelist of the future was to concern himself not with realism but with reality, with discovering the secret self (or selves) beneath the apparent one, with exposing the hidden behind the obvious motive. Thus dreams, daydreams, and fantasies become enormously important as clues to the inner self; the process of free association is more revealing than that of conscious thought; and we learn more about the characters from interior monologues than from the speeches which they exchange with one another.

These ideas were not altogether new to me; they were in the air at the time. I knew that they represented the application to literary theory of some of the principles of Freudian psychology, and that they had already been practiced, at least to some extent, by Proust, Joyce, Woolf, and even Faulkner. But I had never seen them stated in so many words, with such directness and clarity, and they enabled me to view the strange little stories in *Under a Glass Bell* (for notwithstanding my delight I *had* found them strange) in the light of the author's intention – an opportunity for which any reader should be grateful, particularly in the case of a writer as unconventional as Miss Nin, whom it would obviously be unjust to judge by standards she neither respects nor acknowledges. I felt, too, that her prophecy concerning the future of the novel might possibly, some day, be fulfilled.

In 1947, tiring of hack work, I accepted a teaching job at a Midwestern university where I remained for three years and published my first book, a collection of poems. During this time I read only one of Miss Nin's works, a short story titled "Hejda" which appeared in George Leyte's beautiful but short-lived *Circle*. It depicted, with unusual penetration, the relationship of an Arab girl and her Roumanian artist-lover in the Paris Latin Quarter, and it made a profound impression on me; I still think it one of her very best. I was especially interested in her theory of characterization, of arriving, sometimes in a very few words, at the *essence* of a character, either by means of symbol, or by a deliberate flatness, an abstractness of statement that is somehow peculiarly effective:

> A part of her wants to expand. A part of her wants to stay with Molnar. This conflict tears her asunder. The pulling and tearing brings on illness.
> Hejda falls.
> Hejda is ill.
> She cannot move forward because Molnar is tied, and she cannot break with him.
> Because he will not move, his being is stagnant and filled with poison. He infects her every day with his poison.

I spent my summer vacations in New Orleans, and it was here, in either 1948 or 1949, that I conceived the idea of a group of little stories with a French Quarter setting in which I would attempt to practice some of Miss Nin's theories. Conveniently for me, Mr. Tennessee Williams, whom I had met in the summer of 1939 and who was spending the summer in a big old apartment on Orleans Street, was suddenly called to New York before the expiration of his lease, and very generously gave me the use of his place, which was ideal for working. I never finished the project, and only one of the stories has ever been published, but the experience enabled me to appreciate some of the problems inherent in Miss Nin's method and to give me a new respect for her achievement.

Meanwhile, I continued to hear rumors about this author: that she had written the preface to Henry Miller's *Tropic of Cancer*; that she printed her own books on a second-hand foot-power press; that she was breathtakingly beautiful; that she had been a fashion model and also a professional dancer; that she had written a book on D. H. Lawrence; that she had practiced psychoanalysis under the direction of Otto Rank; that since early adolescence she had been writing a monumental diary that according to Henry Miller in T. S. Eliot's *Criterion*, "will take its place beside the revelations of St. Augustine, Petronius, Abelard, Rousseau, Proust, and others" (it was then, in 1937, in its fiftieth volume and is now in its one hundred and third). I had, quite understandably, some difficulty in reconciling these disparate bits of information into a single image, and thus Miss Nin, besides being a symbol of freedom, became for me also a symbol of the enigmatic.

The enigma was dispelled when, in 1950, I left the Midwest to teach at the City College of New York and had an opportunity to meet this legendary creature. At least it was partially dispelled: Miss Nin is still something of an enigma to me – but then, as she herself never tires of pointing out, does not every personality present a mystery? Certainly there was no doubt of her beauty. The rumors, however, had not prepared me for the special quality of her charm: I had expected a febrile intelligence, vehement gestures, Niagara-like monologues, eccentricities of dress and behavior. The woman I met was singularly collected; she spoke but little, and her speech had the curious precision of multilinguists; her diminutive, shapely form was clothed simply but elegantly. Her grey-green eyes were enormous and you felt they did not miss very much – they gave the impression of being as innocent as they were beyond surprise, like the eyes in the portrait of Beatrice Cenci that is attributed to Guido Reni.

It was Tennessee Williams who introduced us, and that year I saw a good bit of Miss Nin. We discovered we had a number of friends in common, like Gore Vidal and Olive Leonhardt, and I showed her my poems and New Orleans stories, some of which she was kind enough to read on a radio program. Then I left for Europe, where I remained several years, out of touch with Miss Nin and with most of my American friends. But wherever I went – Paris, Rome, Barcelona, Tangiers – I continued to hear her named mentioned in literary circles, usually with admiration. If Miss Nin's is not a popular audience, it is at least an international one.

2

An understanding of Miss Nin's theory of fiction, as I have suggested, is indispensable for an appreciation of her work, and she has suffered considerable injustice from critics who were unaware of her intentions. To say (as has sometimes been said) that she does not write about life is absurd; she does, but she writes about it on a level to which very few novelists aspire: in her work, the motivation and characterization are enormously complicated, for what interests her is the ultimate motive behind the apparent ones, the genuine self beneath the many false ones. "Man," she has written, "is his own most elusive impersonator . . . we are all Walter Mittys as described by Thurber, going about our daily living while living a secondary, a third, a fourth life simultaneously as heroes of amazing adventures." It should be obvious that, where several characters are involved, the fictional possibilities become very near infinite, and I think this explains why in a typical Nin novel a single character (always a woman) is explored in very great detail and others are defined in relation to this character: it is her way of limiting material that would otherwise be inexhaustible. I think it can thus be said that Miss Nin conceives of fiction primarily as characterization: theoretically, she requires only a single character, for the others, though they have dimensions of their own, exist primarily for the purpose of defining the protagonists' – they are fictional satellites.

The comparison with astronomy is inevitable, and this is the kind of astronomy that interests Miss Nin: the relation of the central self to the satellite selves, the relation of the central character (with its satellite selves) to the satellite characters (with *their* satellite selves). It is a kind of space fiction, but it is inner rather than outer space, and the spheres are psychological rather than physical. "They sat rotating around each other like nearsighted planets," she writes of the café habitués in *Children of the Albatross*, "mutating, exchanging personalities." And in her latest novel, *Seduction of the Minotaur*, there is a brilliant image, sustained for several pages, in which man's knowledge of the moon is likened to the protagonist's knowledge of her lover:

It was the year when everyone's attention was focussed on the moon. "The first terrestrial body to be explored will undoubtedly be the moon." Yet how little we know about human beings, thought Lillian. All the telescopes were focussed on the distant. No one is willing to turn his vision inward.

"The moon is the earth's nearest neighbor."

They had slept side by side. In the night, or at dawn, his body had been there. She had felt its radiations. . . . In his goodness, a universe. His attentiveness blinded her. If he had another life, other selves, he turned, like a planet, only one face toward Lillian.

"The moon . . . has never been eroded by earth and water. Furthermore, the circular formations that dominate the moon's topography indicate that its crust has never undergone the violent changes which are involved in mountain-building processes on earth."

Larry had sought to present such an undisturbed surface to Lillian's investigations. But this evenness had been a mask . . .

What had sent Larry so far away from human life into the position of a spectator, so far away from the earth? What had made him wrap himself in an unbreathable atmosphere of selflessness and then be absent from his own body? There were incidents she knew. But she had never co-ordinated them. She was landing for the first time on the planet Larry.

"In any case, a planet would be a cool birth."

His mother had not wanted him to be born. This was the first denial. He had arrived unsummoned by love and jealously resented by his father.

"A cool birth does not exclude the later heating and melting of planetary bodies by radioactive elements they contain."

The child, inhibited by such a "cool birth," had sought warmth by running away from home to the huts of negroes living and working nearby for his father . . .

The child has set his planet's course, has chosen his place in outer space, according to the waves of hostility or fear he had encountered. Pain was the instrument which set him afloat and determined his course. The sun, whether gold, white, or black, having failed him he will exist henceforward in a more temperate zone, twilit ones, less exposed to danger . . .

"The relative smoothness of the lunar surface poses a question."

Much of men's energies were being spent on such questions. Lil-

lian's on the formation of Larry's character. Their minds were fixed
on space; hers on the convolutions of Larry's feelings.

The image, it will be noted, is made even more effective by the contrast
between the matter-of-factness of the scientific observations and the deeply
personal quality of the reflections which they suggest and with which they alternate. This passage is interesting also in that it illustrates the use which the
author is constantly making of her training in psychoanalysis.

"It is necessary," Miss Nin has said, "to travel *inwardly*, to find the levels
at which we carry on, in a free-flowing, immensely rich vein, the uninhibited
inner monologue in distinction to the controlled manner in which we con-
verse with others." Her collected novels, appropriately titled *Cities of the Interior*, are all concerned with these inward voyages whose destination is the self;
she is the Magellan of this new world, or rather the Pizarro to whom, after
much painful effort, are finally revealed the dazzling riches of a territory of
extraordinary dimensions and a culture of extra-ordinary refinement.

The contrast between the outside and inside world is nowhere more apparent than in *Children of the Albatross*, where it takes the form of a corresponding contrast between the objective and the subjective, the impersonal
and the personal. Here Paul, the youthful lover, takes refuge from the complexities of the personal into the relative simplicity of the impersonal; however, for Djuna, his mistress, escape is neither necessary nor desirable:

> It was then that he practiced as deftly as older men the great ob-
> jectivity, the long-range view by which men eluded all personal diffi-
> culties: he removed himself from the present and the personal by
> entering into the most abstruse intricacies of a chess game, by ex-
> plaining to her what Darwin had written when comparing the eye to
> a microscope, by dissertating on the pleuronectidae or flat fish, so
> remarkable for their asymmetrical bodies.
> And Djuna followed this safari into his worlds of science, chem-
> istry, geology with an awkwardness which was not due to any lazi-
> ness of mind, but to the fact that the large wave of passion which
> had been roused in her at the prolonged sight of Paul's little finger
> was so difficult to dam, because the feeling of wonder before this
> spectacle was as great as that of the explorers before a new moun-
> tain peak, of the scientists before a new discovery . . .
> A study of anthropological excavations made in Peru was not
> more wonderful to her than the half-formed dreams unearthed with
> patience from Paul's vague words . . . and no forest of precious
> woods could be more varied than the oscillations of his extreme
> vulnerability which forced him to take cover, to disguise his feelings,
> to swing so movingly between the great courage and a secret fear of
> pain.
> The birth of his awareness was to her no lesser miracle than the

discoveries of chemistry; the variations in his temperature, the mysterious energy, the sudden serenities, no less valuable than the studies of remote climates.

Miss Nin's preference of the personal to the impersonal, of the subjective to the objective, is her most characteristic attitude to life, amounting almost to an obsession. In *The Four-Chambered Heart* it creates a dilemma that, on a realistic level, is central to the action of the book. Once more the male, Rango, seeks escape from personal problems by submerging himself in the outside world, this time the world of politics:

> It saddened Djuna that Rango was so eager to go to war, to fight for his ideas, to die for them. It seemed to her that he was ready to live and die for emotional errors as women did, but that like most men he did not call them emotional errors; he called them history, philosophy, metaphysics, science. Her feminine self was sad and smiled, too, at this game of endowing personal and emotional beliefs with the dignity of impersonal names. She smiled at this as men smile at women's enlargement of personal tragedies to a status men do not believe applicable to their personal lives.
> While Rango took the side of wars and revolutions, she took the side of Rango, she took the side of love.
> Parties changed every day, philosophies and science changed, but for Djuna human love alone continued. Great changes in the maps of the world, but none in this need of human love, this tragedy of human love swinging between illusion and human life, sometimes breaking at the dangerous passageway between illusion and human life, sometimes breaking altogether . . .
> She smiled at man's great need to build cities when it was so much harder to build relationships, his need to conquer countries when it was so much harder to conquer one heart, to satisfy a child, to create a perfect human life. Man's need to invent, to circumnavigate space when it is so much harder to overcome space between human beings, man's need to organize systems of philosophy when it is so much harder to understand one human being, and when the greatest depths of human character lay but half explored. . . . Man turned his telescope outward and far, not seeing character emerging at the opposite end of the telescope by subtle accumulations, fragments, accretions, and encrustations.
> Woman turned her telescope to the near, and the warm.

Djuna's ideas (which are the author's) remind us irresistibly of Descartes' dictum, "Conquer yourself rather than the world," and even more forcibly, perhaps, of Whitman:

> The earth, that is sufficient,
> I do not want the constellations any nearer,
> I know they are very well where they are,
> I know they suffice for those who belong to them.

The passages I have quoted from *Children of the Albatross* and *The Four-Chambered Heart* show that Miss Nin accepts almost as a fact of anthropology the traditional notion than women are by nature more subjective than men; in her work it is always the male who, as a means of escape, becomes involved in causes and movements, and the woman who accepts the greater challenge, who turns her eyes inward and discovers the truth of her own nature and who seeks to function on the more significant level of personal relationships. It is on this level, of course, that Miss Nin herself prefers to function as an artist, and those critics who (like Edmund Wilson, Lawrence Durrell, and William Carlos Williams) have commented on the strongly feminine quality of her writing, have also, in so doing, implied an acceptance of this notion.

Quite independently of the sex of the authors involved, however, this theme – the quest for self, the search for identity – has come to dominate much, if not most, of the serious fiction that has been written within the last two decades: Miss Nin is perhaps as much of a pioneer in this direction as Sartre, and may even some day come to be regarded as such by literary historians. Where she differs from orthodox existentialist writers is in the finality with which she rejects the outside world, the world of "current events," in the importance that she assigns to dreams and symbols as clues to the essential self. Sartre's characters achieve identity through alignment with forces outside themselves; Miss Nin's through removal of their false selves. In Sartre man defines himself through his choices ("To make oneself, and to be nothing but the self that one has made" is the motto of the French existentialists), while Miss Nin apparently believes that man must first know what he is not before he knows what he is.

3

So much for Miss Nin's intentions. It now remains to show the means by which she seeks to realize them. I have said that she conceives of fiction primarily as characterization, so that her technique concentrates necessarily on a solutions of the problem of character. She solves this problem in two ways: by directly presenting the reader with the symbols encountered in the character's dreams, daydreams, and fantasies; and by analyzing and interpreting these symbols through the methods of psychoanalysis. However, Miss Nin does not herself play the psychoanalyst; she is too subtle a writer for that. The revelation of character that results from such analysis is achieved either independently, through a series of experiences leading to self-knowledge, or through the assistance of other characters.

The practice of revealing the true identity of a character by divesting him of his outer selves has curiously enough, more in common with that of certain nineteenth-century novelists who did not hesitate to tell the reader, in so many words, what their characters were like – to *judge* them, so to speak – than with the practice of most modern novelists who, in the tradition of Flaubert and Conrad, struggle desperately to maintain a *technical* objectivity toward them, allowing the reader, at least theoretically, to form his own opinions. Miss Nin's, I think, is a more honest method, for the "modern" writer, no less than the nineteenth-century one, wishes the reader to accept his (the writer's) own evaluation of his characters: there is thus a certain hypocrisy – a certain *coyness*, even – in his method of carefully scattering clues and innuendoes that will influence the reader's opinion of them in the direction that he wishes.

A particularly successful example of characterization through dream symbolism occurs in *Seduction of the Minotaur*, whose protagonist, Lillian, has been persistently haunted by the following dream:

> . . . a boat, sometimes large and sometimes small, but invariably caught in a waterless place, in a street, in a jungle, in the desert. When it was large it was in city streets, and the deck reached to the upper windows of the houses. She was in the boat and aware that it could not float unless it were pushed, so she would get down from it and seek to push it along so that it might finally reach the water. The effort of pushing the boat along the street was so immense and she never accomplished her aim. Whether she pushed it along cobblestones or over asphalt, it moved very little, and no matter how much she strained she always felt she would never reach the sea. When the boat was small the pushing was less difficult; nevertheless she never reached the lake or river or the sea in which it could sail. Once the boat was stuck between rocks, another time in a mud bank.

The land-locked ship is Lillian's inhibited self, which has sought unsuccessfully for liberation, for the stream it was destined for and on which it could float effortlessly. Lillian's environment, in other words, has been at war with her nature, or rather it has not permitted her nature its freest expression. She achieves freedom at last in a primitive setting – Golconda, an imaginary town in Mexico.

> Today she was fully aware that the dream of pushing the boat through waterless streets was ended. In Golconda she had achieved a flowing life, a flowing journey. It was not only the presence of water, but the natives' flowing rhythm: they never became caught in the past, or stagnated while awaiting the future.

The symbols Miss Nin chooses to characterize her protagonists are not always from the world of dreams, however. Sometimes the characters form them in their conscious minds, and apply them quite consciously to their own situations. Thus, in *A Spy in the House of Love*, Sabina sees in Duchamp's famous Surrealist painting, *Nude Descending a Staircase*, a symbol of her own multiple selves.

> For the first time, on this bleak early morning walk through New York Streets not yet cleaned of the night people's cigarette butts, she understood Duchamp's painting of a Nude Descending a Staircase. Eight or ten outlines of the same woman, like many multiple exposures of a woman's personality, neatly divided into many layers, walking down the stairs in unison.

And in *The Four-Chambered Heart*, a novel whose action takes place in a houseboat on the Seine, the protagonist, Djuna, decides to sink the boat when it becomes apparent to her that her love affair with Rango is doomed because of the interference of the latter's wife, Zora, who is an hysterical invalid:

> The wish to sink the houseboat had not been a mere nightmare dispelled by the light of the morning, but the only solution to this suicide *à trois*. Zora was sinking them emotionally, and in a far deeper way, and to sink the houseboat would only be a confirmation of the inner drama, an external manifestation of its tensions. But that night, enfevered by nightmares, fantasies, reveries, monologues, Djuna had awakened with a wisdom born of the river; the secret of life was flow.

The water symbolism here, it will be noted, is very similar to that in *Seduction of the Minotaur*.

Concerning the symbolist technique in fiction, Miss Nin has written:

> The meaning of a symbol can penetrate our unconscious before revealing itself to our conscious intelligence, achieving direct communication as music does, by way of the feelings and the senses. The flexibility of interpretation is an invitation to participate in creation exactly as music demands of us response rather than a rational dissection. It is by this very mobility of interpretation that the living quality is preserved, so that one can *feel* and *experience* a novel rather than merely read it as one would a detective story, without feeling, as another pastime of the intelligence.

Her technique has for its object, therefore, not so much the telling of a story as the direct revelation of experience, and her use of rhythmical language has the same object, as a kind of catalyst which (like the drumming at a primitive ceremony) induces in the hearer a state of proper receptivity. This is exactly the effect that her style, through a monotonous accumulation of carefully paralleled constructions, produces: a trance-like state of mind that is in fact a kind of hypnosis, aurally induced. A number of critics have commented that the uncompromising symmetry of her rhetorical constructions suggests the movement of certain dances which (like classical ballet or those Oriental dances which are really elaborate exercises in symbolism) are highly stylized.

While symbolism and psychoanalysis are this author's favorite devices for characterization, she also occasionally resorts to a deliberate abstractness of statement: I gave, in the first part of this essay, an example of this method, at once the most elementary and the most sophisticated of all techniques for characterization; for a more striking illustration, sustained throughout several paragraphs, the interested reader is referred to the first three pages of *Ladders to Fire*, which introduce us to the protagonist (Lillian). This passage is extraordinary; I know of nothing quite like it in modern fiction, and had Miss Nin written not another word about her character she would have remained forever fixed in the reader's mind. But of course this is exactly what she wishes to avoid: characters, if they are to be real (and not merely realistic), cannot be static identities, and so Miss Nin finds it necessary to continue from there – besides which, skillful as it is, this is merely a description of the external Lillian, the Lillian that others see, the self that lies nearest the surface; it is not the self with whom, in *Seduction of the Minotaur*, Lillian finally comes face to face.

4

The publication by Alan Swallow last fall of Miss Nin's collected works is a literary event of the first importance. Miss Nin's audience, though discriminating, has never been a large one: by choosing to concern herself with characters at only their most elusive levels, she has cut herself off from much of the popular recognition that would otherwise certainly have been hers. And she presents other difficulties as well. As in the case of Faulkner, it is a great advantage to have read all her work, since the same characters – and frequently the same symbols – recur in them: it is thus more appropriate to consider the novels as chapters in a continuing chronicle than as autonomous units. Nor can I think of another author, except possibly James Joyce, whom it is so necessary to read more than a single time. The full impact of her work is not receive immediately; the intricacy of its design is not all at once apparent.

These are not conditions that make for an overnight popularity, but they are conditions that frequently make for permanent distinction, and Miss Nin's reputation has been steadily in the ascendant for a good many years. It was not until 1946 that she succeeded in finding a commercial publisher for her novel *Ladders to Fire*; until that year she had, as I have mentioned, printed her work on a foot press. She *knew* that it was good, and now, in 1962, she enjoys the proof that a great many other people know it too. Her integrity and dedication are most impressive, yet what impresses me most of all, apart from the quality of the work itself, is the *obstinacy* – there is no other word for it – that has enabled her, through the years, to ignore advice (well-meant but nevertheless presumptuous) of the Saturday Reviewers of Literature, and to continue writing in her own very special way.

For, following the lead of Proust and Joyce, she really has succeeded in introducing new dimensions into fiction, and critics can afford to ignore her scarcely less than they can those literary astronauts. Among living writers of English, no one, to my knowledge, has searched so relentlessly and with such artistic effect into the ultimate sources of character, or has concerned himself so exclusively and so successfully with the nuances of emotional relationships, the myriad subtle influences – and all constantly changing – which human beings, consciously or unconsciously, exert upon one another.

From *Prairie Schooner* 36 (Fall 1962): 217-31.

Anais Nin and the Feminine Quest for Consciousness: The Quelling of the Devouring Mother and the Ascension of the Sophia

Stephanie A. Demetrakopoulos (Gauper)

This essay is a psychological analysis of the presence of the world mother and her personal mother in Anais Nin's psyche and literary works. I conclude with a related subject: Anais Nin's psychology as metaphysics. My approach grows out of Jungian studies. While I agree with Annis Pratt[1] that Jungian concepts of womanhood need to be radically changed, I think that depth psychology (especially the use of archetypes as a tool of analysis) and Jung's metaphysics articulate better than any other discipline the complexity and profundity of the human psyche. Most criticism now in vogue, such as the Lévi-Strauss anthropological-sociological schools, defines a female character in narrow terms of social role, the slot into which she is forced. Both in my first section on Nin's mother-daughter relationship and my last section on Nin's emergent self as a form of metaphysics, I wish to look at the deep structure of the psyche, the self that wars against societal structures, that has its own *raison d'etre* and internal destiny to fulfill.

Anais Nin has emphasized that anyone approaching her work must study its sources: surrealism and psychoanalysis (6:376).[2] Since her diaries give us the first complete odyssey of a female artist, other women eagerly look for patterns of psychic development that might be universal and hence applicable to themselves. The mass appeal of her diary proves how many women identify with her problems and development. Thus, the aspects of Anais Nin's psyche analyzed here may be seen as typical patterns for women in general.

Several different archetypes or embodiments of the feminine principle will be discussed, hence certain definitions at the onset will be helpful. In *The Great Mother*, Erich Neumann, thoroughly analyzes many images of the transpersonal mother, such as the Devouring Great Mother, the Primordial Great Mother, the Lady of the Plants, the Lady of the Beasts, and the Transformative Mother. He sees the human psyche as born swarming with images of the feminine. Since children's own mothers are the females they most completely experience, they identify their mothers with the all-powerful numinous reality of the goddesses within. Neumann, however, tends to analyze this experience and confusion of the Great Mother with the personal mother from a male point of view. He fails to see that a bountiful, self-sacrificing mother is not so dangerous to the development of autonomy and ego in males since they will be given other models to internalize. I intend to demonstrate the actual impact of this model on girls and women. A woman must develop the Artemis,[3] the asocial aspect of her personality and life, to move toward a realization of the transformative and spiritual mother, the feminine godhead, represented variously as the Sophia, Sapientia, Isis, or Kali (in her positive form). This Great Goddess, "a spiritual whole in which all heaviness and materiality are transcended,"[4] is both intrapsychic and extrapsychic. She flowers from within as the woman matures, and she is projected by whole cultures onto these goddesses. Anais Nin embodies this goddess in her last years, and she forces a redefining of this archetype too. The goddess does embody "the ever-lasting and all-embracing, the healing, sustaining, loving, and saving principle," but she is not "maternally quiescent."[5] In the latter phrase, Neumann again projects his masculine sense of this phase of femininity and not the archetype as it is experienced by women themselves. Thus, while I agree with Neumann that such archetypes exist, I hope that this essay will enlarge the definition. Woman's creation of soul is as active and complex as man's.

One of the greatest obstacles to Nin's full realization of her whole self was her mother, both the personal and the transpersonal mother. A woman's mother – the real, personal mother, the incorporated mother, and the archetypal Great Mother – is more integral and complex, more central to female identity problems than to the male's.[6] For me, the problem of mothers of writers began to brew in a course I took as a graduate student on autobiography and biography. No male writer did more than mention his mother in one or two offhand sentences. Benjamin Franklin, for example, mentions only that she suckled all her many children. Then he goes on to his lengthy admiration for and conflicts with his father. There is not much literary precedent for considering the importance of one's mother in autobiography. Anais Nin's last two diaries should help develop a precedent. Woman is just beginning to articulate her own myths; and woman's own myth will, I believe, emphasize her matrilinearism.

In "What Can a Heroine Do? Or Why Women Can't Write,"[7] Joanna Russ has shown the absence of mythic structure for the heroine in literature. Certain genres like tragedy or romance almost exclusively feature men suffering identity and artistic crises. Both these aspects of culture (mythic and literary gaps in feminine experience) explain why women tend toward autobiographical forms to depict their problems in growing and writing. Nin's diary illustrates still another problem that may be archetypal (i.e. inherently "feminine" – special identity problems for women) or only enculturated. Women trying to come to terms with their growth as persons and artists seem very troubled with despotic mothers whom they have internalized. Is the archetypal world mother, the female dragon, harder to kill for a woman because she is so tied to her mother in seeking for her own image? Or is the nurturing force in a woman's life so identical to herself that killing that overweening tyrant is tantamount to killing one's own motherhood or selfhood?

The aspect of self-sacrifice in her mother is obviously most dangerous to the female artist; she must reject the self-sacrifice asked of her by an often dependent mother who believes that her offspring owes her and her set of values absolute allegiance. This is a double-edged problem for women; they must reject the nurturing aspects of the internalized mother plus the real mother herself. The all-giving mother devours herself as well as her child in terms of giving energy only to the growth and sustenance of another so that the more bountifully maternal one's mother is, the greater the danger of internalizing the mother who stops the artist from giving her time and energy to herself. The overly nurturing woman mothers everyone – her lovers, husbands, children, friends, animals. The artist must confront and discipline the apparently magnanimous and generous mother within if she is to create anything, for this mother would devour her.

The influence of the mother is so deeply ingrained, implanted at such a nonverbal stage, that it takes years of living to gain the perspective to look at one's self and find the mother. The father's influence, usually spoken, articulated values, is much easier to objectify and assess; the father can be separated and evaluated, and his undesirable aspects rejected. This is clearly seen in Anais Nin's diaries. Her father is the first problem she confronts; in order to become an adult woman, she must understand and reject the damaging influence of her father on her sense of her own femininity. Dr. René Allendy replaces the father and reassures her of her desirability as in the poignant moment when she shows him her breasts. Allendy does nothing for her as an artist, but that is not what she needed at that time; he gives her the masculine moral support she needs. Allendy and the Millers are the mentors in her initiation into a full and joyful sense of her own gender. She finally purges her father's negativism in "Winter of Artifice."

But the mother is ultimately more difficult. Nin successfully exorcises the father in volume 1; but up to volume 5 the mother is there, ubiquitous and draining, in Anais's relationships. Nin long seems blissfully unaware of her mother's presence in her self. In volume 1 she mostly thinks of her mother in terms of what went wrong in her parents' marriage (1:103-4, 110, 220, 237, 251, 266, 317); she makes only two evaluative statements about her mother qua mother: on the one hand, her mother is good and generous (1:183); but she is a "devouring maternity" (1:243). This latter would be of some interest except that she never sees this aspect of her mother in relation to her own inner self. In volume 2 Anais makes much of Maruca's corroboration (through her divorce) of Nin's own evaluation of her father; but no mention whatever is made of her mother. The incorporated mother is devastatingly present, however, intrinsic to the Gonzalo-Helba relationship, as I will show. Volume 3 also has no mention of her mother. In volume 4 two slight but significant comments are made; Joaquin, her brother, treats Anais and his mother as interchangeable mother figures (4:50); Nin also speaks of her mother's "indomitable will" and its crippling power in terms of her own personality. But she still makes no concrete connection between her mother and her own maternal qualities.

I have wondered at René Allendy's and Otto Rank's concentration on Nin's father in their analyses of her. Was it unconscious Freudianism or implicit sexism to ignore the ramifications of the mother on her personality? Allendy becomes dependent on her, asking for extra time and reassurance from her. At the same time he insists that she should give up the journal; Rank also asks her to stop her own creative work to translate and edit his works – both men have stereotypic male responses to and demands upon her time and her talent. Allendy cannot understand her artistic and intuitive needs to turn inward, both qualities that make a woman independent of men. Rank obviously saw his work as coming first and Nin as an apprentice-secretary-helper. Both men put pressure on exactly the places that the more mature Nin sees as pathologies that are part of her incorporated mother. In *A Woman Speaks*, Nin says she was afraid that her mother would hate her for her diary; in saying that she needed to mother the artist (Rank, as he saw himself) because her own father was an artist, she seems to want to replay her mother's role toward her father.[8] Both these men reveal anima problems, limitations in their concept of woman; they saw in Nin the need to serve and nurture and then projected their own needs into the care of this all-giving mother in her. Interestingly, Allendy and Rank seem to be what Jung would call, respectively, feeling and intellectual types. Nin, on the other hand, seems to me an intuitive type of personality;[9] it is undoubtedly significant that a woman analyst, Inge Bogner, whom Nin identifies and introduces as an intuitive type, is the first person to help her begin to assess her mother's role in her life.

From the beginning, her mother apparently made a conscious effort to force the masochistically submissive concept of Catholic womanhood upon her. Nin's mother even felt that her daughter's life should have been sacrificed to the child that was stillborn in Paris. This seems to me the ultimate in the negation of selfhood and identity in one's daughter. The emphasis on her mother in volume 5 is thus especially significant. Nin is finally able to face consciously the life-draining influence of her mother:

> Conceding with love and admiration to my mother meant an acceptance of traits inherent in me which I considered a threat to my existence, as, for example, my maternal qualities, and I had to fight them in her. She sought to make of me the woman I did not want to be, who capitulated to wifehood and motherhood, and while she

lived she threatened all my aspirations to escape the servitude of woman. When she died I was forced to take into myself this conflict, and I realized I had long ago lost the battle. I am a woman who takes care of others on the same level my mother did. As soon as she died this rebellion collapsed. I loved my mother, who had visited upon us her own angers and rebellions, who had not known how to escape the feminine servanthood and had not achieved her first wish to be a loved and pampered concert singer. . . . She had to surrender all hope of a career in order to raise and later support her three children. (5:199)

At the same time that she rejects for herself the martyrdom of her mother, both as an artist and as a woman, she admits to the positive feelings and pity she had for her mother and thus seems to expiate the devouring aspect of the mother and acknowledge humanity and individuality in her. She also dreams with devastating clarity of what a life of self-sacrifice did to her mother:

Dream: Atmosphere of gloom and sorrow. I have learned that my mother did not die a natural death but took her own life. Joaquin and I are desperate. She left a valise like a salesman's valise, in which are neatly placed all the parts of a lunch box, Thermos bottles, plastic spoons, sandwiches, *et cetera*. My mother had written under each one: "More picnic boxes to fill. Everyday more lunch boxes. Lunch boxes again. Nothing but lunch boxes."

The implication to me was that my mother had filled too many lunch boxes and had finally gone mad and committed suicide.

I have always felt the role of woman as half-servant or total servant with keen rebellion. (5:223)

Her long life allowed her finally to understand her mother as a person and as part of her. She clearly does not discover this internalized mother during her relationship with Gonzalo. To read of Gonzalo's failure to help her move the houseboat (in volume 2), to sense the terror and violence of unstated anger at this abandonment in her simple statement "He was late" (2:303), is to know that her relationship with him at the time cost her much. She had to reject many idealistic, perhaps romantic views about loyalty and love. At the end of volume 2 she says good-bye to those relationships as she had known them. But for the next two volumes she fights the entanglement, the stifling net of similarly dependent "children." For years after Gonzalo, she did not come to recognize the force in her that made dependent men gravitate toward her.

In *The Four-Chambered Heart*, she sees that she as well as Gonzalo created the complex configuration of their relationship. The novel, written so much later, gives us the context of the characters, the intuitive levels, that even makes us forgive and understand Rango as part of a violent pattern that Djuna (and, we suspect, Nin at that earlier time) so coveted as a severely repressed self. In volume 5 of the diary she begins to assess the matrilinearism that has formed her character; she looks squarely at the internalized mother. She begins also to abandon her "home-made" children – the sons that express maleness through ruthless exploitation of the mother in her and through nonending emotional, intellectual, and economic parasitism. Kenneth Patchen infests volume 3; Gore Vidal hogs her life in volume 4; not until volume 6 does she completely extricate herself from the clutches of James Herlihy. But at least with the latter, through volumes 5 and 6, she shows that he is also reading her work and inspiring her, something missing in her life after Henry Miller and Lawrence Durrell. Changes in one's life are always slow to follow awareness; she does not really act completely in accordance with her awareness in volume 5, but her writing *The Four-Chambered Heart* and her gradual weaning of Herlihy show that she begins to admit consciously that one of her major demons is dependency.

Throughout the fifth volume of the diary she also mentions working on *The Four-Chambered Heart*. By the end of the book, the main character, Djuna, rejects her absolute tolerance and responsibility toward everyone in her life. She realizes that Rango, her lover, and Zora, his wife, are parasites, because she needs them as projections of her own irrationality and dependency; they embody her demons. She needs to be a martyr in order to feel that she is a good person. At the end of the novel, Djuna rejects this simplified view of herself and is reborn, able to see that she must accept responsibility for the trap she lives in. The theme of this novel then correlates with the new, strong strand of self that Nin unravels and ties into place in the fifth diary. She rejects the devouring aspect of her mother and understands (in 1947 to 1955) the relationship she had with Gonzalo and Helba in 1934 to 1939. Volume 2 of the diary treats this relationship; *The Four-Chambered Heart* is a thinly disguised fictionalized account of it. At the end of the novel she kills the self that needs these selfish grown-up children. She also writes a novel with a clear plot, compelling characters, and a stunning climax. The novel reflects a sharper critical judgment that goes hand-in-hand with the ruthless attitude she had to adopt toward her maternal compulsions. She cuts her mother out of her psyche and a lot of mush out of this novel. It still suffers a bit from psychological didacticism, but I find it the most engaging, exciting, even compelling of all her novels.

A closer look at *The Four-Chambered Heart* will illustrate this. The novel depicts a man and a woman who seem to be radically different, Rango and Zora. Yet they are two sides of the same pathological need for dependence. Zora is physically dependent, supposedly unable to deal with the concrete world. She is a confirmed hypochondriac who requires feeding and nursing. She cannot even go to the doctor alone. She claims to have no clothing and dyes anything given to her black, symbolic of her insistent martyrdom. She demands economic and emotional support by a superrational, organized, competent, and pathologically generous Djuna. She needs Djuna as the ordering principle and finally elicits from Djuna a stereotypically male role that Anais played to her mother. Anais was always afraid of her mother's irrationality and inability to cope with everyday economics; we remember that Anais's mother commissioned a sidewalk when the family needed a furnace, much to Anais's despair (5:234). Zora is a tyrant in the same way that Anais's mother was. Like all dependent people, she really seeks to dominate and finally attacks Djuna with a knife. Yet this crudely physical act is easier for Djuna to understand and resolve within herself than Rango's more psychological attacks.

It is Rango who pushes Djuna to her final suicide attempt. He also enjoys the physical comfort that Zora almost exclusively demands; Djuna ends up lighting the fire and the lamps, and waiting on street corners no matter how late he is. But worse, he demands intellectual and emotional support in ways that would negate her whole being. He wants her to follow him blindly as he tries on new selves (like the Spanish revolutionary). He objects to sides of her that he cannot understand or possess. He burns her books, objects to personal fantasy worlds symbolized by Paul, rages against her normal urges toward other men as reflected by her fascination with Sabina and her affairs. He demands all her energy and support. And the mother in her responds, tries to give all he needs and wants. Finally, depleted by his insatiable demands, deeply wounded by his inability to understand her, Djuna attempts suicide. This attempt becomes a formal emotional detachment that saves her. She sees that she has done it to herself. Just as the death of the author's mother set her free to seek the mother within herself, so does the symbolic suicide of this compulsively maternal, supportive self set her free of this triangular relationship that has almost engulfed her identity.

Djuna must kill or exorcise a side of herself that is self-destructive. Esther Harding speaks of the maternal self from which each woman must wean herself in order to grow.[10] This is basically the ritual through which Djuna must pass. For Djuna has become to Rango what Anais's mother was to her husband and what Anais almost became to Gonzalo – a woman who sacrifices her creative energies to the support of an insatiable husband-son. Neither the mother nor the child grows up. Thus, the mature Anais, writing of the Gonzalo-Helba-Anais triangle, is embodying through literature her own deepest demon. The suicide attempt becomes a rebirth, a resurrection of a new self. Djuna transmutes and transcends her past in a dreamlike state as she waits for death. She enters the magnificent epiphany that ends the novel as her creative unconscious portrays her past and its meaning in a series of hallucinatory images and memories.

In the last image in the novel, the water gives up to Djuna's scrutiny and understanding a doll, the little-girl side of Djuna that earlier in the novel still accepted unquestioningly childhood values that trapped her in "goodness."

The doll rises like Venus from the sea, fuzzy hair burned gold like Grünewald's Christ's, whose hair merges with the sunlight. It is a lovely potential; it is featureless and Djuna can now paint any face she wants on this old self through her new self-awareness. She can shape herself and is reborn of waves of free will that now wash over her. The "Noah's ark" (full of potential) has indeed survived.

The new self must sacrifice old illusions, and Nin carefully places this story within the context of other destructively passionate, foolish romantic tales. Rango is alluded to as both Othello and Heathcliff.[11] These heroes are featured in works that demonstrate what Denis de Rougement in *Love in the Western World* would call the inclination to love passion more than the beloved. For Djuna has loved her ability to love and give in superhuman terms more than she loved Rango and Zora, who only become weaker as she becomes more supportive. Djuna must learn to love more critically and to restrain herself from giving too much of herself. Instead of the absolutes of Heathcliff-Othello-Rango, she embraces the reality that Duchamp's *Nude Descending a Staircase* symbolizes, "multiple selves . . . composed of multiple juxtapositions revealing endless spirals of character."[12] She releases herself from the monomaniacal mother within and the need to idealize the male in order to sacrifice selfhood for him. Freed, she will realize many sides of herself; she has exorcised the Devouring Mother.

Several interesting points can be made about this. First, many women in literature consider or commit suicide by drowning: Edna in Kate Chopin's *The Awakening*; Zenobia in *The Blithedale Romance*; Sylvia Plath and Anne Sexton both invoke the sea in their last poems; Virginia Woolf drowns herself. When women are weary of the toil and pain of consciousness, does the sea hold a special affinity for them? (The theory of evolution advanced by Elaine Morgan in *The Descent of Woman* seems strangely applicable: Morgan believes that women were first to stand upright and became hairless because they used the water as a place of protection for themselves and their young.) At any rate, Anais Nin stands with the tougher among us who say that life must be lived through no matter what. Lillian Hellman in *Pentimento* uses her near-drowning to illustrate her endurance and ability to survive; she is like the turtle that even Dashiell Hammett could not kill. *The Four-Chambered Heart* should quell those critics who accuse Nin of too sanguine a view of life. She shows a clear understanding of the roots and depths of a particularly feminine brand of despair, but she does not allow women to succumb to it.

More interesting still is what this pattern of the mature woman exorcising the mother demonstrates about the feminine quest for consciousness. Certainly one of the most fascinating aspects of the diary is its detailed story of a woman artist fervently groping among alter egos to find herself. Each volume is a giant step toward the quest for self, a stripping away of artificial layers. I am preparing a very long paper on the diaries, but here I want to treat only the pattern of quelling first the world father, then the world mother that we find in Anais Nin's diaries and novels. According to Erich Neumann, who usually uses only male-propagated myths to establish patterns, this is the reverse of the normal pattern.[13] He says that consciousness (which he terms *masculine*) is born as the great mother (the biological matrix and the unconscious) is rejected and killed symbolically; the great mother is embodied in our personal mothers, who must function for us as transpersonal mothers during our adolescence. Fixation in the matriarchate, he says, features a "preconscious, prelogical, and preindividual way of thinking and feeling."[14] Later, the hero (ego, consciousness, self) must slay the world father in order to forge her-his own new values: "The world of the fathers is thus the world of collective values; it is historical and related to the fluctuating level of conscious and cultural development within the group . . . the religious, ethical, political, and social structure of the collective."[15] The world father, also embodied in the personal father, must be symbolically slain or the individual will be stifled with "sterile conservatism and a reactionary identification with the father, which lacks the living, dialectical struggle between the generations."[16] For Neumann the slaying of the world mother always precedes the slaying of the world father.

If Anais Nin's pattern of development is normal, it reveals that Neumann does not really know much about feminine development. In his *Amor and Psyche: The Psychic Development of the Feminine*, he does suggest in one tantalizing sentence that the pattern may be reversed for women:

> After becoming conscious of her masculine components and realizing them, and having become whole through development of her masculine aspect, Psyche was in a position to confront the totality of the Great Mother in her two-fold aspect as Aphrodite-Persephone.[17]

Does this mean that as a lover and daughter she confronts her incorporated mother? Neumann is cryptic, to say the least.

Both literature and the psychic development of real women need to be plumbed for what they say about mother-daughter relationships – we know so little. May Sarton in *Mrs. Stevens Hears the Mermaids Singing* features an aged heroine who sees coming to terms with the meaning of her mother as her last and most arduous task. Martha (in her forties) in Lessing's *Four-Gated City* descends into madness when confronted with her mother's final visit. A major theme in Anne Sexton's first book, *To Bedlam and Halfway Back*, is her matrilineal source of being; her creative self seems born of that assessment. These women, both real and fictional, are far from adolescents.

My final conclusion is my contention that in Anais Nin we see the masculine principle come to the fore with the death of her mother. This means an exercising of the analytic aspect of the brain[18] that is culturally suppressed in women. *The Four-Chambered Heart* is, I believe, her most enduring novel. She pares away detail and digressions to give the novel classical lines and focus. The masculine principle in this case is the ability to kill the part of the created work that is imperfect; the feminine principle is that part of the psyche that allows the images and ideas to flow freely from the creative unconscious. The masculine principle is the opposite of that which it nurtures. In a way this is curious. I think that Nin could be seen as implicitly sexist early in her life, in the earlier diaries, in that she ignores the matrilineal roots of her womanhood and constantly emphasizes her connections with her father. Yet with the admission of the power her mother's image has over her and also the love she has for her mother, the masculine principle is, paradoxically, released, and she produces her most balanced and structurally excellent novel.

This is not the only example of the relationship between the quelling of the mother and the better quality of writing in her canon. "Birth," perhaps her finest story, is primordial in its clarity. A woman forces out of her womb a dead child that she wishes still to protect and envelop. She considers, instead, sacrificing her own life, the life of an adult artist, rather than forcing the dead child into the world to be disposed of. She would sacrifice the quality of her own mind and life for a mindless (and paradoxically, dead) addition to the quantity of life. Perhaps in forcing the dead infant out, Nin symbolically, although unconsciously, rejected the devouring mother within and without. Just as she finally acted with judgment and ruthless strength during the birth, so does the story reflect fine editing and shaping, that is, critical judgment.

In other words, I think that her inability to delineate ego territory in her life and cut out selfish demands from others corresponds to an often damaging lack of structure and editing in some of her fiction. As she rejects the maternal, all-encompassing personal attitude, she gains critical judgment in her art. When she spoke in Kalamazoo in 1974, she said that she would like to change her fiction by adding narrative structure, more setting, more dialogue. She saw her novels as being so subjective as to lack clarity. She would eliminate some of her characters' spiraling within for a more clear-cut relationship with the outside world and social reality. Her own passiveness with others seems to be reflected by the almost wholly subjective and internal world of her characters. Toward the end of her life, she began to reject this almost unilateral, subjective mode of being.

It is, however, this very subjectivity that underlies the psychological and metaphysical importance of Nin's diaries. I have to this point defined a narrower aspect of Nin's development, her conscious coming to terms with the matrilinear source of her being. We now turn to another and broader aspect of Nin's diaries that is also psychologically important, her "feminine metaphysics." Her exorcism of a demonic biological, psychic, and matrilineal matrix synchronizes with her consolidation of the Sophia.

The most exciting theology of the last decade rejects what Mary Daly calls

> the eternal masculine stereotype, which implies hyper-rationality (in reality, frequently reducible to pseudo-rationality), "objectivity," aggressivity, the possession of dominating and manipulative attitudes towards persons and the environment, and the tendency to construct boundaries between the self (and those identified with the self) and "the Other."[19]

Schubert Ogden, a founder of "Process" theology, puts it this way:

> The characteristics of classical philosophy all derive from its virtually exclusive orientation away from the primal phenomenon of selfhood toward the secondary phenomenon of the world constituted by the experience of our senses . . . . As soon, however, as we orient our metaphysical reflection to the self as we actually experience it, as itself the primal ground of our world of perceived objects, this whole classical approach is, in the Heideggerian sense of the word, "dismantled."[20]

In a way, this subjective orientation to reality is like the macrocosm-microcosm parallels of the Renaissance; or again, like Leibniz's theories of the universe of mirrorlike monads, each reflecting the whole but slightly differently since each is in a different position. Carl Jung's metaphysics, called *synchronicity*, is based on his study of archetypes as revealed in dreams, art, and literature.[21] Because these archetypes transcend time and space (cause and effect as we know it), he began, toward the end of his life, to guess at a master principle of the cosmos as a subtle, hidden principle of an acausal correspondence.[22] Jung saw the self as a sort of interior cohesion that operates within and across the prevailing pattern of archetypes.[23] Through constant delving within the self, we find the macrocosm manifest in the microcosm, and thus the psyche reaches beyond itself. In other words, the kind of delving within that Anais Nin's diaries demonstrate will put us in touch with ultimate reality. Although her diaries show her changing her mind, sometimes drastically, and moving through radical stages of experimental living, they also demonstrate that moving behind this unfolding, this becoming, is an indestructible substrate of reality – what Jung would call the archetype of the self. Her diaries should reassure a modern person, so afraid that she/he is only socially determined and has no special identity, that the self cannot be lost, that it is unique and integral to each of us, a sort of becoming that is being. I think the overwhelming response to the diaries, by so many women also searching for their identity, illustrates its "numinosity carrying a sense of transcendent validity, authenticity, and essential divinity."[24] Nin shows us that flexibility and change are, in a way, sacred.

This takes us to the second theological aspect of Nin's diaries. Whether ultimate reality is polytheistic[25] or whether polytheism merely expresses the great breadth of becoming that God is, it is undeniable that Anais Nin has helped to give us back feminine deity. She experiences the female body and earthliness as divine, as in the Fez journey. She also experiences the feminine approach to reality as divine:

> She [woman] has to create something different from man. Man created a world cut off from nature. Woman has to create within the mystery, storms, terrors, the infernos of sex, the battle against abstraction and art. She has to sever herself from the myth man creates, from being created by him, she has to struggle with her own cycles, storms, terrors which man does not understand. Woman wants to destroy aloneness, recover the original paradise. The art of woman must be born in the womb-cells of the mind. She must be the link between the synthetic products of man's mind and the elements. (2:234)

One of the damaging dogmatic stances of many modern feminists, from my point of view, is the insistence that men and women are exactly alike psychically, that we are beings different only be virtue of a slight detail of genitalia. I think that this insistence on sameness stems from the fear that any admission of inherent differences will be leaped upon by most men and many women as proof of inferiority. But if, as Jungians believe, women are, generally, more intuitive, flexible, open than men, then surely Anais embodies the fullest development of this aspect of woman. If, as Jung said, "archetypes are mediators between the individual and the cosmos,"[26] Nin can be seen as a mediator between woman and the universe – an articulated link of the feminine One. I hope the feminist movement results in many paths for both men and women. The diaries show us how important the uniqueness of each inner voice is. Anais shows us that listening to the inner self rather than to others, no matter how friendly they seem (Henry Miller, Otto Rank, Lawrence Durrell all try to make her give up the diary), is the way to wholeness and transformation. Anais is far more open to others than most people (sometimes to her own misfortune), but she never loses touch with her own intuitive knowledge of self.

She thus demonstrates the third point I want to make, that there are no absolute paths because there are no absolute forms of being. She demonstrates that all paths are relative to who one is. As a corollary to this, she also demonstrates what Jungians calls the feminine Eros, the quality of "relatedness," in her openness to the becoming of others as well as to herself. She rejects people only when they become absolutely bludgeoning in their attitudes toward her. The "Process" theologian's theory of God is that He (or She/It) is Absolute Relatedness rather than simply an Absolute: "The Thou with the greatest conceivable degree of real relatedness to others – namely, relatedness to *all* others – is for that very reason the most truly absolute Thou any mind can conceive."[27] This concept of God shows

> how maximum temporality entails strict eternity; maximum capacity for change, unsurpassable immutability; and maximum passivity to the actions of others, the greatest possible activity in all their numberless processes of self-creation.[28]

Because of Nin's deep relatedness to her own self, she is able to connect safely and deeply with others very different from herself. She exhibits *caritas*, the medieval concept that the truest godliness is that which loves all God's creatures. She becomes life-enhancing and nourishes growth that is psychic and spiritual as well as biological.

Perhaps what is most important, she embodies the archetype of hope, the psychic configuration that Jung sees as activated in Rhine's experiments at Duke University: "The primary characteristic of successful results, then, was that they coincided with an exceedingly affirmative condition of the psyche, a condition in which the psyche was pervaded by an attitude of hopeful expectancy."[29] Jung also talks about the "archetype of the miracle" in this connection, "the particular quality of expectation that human beings intuitively feel with respect to the capacity that the life process possesses to bring changes in its own functioning."[30] In other words, Nin's life is an argument for free will and self-transformation. She has known despair but never succumbed to it. She endured and celebrated life to the end.

Finally, Nin becomes in her full maturity a living example of the feminine Godhead. In her last diary she begins to transcend her earlier selves in the way she energizes herself through lectures and letters. She begins to turn out to the world more and more. I believe that a transformation much like what Neumann calls the highest stage of the feminine principle, the Sophia, is demonstrated in her attitudes and personality. Neumann defines the Sophia this way:

> Sophia, who achieves her supreme visible form as a flower, does not vanish in the nirvanalike abstraction of a masculine spirit; like the scent of a blossom, her spirit always remains attached to the earthly foundation of reality.[31]

> Her overflowing heart is wisdom and food as once. The nourishing life that she communicates is life of the spirit and of transformation,

not one of earthbound materiality.[32]

Nin is, then, in every sense of the word, prophetic, demonstrating new levels of consciousness as she unfolds her life. Her diaries are an emblem of individuation and selfhood, and they also demonstrate the importance of dreams, the unconscious, and the depths of the imaginal, rich, inarticulate, and unique human psyche. I think her dream of blinding light when she began to publish the diaries was possibly a collective dream; her feminine light in a world so fraught with darkness of the masculine principle gone black with dominion may seem blinding, but only because it is at first new and shocking. It will harm only those who cannot incorporate its power.

NOTES

[1]"Archetypal Approaches to the New Feminist Criticism," *Bucknell Review* 21 (1973): 3-15.
[2]*The Diary of Anais Nin*, ed. Gunther Stuhlmann, 6 vols. (New York: Swallow Press and Harcourt Brace Jovanovich). References to the diaries appear in the text.
[3]For an excellent and intriguing article on each of the Olympian goddesses as a type of feminine personality and as a type of anima, see Philip T. Zabriskie, "Goddesses in Our Midst," *Quadrant* 17 (Fall 1974): 34-46.
[4]*The Great Mother: An Analysis of the Archetype*, trans. Ralph Manheim (New York: Pantheon Books, 1963), p.325.
[5]Erich Neumann, *The Origins and History of Consciousness*, trans. R. F. C. Hull (New York: Random House, 1954), p. 170.
[6]The best treatment of this is Nancy Chodorow, "Family Structure and Feminine Personality" in *Woman, Culture, and Society*, ed. Michelle Rosaldo and Louise Lamphere (Stanford, Calif.: Stanford University Press, 1974), pp. 43-67.
[7]"What Can a Heroine Do? Or Why Women Can't Write," in *Images of Women in Fiction: Feminist Perspectives*, ed. Susan Koppelman Cornillon (Bowling Green, Ohio: Bowling Green University Popular Press, 1972), pp. 2-21.
[8]*A Woman Speaks*, ed. Evelyn J. Hinz (Chicago: Swallow Press, 1975), pp. 52, 216.
[9]Although Anais Nin denies it, Djuna seems the closest to her of all her female characters. Their emotional problems are similar, they are both intuitive types with the corresponding demon of sensation; they both related to men and women in the same positive and negative ways. I do not wish in any way to denigrate Nin's judgments and perceptions about herself, but because a writer's most powerful images and characters often break out of the uncon-

scious, more appears in the writing than the author necessarily meant. Even Hawthorne said that Hester and Zenobia got out of hand and developed more attractive magnitude than he originally planned. Evelyn Hinz, the major Nin scholar, agrees with me. See *The Mirror and the Garden* (New York: Harcourt Brace Jovanovich, 1971), p. 71. For a full description of these personality types (actually orientations to reality), see Marie-Louise von Franz and James Hillman, *Lectures on Jung's Typology* (Zurich: Spring Publications, 1971).

[10]*Women's Mysteries: Ancient and Modern* (New York: Bantam Books, 1971), p. 242.

[11]*The Four-Chambered Heart* (Chicago: Swallow Press, 1959), pp. 127, 150.

[12]Ibid., p. 168.

[13]*The Origins and History of Consciousness*, see especially pp. 152-91.

[14]Ibid., p. 168.

[15]Ibid., p. 173.

[16]Ibid., p. 190.

[17]Trans. Ralph Manheim (New York: Pantheon Books, 1956), p. 136.

[18]The right side of the brain has been identified as the analytical, aggressive side by modern research psychologists. In other words, what Jung had postulated from his studies of patients, dreams, and myths has been validated by physical evidence. See Robert E. Ornstein, *The Psychology of Consciousness* (New York: Viking Press, 1972), pp. 64, 219.

[19]*Beyond God the Father* (Boston: Beacon Press, 1973), p. 15.

[20]Schubert M. Ogden, *The Reality of God and Other Essays* (New York: Harper and Row, 1966), p. 57.

[21]C. G. Jung, "Synchronicity: An Acausal Connecting Principle," in *The Collected Works of C. G. Jung*, ed. Herbert Read, Michael Fordham, Gerhard Adler (New York: Pantheon Books, 1953-), 8: 417-533.

[22]Ira Progoff, *Jung, Synchronicity, and Human Destiny* (New York: Julian Press, 1973), p. 74.

[23]Ibid., p. 87.

[24]Ibid., p. 83.

[25]David L. Miller, in *The New Polytheism: Rebirth of the Gods and Goddesses* (New York: Harper and Row, 1974), forces us to see that "psychologically, polytheism is a matter of the radical experience of equally real, but mutually exclusive aspects of the self" (p. 5).

[26]Progoff, p. 325.

[27]Ogden, p. 65.

[28]Ibid., p. 65.

[29]Progoff, p. 104.

[30]Ibid., p. 105.

[31]Neumann, p. 325.

[32]Ibid., p. 331.

From *Women, Literature, Criticism*, ed. Harry R. Garvin. Lewisburg, Penn.: Bucknell University Press, 1978. This volume was also published as *The Bucknell Review* 24.1 (Spring 1978): 119-36.

Anais Nin: A Critical Evaluation

Estelle C. Jelinek

It must have been early in 1971 that I began hearing Anais Nin's name put forth by my friends in the women's liberation movement. I couldn't pin them down when I asked why they adored her; they said I had to read her to understand. So I read *A Spy in the House of Love* first, and I found its style impressionistic, its content repetitious, and its heroine unsympathetic. She is in a constant state of flux, living now in one role, now in another, play-acting, fantasizing, going from one man to another for her identity, but returning like a child, always to a husband who was like a father to her. *Ladders to Fire* was my second attempt at a Nin "novel"; I wanted so much to "catch fire" as my friends had. I was disappointed again. *Ladders* was not more than a variation of the theme and plot of *Spy* – another actress playing roles, lying, and taking her identity from men.

But I didn't give up. I began reading Nin's diaries. Although I appreciated her honesty and her struggle for a personal identity, I was bored by her vanity and her endless descriptions of adoring and adored men. These early diaries seemed to me merely sourcebooks for her rather inept and inane novels. Nonetheless, I kept looking for the *real* Nin. When an "Anais Nin Celebration" was held at the University of California, Berkeley, in December 1971, I paid my $15, convinced that I could not help but be turned on by her if only I saw and heard her "in the flesh." During that weekend, my initial reaction to Nin shifted from a tentative disapproval to outright rage. Now, three years later, having seen Nin in the flesh again, I realize that my anger has diminished, but my disapproval of her is just as keen.

In the years that have passed, Nin has traveled across the country speaking at colleges and feminist events, sometimes solo, sometimes in conjunction with other women. Always it is she, however, who is billed as the main attraction; it is her picture that accompanies announcements of the events in local newspapers. And it is her performance that the thousands of women, overwhelmingly white and middle class, wait for in awed expectation. Radicals, conservatives, feminists, Marxists, librarians, teachers, housewives, students, poets – all come to celebrate the idol. When Nin appears on stage, the audience seems to gasp in unison and pay homage to her with "Ooh" and "Aah" and "Isn't she lovely!"

The response to her was the same in 1974 as it was in 1971. And her style and message have not altered either. She reads from her diaries – now her fifth one, whose contents are hardly distinguishable from the previous four. Her heroes and mentors are always men: D. H. Lawrence, Henry Miller, Ingmar Bergman, Otto Rank, Picasso, Casals, Dali, Antonin Artaud, André Breton, Max Ernst, and others. At some celebrations the audience is treated to a video portion as well. It may be slides of the architecture of Lloyd Wright, the "master builder," who, as Nin says, has been overshadowed by his famous father; or perhaps a film on Jean Varda, the Sausalito painter and "poet of collages," who adored women and "turned them into myths of all kinds"; or it may be that film of unmistakable adoration, *Anais Observed*, by Robert Snyder.

In the slides designed to show the architecture of Wright's Wayfarers' Chapel in Southern California, we see Nin strolling through the chapel wearing a flowing white gown, then draped in a white cape, posing under the medieval arch that marks the entrance to the chapel. In Snyder's film we see her posing seductively in a field or sitting in her (now familiar) long red velvet dress, serenely reclining on a couch under a collage by Varda. Snyder often says, I am told, as he did at that 1971 celebration I attended: "I guess we're here to celebrate her sweet sixteen."

Between Nin's readings from her diaries about her male heroes and scenes of "Nin the Hero," we may be fortunate enough to hear contributions from other women, some reading critical interpretations of Nin's writings, others reading their own creative efforts. The women are talented and deserve recognition; Nin herself deserves credit for encouraging them. But when Nin introduces one woman as "a critic, unusual in women – she has her own point of view, she is sensitive, and she is feminine and still objective," I must then question Nin's feminism. From reading her diaries and novels and now having heard her in person, I can see, despite what I have been told, that she holds views that are anathema to me and the women's liberation movement.

As long as she continues to read from her diaries and speak of her male heroes and to tell us that her heroes today are Daniel Ellsberg and Ralph Nader (and, *by the way*, that she is looking for women to worship as well), any woman who takes her feminism seriously must at least question Nin's attitudes. Equally to the point I am making is Nin's belief that women have a special and unique nature, one that will transform the world. In 1971, one poet, reiterating Nin's own views in the diaries, spoke of her as validating the "female principle" in society: fusion, anti-war, earth-mother, gentleness. Nin herself said that women "should dominate, and men should let them because she has something special to give." The future of our society, Nin declared, depends on women's finding themselves, being free, for only by finding the truly feminine in themselves can they "give rebirth to everything that is divided." In 1974 her message had not changed; in speaking of the woman of the future, her theme, Nin said that she would be a "better fusion," she would make a "totally better world"; she will combine the "intellectual with intuition and a sense of personal intimacy." Woman, she said, has developed the intimacy quality, which she should keep, and man will have that quality too when he recognizes the femininity in himself. But woman must not neglect the intellectual in herself, Nin said, which, by implication, is man's realm.

In her diaries, especially, Nin speaks to these sexist notions, which are offshoots of her mentors Lawrence and Jung:

It is feminine to be oblique. It is not trickery. (I, 58)

Or

When man lies in her womb, she is fulfilled, each act of love is a taking man within her, an act of birth and rebirth, of child-bearing and man-bearing. Man lies in her womb and is reborn each time anew with a desire to act, to BE. But for woman, the climax is not in the birth, but in the moment when man rests inside her. (I, 106)

Or

The territory of woman is that which lies untouched by the direct desire of man. Man attacks the vital center. Woman fills out the circumference. (I, 184)

Or

Feminine vision is usually myopic. I do not think mine is. But I do not understand abstract ideas. (I, 190)

Nin's concept of woman is really an alternate form of sexism. Where usually men have used the traits she celebrates against women, Nin puts women on a pedestal because they (seemingly) possess these traits, as though they were innate in women and absent in men. I don't find it at all justifiable to call women better than men because their thinking is intuitive and not logical, or that they are earth-mothers and creators (which perhaps men envy), or that they are more sensitive and compassionate. This kind of sexism makes logical women "masculine" and intuitive men "feminine," women who do not want to have children "unnatural," men who are compassionate and sensitive "effeminate."

Even the women in her novels are not models for feminists. We may

identify with their search for an individual identity, but ultimately these protagonists are searching for their identity through men. They go from one man
to another, looking for the hero who will fill all their needs. Each is helpless,
lost, playing a part. Their roles become second nature to them, so much so
that they are never sure who they really are without this external, male validation of themselves. In the last analysis, Nin's protagonists are variations of
Nin herself. When one sees her performing today, whether reading from her
diaries or posing in films, the theatrical effect is dominant. Even *she* has
questioned her authenticity, her need to play roles:

> ... I begin to imagine that I am also a fake – that maybe all my
> journals, books, and personality are fakes. When I'm admired I
> think I am duping the world. . . . And I see the question of my sin-
> cerity could easily drive me insane if I studied it continuously. My
> imagination entangles me hopelessly. I lose myself. What distresses
> me is that I seem to play on the feelings of people. (I, 205)

Artaud felt her insincerity acutely: "You give everyone the illusion of maximum love" (I, 245). I, too, question Nin's sincerity acutely; she is still playing
roles. Currently, it is that of a feminist.

In her diaries, Nin has also written of her distaste for anything but the extraordinary life:

> Ordinary life does not interest me. I seek only the high moments.
> (I, 5)

And she is not interested in politics:

> I don't rave against politics. I ignore it. (I, 12)

> ... politics to me, all of them, seem rotten to the core and all based
> on economics, not humanitarianism. (II, viii)

In seeking her individual solution, she is revolted by "realism" – the concern
with externals, the world around us: things, the world of science, facts, and so
on. The literature of realism, to her, is crude and absurd; why write about
opening doors, she says, refrigerators, the "ugly" in life? There is no room
for despair, only joy. As she globalized her position in her diary, if everyone
were like her, there would be no wars, no poverty.

In "Notes on Feminism" (1972), Nin writes:

> Poverty and injustice and prejudice are not solved by any man-
> made system. I want them to be solved by a higher quality of human
> being who, by his own law of valuation upon human life will not

permit such inequalities. (*Woman: An Issue*, Boston: Little, Brown, 1972)

And that human being must struggle individually, from within, to change the world. The group solution is out as far as Nin is concerned. Tillie Olsen asks her students how many servants go into making Nin's life possible: in her villas in France, in her bohemian salons in New York, and now on the West Coast? Naturally, anyone who cannot tolerate ugliness, who lives in a world of admirers, who is a goddess courting her worshippers, who lives for individual solutions, is not going to believe in any form of collective action. In one interview she said:

> This is sometimes the only difficult thing I have to bridge when I speak to women's liberation: That having been made responsible for their situation, they refuse the idea that we can help ourselves individually. (*Everywoman*, 1972)

For Nin, politics deal with external realities, whereas she is interested only in the internal, creative ones. This makes her selective in her choice of friends, in the women she encourages, in the males she worships, in the privileged world she not only lives in but approves of to the exclusion of all others. She doesn't really care about anyone by artists. Somehow, she feels she can affect the whole world with her personalized aesthetics:

> I am not committed to any of the political movements which I find full of fanaticism and injustice, but in the face of each human being, I act democratically and humanly. I give each human being his due. I disregard class and possessions. It is the value of their spirit, of their human qualities I pay my respect to . . . (I, vii)

But in "Notes on Feminism" [collected in *In Favor of the Sensitive Man and Other Essays*] Nin attacks the women's liberation movement for being negative, for attacking male writers and male-dominated films or for "group thinking":

> I see so many women in the movement thinking in obsessional circles about problems which are solvable when one is emotionally free to think and act clearly.

She sees women's "undirected, blind anger and hostility" as ineffective weapons. "Slogans," she writes,

> do not give strength because generalizations are untrue. . . . The group does not always give strength because it moves only accord-

ing to the lowest denominator of understanding. The group weakens
the individual will and annihilates the individual contribution.

Ayn Rand upheld this personal vision of the creative artist as a superior
being and, concomitantly the inferiority of the masses in *The Fountainhead*.
One could see Nin's individualism carried to the fascistic extremes that Ayn
Rand articulated in her later books and in her philosophy of objectivism.
How can feminists and radicals of all types accept uncritically this elitism and
miss the incompatibility with the rest of their lives? To Nin, realism is dis-
tasteful: that means the poverty in ghettos and barrios; that means the inhu-
manity in prisons; that means the day-to-day practical efforts to get equal pay
for equal work or, even more difficult, getting welfare or food stamps when
one has no permanent address. Nin is appealing to middle-class women who
have the leisure to lavish attention upon their creative talents. Nin is not essentially interested in the struggle of poor women or women who haven't her
talents.
   But, one may say, there are other women doing that and her interests are
different. Granted. But Nin would be *repelled* by that kind of work; she would
feel above these uncreative, untalented, "ugly" people for whom the "ugly" is
their everyday reality. That is the difference between Nin and other women
artists who work in their chosen profession exclusively. It's the snobbishness
and elitist attitude that differentiates her from these others. Nonetheless,
women who call themselves feminists or Marxists swoon at her words and
applaud her "feminine" virtues. These women seem incapable of discerning
the inherent contradictions between their sexual and/or radical politics and
her views: her emphasis on, and embodiment of, conventional femininity, her
hatred of the ugly and the ordinary, her touting of the individual solution, and
her disdain of collective endeavors.
   It took me a long time to understand my rejection of Anais Nin and to
analyze the reactions of my friends to her writings. In recent months, I've
been getting support from some women whose reactions to her are similar to
mine, but I am still meeting women who either give a long sigh at the sound
of her name or react defensively to my tentative questioning of the implications of her views. Some women's reactions to my ideas on Nin's sexism are
quite dramatic, as though I were, by attacking Nin, attacking their own femininity. This must be, at least partially, at the root of the adoration for Nin: the
burden women still feel to prove their "femininity" in spite of their individuality.
   I can understand the model Nin herself presents to other women who are
struggling to realize a creative identity. The validation she gives to the personal growth process, to using the material of one's own life and one's own
self in creative expression is certainly reason for admiring her and her diaries.
But admiration is a far cry from adulation. We may admire Zelda Fitzgerald
for her struggle to realize her artistic potential or Isadora Duncan for her pi-

oneer work in liberating the human body through dance. But we must certainly not distort a woman's contribution to the arts just because she is a woman.

The blindness I see in Nin's readers and audiences is also evident in the many articles written about her. I have yet to read an article that questions her place in the women's movement, her feminism, or the relevance (or irrelevance) of the politics of her aesthetics. In a *New York Times* guest editorial on the women's movement, it is Nin who is called on to define our origins. She writes: "Several developments accelerated the growth and expansion of the woman. One was psychoanalysis which gave her self-confidence and guidance in the creation of herself as an individual . . . . The second development was political; women working in groups and organized efforts to change laws detrimental to the equality of woman, her economic independence, her happiness. The third was the formation of consciousness-raising groups. Women gathered to discuss their problems openly, to discuss solutions, to strengthen each other's confidence, to establish solidarity" (Jan. 14, 1972).

Nin's *Times* article points up two significant factors. The first is that she knows very little about the women's movement. Anyone who has had any involvement in it knows that consciousness-raising groups were the first and basic foundation of the current movement; that political organizing and efforts to change laws have been going on for decades on a small scale, often hidden from the public eye, until their emergence on a large scale because of the thousands of women who joined the movement through consciousness-raising groups. As for psychoanalysis, the women's movement has had to work doubly hard, in fact, to try to erase the damage that has been done by psychiatrists, predominantly influenced by Freud's often harsh and belittling judgments of women. The fact that Nin, who was told by one psychiatrist (Allendy) that she was trying to "surpass men in their own work, to have more success" and by another (Rank) that she must discover which she wants to be, either "a woman or an artist," can still extol psychoanalysis shows how dated and unfeminist she really is. Certainly analysis never made her a feminist, for she still needs her male heroes and her identification with them – even those she had forty years ago. She still needs to present herself as almost professionally seductive. She has not overcome her adoration of her father, her need for men to define and worship her.

The second significant factor concerning the *Times* article is that the press has been hoodwinked, just as her readers have been, into thinking Nin is a feminist; and the nation's most prestigious establishment newspaper prints her opinions on the women's liberation movement as though she represents that movement. Both the feminist and straight press have responded to her in much the same way that her naive readers have: with awe and blindness to the facts of her sexism and elitism.

In all the articles I have read about her, I see three distinct approaches to Nin. The most typical is that represented by an adoring article in the November 1971 issue of *Off Our Backs*, "Anais Nin: Two Women React," by Linda M. McGonigal and Sheri A. Maeda. These women approached their interview with the venerable Nin with the "anxiety of meeting someone your gut already knows," hoping "for a miraculous flow." When they left Nin, they "walked further into the reality, into the dream, and the becoming awareness of being Woman." In between, Nin expressed views that her interviewers were obviously in too much of a daze to realize were sexist: "Woman perceives reality via her emotions, spirit and mind, while man abstracts realism from reality, a process limited to the mind. Woman's closer contact with and belief in the unconscious and emotional has produced a different view of reality, one more real than that of man, who goes about setting things in logical, rational schemes." This article, coming as it did from a feminist newspaper, most accurately typifies the blind reaction of Nin's readers.

In the second type of article, which appears in both movement and establishment publications, the authors may raise questions rhetorically about Nin's views, but they do not explore them, out of fear, perhaps, of incurring the wrath of the Nin cult. In her article in *Notes from the Third Year*, Ann Snitow does mention that "it's fairly plain [that] Anais Nin isn't a conscious feminist as we understand the term now," but Snitow never speaks to that point; instead she praises the diaries for telling us the "painful truth." Nin's honesty becomes the criterion for acceptance, no matter what views are expressed. The diary becomes for Nin "the place where a woman can speak the truth without hurting all those people she is supposed to protect and support." Therefore, how can we scoff, when Nin truthfully tells us that she feels forgiving and compassionate toward Henry Miller when he sells the typewriter she had given him for his writing in order to buy some wine. The question is: truth about what?

Others like Snitow handle a negative appraisal of Nin by merely raising the issue, then dropping it. In the *San Francisco Chronicle* article (December 6, 1971) covering the first celebration I attended, the headline read, "A Heroine for Feminists." Beverly Stephen led of her report with this statement:

> Who could have guessed that many new feminists would find a heroine in a soft-spoken 68-year-old woman who refuses to generalize about men as 'oppressors.' Who doesn't have much sympathy for slogans like 'male chauvinist pig.' Who feels no need for drugs. Who can wear a long black dress in the middle of the afternoon. Who can befriend a man like Henry Miller.

But Stephen never pursues the point; the rest of the article is merely a factual account of the celebration.

In a feature story on January 16, 1972, about the same event, Jean Dickinson notes, in "Celebrating Anais Nin" (San Francisco *Examiner and Chronicle*): "So, no one asks about her husband and how she integrated him into a life filled with writing and Henry Miller. No one asks about her relationship to the Women's Movement, or about her attitude towards Kate Millett and other militant voices. No one questions her belief that women are more intuitive than men. No one challenges her 'Everywhere I look I am living in a world made by man as he wants it, and I am being what man wants . . . ' (I, 46), [her] rejection of political solutions or her conviction that it is enough to build 'private shelters.' " But Dickinson does not pursue these points either. Again I suspect it is out of fear of antagonizing such a popular figure and her admirers.

In an *Everywoman* interview in 1972, Karla Jay did have the courage to question Nin on some of her views on psychoanalysis and individual solutions as opposed to the group process of consciousness raising. Nin's reaction was, "we can help ourselves individually," but then she deftly concedes that "we need both because there are some cases where the social has so twisted an individual that all he can bring is already a damaged human being, and a damaged human being doesn't get repaired by political methods." I wonder who she would consider damaged – anyone who was not creative? anyone who did not dream? – for certainly these are the only qualities in people to which she seems to relate. Jay's format is a question-and-answer interview so that the intention may have been to let readers draw their own conclusions. But the fact that Jay does not follow up some of Nin's obviously elitist responses is further evidence of how tenderly women treat this delicate "feminine" object. Hidden among the routine questions and answers, Jay's probing is lost in the final positive impression left of Nin.

The third type of response to Nin by the press is represented by Anna Balakian's review of the fourth diary (*New York Times Book Review*, January 16, 1972). This type is actually rare, but it does exist. What Balakian does is *deny* that Nin possesses those traits of sexism or elitism, without investigating them: "Though she was placed by birth in an international milieu, made up mainly of musicians, artists and writers, there is no elitism in the world of Anais Nin." In the fourth diary, there is room for unknowns, as well as people like "Gore Vidal, Edmund Wilson, Truman Capote, Richard Wright, Salvador Dali, Martha Graham and the surrealist Andre Breton, . . . "!

Balakian describes Nin as "Ariadne leading man through the labyrinth. . . . She belongs to that almost extinct breed that still espouses the doctrine: 'I am my brother's keeper.' " Balakian does not question Nin's status in the women's movement: "Is she a symbol of the liberated woman? She has been for so long a free spirit that it is hard to think of her as 'liberated.' Her so-called feminine intuition is really a combination of poetic perception, acumen and the wisdom gained from a wealth of encounters."

What we have in the cult surrounding Anais Nin is a regressive aspect of the women's liberation movement. I am not impressed with her appearances at fund-raising events for women's centers or her promotion of women's journals because I see these, just as I view those "celebrations," as opportunistic efforts to spread her name and sell her books. At her appearance in San Francisco in the spring of 1974, she asked to be introduced with the announcement of the publication of the fifth volume of her diaries, and she offered to sign this book afterward in the lobby where her works were the only ones on display (at a feminist event attended by 1000 women!).

I believe Nin's involvement in the women's movement is insincere because she is not a feminist. She holds views that are contrary to those held by true feminists: the glorification of male heroes, the belief in the special nature of women that makes them superior to men, her repulsion to the ordinary, everyday struggles of oppressed peoples, her reliance on the individual solution, and her own self-glorification. Women will be poets and free thinkers without the Anais Nins. I think it is time women began to look at Anais Nin with some objectivity. She may be an inspiration and model for the struggling creative artist, but she is not a feminist; in fact, some of her views are outright sexist. She sees little if any value in collective efforts and is blind to the economic realities of most of society. Nin is using the women's movement for her own ends – to sell her books. We must not weaken our cause by nearsightedness; hero-worshipping should be anathema to all serious radicals and feminists.

From *Feminist Criticism*, edited by Cheryl L. Brown and Karen Olson. Scarecrow Press, 1978, pp. 312-23.

The Music of the Womb: Anais Nin's "Feminine Writing"

Sharon Spencer

The woman artist has to fuse creation and life in her own way, or in her own womb if you prefer. She has to create something different from man. Man created a world cut off from nature. Woman has to create within the mystery, storms, terrors, the infernos of sex, the battle against abstractions and art. She has to sever herself from the myth man creates, from being created by him, she has to struggle with her own cycles, storms, terrors which man does not understand. Woman wants to destroy aloneness, recover the original paradise. The art of woman must be born in the womb-cells of the mind. She must be the link between the synthetic products of man's mind and the elements.   (*Diary 1934-1939* 234)

This passage was written by Nin in 1937 when she was deeply involved in the process of articulating a philosophy of writing that would serve her specific needs as a woman writer. She described her unique approach to writing fiction in various ways: as "symphonic writing," as "the language of emotions," and as "the language of the womb." The phrase "music of the womb" unites the two most original – and most basic – characteristics of Anais Nin's body of fiction. Her writing is "musical" because it achieves its experiential impact through carefully constructed lyrical passages built up of textured, interrelated images; it is a "music of the womb" because it became (in the late 1930s) a consciously articulated expression of woman's experience, aspirations, and values. Nin wanted to endow words with flesh and blood, so to speak, to instill an inner dynamism, or *élan vital*, to demonstrate the value of sensitivity, empathy, compassion, eroticism, sensual pleasure and love of all kinds, as well as an appreciation of the arts. She believed that these qualities had been killed by many male writers' "cerebral" approach to fiction, their tendency to dissect and analyze (to "kill" their materials), and their puritanical judgmental attitudes, defensive postures arising – she believed – from a fear of yielding to feeling. When Nin set out to create an authentically "feminine" fiction, she conceived and initiated an ambitious project, the "continuous novel" *Cities of the Interior*. The five individual titles are *Ladders to Fire* (1946), *Children of the Albatross* (1947), *The Four-Chambered Heart* (1950), *A Spy in the House of Love*, 1954), and *Seduction of the Minotaur* (1959).[1]

The "music of the womb" is radical in three distinct ways. First and most obvious, in the 1930s, 1940s, and 1950s Nin was unveiling and exploring themes that few women writers except Colette had taken on, tabooed subjects: love affairs between older women and younger men; single women's entanglements with married men; women's friendships with homosexual men; white women's attraction to black men; a woman's attempt to attain erotic self-expression in the absence or love or emotional attachment; father-daughter and brother-sister incest; motivations causing lesbianism. Technically as well, Nin's earliest published works were boldly experimental. Both *House of Incest* and *Winter of Artifice* were written while Nin was working out her ideas for the "music of the womb." For a time, beginning in 1933, she was working on both manuscripts simultaneously, but *Winter of Artifice* was not completed until 1939. In both books she abandoned realistic conventions of style, structure, plot, and characterization, choosing instead to create free, autonomous, and organic forms. Each book is unique; each has a distinctive conception and form. What unites these works, making them cohere as a unified *oeuvre* is the "music of the womb": their musicality (the lyrical and rhythmical organization of all literary units, ranging from the phrase to the chapter or episode) and their devoted excavation and articulation of woman's experience.[2] Although Nin has often been labeled a Surrealist, she is closer to the fundamental impulse of Expressionism; she did not want to portray appearances but *essences*, and her literary forms were dictated not by tradition, but by the special individuality of each work, by "inner necessity" (to borrow a phrase from Vassily Kandinsky).

Inspired by Rimbaud's *Une saison en enfer*, Nin wrote *House of Incest* to express woman's psychic suffering: "I felt obsessions and anxieties were just as cruel and painful, only no one had described them vividly, as vividly as physical tortures. I wanted to do, in *House of Incest*, the counterpart to physical torture in the psychic world, in the psychological realm" (*Diary, 1931-1934* 265). A confession, *House of Incest* has an organic structure of seven parts that are set off from one another by calligraphs that resemble ancient runes; this design effectively enhances the overall air of torment and mystery. Throughout 72 pages densely filled with images, a nameless woman narrator broods obsessively on her state of dissociation, alienation, and emotional and sexual paralysis. She is attracted, on the one hand, to the irresponsible sensuality of a figure named Sabina and, on the other, to a pathetic and sinister aristocrat called Jeanne, who is in love with her brother.

In this book, the idea of incest is a controlling metaphor for all doomed, impossible loves, or for narcissistic self-love. The isolated and emotionally paralyzed narrator is split into parts, body separated from spirit, feeling from intelligence, love from desire. Jeanne is the narrator's guide on the perilous journey into the house of incest, a ghastly place of infertility and death. Powerful images piled on one another betray the energy of the frantic plunge: "The rooms were chained together by steps . . . . The windows gave out on a static sea, where immobile fishes had been glued to painted backgrounds. Everything had been made to stand still in the house of incest, because they all had such a fear of movement and warmth, such a fear that all love and all life should flow out of reach and be lost" (51-52). Typical of the many images of infertility is a white plaster forest, a "forest of decapitated trees, women carved out of bamboo, flesh slatted like that of slaves in joyless slavery, faces cut in two by the sculptor's knife, showing two sides forever separate, eternally two-faced . . . " (55). The book has a nightmarish intensity and a quality of suffocation. It is a nocturne: dark, foreboding, and also cruel.

Winter of Artifice is among Nin's finest novellas, both because of its unique mode of lyrical exposition – its technical distinction – and its sensitive, profound treatment of a perilous subject: incest between adults. Published in 1939, *Winter of Artifice* may well be the first work by a woman to probe deeply the nature of this attraction and its emotionally crippling bondage. After 20 years of separation, an adult daughter is reunited with her still youthful father. Naturally she experiences an almost irresistible pressure to hurl herself emotionally into the past to recapture the period of intimacy with him that she was denied at the appropriate age. (Like Nin's own father, the woman's father abandoned his family when she was a young girl.) Gradually, by accumulating intelligent insights into his character, the young woman withstands the threat to her adult autonomy that is contained in her desire to merge or fuse with her seductive father. Her womanly way of "conquering" her vain father is to offer a form of mothering that this narcissistic man cannot bring himself to refuse. His strategy for continuing to withhold love from his daughter is to typecast her as an "Amazon," a woman who does not need men. As long as the daughter collaborates in this distorted perception of herself as self-sufficient, she tacitly permits her father to refuse any responsibility to love her. The only solution is to accept her father's inability to love anyone but himself and to relinquish the fantasy of obtaining anything from him except deceptive flattery. This accomplishment is, inevitably, the result of a long struggle during which the daughter strips away her father's masks, one after another, revealing a frightened, lonely, aging man.

An extremely sophisticated piece, *Winter of Artifice* resembles a musical composition more closely than Nin's other works. Its 64 pages are woven into 13 movements of unequal length whose theme is "Musique Ancienne," one woman's experience with the Electra complex. In the sixth – central – section, the novella rises to an emotional climax and crisis. The daughter allows herself to imagine total union with her father:

> Inside both their heads, as they sat there, he leaning against a pillow
> and she against the foot of the bed there was a concert going
> on . . . . Two long spools of flutethreads interweaving between his
> past and hers, the strings of the violin constantly trembling like the
> strings inside their bodies, the nerves never still, the heavy pound-
> ings on the drum like the heavy pounding of sex, the throb of blood,
> the beat of desire which drowned all the vibrations, louder than any
> instrument . . . . (84-85)

This rhapsody is extended and buoyantly sustained, subsiding into a
slower rhythm and more muted tone. The dangerous dance of father and
daughter now becomes a solo performance for the daughter, who begins to
glide away. In the seventh section she recalls having given a dance performance when she was sixteen during which she imagined that she saw her father
in the audience, approving her performance. When she asks him to verify
this, "He answered that not only was he not there but that if he had had the
power he would have prevented her from dancing because he did not want
his daughter on the stage" (99). Assured that her father wants to bind her
with limitations, she tastes the foreknowledge of freedom. Regarding his
"feminine-looking" foot, she fantasizes that it is really *her* foot, which he has
stolen. This enables her to glimpse the truth that he wants to steal her mobility and freedom for himself. Literally, "tired of his ballet dancing" (113) (a
traditional, formally patterned dance contrasted to her more modern freer
way of moving), she demands the return of her own foot, and with it she re-
claims the capacity to run from him.
    While working simultaneously on *House of Incest* and *Winter of Artifice*,
Nin wrote:

> *It is the woman who has to speak.* And it is not only the Woman
> Anais who has to speak, but I who have to speak for many women.
> As I discover myself, I feel I am merely one of many, a symbol. I
> begin to understand June, Jeanne, and many others. George Sand,
> Georgette Leblanc, Eleonora Duse, women of yesterday and today.
> The mute ones of the past, the inarticulate, who took refuge behind
> wordless intuitions . . . (*Diary, 1931-1934* 289)

In 1937 she articulated the characteristics of "womb oriented writing,"
thereby becoming the third woman writing in English (as far as I am aware)
to have committed to paper the need for a feminine theory and practice of
literature. Dorothy Richardson, of course, was the first, and Virginia Woolf
the second.
    In August 1937, a conversation with Henry Miller, Lawrence Durrell,
and his wife, Nancy, provoked Nin to defend her subjective, lyrical, flowing
fiction. Later, she reflected:

Henry and Larry tried to lure me out of the womb. They call it objectivity. But what neither Larry nor Henry understands is that
woman's creation, far from being like a man's, must be exactly like
her creation of children, that is it must come of her own blood, en-
globed by her womb, nourished by her own milk. It must be a human creation, of flesh, it must be different from man's abstractions.
(*Diary, 1934-1939* 235)

The writing of the womb must be alive: that is, natural, spontaneous,
flowing (to use one of Nin's favorite words). It must have warmth, color, vibrancy, and it must convey a sense of movement (often Nin's characters are
stuck, immobile, or paralyzed), the momentum of growth. Woman's literature (a literature of flesh and blood) must create synthesis; it must reconnect
what has been fragmented by excessive intellectual analysis. Woman's creative works must be deep; they must trace expeditions into dangerous terrain.
They must explore tabooed topics and forbidden relationships. Woman's art
must be honest, even if the search for truth causes pain:

Woman's role in creation would be parallel to her role in life. I
don't mean the good earth. I mean the bad earth too, the demon,
the instincts, the storms of nature. . . . Woman must not fabricate.
She must descend into the real womb and expose its secrets and its
labyrinths. . . . My work must be the closest to the life flow. I must
install myself inside of the seed, growth, mysteries. I must prove the
possibility of instantaneous, immediate, spontaneous art. My art
must be like a miracle. Before it goes through conduits of the brain
and becomes an abstraction, a fiction, a lie. It must be for woman,
more like a personified ancient ritual, where every spiritual thought
was made visible, enacted, represented. (235)

Nin now conceived the multivolume "continuous novel," *Cities of the Interior*, a project that involved transforming the diary, or parts of it, into fiction. Characterized by a richly inventive feminine imagery (drawn from wom-
en's preoccupations and occupations like work, cooking, decorating a home,
feelings about pregnancy, clothing and makeup)[3] and an organic spontaneous
(thus unpredictable) structure, *Cities* takes as its theme the psychology of
woman: "Theme of the development of woman in her own terms, not as an
imitation of man. This will become in the end the predominant theme of the
novel: the effort of woman to find her own psychology, and her own significance, in contradiction to man-made psychology and interpretation. Woman,
finding her own language, and articulating her own feelings, discovering her
own perceptions. Woman's role in the reconstruction of the world" (*Diary,
1944-1947* 25).

The originality of *Cities of the Interior* lies partly in its use of lyricism to convey character, situation, and action but even more definitively, in its radical concept of structure. It is a group of distinctly discreet but related volumes with individual titles, in Nin's words, "a continuous novel." The various women artist protagonists appear and reappear, now one and now another occupying the central position as "main character." The individual volumes can stand alone wholly without reference to the others, or they can be read as parts of an unfinished whole. The order of the component parts of the continuous novel does not affect the reader's comprehension of the whole. The volumes can be considered interchangeable. Nin achieved this by avoiding specific chronological references, which would have established a sequence, and by writing fluid open endings that provide links moving simultaneously forward and backward in time.

This relativistic concept of structure underscores Nin's fluid concept of personality. In her books, being is always dynamic, the focus always on the process of becoming. Therefore, the ever-developing and self-modifying structure of the "continuous novel" is the ideal enclosure, because it destroys the very possibility of closure. New "cities" can always be prefixed, inserted in the middle or added at the end. The shape of *Cities of the Interior* need not be imagined as final, because the characters possess never-ending transformational possibilities. The organic structure of *Cities of the Interior* makes it at once abstract and yet intensely personal. Because it explores the psyche of woman with unprecedented depth, the work can be considered theoretical, and because it creates memorable characters, demonstrating what Nin meant by stressing subjectivity as the means of attaining the more general, or universal level of experience. "Because I could identify with characters unlike myself, [I could] enter their vision of the universe and in essence achieve the truest objectivity of all, *which is to be able to see what the other sees, to feel what the other feels*" (*Novel* 68).

Of the five novels, *Seduction of the Minotaur* (1959) is the most fully developed, the deepest in emotional range as well as the most technically accomplished. This novel derives its leisurely organic structure from the archetype of the journey; the several parts of the novel are journeys within the larger journey. *Seduction* begins with Lillian's arrival in Golconda where the people, whose "religion was timelessness" (92) "exuded a more ardent life" (14), and it ends with her "journey homeward" (95). Golconda is Lillian's "territory of pleasure" (9). Escaping from her "incompletely drowned marriage" with Larry (96), she is "maintained in a net of music, suspended in a realm of festivities" (12). Between her arrival and her "journey homeward," she reluctantly undertakes a perilous inner journey. (Now we are in the "labyrinth" Nin mentioned when she expressed the need for women to confront dangers.)

Once a classical pianist, the Lillian of *Seduction of the Minotaur* has exchanged traditional art for a more spontaneous one – jazz: "Classical music could not contain her improvisations, her tempo, her vehemence." (115). But "jazz was the music of the body . . . . It was the body's vibrations which rippled from the fingers. And the mystery of the withheld theme known to the musicians alone was like the mystery of our secret life" (18-19). Some of the novel's most brilliant passages approximate the technique of improvisation. Perhaps the most striking is the initial description of Golconda (a Mexican resort probably based on Acapulco): "She had landed in the city of Golconda, where the sun painted everything with gold, the lining of her thoughts, the worn valises, the plain beetles, Golconda of the golden age, the golden aster, the golden eagle, the golden goose, the golden fleece, the golden robin, the goldenrod, the goldenseal, the golden warbler, the golden wattles, the golden wedding, and the gold fish, and the gold of pleasure, the goldstone, the gold thread, the fool's gold" (6).[4]

The novel's major discovery (the goal of the dangerous journey) is the minotaur in Lillian's own personal labyrinth (unconscious), and this monster is none other than herself: "a reflection upon a mirror, a masked woman, Lillian herself, the hidden masked part of herself unknown to her, who had ruled her acts. She extended her hand toward this tyrant who could no longer harm her" (111). (In contrast, Theseus murdered the minotaur, and exploited and abandoned Ariadne.) Lillian discovers that her belief in our own freedom is an illusion; still bound, she must rediscover vital aspects of the "primitive." She must learn to dance to "the music of the body" before summoning the emotional and spiritual power to reignite her love of Larry through enlightened understanding. Before she can be reconciled with Larry, she must seek and submit to the rite, to a *participation mystique*.

Lillian loves to walk around Golconda barefooted. But when she is dancing with Fred, he clumsily steps on her foot. Another man, Michael Lomax, tries to prevent her from dancing with the natives, but Lillian defies him. In one of several scenes depicting dancing, Lillian also defies Dr. Hernandez. Determined to touch earth's "fiery core" (106), Lillian seeks fusion, not with any of the male characters, but with Golconda itself. This is the essence of her betrayal of Larry, but it is an impersonal betrayal and its ultimate effect makes healing possible:

> A singer was chanting the Mexican plainsong, a lamentation on the woes of passion. Tequila ran freely, sharpened by lemon and salt on the tongue. The voices grew husky and the figures blurred. The naked feet trampled the dirt, and the bodies lost their identities and flowered into a single dance, moved by one beat . . . .
>
> Dr. Hernandez frowned and said: "Lillian, put your sandals on!" His tone was protective; she knew he could justify this as a grave medical counsel. But she felt fiercely rebellious at anyone who might put an end to this magnetic connection with others, with the earth, and with the dance, and with the messages of sensuality passing between them. (105-06)

Lillian has become strong enough to resist attempts to inhibit her, even in the guise of protectiveness. She exults: "The time was past when her body could be ravished . . . by visitations from the world of guilt" (107).

At its most exalted, music was for Nin, as for many European writers, a way of entering the transcendent, even the sublime realm of experience. While "music of the body" may represent a parallel to the élan vital described by Henri Bergson (the basic dynamism of life), more sophisticated musical expressions represent parallels to more complex and intricate modes of experience: The "rhythm of life" (breathing, walking, the heart beat, dancing) has its counterpoint, or counterpart, in a more spiritual music. This more intricate, more subtle music provides "the continuity . . . which prevents thoughts from arresting the flow of life" (24) as well as "a higher organization of experience" (84).

This "higher organization of experience" (transcendence, the forgiveness, the revitalized and renewed love Lillian feels for Larry at the novel's end) becomes accessible to her only after the ritual *participation mystique* has been consummated. Only then it is possible for her to leave the labyrinth, not retracing Ariadne's thread, but by simply rising above the maze. Several transformations occur, enabling Lillian to soar at last. One such transformation (and it is crucial) is her temporary change of relationship to Larry. Becoming his mother instead of his wife, she re-*imagines* Larry, thus giving birth to him in a new, more complex form.

Finally, then, the most richly embroidered theme of "music of the womb" is the need for love, not only the power of maternal love, with its transformative powers, but also agape, the love of friends, which is the essence of Nin's fraternal vision of marriage, viewed more as lifelong friendship than erotic coupling. All the themes that appear and reappear in Nin's writings are related to the principle of Eros, or relatedness, as well as to the need for human beings to nurture and, when necessary, to heal one another.

Having departed from the labyrinth by air (in a plane), Lillian becomes absorbed in a sustained meditation on her relationship with Larry; this occupies the duration of her "journey homeward," the novel's concluding section. Admitting that she has not listened carefully to Larry because "he did not employ the most obvious means of communication" (99), Lillian traces their relationship back to its origins and their personalities back to their respective childhoods. Earlier imagery of earth, water, and fire is replaced by celestial figurations. Painful childhood incidents caused Larry to "be flung into outer space" (134). Lillian knows that she must find a way to bring him back to human orbit. To do this, she envisions Larry as the moon, a symbol of feminine receptivity: "How slender was the form he offered to the world's vision, how slender a slice of his self, a thin sliver of an eighth of moon on certain nights. She was not deceived as to the dangers of another eclipse" (136).

Even though she is elated by her newly created vision of Larry, Lillian acknowledges the difficulty of maintaining this vision with consistency and fidelity. The novel presents marriage as a process in which the struggle to fuse or to create a union of two must be balanced by the need to maintain individual integrity or selfhood. For this, periods of separation are required (like Lillian's three-month stay in Golconda). Nin's concept involves an important duality; one always lives, she believes, in two cities as the same time (the conscious and the unconscious realms of being). Lillian recognizes that "the farther she traveled into unknown places, unfamiliar places, the more precisely she could find within herself a map showing only the cities of the interior" (80).

Seduction of the Minotaur concludes with one of Nin's most tender passages, reminding us that however exciting the daring act of exploration, the greatest challenge of all is to explore the most familiar territories, those that lie closest to home, the cities of the interior. It is only by descending in an attempt to learn the truth that we can rise again, to embrace those we have loved perhaps but have never loved well enough: "Such obsession with reaching the moon, because they had failed to reach each other, each solitary planet! In silence, in mystery, a human being was formed, was exploded, was struck by other passing bodies, was burned, was deserted. And then it was born in the molten love of the one who cared" (136).

The tenderness, solicitude, and acceptance of the human need to nurture and to be nurtured characterize Nin's last "novel" as strongly as *Seduction of the Minotaur*. If *Seduction* is the most mature, the most fully developed and richly detailed example of the "music of the womb," *Collages* (1964) may be her most original book. Less musical than visual, as its title indicates, *Collages* is a composition of 19 juxtaposed vignettes. There are no narrative passages, no transitions between vignettes, no plot. Unit and overall coherence are provided by the dominant presence of Renate, a painter, and by the recurrence of related themes in the vignettes. There are many settings and many "characters"; all are swiftly sketched in Nin's vibrant, imagistic prose. Among them are Leontine, a buoyant black singer; Henri, a master chef; the deliriously mad actress Nina Gitana de la Primavera; Nobuko, who every day selected her kimono to harmonize with the weather; Varda, creator of exquisite airy collages of women; the betrayed wife of a French consul, who invents a new love for herself. Although all have been wounded in some way (Renate by her selfish lover Bruce), all are resourceful and imaginative; they have woven self-sustaining worlds of fantasy around themselves.

The situations depicted in the 19 vignettes are varied, but each demonstrates transformation achieved through imagination. All celebrate the vital role of creativity, whether it is the charm of playing "make-believe," the power of fantasy to invent new personalities and lives for oneself when reality becomes unbearable, or specific artistic creativity such as that represented by the book's artists: Renate, Leontine, Varda, and a writer named Judith Sands.

In a typical nurturing act, Renate rescues the neglected and bitter Judith

Sands (easily recognizable as a portrait of Djuna Barnes) from her lonely garret-like hideout. In the book's witty final vignette, the name of Judith Sands is saved from the jaws of a self-destructing apparatus that "eats" the names of artists and writers before exploding and burning. Symbolically, Nin alludes to the continuity of a tradition of women writers and restores Djuna Barnes to her place in that tradition.

To look back at *House of Incest* – an expression of entrapment, isolation, fragmentation, and suffering – and then to look at *Collages* – with its light, airy, confident tone and frequent examples of mobility – is to see the trajectory of Nin's growth as a woman and artist. Renate is assured and confident, entirely comfortable with her role as woman artist and with her many friendships; she is not at all dependent on her lover for her sense of value. When someone suggests that Varda make a portrait of Renate, he declines, explaining that she is *"femme toute faite."* He adds: "A woman artist makes her own patterns." Indeed, a definitively female narrative was Nin's ideal. It preceded by 40 years the theories of contemporary French writers, such as Annie Leclerc and Hélène Cixous, who argue the need for "writing the body," as Nin argued the need for writing the womb.[5]

NOTES

[1]The first book-length study of Nin's writings appeared in 1968: Oliver Evans's *Anais Nin*. Since then, there have been a number of studies and collections, including those by Hinz, Zaller, Knapp, Scholar, and Spencer. Also see Benstock (which includes a discussion of *House of Incest*) and *Anais: An International Journal* (Los Angeles), an annual begun in 1983.
[2]Thoroughly Latin, Nin had a personal perspective on the "Calvinist" approach to language: "Elaborate language, said the action novelist, was not necessary for our daily relationships. It was a luxury and an affectation we could dispense with. Simplifying it to basic English would lead to better communication. What it led to was an almost total atrophy of verbal expression. The Calvinist puritanism of speech weighed heavily also on color, rhythm, musicality of language which were equated with romanticism, baroque architecture and aristocracy" (*Novel* 94).

Music was important to Nin: her mother was a singer, her father a pianist and composer, and her brother Joaquin Nin-Culmell is a composer. Nin herself experimented with a career as a dancer. Moreover, she was particularly sensitive to the musical qualities of the English language. For instance, she felt a strong affinity with jazz: "Poetic prose might be compared to jazz. Jazz does not work unless it swings. The beat must be constantly tugged and pushed across the familiar line of the four-four balance until the real rhythmic message is *felt more than heard*" (*Novel* 171).

[3]Almost any page of Nin's fiction offers examples of her "feminine" imagery. When Lillian cooks, "the fruit was stabbed, assassinated, the lettuce was murdered with a machete. The flavoring was poured like hot lava and one expected the salad to wither, to shrivel instantly" (*Cities*, "Ladders" 4). Lillian's mode of dressing created "tumult in orange, red and yellow and green quarreling with each other. The rose devoured the orange, the green and blue devoured the purple. The sport jacket was irritated to be in company with the silk dress, the tailored coat at war with the embroidery" (5).

[4]Gold is associated with the highest plane of existence in the symbolism of medieval alchemy, a process that became for Nin a convenient analogy for creative transformation in both art and life. Most of the images of Golconda are drawn from nature, from the world of birds, insects, and herbs. One striking exception is "golden wedding"; continuity in relationship, especially marriage, is one of the novel's several interconnected problems. Another exception is "the golden thread," which suggests the thread that Ariadne gives Theseus to help him find his way out of the labyrinth. It is the sun that makes everything golden (the vibrancy of the light is a recurrent reference in *Seduction*). And Golconda itself suggests "gondola," which is a specific type of boat, a variation on the landlocked ship in the book's directive dream, described in the opening passage, expressing Lillian's psychological difficulty in terms of the dream of a landlocked boat. Consequently, the seemingly random associations of the passage are actually connected in ways that sustain and strengthen the novel's major themes.

[5]Readers may wish to consult *New French Feminisms* edited by Marks and de Courtivron and *The Newly Born Woman* by Cixous and Clément. Also see Margret Andersen who connects the work of Nin and Annie Leclerc.

WORKS CITED

Andersen, Margret. "Critical Approaches to Anais Nin." *The Canadian Review of American Studies* 10 (1979): 255-65.

Benstock, Shari. *Women of the Left Bank: Paris, 1900-1940*. Austin: U of Texas P, 1986.

Cixous, Hélène, and Catherine Clément. *The Newly Born Woman (La jeune née)*. Trans. Betsy Wing. Minneapolis: U of Minnesota P, 1986.

Evans, Oliver. *Anais Nin*. Carbondale: Southern Illinois UP, 1968.

Hinz, Evelyn J. *The Mirror and the Garden: Realism and Reality in the Writings of Anais Nin*. [Columbus]: Publications Committee of Ohio U Libraries, 1971.

_____, ed. *The World of Anais Nin: Critical and Cultural Perspectives*. *Mosaic* 11.2 (Winter 1978).

Knapp, Bettina. *Anais Nin* New York: Ungar, 1978.

Marks, Elaine, and Isabelle de Courtivron, eds. *New French Feminism: An Anthology*. Amherst: U of Massachusetts P, 1980.

Nin, Anais. *Cities of the Interior* (*Ladders to Fire, Children of the Albatross, The Four-Chambered Heart, A Spy in the House of Love, Seduction of the Minotaur*). Collective title first published 1959 (with *Solar Barque* instead of the yet incomplete *Seduction*). *Seduction* published separately 1961. Complete edition with Introduction by Sharon Spencer, Chicago: Swallow, 1974.

_____. *Collages*. Denver: Swallow, 1964.

_____. *The Diary of Anais Nin, 1931-1934*; *The Diary of Anais Nin, 1934-1939*; *The Diary of Anais Nin, 1944-47*. All edited by Gunther Stuhlmann. New York: Harcourt, 1966, 1967, 1971.

_____. *House of Incest*. 1936. Denver: Swallow, 1961.

_____. *The Novel of the Future*. 1968. Athens: Ohio UP, 1985.

_____. *Winter of Artifice*. 1939. Denver: Swallow, 1961.

Scholar, Nancy. *Anais Nin*. Boston: Twayne, 1984.

Spencer, Sharon, ed. *Anais, Art and Artists*. Greenwood, FL: Penkevill, 1986.

_____. *Collage of Dreams: The Writings of Anais Nin*. 1977. Expanded ed. New York: Harcourt, 1981.

Stuhlmann, Gunther, ed. *Anais: An International Journal*. Los Angeles.

Woolf, Virginia. *A Room of One's Own*. 1929. New York: Harcourt, 1963.

Zaller, Robert, ed. *A Casebook on Anais Nin*. New York: NAL, 1974.

From *Breaking the Sequence: Women's Experimental Fiction*. Eds. Ellen G. Friedman and Miriam Fuchs. Princeton: Princeton University Press, 1989, pp. 161-73.

Nin's Shorter Fiction

Passion in Parenthesis

Stuart Gilbert

In an earlier age the author of the *House of Incest* would probably have ended her career at the stake – in good company, needless to say, beginning with Joan of Arc. For there is something uncanny in her clairvoyance. It is as if she had drunk a potion, or contrived a spell giving her access to that underworld whose entry bears the prohibition: *All consciousness abandon, ye who enter here!* Courage was needed to embark on such a quest, and, with courage, shrewdness and a delicate sense of balance, enabling the clairvoyant to walk the tight-rope between self-analysis and self-abandonment. All these qualities, and with them no ordinary skill in the manipulation of words and rhythms, are manifest in the work of Anais Nin.

The act of love might seem relatively accessible and open to analysis as a physical event; yet a *petite mort* seems to obliterate cognition almost as thoroughly as death *tout court*. In the moment when desire rises to white heat, the conscious mind goes up in flames; forces older and stronger than the intellect, most fragile of man's attributes, disintegrate it. Inevitably there are no ready made phrases for such an experience, which, like the ecstasy of the mystic, can be described only in metaphor, conveyed by implication.

In this amazing work Anais Nin sets boldly out to describe these experiences which to most writers seem to lie beyond the range of words. She has succeeded, as nearly as success is possible – given the limitations of our modes of thinking and expressing thought – in the attempt. The title refers, I think, to one of her discoveries in this uncharted land; that ultimately such experience is self-centered, the lover is thrown back on himself or herself, while the partner dwindles to a lay figure draped in the vestments of creative passion. Thus, in a sense, the beloved is a projection of the lover, a phantom born of his imagination; and the act of love becomes an act of incest.

To my belief, nothing quite like this has been done before; previous attempts to scale these heights have had a way of falling into bathos. For, seen from the outside, such experience looks merely grotesque; hence the absurdity of so-called realism in erotic literature. To see love steady and see it whole, the observer must be posted, as Anais Nin posts herself, in the center of its action, in the heart of ecstasy; and he must have the poet's gift.

From *Reading and Collecting* 1.12 (November 1937): 23.

Refinements on a Journal

Paul Rosenfeld

The father of Anais Nin was an elegant, spoiled Spanish musician and composer whom some authorities set in an artistic category above Manuel de Falla's. In her twelfth year he brought her, his wife, and his small sons to New York and deserted them. The little girl was in love or fancied herself in love with her father, possibly because she had received little understanding from him. His brutality profoundly shocked her. To help make the desolation of life endurable she began keeping a journal. She has told us that it was a monologue or dialogue dedicated to him, inspired by the superabundance of thoughts and feelings caused by the pain of his leaving. In her own words, "little by little she shut herself up within the walls of her diary. She talked to it, addressed it by name as though it were a living person, her own self, perhaps. . . . Only in her diary could she reveal her true self, her true feelings. What she really desired was to be left alone with her diary and her dreams of her father. In solitude she was happy."

The diary grew, persisted in the process of development. It is said actually to comprise fifty-odd sections or notebooks. Fragments which have been circulated suggest that despite monotonies it belongs to literature more thoroughly than does the famous journal of Marie Bashkirtseff. Romantic posturing, narcissistic self-portraiture seem fairly absent here. One feels the effort of truth in the face of curious reticences and obscurities. The vast congeries of prose is lyrically expressive of certain feminine, in instances almost imperceptible, feelings connected with an aesthetic world mainly that of decadent Paris; expressive even more of a feminine self-consciousness strangely enamored of the very state of feeling, yet singularly perceptive of the subliminal and marvelous. The element of the irrational, germane to all lyricism, is included in the style: it is prevalently surrealistic. Audaciously it exploits the connotative power of language while presenting the unseen through wild, often far-flung analogies. Still many of these analogies are remarkably exact: that, for example, which reveals the semi-conscious rhythmic unity of feeling between two intimates – almost on the musical level – through an image of orchestral sonorities; or that shadowing forth neurotic conflicts with the symbol of the high strain and hubbub of a giant New York hotel. Taste, indeed, remains in evidence throughout: plainly in the style's refusal, for all its periodic exaltation, to violate the genius of prose, the tone of speech, and fully commit oratory or prose-poetry.

Frequently in these years, we feel, the author must have entertained an impulse to improve on her lyrical diary in the way of unification and impersonality by recasting some of its materials in narrative shape, with herself as the center of an epical event. As frequently, we guess, she must have had moments which revealed not only the growing difference between the imago who was the recipient of her confidences and her actual father but the former's steady tendency to sublimation. Both hunches are corroborated by "Winter of Artifice," the present little volume – sensuously so attractive with its shapely typography, good ink, softly toned paper, and the delicate line drawings by Ian Hugo. With the disposition of some of the material of the journal at a certain distance from her own center of gravity, it exhibits – awkwardly at times but altogether fluently and touchingly – two of these moments of revelation. The first was incidental to her seductive parent's long-looked-for reappearance in her life. In the course of an effective portrait of him we see Joaquin Nin take her to stay in the south of France and her conception of a temporary feeling that he is the person closest to herself. Shortly the disharmony which always had existed between their ways of living grows plain. She becomes aware that she has outgrown her need of him.

The second experience reaches us in the course of an ingenious account of a psychoanalysis. We grasp the event of the partial transference to the physician of the patient's discovery of her own poles of warmth and coldness under different feminine names. We see her new enjoyment of her own body and final disinclination or inability to dissolve her early fixation and completely accept normality in the orthodox sense. The final charmingly imaginative pages tragically reidentify the fixated being who imperiously and jealously holds her allegiance in torment and bliss, in living and keeping her journal. She calls it "the dream": it wears the look of her own individuality, in which as if it were a shell she hears the murmur of life. The suspicion that from the first Anais Nin was both something of an artist and a solitary, that her *"beata solitudo, sola beatitudo"* in keeping a journal made her more of both, is inevitable. Journals famously are a resource in solitude, a means of breathing in the desert. Fatally they also are its co-creators.

From *The Nation*, September 26, 1942: 276-77.

"Men . . . Have No Tenderness": Anais Nin's *Winter of Artifice*

William Carlos Williams

When women as writers finally get over the tendency to cut their meat so fine, really "give" out of the abundance of their unique opportunity, as women, to exploit the female in the arts, Anais Nin may well be considered to have been one of the pioneers. I speak of her new book, *The Winter of Artifice*, hand printed by herself.

It's hard to praise a book of this sort. Either you say too much and overdo it or you say too little and seem to condemn. And I want to praise. To face an accusation of artiness would be its danger and nothing in a writer is more damnable. But if there is that that seems superlative, in the use of the words, in the writing, spotted like a toad though it may be or a lily's throat – then go ahead. Make the blunder. This is a woman in her own right.

In *The Winter of Artifice*, the first of these stories, from which the general title is taken, a man is carefully, lovingly placed in his living grave by a devoted daughter. In the second, *The Voice*, a woman destroys a psycho-analyst who is rather a baby – or perhaps shrewd enough, professionally, never to fall in love with a woman he knows he can get.

This doesn't sound too good: the familiar pattern common among female writers in recent years. The mantis that takes her mate in her arms, bites an eye out then consumes him to the last whisker. Transformed to a varnished packet of eggs he will be fastened anon to the thorn of some nearby rose bush. Women enjoy this sort of thing. With Anais Nin it is a means and not an end.

Women in the arts have had many special difficulties to overcome. First it was the time lag between the general ascendancy of man as against woman to intellectual distinction, particularly in the arts. This placed woman too much on the defensive in a world lacking much that she had to offer, by which an astringency was forced upon her from which she could neither gain satisfaction nor escape. Some of them get tough and want to throw it around like men. What the hell? It's only a sort of boil anyway. Others take other means of escape. But until they recover completely from this negative combative stage they will fail to realize their full opportunity.

In these two stories of Anais Nin a titanic struggle is taking place below the surface not to succumb to just that maelstrom of hidden embitterment which engulfs so many other women as writers. I feel the struggle and find myself deeply moved by it. It's the writing itself which effects this sense of doomed love striving for emergence against great odds. It is in the words, a determination toward the most complete truth of expression, clean observation, accurately drawn edges and contours – at the best. But the characters of the story, do what they may, are drawn down. Something in the writing is not drawn down, survives.

To me the leading character of Anais Nin's first story and Lilith of the second are the same person though not spoken of as though they were, in the telling. They, as a matter of fact, complement each other: if the outcome of the first story had not been what it is the second would have missed its occasion for being. The young woman of *The Winter of Artifice* not having achieved what she set out to do, repossess the father, the development found in the second story becomes all but inevitable.

It is woman trying to emerge into a desired world, a woman trying to lift herself from a minor key of tenderness and affection to a major love in which all her potentials will find employment, qualities she senses but cannot bring into play. The age and times are against her. But if I speak of discovery here I mean that the strain, the very failures of the characters in both these stories tell of something beyond ordinary desiring. Whether Anais Nin is correct in her final analysis of what that is is something else again.

It is hard to say: the effect is, from my viewpoint, of a full vigor striving to emerge through a minor perversity. Another might read it the other way. Let it not be forgot that the girl's father of *The Winter of Artifice*, on whom she lavished her love (not forgetting that without a quiver she abandons a resourceful mother who had made a home for her during her infant years) is not destroyed willingly. The girl who has lived for him, who has welcomed him a visitor in her dreams and flies to his side at the first opportunity, puts up a real fight to rescue him from his self-destroying lies. But he will not have it. He either won't or can't come clean with her until, after a tremendous effort, she gives him up and goes her way.

What might have happened had she won? What might not have come out of the association between father and daughter, for truth, for relief from a besotted world *had* the man allowed the daughter's pure and devoted love to triumph? Light was refused, he preferred his enshrouding lies. She was the true light bringer for him but he failed to receive it. She did not falter, it was he not she who was perverse.

The second story grows out of this failure. This time it is another person but the character is about the same. Lilith releases herself to her fate and who shall say whether she or The Voice is at fault at the end. She has been conditioned in the first story, or we have, and this second is the result of it.

These might easily be the two first chapters of a longer novel of great promise.

Maximum vigor lies in two strong poles between which a spark shall leap to produce equilibrium in the end. When we get a piling up at one pole without the relief the feeling is transitional. A passage from the second story, *The Voice*, will show this piling up at the negative pole: "Lilith entered Djuna's room tumultuously, throwing her little serpent skin bag on the desk, her undulating scarf on the bed, her gloves on the bookshelf, and talking with fever and excitement: . . . What softness between women. The marvelous silences of twinship. To turn and watch the rivulets of shadows between the breasts, . . . the marvelous silence of woman's thoughts, the secret and the mystery of night and woman become air, sun, water, plant . . . When you press against the body of the other you feel this joy of the roots compressed, sustained, enwrapped in its brownness with only the seeds of joy stirring . . . The back of Lilith, this soft, musical wall of flesh, the being floating in the waves of silence, enclosed by the presence of what can be touched." This is the mood and the background, a stasis, an absolute arrest. Proust is one of its triumphs. But were that all, frankly, I shouldn't bother with the book though good writing will be good writing to the end of time. To me Anais Nin carries the impetus a little further; from that undertone a new melody tries to lift itself, tries and fails in what constitutes, I believe, an upturn in the writing.

For much of the confusion and all the "mysteries" concerned in a certain pseudo-psychologic profundity of style well known among women comes from a failure to recognize that there is an authentic female approach to the arts. It has been submerged, true enough; men have been far too prone to point out that all the greatest masterpieces are the work of males as well as of the male viewpoint or nearly so. Women swallow this glibly, they are the worst offenders. But the fact is, without "mystery" of any sort, that an elementary opportunity to approach the arts from a female viewpoint has been badly neglected by women. More important, without a fully developed female approach neither male nor female can properly offset each other. Am I right in presuming that Anais Nin cares a fig about that or even agrees with me in my main premise?

The male scatters his element recklessly as if there were to be no end to it. Balzac is a case in point. That profusion you do not find in the female but the equal infinity of the single cell. This at her best she harbors, warms and implants that it may proliferate. Curie in her sphere was the perfect example of that principle. Naturally some men write like women and some women like men, proving the point; two phases with a reciprocal relationship. This female approach has only recently been recognized in its full dignity by women of distinction, in the past by them signally neglected. The term "female" has been too tied up with weakness, with effeminacy, suggestive of sickness to bear the close scrutiny necessary to get to the elemental worth out of the thing.

It begets a style beset with dangers which Anais Nin has far from escaped but from which I think she shows she is escaping or might escape to perform a completely outstanding work. It is a style whose faults made Virginia Woolf at times all but unreadable. Our own Kay Boyle stood on the brink many years ago: a careful arrangement of polished pebbles to simulate the shore of the sea, a fine-combing for effects, and words, words, words dusted and dressed – an inability, in short, to give the theme its head in a major (female) key and let the writing rest on that.

But where is there such a theme for a woman? Certainly not sand which cannot possibly be made to stand as a tower without a cement of understanding to hold it together. In a woman, something that links up her womanhood with abilities as a writer will allow her to draw abundantly upon that for her material. Its development, looking at the failures, appears to be a slow process, today like a bird half out of an egg. A young poet, Marcia Nardi, succeeds in it more seriously and unaffectedly than any woman writer I can recall at the moment.

It's the *female* of the thing that still goes against the grain. To follow the prevailing myth: no one wants to be female but a few discerning men. Men, it is said, make the best modistes, the best cooks, the best little whores, the best, the best, etc. Women eat it up. Or fight against it. None wants it unless I am correct in believing that Anais Nin, much to her credit, begins to show the change in a positive attitude toward her opportunities and not a defeatist, reactionary one.

Anais Nin is in nothing that I can detect a man. From this courage and it seems to require courage in a woman to be a woman in the arts consciously, basically and . . . tenderly! without rancour! I say, from this courage Anais Nin is developing her newness, her security.

It must be something of this to account for the confidence and vigor of the woman. Her style, when she doesn't start off into wordy symphonies which are after all derivative and which I do not like in her, has assurance, a unique assurance. It breaks down at times as I have asserted, runs off into "subtleties," attenuations, sound effects – the old difficulty. But when it speaks direct it transmits a feeling of depth. Reading, I feel free to enjoy. Nobody is slashing my legs under the table, maliciously, as with so many women who imitate men. Anais Nin gives the impression of a woman for once sailing free in her own element, undisturbed.

Anais Nin hasn't written very much but I think everyone has read what she has written. We all remember the house-boat on the Seine, the shrieks and blinding pain of that childbirth with its gargantuan shadows and lightnings – that were not false. It has become an established image.

The thing is that though such writing is full of violence we do not find or seldom find, in this case, a straining after effects. Or if we do it is *that* which must be discounted. The only way anyone, male or female, can ever get away from that is by having something momentous to say and saying it to the full exclusion of all else. The style may be florid or it may be lean, that isn't the point, but it must never slide off irrelevantly into unnecessary matter.

It isn't the individual piece that we are doing either, it's not one series of images, any one story or material; they are the forms the imagination assumes under contemporary pressure. But it is that thing in ourselves which should we uncover it suddenly and completely we might shrivel up and be made impotent, forces us breathlessly on. Joyce speaks of the simultaneous straining and holding back; not because we will but because we must.

If I say Anais Nin is a good writer I mean that at her best she writes devotedly, without lie or excess baggage, from some such secret source of power which I have been trying to disclose, like a pig buried under a rosebush, a secret having to do profoundly with her sex. No doubt I am more than half wrong in defining it, if I have done so.

But Anais Nin herself indicates in one passage, I think, that she is almost fully conscious in herself of what I have been saying. Look at this: "The telephone range and there was someone downstairs to see The Voice. It is urgent. This someone came up, shaking an umbrella dripping with melted snow. She entered the room walking sideways like a crab, and bundled her coat as if she were a package, not a body. Between each word there was a hesitancy. In each gesture a swing intended to be masculine, but as soon as she sat on the couch, looking up at The Voice, flushed with timidity, saying: Shall I take off my shoes and lie down, he knew already that she was not masculine. She was deluding herself and others about it, etc., etc. . . . " The entire passage is worth studying carefully.

In the first place it's good writing. No hesitancy here. No posturing. No over-elaboration. The sentences are well formed, the observation is accurate, the sensitivity is unstrained. Absolutely not a touch of neurosis *in the writing.* Something the writer has observed and understood, something important, important enough to write about it truthfully. The subject matter itself is also interesting.

I have hazarded what I have had to say here on what is perhaps a somewhat unsupported opinion. Be that as it may this is the sort of thing, the sort of writing I have just quoted, that interests me, in detail, gives me the feeling that what I have been guessing about Anais Nin is right, permits me to take her most seriously. It is the sort of writing makes me think that Anais Nin knows what she has hold of. Something that steadies her hand, keeps her from slipping into detached adjectives for effects; says, finishes, and quits saying. That it is woman, surmounting her own history and turning to the arts for justification and relief, that is at stake. The final passage of the book is very moving:

"When she found the place, she sat very still and content. She was remembering the dream and seeking to recapture the lost pieces. She had caught her dream. Then it seemed to her that all the clocks in the world chimed in unison for a miracle. As the clocks chimed at midnight for all metamorphoses. The dream was synchronized. The miracle was accomplished. All the clocks chimed at midnight for the metamorphosis. It was not time they chimed for, but the catching up with the dream. The dream was always running ahead of one. To catch up. To live for a moment in unison with it, that was the miracle. The life on the stage, the life of the legend dovetailed with the daylight, and out of this marriage sparked the great birds of divinity, the eternal moments."

Moving as this may be it is not, for all that, the end of the story, not if what I have been saying holds water – but there is always a possibility that it does not. It may be that I am thoroughly mistaken.

From *New Directions No. 7* (1942): 429-36.

Review of *Under a Glass Bell*

Edmund Wilson

The unpublished dairy of Anais Nin has long been a legend of the literary world, but a project to have it published by subscription seems never to have come to anything, and the books that she has brought out, rather fragmentary examples of a kind of autobiographical fantasy, have been a little disappointing. She has now, however, published a small volume called *Under a Glass Bell*, which gives a better impression of her talent.

The pieces in this collection belong to a peculiar genre sometimes cultivated by the late Virginia Woolf. They are half short stories, half dreams, and they mix sometimes exquisite poetry with a homely realistic observation. They take place in a special world, a world of feminine perception and fancy, which is all the more curious for being innocently international. Miss Nin is the daughter of a Spanish musician, but has spent much of her life in France and in the United States. She writes in English, but mostly about Paris, though you occasionally find yourself in other countries. There are passages in her prose which may perhaps suffer a little from an hallucinatory vein of writing which the Surrealists have overdone: a mere reeling-out of images, each of which is designed to be surprising but which, strung together, simply fatigue. In Miss Nin's case, however, the imagery does convey something and is always appropriate. The spun glass is also alive: it is the abode of a secret creature. Half woman, half childlike spirit, she shops, employs servants, wears dresses, suffers the pains of childbirth, yet is likely at any moment to be volatized into a superterrestrial being who feels things we cannot feel.

But perhaps the main thing to say is that Miss Nin is a very good artist, as perhaps none of the literary Surrealists is. "The Mouse," "Under a Glass Bell," "Rag Time," and "Birth" are really beautiful little pieces. "These stories," says Miss Nin in a foreword, "represent the moment when many like myself had found only one answer to the suffering of the world: to dream, to tell fairy tales, to elaborate and to follow the Labyrinth of fantasy. All this I see now was the passive poet's only answer to the torments he witnessed. . . . I am in the difficult position of presenting stories which are dreams and of having to say: but now, although I give you these, I am awake!" Yet this poet has no need to apologize: her dreams reflect the torment, too.

The book has been printed by Miss Nin herself and is distributed through the Gotham Book Mart, 51 West Forty-Seventh Street. It is well worth the trouble of sending for.

From "Doubts and Dreams: *Dangling Man* and *Under a Glass Bell*," *The New Yorker*, April 1, 1944: 70, 73-74.

Review of *Under a Glass Bell*

Isaac Rosenfeld

According to what Henry Miller and William Carlos Williams have written about her, Anais Nin is a pioneer among women writers, striking out into a new area in the experience and expression of her sex. There are two reasons why "Under a Glass Bell" fails to present evidence for this claim. The first is that a truly pioneer figure, the equivalent for the feminine sex of Daniel Boone or Natty Bumpo, will never be found. And not because the will or the temperament is lacking, but because the wilderness is lacking. There are no regions of sex where a few well equipped masculine surrealists cannot penetrate, or to which, even if women be the ultimate discoverers, Freud, D. H. Lawrence and James Joyce cannot be taken as guides. I do not deny that Djuna Barnes, for example, inhabits a unique place; she does, however, have neighbors. Literary discoveries in sex, granting their indebtedness to the work that has already been done both in modern writing and psychology, no longer come as a complete surprise, but rather, as the fulfillment of our expectations. (This, I admit, is a-priori reasoning, for I have not read Anais Nin's unpublished journals on the basis of which the above claim is made.)

The second reason why "Under a Glass Bell" does not advance Anais Nin as a pathfinder has to do with the very writing of her book. It is the sort of writing which conveys more about the author, in a general sense, than it does, specifically, about itself. There are eight short stories or sketches in her book dealing with life in a house boat on the Seine, schizophrenia, the relations between the author and a servant girl, and the experience of childbirth. There is a delicacy in all these stories which resembles the lines of the semi-abstract copper engravings (by Ian Hugo) which so suitably accompany this book. There is delicacy even in "Birth," the story of a woman in labor with her dead child, her prolonged, intolerable pain resulting from her unconscious refusal to part with the child. It is the delicacy of the small scope, the needle point, confining the emotion exactly to the scale Anais Nin is working in – and naturally, it is better suited to concentration than discovery. Even the fantastic overtones she strikes in her sketches of schizophrenia, such as "Je Suis le Plus Malades des Surrealistes" and the title story, suggest an approach determined more by the conscious selection of sensibility that the instinctual imagery of sex.

What the stories in "Under a Glass Bell" do convey is a sense of craftsmanship and design, a set of values rarely imposed upon writing. Most short-story writers now practising their trade in this country are content with the ready-made design which follows the conventional beginning-middle-climax-end pattern suitable to conventional dramatic narrative. While experiments in focus, scale and design are interesting for their own sake, they turn out successfully only when the writer can make them conform to the demands of his craft. This Anais Nin has done, profiting even from the occasional lapses, like a stitch gone astray in embroidery, which appear in her work with the imperfection of an intimate product.

"Under a Glass Bell" was hand set by the author – a fact well in keeping with the non-commercial intent and quality of her writing.

From "The Eternal Feminine," *The New Republic*, April 17, 1944: 541.

Review of *Under a Glass Bell*

Violet R. Lang

Last fall Dutton published *Children of the Albatross*, by Anais Nin, without any of the usual publisher's ballyhoo – the commercial or the avant-garde variety. This winter they republished her collected short stories together with the novelette, *Winter of Artifice* (the stories have had both an English and a private edition). It may be that we have grown able, in this country, to recognize and accept this specialized and deeply private kind of experience – the kind of experience that a Surrealist painting commands and evaluates, the kind of experience found crystallized in *Winter of Artifice* – without our old reaction of scorn or of indignation at the baffling in art: the past decade has forced us into the recognition of the internal drama.

I think some part of the hostility with which Anais Nin has been dismissed by some readers may be attributed to this betrayal of objectivity; she is *embarrassing*. She has discredited the importance of environment of place and time; her streets are alike in New York or in Paris; she has returned to the natural city. Her emphasis is upon emotional interdependence, upon creation and upon destruction, upon the familial situation. Because these written lives are not lived in the language or seen from the perspective we are accustomed to assume, in the act of recognition, we are caught unawares. This is unsettling, and we are not used to it. We have not the conventions to do so. We look for a careful balance between reality and poised mentality in our novels; we look for a habit of intelligence, an intellectual capacity, which we identify readily as insight, character, typical behavior of a familiar type. Anais Nin upsets all this; she dismays the balance; the vivid discord of this painful inner reality must rise to create its own balance, demand its own perspective.

It is possible, on the other hand, to deny that the adjustment must be made, or that participation is required of the reader; it is possible to condemn the whole, discomfiting assumption of experience by unquestionable critical principles. She can be condemned for indiscretions of plot-manipulation (which have little importance to her), for repetitions and exaggerations, too rich characterizations, or even for her overwhelming use of emotional and connotative language – but this condemnation is pointless. She is not an objective writer; she is not trying to tell a good story; she is above all not attempting to manipulate social action.

What she is trying to do, and does very well, is to interpret deep personal relationships by writing of them in those circumstances which interpret them, the moments of change, the moments of revelation, the time of terrible intensity. She does this with deep sincerity, and with humility.

* * *

"The Mouse," "Rag Time," "The Labyrinth," and "Birth," to name several of the most extraordinary stories in the collection, are remarkable for precisely this fusion [of poetic impulse and the conventions of realism]. It is certain that her influence has already been felt, that she has affected many young writers and will continue to do so – and that the infusion, amidst the current dried-out imitations of Faulkner and Hemingway, enriches contemporary writing here and abroad.

She is a courageous writer, never leaning on the props of humor or colloquial speech, never having to reinforce the written situation with direct allusions to place or contemporary, physical detail. Indeed, one occasionally suspects that she has no sense of humor, and wonders where she has written or lived, in what time and in what place. And bound by her sincerity as she is to the real feeling, the essential situation, she must wander by night through the dark wood of neurosis, obeying that obligation of distortion and bedevilment, approaching the moment of dread, or the moment of realization.

So it is that she has this faculty for embarrassment. With other writers, in the portrayal of the personal drama, there is the indication on the writer's part of his authority, the convention of objectivity; there is a formal affiliation possible, between the author and the reader, in the examination of the text.

With Anais Nin this is not possible. There is no longer the framework of author, reader, people-in-a-book. The children of the albatross are living – threatening. There is no definable distance between them, the writer and the reader. These are marine characters of perilous delicacy, but they are real. Their reality exists outside of language, outside of description, dependent on the synthesis of these intense moments for the revelation of who they are.

Recognition is slow at first; then the first, familiar undertones of personality begin to merge into a whole, the whole of dream and consciousness, of spoken word and myth, of symbol and action. When it touches and at last affects, this recognition is a little frightening.

From *Chicago Review* 2.4 (Spring 1948): 162-63.

The Textual Evolution of
the First Section of "Houseboat"

Benjamin Franklin V

Her public posture led one to suspect that Anais Nin had thoughts and experiences that somehow but effortlessly resulted in stories, novels, diary entries, or pieces of criticism of uniformly high quality. But the persona of the lecture circuit belied the serious author who worked diligently to create a similar persona named Anais Nin in the *Diary* and who consciously fashioned her non-fiction into fiction and perhaps fiction into non-fiction. Nin was a diligent craftsman, and she was frequently dissatisfied with her work as it was originally published: she revised titles and contents, and in one instance she rewrote a novelette from a new point of view. I am concerned with Nin's revisions of her stories that were published first in the late 1930's and early 1940's and then became part of the various editions of *Under a Glass Bell* beginning in 1944. To trace the textual evolution of even one of her best stories would be too lengthy in this context, but an examination of the first section of "Houseboat" will go far to suggest the nature of Nin as a reviser.

I

"Houseboat" has always been placed first in *Under a Glass Bell*, yet it was not published as a whole outside that collection until 1971 when it appeared in *MD Medical Newsmagazine*. What amounts to a draft of the first section of the story appeared as "Life on the Seine" in 1941,[1] however, and by examining it and the corresponding parts of the subsequent editions of "Houseboat" one may glean a picture of Nin at work refining one of her creations. I hope to show that the original composition was roughly written; that Nin revised it substantively before establishing the standard, accepted text in 1948; that this finished product still needed work; that someone – and probably someone other than Nin – provided those refinements in the edition of the story published in the unlikely medical magazine; and that this best text has for some reason since been ignored. Underlying this paper is a belief that try as she did, both in this story and in the rest of her fiction, Nin never became the consummate artist comfortable with the basics of the English language or the American idiom, a fact that is obscured by the incandescent exoticism of her diction and her psychological subject matter.[2] Nin's work offers keen and valuable insight into the cities of one's interior, but she was unable fully to master the *craft* of fiction.

Nin made the major revisions of "Life on the Seine" in the first appearance of the complete story in 1944. The changes improve the original text noticeably, and while many were intended to tighten loose syntax, change capitalization, or insert, delete, or regularize punctuation, there are numerous substantive changes as well, and it is only with them that I shall deal in this paper. The first alteration is the deletion of an entire paragraph from the 1941 text. Placed between what are now the first and second paragraphs of the story[3] was another in "Life on the Seine" that reads as follows:

> Below me flowed the river welded and unified even in its anger. The sky threw its deflected rancour down over it, the clay bottom was stirred and colored the water with the tones of resentment, but the river flowed whole and complete with the same ease as music.

In the first paragraph the narrator tells of her escape from the current of the crowd to the houseboat on the Seine; the land is oppressive and the water, she hopes, offers her freedom. But after writing and publishing the paragraph just quoted Nin wisely chose to delete it from subsequent editions because it, much like the current of the crowd, is too prescriptive. Her original instinct was to describe the river's situation – free-flowing and whole despite turmoil above and below it – but one of the hallmarks of her fiction is that it shows and does not tell,[4] and being specific about the dominant symbol violated the story's subtlety. The attentive reader will grasp the parallel between the narrator and the river without such obvious and heavy-handed assistance. Further, the first five words of the 1941 paragraph are those of the entire penultimate sentence of the same text's second paragraph. While Nin often used repetition to good effect, she did not in this instance, and the revised text is therefore a considerable improvement over the original.

Nin next changed three key words in the present second paragraph. When the narrator compares herself to the derelicts ("wrecked mariners") who live on the quays she describes them as practically sub-human, yet Nin had the narrator originally attribute a positive quality to them that was at best ironical. The third sentence – the one describing the mariners – ended "sleeping, drinking, dreaming" in "Life on the Seine," but Nin deleted the last word, probably because it is one closely associated with the narrator and because it allows too much hope for the mariners. "Dream" is one of Nin's most important words, and using it imprecisely subverts the essence of her art. The mariners are also described in the eighth and ninth sentences, and in the former they have become similar to each other because of the weather, a likeness that extends to "the same *colored* skin" that became "the same *erod-*

ed skin,"[5] with the latter adjective much more in keeping with the mariners' unfortunate wasted state than the bland and general "colored." Their eyes were originally filled with "cold tears" that hint at the inability to express emotion, but Nin revised that to "stale tears," suggesting not a lack of feeling but expressed emotion that is ignored by others. In each of these instances Nin improved upon the original either by deleting or changing words that did not connote what she truly intended.

She also improved the text of the first sentence in what is now the second full paragraph on page 12 of the Dutton edition when she excised the last six words from the following in "Life on the Seine": "While the tramps slept, or ate bread and drank wine. . . ." In the short paragraph preceding this one Nin establishes the tramps desire for a somnolent existence (which is similar to what the narrator desires and attempts to attain), and the logical extension of their wish to have "no shocks, no violence, no awakening" is to have them asleep where such escape from reality is possible. Their eating bread and drinking wine contradicts what has already been established, so Nin once again was wise to alter the original text.

The last sentence on the present page 13 deletes a word and changes another from "Life on the Seine," both beneficially. The context is this: the narrator is leaving the city for the seclusion of the houseboat and her dreams, and this paragraph recounts her thoughts as she crosses the gangplank and prepares to unlock the door to the boat. She is troubled, and with good reason: to leave a known and socially accepted (and rational and awake) existence for one that is unknown or misunderstood and disparaged by society (the subconscious, the dream) is a bold step about which the narrator comments ambivalently in this story, but the narrator makes a courageous decision and prepares to enter the boat. Above all else she fears the houseboat will break its moorings and float away as it did once before (and one shortcoming of the story is that the narrator's earlier experience is alluded to at all) when, originally, "*only the* chain at the prow" breaks, but revised, when "*the* chain at the prow" breaks. Nin at first diminished the importance of the chain, but her decision to delete "only" was correct because the breaking of the tie between river and shore, dream and consciousness – the umbilical, as it were – is all that is needed to send the narrator exclusively into life on the boat and all that it represents. Only with the help of the wrecked mariners was she earlier able to save herself from such an existence.

In its original published form the final clause in the same sentence reads: ". . . the tramps had helped to swing *her* back in place." Evidently without realizing it Nin had equated too specifically the houseboat and the narrator, and, as I have already observed, Nin generally avoided stating the obvious. Boats have traditionally been referred to as feminine, but in this case it is crucial that the neuter be used, as Nin does in the revised text: ". . . the tramps helped to swing *it* back into place." In addition to being grammatically correct Nin's use of this pronoun also leaves the reader the job of equating the narrator and the houseboat, a process that engages the reader actively in the story while preserving its subtlety.

Another instance of Nin's deleting a word that too obviously attributed a quality of the narrator to an inanimate object is to be found in the last sentence of the final paragraph of page 13 of the Dutton edition. One knows that the narrator is justifiably fearful of her existence on the houseboat apart from life in society on shore, and when she originally wrote of the narrator's observation of the shadows on the quays Nin attributed fright to them: "It was only when the window rustled that the shadows which seemed to be one shadow split into two, swiftly *and frightenedly,* and then in the silence melted into one again." Attributing fright to the shadows borders on telling rather than showing the reader the similarities between the narrator and her external world, and Nin was astute in permitting the reader to see for himself the narrator's fear as she "splits" from her conscious to unconscious state in the revised text. (It is for this same reason that Nin chose to delete two sentences that concluded what is now the first paragraph on page 14: "The lights on the stairways to the street trembled. Shadows moved behind the trees on the quays, shadows dressed in petticoats.")

The episode with the revolver is one of the most perplexing in the story (does it have positive or negative connotations for the narrator? for Nin?), and here too the author was at first specific and obviously misleading but later general and accurate in her description of the narrator's face. The third sentence of the second paragraph on page 14 of the Dutton text originally read, in "Life on the Seine": "I looked at it *exactly* as if it reminded me of a crime I had committed, with an irrepressible smile *of great finesse, the kind of smile which* rises sometimes to people's lips in the face of great catastrophes which are beyond their grasp, the smile which comes at times on certain women's faces while they are saying they regret the harm they have done." The narrator of this story is incapable of finesse, and attributing that quality to her destroys the hesitancy, indecision, and fear that make her a complex and genuinely human being. As its was originally written this sentence stood as the sole description of the narrator's smile, but after Nin wisely altered it, she felt that some description of the smile was needed, so she added this line as the fourth sentence in the paragraph: "It is the smile of nature quietly and proudly asserting its natural right to kill, the smile which the animal in the jungle never shows but by which man reveals when the animal re-enters his being and reasserts its presence." The syntax here is jumbled and it is therefore difficult to understand exactly what Nin means, but this sentence represents an attempt on her part to refine the concept of finesse to something like animal instinct. The focus is clearly on nature, but Nin is also concerned with the nature of man; that is, just as animals in nature kill by instinct and thereby do whatever is necessary to preserve themselves, so too does the narrator, by entering the houseboat and firing the revolver, do what she must (enter her subconscious, her dreams) to preserve herself. This is obviously not conscious finesse, but rather a quality – or an instinct – that all animals including humans possess. The narrator has been injured in life and protects herself by fleeing from society to the houseboat. With this revision Nin attempted to make a glib and inaccurate description of the narrator's smile into something much more profound and universal, although, while her attempt was laudable, it was not totally successful because of the difficult syntax of the added sentence.

Nin also repositioned some sentences she had placed ineffectively in the 1941 version of the story. In the Dutton edition, the last two sentences in the first paragraph on page 15 originally appeared as the final sentences of what is now the second paragraph on that page, and the change was a fortunate one. At this point in the story the narrator is describing her view of the river from the houseboat (the windows facing the shore are closed) and how the breeze from the water caresses her bedroom, her "room of shadows," her "bower of the night." In the original version the narrator goes directly from her description of the view, breeze, and bedroom to a statement of what happens as she prepares to dream in her bedroom, but in the revised text she first describes her room ("Heavy beams overhead. . . .") before stating *parenthetically* what happens when she lies down to dream. Here the specific, exotic description of the bedroom logically sets the stage for the dream that will follow, and it is this establishing of a logical sequence bordering on cause and effect that makes the revision not only acceptable but mandatory.

An important change in the next paragraph also improves the text. At this point in the story the narrator reclines on her bed feeling certain that it would save her life if the houseboat were to sink. Nin herself, however, regularly cautions against a life lived exclusively in the dream, and the narrator here is oblivious to any of its dangers (not forgetting her original trepidation upon boarding the boat), thinking the dream state one solely of ecstasy. When Nin first wrote this paragraph she began the last sentence with "Burying" but late revised to "Burrowing": "Burrowing myself into the bed only to spread fanwise and float into a moss-carpeted tunnel of caresses." Once again the original word does more than hint at the relationship of the narrator and the houseboat, and "burying" herself in the bed tells of her necessary death. "Burrowing," on the other hand, while bordering on cuteness, nonetheless eliminates any connotations of death and challenges the reader anew to establish for himself the relationship between the narrator and the houseboat.

Toward the conclusion of "Life on the Seine" (Dutton, 15.6) Nin introduces a religious element that is unexpected and undeveloped. The situation is one in which the narrator is observing candles battling futilely to destroy darkness (society attempting to subdue the narrator, consciousness trying to obscure subconsciousness), and the final two sentences of that description are these: "The candles never conquered darkness but maintained a disquieting duel *of halos and holy ghost tongues on the eve of expiring. Their trembling breathless duel with the night.*" Nin abruptly introduces similar religious elements at the end of *House of Incest* with uncertain results, but placing them without warning or development in the brief first section of "Houseboat" is certainly more than the piece can bear. She improved the story by deleting the religious elements and compressing the two sentences into one: "The candles never conquered the darkness but maintained a disquieting duel with the night."

The last full paragraph on page 15 of the Dutton edition contains another major revision of the 1941 text. This is the penultimate paragraph of the first part of the story, and here the narrator is reminded of life on shore when she hears sounds emanating from that direction. Until this point she has walked hesitantly to the houseboat, succumbed to its charms, and begun her dream; now she is emerging from it. This paragraph hints at the narrator's emotional state, but Nin used two awkward and perplexing paragraphs to make a less effective comment in the earlier piece:

> I heard a sound on the river. *In my bare feet* I leaned out of the window. But the river was silent again. *I lay on the bed trying to remember where I had seen the windows before. Where had I seen these small casement windows divided into six little squares of glass and covered with small colored stones? It was in Grimm's Fairytales, in the house of the dwarfs.*
>
> Now I heard the sound of oars. Softly, softly coming from the shore. A boat knocked against the barge. There was a sound of chains being tied.

In this original version Nin has the unnecessarily barefooted narrator viewing herself as a small, inconsequential person, much like the Mouse and Stella in other stories, and while the intended effect was to relate this present, adult experience with the dream to the dreams the narrator had as a child (as inspired by the brothers Grimm), it is unsuccessful largely because it is superfluous. The reader does not need to know that the narrator was a dreamer as a child; all that matters is that she desires and is able to attain the dream. To provide this historical detail is to destroy much of the charm of Nin's art, and she was wise to rewrite the two 1941 paragraphs.

The last paragraph of this part of the story (Dutton, pp. 15-16) ends with the narrator awaiting the phantom lover who represents the ideal man. She is pleased that she will accept only perfection, but Nin obviously believed and the reader knows that to await the ideal is to wait forever for the unattainable (Hawthorne's Aylmer is just one of many other characters who desires with disastrous results what the narrator does here). One may of course attain the ideal in a dream, but transferring that quest to one's daily life is dangerous and self-defeating. Both "Life on the Seine" and the first part of "Houseboat" end with this comment on the phantom lover, but the former contains a final sentence that Nin later struck:

> I await the phantom lover – the one who haunts all women, the one I dream of, who stands behind every man with a finger and

head shaking, "Not him; he is not the one." Forbidding me each
time to love. *I await him*.

This last sentence is obviously redundant, and because of this protestation
one thinks the narrator is attempting to convince herself of the validity of her
own desire. Once again Nin's revised text is superior to the original.

Of the revisions discussed above, only two − swing it back] swing her
back; Burrowing] Burying − did not appear in the first Gemor edition of the
story in February, 1944, and they appeared in the second Gemor edition in
June of that year. One may therefore conclude that Nin made most of her
major revisions after the ephemeral little magazine *Matrix* published "Life on
the Seine" in 1941 and before she personally set type for the first publication
of the story in 1944. She made a few revisions in the first Gemor text before
setting type for the second (rods] shoots, Dutton, 12.2, and looking] opening, Dutton, 15.2, are the most significant of the changes not discussed in this
paper), but it is obvious that after the first group of revisions she gave most
serious attention to the text when she prepared it for the Dutton edition of
1948. There are innumerable instances of uniform readings in the first four
editions that are altered in the 1948 text, and while few of the revisions are
substantive, they do indicate that Nin had become more aware than previously of the mechanics of language, and she made a special attempt to make uniform her spelling (anesthetic] anaesthetic; houseboat] house boat) and
punctuation. After 1948 Nin had opportunities to make further revisions in
the Owen text (1968), in the periodical *MD Medical Newsmagazine* (1971),
and in the two editions of the *Anais Nin Reader* (1973, 1974), but aside from
a few minor changes that were editorial and not authorial − and also considering a typesetter's error in the two editions of the *Anais Nin Reader* (boat [
moat, Dutton, 15.29) − the 1968, 1973, and 1974 texts are those of the 1948
edition. Of the editions published after 1948, only one − the 1971 − differs
substantively from it. The development of the "Houseboat" text, then, is, with
the exception of the 1971 edition, logical: as Nin matured as a literary artist
she refined it effectively several times until she produced a text thirty years
ago with which she was satisfied.

By far the most changes occurred between the texts of 1941 and 1944,
but the next greatest number appeared between those of 1968 and 1971
(there are almost twice as many revisions there as between the 1947 and 1948
texts, for example), and judging by their nature, these last changes were made
by someone more sophisticated than Nin showed herself to be in the use of
language. Here special attention was given to capitalization, spelling, compound words, possessives, punctuation, prepositions, tense, and the substitution of "that" in restrictive clauses for the awkward "which." These revisions
without exception improve the text and make it, finally, complete and effective stylistically, but its existence raises several troublesome questions. Who
made the changes? If Nin, then why, after such assiduous attention to the text
did she not use it as the basis for the most recent printing of the Dutton edi-

tion (fourth Swallow printing) or the two editions of the *Anais Nin Reader*? If not Nin, did this unknown person make the revisions with her authorization? A line on the first page of the *MD Medical Newsmagazine* text reads as follows: "From *Under a Glass Bell*, copyright (c) 1948 by Anais Nin. Reprinted by permission of the author's representative, Gunther Stuhlmann," but in a letter to me dated 8-10-76, Stuhlmann states that he did not revise the text and that "the MD reprint was a routine permission request which did not imply that any changes in the text were to be made . . . ." If the reviser was neither Nin nor Stuhlmann, then it must have been an editor at MD Publications, and if that is the case, there is cause for concern, even though the revisions improved the text.[6] I do not know the answers to the problems presented by the 1971 edition of "Houseboat," but they need to be discovered.

Such a study as this one of Nin's revisions leads to the conclusion that she was a serious and careful but imperfect examiner of her own work. She was still fairly new to fiction-writing when she published "Life on the Seine" in 1941, but as she matured artistically she was able to evaluate and reevaluate her early work and make revisions that invariably improved the texts. Nevertheless, it must still be said that with the exception of *House of Incest* and "Birth" (the latter lifted practically verbatim from the *Diary*, at least as we have it in its published form), all of Nin's fiction could have benefited from more textual revision; she, however, must have been content with it as it stands. I believe that Nin's fiction constitutes a substantial body of largely and undeservedly ignored literature that suffers slightly but noticeably from her inability to hone her prose to the necessary degree of sharpness.[*]

NOTES

[1]"Life on the Seine," *Matrix* 3.2 (1941), 12-16. This should be inserted as item C21a in my *Anais Nin: A Bibliography* (Kent, 1973). The second and third parts, about the landscape of despair and the isle of joy, apparently were never published apart from "Houseboat," but the last section appeared as "I Shall Never Forgive the King of England," *Matrix* 3.3 (1941), 28-33. Even though the complete story was first published as "House Boat," I refer to it throughout this essay as "Houseboat," honoring Nin's final decision with respect to the title.

[2]Nin came closest to fusing manner and matter in *House of Incest*, her first piece of fiction.

[3]All references to the final text of "Houseboat" are to *Under a Glass Bell and Other Stories* (New York: Dutton, 1948), pp. 11-16.3. See II for a list of and comment on the different editions and printings of this story.[*]

[4]It is because it tells too much that the story "Hejda," for example, is not as effective as it might have been.

[5]All emphases within quotations in this paper are my own.

[6]In a telephone conversation with MD Publications in New York City on

March 17, 1977, I was informed that their editors occasionally alter a submitted text (in this case a Swallow printing of the Dutton edition) to make spelling uniform, correct grammar, and change "which" to "that" in restrictive clauses. The revised text is sent to the author or his representative before publication, and since Gunther Stuhlmann does not recollect knowing of revisions in this edition of "Houseboat," it is possible that Nin saw the modified text and endorsed it.

*Editor's note: Parts II and III of Franklin's article, not reproduced here, list the nine editions of "Houseboat," the eight printings of the "Dutton" edition, and textual variations that support his "evolution" argument. Of course, additional printings have appeared since his article was first published.

From *The World of Anais Nin: Critical and Cultural Perspectives*, ed. Evelyn J. Hinz. A Special Issue of *Mosaic* 11.2 (Winter 1978): 95-106.

Discourse and Intercourse, Design and Desire in the Erotica of Anais Nin

Smaro Kamboureli

Dis-cursus – originally the action of running here and there, com-
ings and goings, measures taken, "plots and plans": the lover, in
fact, cannot keep his mind from racing, taking new measures and
plotting against himself. His discourse exists only in outbursts of
language, which occur at the whim of trivial, or aleatory circumstances.

            Roland Barthes, *A Lover's Discourse*

Sexuality is only decisive for our culture as spoken, and to the degree it is spoken.

            Michael Foucault, *Language, Counter-Memory, Practice*

In the following excerpt from the "Preface" to *Little Birds*, Anais Nin distinguishes between erotica and pornography:

> It is one thing to include eroticism in a novel or a story and quite
> another to focus one's whole attention on it. The first is like life it-
> self. It is, I might say, natural, sincere, as in the sensual pages of
> Zola or Lawrence. But focusing wholly on the sexual life is not nat-
> ural. It becomes something like the life of the prostitute, an abnor-
> mal activity that ends up turning the prostitute away from the sex-
> ual. Writers perhaps know this.[1]

While both erotica and pornography acknowledge the significance of sexuality and aim to arouse sexual feelings, they differ from each other insofar as
their aesthetic and socio-cultural perspectives are concerned. Erotica deals
primarily with the dialectics of desire: desire as the articulation of the tension
that exists between a lover's emotions and the cravings of his body, and desire
as the tendency to give aesthetic form to sexual experience. Erotics and aesthetics, then, depend on each other: as desire gives shape to man's life so

does language enact or amplify the semantics of his sensual gestures. Sexuality is evoked both by the depiction of entangled bodies and by devices that enhance the lover's identity. Thus the sexual act in erotica is not an end in itself: it is only one of the forms that eroticism takes. Pornography, on the other hand, according to the *OED*, is about the "description of the life, manners, etc. of prostitutes and their patrons." Pornography reduces the ramifications of desire to one aspect of sexuality. Its material is located within a minimal context which not only undermines the complexities of sexuality, but also deprives man of the feelings necessary for the arousal of "natural" desire.[2]

These differences between erotica and pornography, as Nin is implicitly aware, make *Delta of Venus* and *Little Birds* more pornographic than erotic. In an oblique way, she advises her readers against comparing or confusing these stories with her other writings. In this respect, *Erotica*, the collective title of *Delta of Venus* and *Little Birds*, is a misleading index of their contents.[3] Yet Nin has deliberately chosen to call her pornographic stories erotic, for, as I intend to show, she is innovative within the genre of pornography. She creates a context where, even though the focus is exclusively on the sexual life, sexuality is far from being "not natural." Nin, however, does not allow her readers to wonder why she is engaged in an "abnormal activity."

The two volumes of her stories open with prefaces that both obfuscate and illuminate this engagement. The prefaces come as a surprise to a reader who has been already initiated into pornography or to a novice who is solely interested in titillating experiences. It is not conventional to find literary prefaces to pornographic stories or novels, first, because they cause a confusion of the pornographic genre with more serious literature and, second, and more importantly, because they delay the promised pleasure. A notable exception is Pauline Réage's *The Story of O* which bears a "Note" by its translator Sabine d'Estrée, a "Note" by the critic Mandiargues, and lastly a "Preface" by Jean Paulhan, a member of L'Académie Francaise. But this is France, where erotica and pornography have a long and serious tradition, claiming, among others, George Bataille whose novels *Madame Edwarda, Histoire de l'Oeil,* and his studies *L'Eroticisme, Les Larmes d'Eros* and *La Literature et le Mal* deserve an important place in the history of sexuality as an expression of human nature.

Nin, having lived both in France and in the States, is familiar with the differences that characterize the traditions of the two countries in terms of perceiving, and writing about, sexuality. As she notes in her *Diary*,

> The joke on me is that France had a tradition of literary erotic writing, in fine elegant style, written by the best writers. When I first began to write for the collector I thought there was a similar tradition here, but found none at all. All I have seen is badly written, shoddy, and by second-rate writers. No fine writer seems ever to have tried his hand at erotica.[4]

In writing her *Erotica*, Nin confronts the established French tradition of erotic writing and the American tradition of pornography that makes no claims whatsoever as literature. She is conscious of addressing an American audience. Given this, the two prefaces reveal her intent to present *Delta of Venus* and *Little Birds* in a different light: they read as apologias and as disguised manifestos about pornography.

In the "Preface" to *Delta of Venus*, which is an excerpt from the third volume of the *Diary*, Nin provides us with the context that generated the writing of these stories. Henry Miller was writing erotica "at a dollar a page" for an old collector and one of his rich clients (vii). But because he found this "writing to order . . . a castrating occupation" (ix), he quit after a while and asked Nin, who also claimed to be in financial need, to continue. This incident constitutes not only the occasion of her pornographic stories, but also the beginning of her apologia.

In the "Preface" to *Little Birds* we read,

> In New York everything becomes harder, more cruel. I had many people to take care of, many problems, and since I was in character very much like George Sand, who wrote all night to take care of her children, lovers, friends, I had to find work. I became what I shall call the Madame of an unusual house of literary prostitution. It was a very artistic "maison" . . . .
>
> Before I took up my new profession I was known as a poet, as a woman who was independent and wrote for her own pleasure. . . . Yet my real writing was put aside when I set out in search of the erotic. (*LB*, viii, ix)

Nin presents the conditions that led her to the writing of *Erotica* as the continuation of two cultural paradigms. The first one is, of course, New York City which, besides offering artists an exciting environment to live in, makes life "harder" for them. In short, Nin justifies herself by evoking the theme of survival: the poor artist sacrifices her moral principles for the sake of her altruism. The second cultural paradigm she employs is notably French again, that of George Sand. Nin is not alone in the game that "cruel" conditions force her to play. George Sand, a writer of status, was engaged in, more or less, the same activity. Nin feels that by writing pornography her reputation as a literary writer is at stake. The analogy she draws between herself and Sand and her statement that she put aside her "real writing" when she "set out in search of the erotic" make her latent anxiety quite obvious.

Nin "prostitutes" herself by writing, as she claims, not for her "own pleasure," but for the pleasure of the collector. The result is that she becomes a "Madame" who is, paradoxically, not a lover or a friend, but a mother figure as "matron." J. S. Atherton, in his review of *Delta of Venus* titled "The Maternal Instinct," says that "It is rather unfortunate that the latest book by her to appear here [Britain] is a book of frankly dirty stories of which she herself disapproved and only produced *under pressure*."[5] Atherton emphasizes, to a greater extent than Nin, the occasion of the stories in order to justify their "dirtiness." He has obviously read the "Preface" only as an apologia.

In the story of "The Basque and the Bijou," the madame of the house in a red-light district is described as "A maternal woman . . . but a maternal woman whose cold eyes travelled almost immediately to the man's shoes, for she judged from them how much he could afford to pay for his pleasure. Then for her own satisfaction, her eyes rested for a while on the trouser buttons" (*DV*, 159). The profession of this madame is apparently different from Nin's profession of "literary prostitution"; Nin does not apply this "maternal" image to herself. As a mother figure, she has different intentions.

Although Nin was undoubtedly taking care of her lovers and her friends whenever needed, as her *Diary* testifies, she is obviously manipulating in the "Preface" the nurturing aspects of the maternal role because of their positive ethical connotations. Thus Nin exonerates herself socially.

As for her literary role, she makes it clear that she is the "madame" of a "very artistic 'maison.' " She is engaged in "literary prostitution." The word "literary" is revealing both of her intent to justify herself and of the changes she brings in the pornographic genre.

Even though Nin "hated" the old collector, and could not afford typing paper or the repairs of broken windows, and could not pay the expenses of Miller, Duncan, Gonzalo, etc., she could somehow afford the time for background research. She proceeded to write the stories in an almost scholarly fashion: she "spent days in the library studying the *Kama Sutra*, listened to friends' most extreme adventures" (*DV*, ix). In spite of her reservations, Nin is not writing pornography "tongue-in-cheek"; she "caricatur[es] sexuality," but she does so only to the extent that she makes it the single theme of *Delta of Venus* and *Little Birds* (*DV*, ix).

Nin's focus on sexuality emphasizes the pornographic aspect of *Erotica*. Yet the biographical elements that occasionally permeate her stories cause a shift of her gaze from the mere pornographic to a more inciting look at the sexual lives of the people she knows. Nin is being deceptive when she says that "I did not want to give anything genuine, and decided to create a mixture of stories I had heard and inventions, pretending they were from the diary of a woman" (*DV*, ix). This straightforward statement becomes baffling when we see it in its original context which is the third volume of the *Diary*. In the same volume, we read about incidents which echo almost identical incidents in the *Erotica*. I will limit myself to two examples of this kind:

(from the *Diary*, vol. III)

> I visited Hugh and Brigitte Chisholm in their East River apartment.
> The place is so near the water that it gave me the illusion of a boat.
> The barges passed down the river while we talked. . . . Hugh is

small in stature, with curly hair, soft greenish eyes, an impish air. He is a good poet.

As I enter they treat me like an *objet d'art*. . . .

She shines steadily, under any circumstance. Not intermittently as I do, because I can only bloom in a certain . . . warmth. . . . That afternoon, in the warmth of their appreciation, I blossomed. . . .

From the objects I could divine their life in Rome, Paris, Florence; Brigitte's mother; the famous *haute couture* designer, Coco Chanel; *Vogue*; the pompousness of their family background and their effort to laugh at it. (21-22)

(from "Mandra" in *Little Birds*)

I am invited one night to the apartment of a young society couple, the H's. It is like being on a boat because it is near the East River and the barges pass while we talk. . . . Her husband, Paul, is small and of the race of imps. Not a man but a faun – a lyrical animal, quick and humorous. He thinks I am beautiful. He treats me like an objet d'art.
. . . She is a natural beauty, whereas I, an artificial one, need a setting and warmth to bloom successfully. . . .

Everything is touched with aristocratic impudence, through which I can sense the Hs' fabulous life in Rome, Florence; Miriam's frequent appearances in *Vogue* wearing Chanel dresses; the pompousness of their families; their efforts to be elegantly bohemian; and their obsession with the word that is the key to society – everything must be "amusing." (144)

(from the *Diary*, vol. III)

I knew no woman as easily persuaded to go to bed who had obtained so little from her play-acting. The extent of her frigidity appalled me, and I persuaded her it would get worse, and finally become incurable if she so deadened her contact with men. I gently took her by the hand and led her to an analyst.

But this woman, who could undress at the request of any man, make love with anyone, go to orgies, act as a call girl in a professional house, this Beth told me she found it actually difficult to *talk* about sex! (24)

(from "Mandra" in *Little Birds*)

She is being analyzed and has discovered what I sensed long ago: that she has never known a real orgasm, at thirty-four, after a

sexual life that only an expert accountant could keep track of. I am
discovering her pretenses. She is always smiling, gay, but under-
neath she feels unreal, remote, detached from experience. She acts
as if she were asleep. . . .

Mary says, "It is very hard to talk about sex, I am so ashamed."
She is not ashamed of doing anything at all, but she cannot talk
about it. She can talk to me. We sit for hours in perfumed places
where there is music. She likes places where actors go. (140-41).

The diary which Nin "pretends" to have invented is actually her published
Diary, the edited version of the diaries she kept all her life. She uses some of
its material concerning her friends practically verbatim, an act that suggests
that she is far from writing a caricature of sexuality; she records in detail sensual settings and recollects the way sexuality manifests itself in her milieu.
Reality is embedded in fantasy and vice versa.

But Nin does not limit herself to using only her friends' sexual adventures. What enhances her fusion of the real with the imaginary is her personal presence in *Erotica*, a presence hardly disguised. In "Marcel" we read
about a woman who lives in a houseboat (*DV*, 250); in "A Model" we read
about young girls "who had never read anything but literary novels" (*LB*, 67),
who "knew languages," who also "knew Spanish dancing," who "had an exotic face" and "accent," who posed as a model for New York artists (*LB*, 68).
A reader of Nin's *Diary* will recognize immediately Nin herself. I am not arguing here that *Delta of Venus* and *Little Birds* are Nin's disguised, or
"anonymous" (*DV*, xii) autobiography. What is of great interest is that Nin
does not distance herself from pornographic writing, a distance she should
have kept had she thought of her pornography in purely negative terms. Nin's
self-portrait in *Erotica* is her signature as artist. It is a signature that falsifies
her apologetic tone while it verifies her belief that her pornography is not
completely devoid of art.

This brings us back to the occasion of *Erotica*. Nin has to comply with the
collector's persistent demand: "leave out the poetry . . . [c]oncentrate on sex"
(*DV*, ix). In Nin's words, he wants her to "exclude" from her writing her
"own aphrodisiac – poetry" (*DV*, x). Here we have two different attitudes
toward pornography. As D. H. Lawrence says, "What they are [pornography
and obscenity] depends, as usual, entirely on the individual. What is pornography to one man is the laughter of genius to another."[6] The collector, in this
respect, and his client (whether real or fabricated, he is an extra-textual device designed to create the occasion) deprive Nin of her sensuality. They col-
lect (steal) her fantasies, her longings, her actual experiences. They deprive
her of her memories, and of her imagination as a person and as an artist.

The collector wants Nin to reduce discourse to the level of mere intercourse. Yet, ironically, it is language he is solely interested in. He is not like
Elena and Pierre in "Elena" whose reading of erotic books keeps them in
touch with their bodies:

> He bought her erotic books, which they read together. . . . As they lay on the couch together and read, their hands wandered over each other's body, to the places described in the book. . . .
>
> They would lie on their stomachs, still dressed, open a new book and read together, with their hands caressing each other. They kissed over erotic pictures. (*DV*, 115-16)

The process of reading erotica amplifies Elena's and Pierre's desire. The real (Elena's and Pierre's lovemaking) merges with the imaginary (the content of the books). They not only re-enact what they read, but they also "embrace" the books themselves. Their response to erotica is different from the response of the pornographic reader, which usually results in vicarious sexuality.

In contrast, the collector represents one of the two stereotypes of the pornographic mind. He is the one who fears, and thus has to forget, the reality of the body. His stance toward sexuality divorces the body (eros) from the head (logos). Not being able (potent) to face the body naked, he wants the pornographic discourse to be naked instead, namely unadorned with poetry. By avoiding, therefore, an encounter with the presence of a real lover, the collector, or the stereotype he represents, destroys the flesh of the body: he goes to a skeletal outline which is a fabrication and as such empty of spirit. As Nin says when she addresses him in the *Diary*, "You are shrinking your world of sensations. You are withering it, starving it, draining its blood" (*DV*, xiii). The collector is not like Donald who says to Elena that "[t]alking together is a *form* of intercourse" (*DV*, 104; my emphasis). The collector desires a discourse that will entirely replace intercourse.

The second stereotype of the pornographic mind is the lover who worships the body while, at the same time, wanting to silence it. Nin provides us with an example of this in "The Queen." The narrator of the story talks about a painter who sees women only as whores:

> He was saying, "I like a whore best of all because I feel she will never cling to me, never get entangled with me. It makes me feel free. I do not have to make love to her. . . .
>
> The women who are unabashedly sexual, with *the womb written all over their faces* . . . the women who throw their sex out at us, from the hair, the eyes, the nose, the *mouth*, the whole body – these are the women I love." (*LB*, 101, 104; my emphasis)

This character is receptive only to the sexuality of the body. His exclusive love for its sensual qualities erases all the features that give life and character to a woman. Unlike the collector, whose fear of the body makes him a lover of a surrogate body, the body of language, the painter of this story reduces discourse to one level only of signification, that of sex. Accordingly, the sexual act for him is solipsistic. This solipsism expresses the painter's narcissism as well as his reluctance to accept the presence of woman during the act of lovemaking. He is afraid of the feminine psyche.

This kind of pornographer, as Susan Griffin says in *Pornography and Silence*, "reduces a woman to a mere thing, to an entirely material object without a soul, who can only be 'loved' physically."[7] The painter, afraid of the loss of his freedom, kills the individuality of woman: he sees her mouth only as the surfacing of her sex. Yet this phenomenology of female sexuality and pleasure is deceptive. The mouth seen only as metaphor is reduced to an orifice, an orifice though that remains mute. Nin, aware of this, renounces this attitude toward pornography within the story itself: the painter's most favorite whore, Bijou, is "colder than a statue" (*LB*, 101); her sexuality is static; moreover, it is the painter who "clings" to her as he follows the "tiny trail of semen" that she leaves behind her from all the lovers she took, except him (*LB*, 106). The painter is betrayed both by his whore and by his own erotics of detachment.

Nin herself is a pornographer of a different kind. She transforms her contempt for those who focus "only on sexuality" into "violent explosions of poetry" (*DV*, xii). The metaphor of explosion is pertinent here. What is a physical orgasm for the pornographic mind is for Nin both a physical act and the release of poetic language. As Roland Barthes says in talking about Sade's writings, "there [is] no distinction between the structure of ejaculation and that of language."[8] Nin's fusion of discourse and intercourse is evident in most of the stories in *Delta of Venus* and *Little Birds*.

We read, for instance, in "Linda":

> André had a particular passion for the mouth. In the street he looked at women's mouths. To him the mouth was indicative of sex. A tightness of a lip, thinness, augured nothing rich or voluptuous. A full mouth promised an open, generous sex. . . .
>
> Linda's mouth had seduced him from the first. . . . There was something about the way she moved it, a passionate unfolding of the lips, promising a person who would lash around the beloved like a storm. When he first saw Linda, he was taken into her through this mouth, as if he were already making love to her. And so it was on their wedding night. (*DV*, 232-33)

There are some subtle differences here between André and the painter mentioned earlier. For André, the mouth is not a projection of the female sex, but the entrance itself into the being of the woman. The mouth as the source of language reveals a woman's potentiality both as a lover and as a person who can articulate her imaginings. Thus André does not see woman as a whore, as the painter does, but as a "beloved" who eventually becomes his wife.

What illustrates even better the relationship that Nin established between discourse and intercourse is, again, the story of "Elena":

She [Elena] moved quicker to bring the climax, and when he saw this, he hastened his motions inside of her and incited her to come with him, with *words*, with his *hands* caressing her, and finally with his *mouth* soldered to hers, so that the *tongues* moved in the same rhythm as the *womb* and *penis*, and the climax was spreading between her *mouth* and her sex, in *crosscurrents* of increasing pleasure, until she *cried out*, half *sob* and half *laughter*, from the overflow of *joy* through her body. (*DV*, 96; my emphasis)

Here erotics and poetics merge. The lovers' desire for each other engulfs their whole selves. Intercourse is not a mechanical operation but an act of both love and speech. As George Steiner notes, "Sex is a profoundly semantic act."[9] The semantics of lovemaking communicates the lovers' sexuality in language that has a dialectic structure: it is the "crosscurrent" of the body (the sexual organs/the tongues) and of the spirit (the sob/the laughter/the joy); it is the expression of sexuality as it is contained in the psyche.

By presenting the sexual face of the psyche, Nin reveals the animal in man. The fiercer the desire the lovers and the greater their abandonment, the closer they come to the instinctive world of the animals. Elena and Pierre reach this level of existence:

His caresses had a strange quality, at times soft and melting, at other times fierce, like the caresses she had expected when his eyes fixed on her, the caresses of a wild animal. There was something animallike about his hands, which he kept spread over each part of her body, and which took her sex and hair together as if he would tear them away from the body, as if he grasped earth and grass together. (*DV*, 94)

The two lovers *transgress* their consciousness as their animality manifests itself. They are dehumanized, becoming thus aware of their own limits and consequently of the limits of their sexuality. As Michel Foucault says in his discussion of sexuality and Bataille in the essay "Preface to Transgression," transgression "serves as a glorification of the nature it excludes: the limit opens violently onto the limitless, finds itself suddenly carried away by the content it had rejected and fulfilled by this alien plenitude which invades it to the core of its being."[10] The excess of Elena's and Pierre's desire, like that of most of the characters in Nin's *Erotica*, becomes the measure of a double recognition: they encounter their profanity and its limits, a profanity that designates the finitude of their consciousness, in other words, the effacement of their egos during the sexual act.

What further indicates the prominence of animal profanity and the absence of an overtly conscious self in Nin's *Delta of Venus* and *Little Birds* is her diction, which is pointedly different from the diction we see in traditional pornography. Nin never uses words like "cunt," "cock," and "fuck." Instead, she expresses the profanity of the sexual organs by describing them in terms of natural and animal imagery.

In "Mathilde," Mathilde's sex is "like the gum plant leaf with its secret milk that the pressure of the finger could bring out, odorous moisture that came like the moisture of the sea shells" (*DV*, 15). Similarly, we read in "Two Sisters" that "[t]he fur had opened to reveal her [Dorothy's] whole body, glowing, luminous, rich in the fur, like some jeweled animal. . . . John did not touch the body, he suckled at the breasts, sometimes stopping to feel the fur with his mouth, as if he were kissing a beautiful animal" (*LB*, 44).

The profanity of the body and its multifarious significance are further reinforced by Nin's usage of the word "ass," which is the most apparent word in her sexual discourse, pointing as it does to the boundary line between body and spirit. Octavio Paz in his *Conjunctions and Disjunctions* compares the face with the ass and thus illustrates the "soul-body dualism." He sees the conflict between the two as representing "the (repressive) reality principle and the (explosive) pleasure principle."[11] We find a good example of this dualism in "Mathilde": "she lay on her left side and exposed her ass to the mirror" (*DV*, 15). As Paz says, "the mirror reflects the face of an image";[12] in Mathilde's case, then, the mirror image of her ass is symbolic of the "other" face of *homo eroticus*. Nin reconciles the profanity of the body and the unconscious power it imbues with the self-consciousness of the face.

Nin's sexual discourse avoids the vulgarity of hard-core pornography. Her lyrical language emphasizes the poetics of sexuality. She transgresses the limits of the body's anatomy by stressing its eroticism. The semantics of the sexual act, therefore, signifies the lovers' transgression of the boundary of the human as they enter the realm of the animal. We should not overlook at this point the paradox of the fact that the human element, even when transgressed, is quite often described in utterly civilized terms, for example, the fur of the animal is a sign of luxury, the woman that is a jeweled animal. This civilized form of sexuality indicates that the lovers in Nin's *Erotica* estrange themselves from the familiar (their egos) in order to discover the strangeness that reconciles them with their sexual instincts. Sexual transgression has now come full circle. To quote from Foucault again, "Sexuality points to nothing beyond itself. . . . It marks the limit within us and designates us as a limit."[13] As Elena says, "it [is] a strange transgression" (*DV*, 104).

Transgression destroys the relationship of ethics to sexuality. Foucault observes that "A rigorous language, as it arises from sexuality . . . will say that he [man] exists without God."[14] When Elena notes about Leila that she has "acquired a new sex by growing beyond man and woman," that she is like "a mythic figure, enlarged, magnified" (*DV*, 135), she describes a human condition that signifies the "death of God." The same concept is also implied by the "naked savage woman" that Reynolds is talking about in "A Model" (*LB*, 84). According to Foucault, "it is excess that discovers that sexuality and the death of God are bound to the same experience."[15] Indeed, it takes Leila's fierce desire to experience both male and female sensuality and the "panther" qualities of the "naked savage woman" to annul the unethical connotations of obscenity that make God unnecessary. As Henry Miller observes in *The World of Lawrence*:

> Obscenity is pure and springs from effervescence, excess vitality, joy of life, concord, unanimity, alliance with nature, indifference to God of the healthy sort that takes God down a peg or two in order to reexamine him. . . .
>
> Obscenity figures large and heavily, magnificently and awesomely, in all primitive peoples. . . . The savage is not a sick man. The savage retains his sense of awe, wonder, mystery, his love of action, his right to behave like the animal he is. . . .[16]

This "pure" nature of obscenity explains why Nin's characters, by crossing beyond their limits, challenge the existence of God.

Yet the "death of God" does not imply an absence of the sacred. The lover as transgressor creates his own version of the sacred out of the intensity of his profanity. This is what Elena has in mind when she says to herself, "I talk almost like a saint, to *burn* for love – no mystic love, but for a ravaging sensual meeting" (*DV*, 144; my emphasis). The same "saintly" abandonment is expressed by the clairvoyant in "The Basque and the Bijou":

> His dance for the three women took place one evening when all the clients were gone. He stripped himself, showing his *gleaming goldenbrown body*. To his waist he tied a fake penis modelled like his own and the same color.
>
> He said, "This is a dance from my own country. We do this for the women on *feast* days." . . . He jerked his body as if he were entering a woman. . . . The final spasm was wild, like that of a man *giving up his life in the act of sex*. (*DV*, 184; my emphasis)

The motif of sacrifice that we see in both cases is the natural consequence of the latent presence of the sacred. The light that surrounds the two lovers signifies that they have already gone beyond their profane limits and they are now ready to transgress another boundary, that of death. Sexual transgression as sacrifice reinstates God's presence, only now his presence inspires no awe, for he is experienced as a divine power that dwells within the body. Thus the body as a vehicle of the divine receives all the acts of worship offered to it.

The infliction of death on a lover during the sexual act is the most extreme blow that the lovers' sexual drive can direct against the prohibitions that our culture imposes on sexuality. Bataille, in discussing the nature of sexual prohibition, says,

> What is forbidden urges transgression, without which such an action of transgression would not have had that evil glimmer that

seduces. It is the transgression of what is forbidden that bewitches.

But this glimmer is not only one that radiates from eroticism. It lights up the religious life every time it involves an action of utter violence, an action which is triggered the moment death slits the throat of a victim.

Sacré!

But, as for me, the ultimate form of death brings a strange sense of victory. It bathes me in its light, and stirs within me an infinitely joyous laughter. This is the laughter that allows one to disappear![17]

The disappearance that Bataille talks about is the ultimate form of transgression, a sacred transgression this time, that transforms the sexual act into a miracle: what inhibits sexuality is forced to disappear by the power of sexual desire. It is not accidental, for instance, that Mathilde is given incense; "[i]n Lima she received much of it, it was part of the ritual. She was raised on a pedestal of poetry so that her falling into the final embrace might seem more of a miracle" (*DV*, 12). The incense that Mathilde receives and its rapturous effects present her as a "victim" because they cause her *fall* "into the natural embrace." Contrary to what is observed in traditional pornography – an abuse of the myth of the fallen woman – Nin sees Mathilde's fall through different eyes: Mathilde's profane self disappears in order to emerge (to be "raised") as a source of joy and illumination. Accordingly, death, or orgasm seen as *une petite mort* by Bataille,[18] kills the lover while it restores the power and significance of sexuality.

Thus when Nin says that "[w]riting erotica became a road to sainthood rather than to debauchery" (*DV*, xii), she suggests that man does not necessarily blind himself when he focuses on sexuality if he manages to transgress the sexual limits prescribed by our culture. Transgression, in this context, is ultimately both positive and negative: sexual desire connects but its fulfillment separates.

It is obvious by now that Nin's treatment of pornography results in a sexuality that is considerably different, both in intent and content, from the sexuality described in traditional pornography. Nin explains this herself by saying she "was intuitively using a woman's language, seeing sexual experience from a woman's point of view" (*DV*, xv). Most of the stories, indeed, display a woman's sensibility, and a number of them, when they are not narrated by a third person, which is usually the case, are told in a woman's voice. Nin challenges the assumption that women repress their sexuality and that they do not like reading pornography. The point she tries to make, and I think that she does so successfully, is that there is a difference between pornography and, what I called earlier, the pornographic mind. Pornography as writing pertaining to prostitution, and erotica as writing pertaining to eroticism, can be appealing to both sexes when they take into account both man's and woman's points of view.

But I think that Nin's contribution to the genre of pornography owes less to her feminism and more to the fact that she is an artist. When she says that her own aphrodisiac is poetry and that her pornography consists of explosions of poetry, she announces, I believe, a new kind of pornography which links the lover with the artist and the body with the artist's creative work. The predominant artist figure in *Erotica* is the painter.

The world of the artists and their models in Nin's stories is both erotic and pornographic in the generic sense of the terms. One of the stories that illustrates this is "A Model." Nin works here with the paradox inherent in the male chauvinistic tradition that views woman as an object. The first-person narrator of the story is a young model who poses for New York artists. Some of them see and treat her as an aesthetic and sexual object. Others, like Reynolds, see her in aesthetic (object-ive) terms but in a manner that does not erase her individuality. On the whole, however, Nin's intent is to show that for the artist design and desire, like discourse and intercourse, go together. When the artist depersonalizes the model by focusing solely on the aesthetics of her body, he proves to have a pornographic mind. When, on the other hand, he interprets her external beauty in conjunction with her personal qualities, he is then an artist/lover for whom the aesthetics of his art reveals woman not as a sexual object but as an *objet d'art*. He sees her as subject matter, as a person out of whom art is made.

The story that illustrates this conflict of woman-as-object versus woman-as-subject is "The Maya." "The painter Novalis was newly married to Maria . . . with whom he had fallen in love because she resembled the painting he most loved, the *Maja Desnuda*, by Goya" (*LB*, 59). Novalis cannot make love with his wife because he sees her not as a real woman but as the projection of his favorite painting. What he asks of her is "not the caprice of a lover, but the desire of a painter, of an artist" (60). The result is that he can make love only to the paintings he makes of Maria. He is, in short, the artist as Pygmalion reversed.

Novalis' resistance to the real Maria derives from his belief that she is art personified. Besides evoking Goya's *Maja*, Maria is the muse who opens Novalis' way toward his desired subject matter, namely herself. Nevertheless, the identification of these two orders of reality, art and life, is a form of fulfillment that threatens Novalis with the elimination of his concept of the muse as a figure that stands somehow outside the territories of his life and art. Only when Maria unfolds her controlled sexuality does she manage to "efface the paintings from his emotions, to surpass them" (64).

Sexuality, as it is presented here, is the artist's inspiration. Yet the artist has to transgress the limits of his medium before he is able to realize this inspiration. He has to demystify the figure of the erotic muse by sacrificing it to his real lover. Moreover, he has to distinguish between the woman he paints and her image on canvas. he has to destroy this frozen image in order to be able to embrace the real woman. The sacredness of sexuality is to be found at the point where the limits of the real and the imaginary meet. The artist must realize that his art is meaningful only when grounded in life.

Nin realizes this point by having many women characters evoke actual erotic paintings. In "Pierre," the visitor to Pierre's mother who has to dry her clothes and thus takes of her stockings, evokes, for me, Courbet's *Woman with White Stockings*. Pierre, when he looks at her, discovers the "pose he had pictured. . . . [T]the first naked woman he has seen, so much like paintings he had studied in the museum" (*DV*, 208). In "Elena," when Elena goes with Leila to an opium den which is like an "Arabian mosque," they hear the "voice of a woman which began what seemed to be at first a song, and then turned out to be another sort of vocalizing . . . a vaginal song" (*DV*, 128). Nin might have had in mind Ingres' *Odalisques with the Slave* which makes material the two pairs of concepts she is working with in *Delta of Venus* and *Little Birds*: discourse and intercourse and design and desire.

This intermingling of works of art with Nin's discourse amplifies her signature in *Erotica*. The allusions to Goya, Lawrence, Balzac, and Freud, to mention only a few, give to *Delta of Venus* and *Little Birds* a greater perspective than is normally given to pornographic writings. Had Nin been "exclusively" interested in the mechanics of the sexual act, she would neither have written in lyrical language nor would she have made the artist the focus of her stories. As her own aphrodisiac is poetry, so her stories are exciting to her readers because their sexual content is enriched by her poetic sensibility.

NOTES

[1]Anais Nin, *Little Birds* (Bantam Books, 1979), p. viii. All further references to this book, abbreviated *LB*, will hereafter appear parenthetically in the text.

[2]See Peter Michelson, *The Aesthetics of Pornography* (Herder and Herder, 1971), for an indepth analysis of the genre. See also Cathy Schwichtenberg's semotic analysis of Nin's *Delta of Venus*, "Erotica: The Semey Side of Semiotics," *Sub-Stance*, No. 32 (1981), pp. 26-38.

[3]Nin's *Erotica* consists of two volumes. *Little Birds*, mentioned above, and *Delta of Venus* (Bantam Books, 1978), cited hereafter in the text under the abbreviation *DV*.

[4]*The Diary of Anais Nin*, Vol. III, edited and with a preface by Gunther Stuhlmann (Harcourt Brace Jovanovich, 1969). Further references to the book will appear in the text.

[5]J. S. Atherton, "The Maternal Instinct," *Times Literary Supplement*, July 1978, p. 756.

[6]D. H. Lawrence, "Pornography and Obscenity," in *Selected Literary Criticism*, ed. Anthony Beal (London: Mercury Books, 1956), p. 32.

[7]Susan Griffin, *Pornography and Silence* (Harper and Row, 1981), p. 3.

[8]Roland Barthes, *Sade, Fourier, Loyola*, trans. Richard Miller (Hill and Wang, 1976), p. 129.

[9]George Steiner, *After Babel: Aspects of Language and Translation* (London: Oxford University Press, 1977), p. 38.

[10]Michel Foucault, "Preface to Transgression," in *Language, Counter-Memory, Practice: Selected Essays and Interviews*, ed. and introduction Donald F. Bouchard, trans. Donald F. Bouchard and Sherry Simon (1977; rpt. Cornell University Press, 1980), p. 34

[11]Octavio Paz, *Conjunctions and Disjunctions*, trans. Helen R. Lane (Viking Press, 1974), p. 4. Paz's study has as its point of departure a woodcut by Jose Guadalupe Posada titled "The Phenomenon," which shows "a dwarf seen from the back, but with his face turned toward the spectator, and shown with another face down by his buttocks," and Francisco Quevedo's *Gracias y Degracias del Ojo Culo* [*Graces and Disgraces of the Eye of the Ass*], which is "a long comparison between an ass and a face" (3).

[12]Paz, p. 11. Paz uses here as a paradigm Velazquez's "Venus and Mirror," and "a variant of the sex/face metaphor," in order to discuss the "miraculous concord" of the face and the ass.

[13]Foucault, p. 30.

[14]Foucault, p. 30

[15]Foucault, p. 33.

[16]Henry Miller, *The World of Lawrence: A Passionate Appreciation*, ed. with an introduction and notes by Evelyn J. Hinz and John J. Teunissen (Capra Press, 1980), pp. 175-76.

[17]George Bataille, *Les Larmes d'Eros* (Paris: Jean-Jacques Pauvert, 1964), p. 60 (my translation).

[18]Bataille, p. 35.

From *Journal of Modern Literature* 11.1 (March 1984): 143-58.

Nin's Novels

Surrealist Soap Opera

Herbert Lyons

A writer of uncommon initiative, Miss Nin has had earlier works privately printed, and even printed several herself, by hand. In so doing she has obtained a small but not undistinguished audience and won acclaim from what her present publishers [E. P. Dutton] call the "avant garde." It must be reported, with regret, that in this instance the "avant garde" seems to have more enthusiasm than taste and Miss Nin more enterprise than talent.

In a reasonably coherent prologue to her novel, Miss Nin states that she is concerned with "woman's struggle to understand her own nature. . . . Man appears only partially in this volume because for the woman at war with herself, he can only appear thus, not as an entity. Woman at war with herself has not yet been related to man, being capable only of maternity." As becomes an advanced writer, the author is naturally less lucid in the actual exposition of her plot. But despite the to-be-expected obscurities, the plot is not difficult to follow. Miss Nin is a natural storyteller and, try as she will, she cannot succeed in preventing the reader from recognizing the tale.

The first character introduced in *Ladders to Fire* is a female movie star who is understandably upset because, while everybody loves her on the screen, almost nobody loves her off. Even for a lady making thousands of dollars a week this is a sad predicament, and one is sorry that at the end of Stella's story she is not better off than at the beginning: "People sent her enormous bouquets of rare flowers. Continued to send them. She signed the receipts, she even signed notes of thanks. Flowers for the dead, she murmured. With only a little wire, and a round frame, they would do as well."

The novel's second section is somewhat more complex. There is a lady named Lillian, who "was always in a state of fermentation" and who has a bad time of it with several gentlemen, including her husband.

Next comes Djuna who has an even worse time with shadowy gentlemen that Lillian. In the final section Stella, Lillian, and Djuna wind up at a party in Paris and encounter a lady named Sabina, who may be Miss Nin's conception of the New Woman. There are a number of surrealist revelations, and that's all.

Inasmuch as the "avant garde" may not listen to the radio, it is perhaps worth noting that numerous daytime serials are almost exclusively devoted to less fancy variations on this same theme. In soap opera the men are generally pale and weak, the woman, as the author has one of her characters say, "are moving from one circle to another, rising toward independence and self-creation." And like Miss Nin's novels, the radio serial never stops. Unless the sponsor kills the program, the ladies just move and rise, endlessly.

Miss Nin has this to say of her technique: "I write as a poet in a framework of prose. I intend the greater part of my writing to be received through the senses, as one receives painting and music." And, like some modern painters, she covers the canvas too thickly, so that it tends to look like a used palette: the resulting abstraction is murky, meaningless and too often in bad taste. As in much modern music, there is little originality. The novel contains traces of Djuna Barnes, Henry Miller and Edmund Wilson and a large deposit of French surrealism. These days, many things get by under the banner of complexity and super-sensitivity; artiness and obscurantism, as always, are sometimes disguises for second-rate talents. But Miss Nin's novel has a certain interest as a pastiche of contemporary preciousness.

From *New York Times Book Review*, October 20, 1946: 16.

Freudian Noah's Ark

René Fülop-Miller

In that church of modern literature which was set up in the magazine *Transition* between the two world wars, Anais Nin received her baptism as a writer. *Transition's* new religion of art leaned heavily on "magic realism" and "the imaginative power of the word" in the spirit of Rimbaud. Miss Nin's fragmentary "House of Incest," published in *Transition* at the same time as Joyce's "Work in Progress" and Kafka's "Metamorphosis," was a Niagara of formless associations of a psyche obsessed by fantasies. Her later works won the attention of such critics as Edmund Wilson and Rebecca West.

A maturer artist now, Miss Nin has been able in her new book to give form to psychic tensions and to translate inner events into narration. *The Four-Chambered Heart* deals with a man of primitive and natural force who destroys himself. Rango, who grew up in the spacious high plateaus of Guatemala, is plunged into the decadent night live of Paris and goes to pieces.

His disintegration reaches its tragic climax in his marriage with Zora, a gypsy-like Strindberg woman who uses the witchcraft of a frigid hysteric to keep Rango enslaved. By dramatizing her invalid state, she puts great weight upon Rango's conscience. He is struck with a sorry weakness, in the manner of men with the strength of Samson when they have been shorn by a woman.

Opposed to the pathological Zora, who symbolizes the destructive elements in Rango's nature, is the constructive character of Djuna – a wholly feminine person who tries to save Rango from perdition by offering him an honest and healing love. Miss Nin's creative powers are demonstrated most impressively in her characterization of Djuna.

The struggle between negative and positive forces for the soul of Rango, who is torn between Djuna and Zora, ends in his seeking escape in political action. But the cold disciplinaries of the party have little use for wayward visionaries like Rango, and he is expelled. At a loss, he returns to the houseboat on the Seine where he and Djuna keep their rendezvous. Djuna, cheated of romantic love with him, decides to sink the houseboat. The book ends with a rescue that leaves us in doubt whether this "Noah's Ark" has preserved the people aboard it for a new beginning, or for a continuation of their old hopeless life.

To describe the course of the action is to convey only a part of *The Four-Chambered Heart*. For to Miss Nin external events form only one side of true reality, in which two realms – the inward and the outward, the world of dream and of waking – are united.

Miss Nin has the gift of communicating this unity directly. External action is deepened by being converted to inward experience; the visionary and hallucinatory become integral parts of reality. The River Seine and the flowing Seine of the psyche are thus presented as one stream of life.

The author has drawn on psychoanalysis – on Freud and on Jung as well. It is a pleasure to note that her knowledge is not flaunted, but creatively used.

From *New York Times Book Review*, January 29, 1950: 4.

Temperament vs. Conscience

Maxwell Geismar

Anais Nin is as well known to literary circles here and abroad as she has been little known to the general reading public. Her unpublished diary is something of a legend, and the present book [*A Spy in the House of Love*] is the best of her series of novels published in this country. The craft moves directly toward the area of psychological realism; the prose is a pleasure to read. This is, in short, a sensitive and discerning fable of a woman's love life, which manages to compress within a very brief compass some of the rewards and almost too many of the anguishes of passion for its own sake.

It is almost a terrifying book – saved by the humor with which Miss Nin endows her theme, which raises it finally to the level of an artistic tragicomedy. The story concerns the amorous exploits of the heroine, Sabina, a veteran of these battles, pursued by her own guilt and fear, caught between her temperament and her conscience. In the symbolism of the narrative she is pursued by the "lie-detector," a sort of F.B.I. of the heart. (This figure is an amusing mixture of psychoanalytic and conventional morality.) The heroine evades him, and we begin to realize that Miss Nin is one of the few women writers in our literary tradition to affirm the centrality of the biological impulses for her own sex, and on the same terms, as for men.

The point is also that she is prepared to describe these emotions from the feminine point of view with the same ruthless honesty that marked a D. H. Lawrence or a Dreiser. And what a price is paid by the protagonist – or the victim – of the present story for her moments of ecstasy and conquest! She must move on a superficial level of lies, tricks, evasions in each new case of love; the tactics of feminine deceit are exposed here in a manual of love's subterfuges. On a deeper level of genuine affection she must still prepare to wound before she is wounded, to betray so that she may not be betrayed, to make her escape before the lover makes his. The price of impulse is eternal anxiety, Miss Nin implies. This spy, like all spies, must be prepared for treason, for flight, for ignoble death.

This theme is dramatized in a series of separate episodes with rather shadowy masculine figures who operate mainly to project various roles a woman also plays in love – or is forced to play. In the end Miss Nin's heroine turns for comfort and wisdom to another woman, Djuna, who has figured in the previous novels in the series. Friendship is the solace for passion perhaps, as art is the crystallization of imperfect human desire.

From *The Nation*, July 24, 1954: 75-76.

Humanity Is the Principle

Malcolm Mudrick

A Spy in the House of Love . . . is a touchingly battered innocent survival of the 'twenties and great fun. Here is a representative passage from the end of one chapter and the beginning of the next:

> The trembling premonitions shaking the hand, the body, made
> dancing unbearable, waiting unbearable, smoking and talking un-

bearable, soon would come the untamable seizure of sensual canni-
balism, the joyous epilepsies.

They fled from the eyes of the world, the singer's prophetic,
harsh, ovarian prologues. Down the rusty bars of ladders to the un-
dergrounds of night propitious to the first man and woman at the
beginning of the world, where there were no words by which to possess each other, no music for serenades, no presents to court with,
no tournaments to impress and force a yielding, no secondary instruments, nor adornments, necklaces, crowns to subdue, but only
one ritual, a joyous, joyous, joyous, joyous impaling of woman on
man's sensual mast.

***

She reopened her eyes to find herself lying at the bottom of a
sail boat, lying over Philip's coat gallantly protecting her from sedi-
ments, water seepage and barnacles. Philip lies beside her, only his
head is above hers, and his feet extend further down than hers. He
lies asleep, content, breathing very deeply. She sits up in the moon-
light, angry, restless, defeated. The fever had reached its peak, and
waned separately from her desire, leaving it unfulfilled, stranded.
High fever and no climax, – Anger, Anger – at this core which will
not melt, while Sabina wills to be like man, free to possess and desire adventure, to enjoy a stranger.

Sabina is just a girl in search of an ideal mate; and – shadowed by a lie
detector – she tries out five different men, one of them her husband, a quiet
gentle fellow who never seems to worry about his wife's frequent week-at-a-
time absences (he thinks she's an actress on tour), and on her reappearances
"never understood her eagerness to take a bath, her immediate need to
change her clothes, to wash off the old make up." Then there is Philip, the
movie-idol type, who strolls the beach singing an aria from *Tristan*, and who
complains that "Women are so offended if you are not always ready and in
the mood to play the romantic lover, when you look the part." There is a jazz
drummer ("Drum – drum – drum – drum – drum – upon her heart, she was a
drum, her skin was taut under his hands, and the drumming vibrated through
the rest of her body. Wherever he rested his eyes, she felt the drumming of
his fingers upon her stomach, her breasts, her hips"); and though he lives on
the same street as E. E. Cummings and Djuna Barnes, though he combines
with Sabina in "caresses . . . acutely marvelous, like the multicolored flames
from an artful fireworks, bursts of explodes suns and neons within the body,
flying comets aimed at all the centers of delight, shooting stars of piercing
joys," he won't do. There is John, the war-vet aviator who broods, whom "she
wanted to rescue . . . from the distortion she knew led to madness. She wanted to prove to him that his guilt was a distortion, that his vision of her and

desire as bad, and of his hunger as bad, was a sickness." Having achieved in his vicinity "a long, prolonged, deep thrusting ecstasy," she nevertheless can't save him from himself. Finally, there is Donald, the slinky mother-seeking pansy who, "touching her naked foot . . . had felt a unity resembling the first unity of the world, unity with nature, unity with the mother, early memories of an existence within the silk, warmth and effortlessness of a vast love"; but he doesn't work out either.

It would be unfair to imply that Miss Nin is incapable of straightforward inanities. The dialogue, for example, is out of *John's Other Wife*; descriptions of characters are breathtakingly trite; and – most touching throwback of all – Debussy and early Stravinsky flow from aphrodisiacal phonographs over lovers on studio couches in the Village, just as though nothing has changed since Coolidge. Sabina ultimately undergoes a night-club analysis by Djuna ("You probably see . . . [your] guilt mirrored in every policeman, every judge, every parent, every personage in authority"), and completes the treatment by listening, at Djuna's studio, to a Beethoven quartet, unspecified, which "began to tell Sabina as Djuna could not, of what they both knew for an absolute certainty: the continuity of existence and of the chain of summits, of elevations by which such continuity is reached." She weeps, and the benignant lie detector closes the book saying: "In homeopathy there is a remedy called pulsatile for those who weep at music." From the dust jacket, we learn that Mr. Edmund Wilson has called Miss Nin "a very great artist, who feels things we cannot feel," and that a collection of her short stories "is on the required reading list at Columbia University."

From *The Hudson Review* 7.4 (Winter 1955): 612-14.

Nin: The Topic of Paris

James Korges

Among the curiosities in contemporary reviewing has been the critical reception of Anais Nin, something that has misled a good many readers into believing her a good novelist. For a time, in 1945, the critical wars about Miss Nin were being fought by giants: Edmund Wilson, with the full weight of his reputation behind him, praised her work; Isaac Rosenfeld, with the vigor of a minority position, denounced her work. It was *The New Yorker* versus *The New Republic*. As quite often happens, the position of *The New Republic* has proved right, whereas the mid-cult views of *The New Yorker* pall.

Nin's most recent work, *Collages*, was praised by of all things, the *Times Literary Supplement* as "a handful of perfectly told fables," the prose of which is said to be "daringly elaborate, . . . accurately timed, . . . colorful, evocative." One opens the book to find only another presentation of some typical situations in Nin's fiction: a girl in a foreign country (part of the "alienation *manqué*" so popular in recent novels?), a lovely father, lovers, neuroticism, incoherence in structure, some fairly interesting character sketches, and general verbal inaccuracy: on page 96, for example, a character's "language too was stylized and every word glazed with patina," as though patina were a glaze. Years ago, when I first read a novel by Miss Nin, I hoped that she would improve, that the blemished prose would get better, that the characters would become less puppet-like as she matured into a fuller comprehension of the human condition. This latest book of prose shows that my hopes will not be realized.

If one wonders what Edmund Wilson and others have seen in Nin's books, one can find it. The first part of the vast novel, *Cities of the Interior*, also published by Alan Swallow, sets out to examine this abstraction: "When man imposes his will on woman, she knows how to give him the pleasure of assuming his power is greater and his will becomes her pleasure; but when the woman accomplishes this, the man never gives her a feeling of any pleasure, only of guilt for having spoken first and reversed the roles." This potentially powerful theme might have been an examination of "what Lillian knew," but the theme is dissipated. It remains an abstraction, a "key statement" in a mess of flat character sketches, trite descriptions, surreal actions, lesbian affairs, and so on. The women are all variations of the same character: neurotic but wise, artistic but motherly, curious but aloof, passionate but frustrated (frustrated at least until the climactic scenes of sexual play, rendered in imagery of fireworks!), in love with Father but searching for Love, Love, Love. There is constant insistence on the women's fine perceptions, as though the narrator of the novel needed to play each scene at peak intensity. One's emotional responses fail. The male characters are a travesty, even the character said to be modeled on Henry Miller. Miss Nin explains some of the nonsense about the men in one of her essays, saying that Jay and Lillian reach an "impasse" in their relationship: "because she has to mother the child in him, she cannot have a real child." And we are supposed to take seriously this explanation of Jay's sterility. I cannot. The novel of over 700 pages (unnumbered in the Swallow edition), *Cities of the Interior*, is full of that sort of funny business. For instance: "Lillian was always in a state of fermentation." "Her large teeth were lustful." "She was to play the lover alone." And so on.

Now, I have no intention of supporting the intentional fallacy. (The "intention" of most novelists is a great work of literature; most fail.) But part of the difficulty with Nin's writing is in her theories, as stated in her two essays, "Realism and Reality" (1946) and "On Writing" (1947). Miss Nin defends herself from readers who expect from her what she calls "traditional" novels. Misunderstandings arise, she says, "mostly from the fact that I write as a poet in the framework of prose and appear to claim the rights of the novelist." One doubts the "fact," and one wishes that if she is going to "write as a poet," whatever that may mean, she would not be so prolix, so lax in her concern for language. She also insists that one gets some understanding of her characters be seeing them "as one regards modern painting." One would assume that by 1946 every writer would have known that the techniques of painting and writing are quite distinct, and that one's way of "regarding" painting is different from one's way of reading prose fiction. The confusion of painting and writing only diminishes both arts, as we all saw early in this century when a post-Lessing confusion of the arts was, for a time, fashionable.

Nin speaks honestly of having "left out so much that you are accustomed to find in character novels." But, one objects, there is no narrative device in the novels to justify or explain the omissions. *Children of the Albatross*, for instance, is structured (in so far as it is structured) by relationships of groups of three or four people; but there is no successful use of the point of view, and there is no reason for the isolation of the characters from the normal, day-to-day commerce of the great world. If Miss Nin had looked at a "character novel," such as James' *Turn of the Screw*, to name only one work favored by her great defender Edmund Wilson, or if she had looked at a greater novel, Ford Madox Ford's *The Good Soldier*, she would have seen how accomplished novelists work such situations, putting into the fable itself the narrative devices which isolate the telling of the story. It is no accident that the collection of Miss Nin's stories is titled *Under a Glass Bell.* Her works are perhaps our finest fiction of solipsism without irony.

Perhaps I am making a difficult point obscurely; but we are considering *The Cities of the Interior,* a novel of over 700 pages which has as its controlling notion Miss Nin's belief that "if we accept neurosis as a part of our humanity it will cease to be a case in literature and become one of the richest sources of fiction writing." (The quotation is from "Realism and Reality.") One has that sense of a live fish swimming in one's stomach: the implications of Nin's statement and of her position terrify. She argues that "collective neurosis" – whatever that may mean – "can no longer be dismissed as exceptional" – as if it ever was; for when all men are neurotic, there is no neuroticism. I'm not sure what Nin means; but it is her obscure, her pretentiously vague "thought" that leads, I think, to the muddle of her prose: *le style est l'homme même,* even today. After all, if this collective neurosis is, as she says, "a direct result of our social system," then we had better start doing something about that social system, not start writing novels complacent in their neuroticism.

I am going to deal at some length with one of Nin's novels, *The Four-Chambered Heart,* which I think (quite possibly for the wrong reasons) the best of her books. It is a sort of *Ethan Frome* set in the Paris of the 1920's: here the weakling lover (Rango) and his mistress (Djuna) must care for the lover's invalid wife (Zora), only with a difference: these characters whose names are the very music of an exotic land are not moral New Englanders. What they are, what they represent, and what their relationship is give the novel its curious power. The story is often wonderfully evocative, with the lovers in a houseboat moored on the Seine. And there is pathos in Rango's realization, early in the book, that his family would be ashamed of the life he leads, so unlike the impersonal "families" of the characters in *Children of the Albatross* and other novels by Nin. For the first time, I think, Nin was close to rendering the relationship between two people, rather than reporting monologues and actions, notations copied from a diary set down for psychoanalysis. Nin does not discuss this romance, but instead presents it in some richly romantic images: the apparent stability of the romantic love of Rango and Djuna is not discussed but embodied in the houseboat, tied to the stone shore but floating on the flux and change of the Seine, on the symbol itself.

Djuna, like all Nin heroines, is still a captive of her father. She must sneak away from the houseboat to return to her father's house, to live in the daytime with the man who "exhausts all the loves given to him." Thus both Djuna and Rango are committed to possessive persons, for Zora demands possession of him and his time. Both lovers must struggle to be free – one of the major themes in Nin's novels – and they find the place of freedom in the hold of a houseboat, anchored near a bridge: "The walls of the barge curved like the inside of a whale belly. The old beams were stained with the marks of former cargoes: wood, sand, stone, and coal." And now the cargo is love. Nin is dealing in the clichés of women's magazines and of soap opera; but in this novel she controls the clichés. She lets the characters imagine and begin a great voyage of love; but the voyage does not lead where they expected.

There in the water, in a room like the inside of a whale, Rango lights a lamp. This simple act, in this setting, is finely suggestive. Yet Rango is also responsible for Zora, "awaiting food, awaiting medicines, awaiting Rango to light the fire." This responsibility is one part of his double burden, and the other part is his own flaw, given not as "analysis" by Nin but as an image: "he rubbed [his face] with the fists closed as children do, as bears and cats do." For gradually the great romantic images build to an unsupportable mass, the "lovers' dream of a desert island, a cell, a cocoon, in which to create a world together from the beginning." This is mere Romantic hubris, this wanting to create a world, this living in *isolated* love. Rango is, after all, a man whose secret flaw is given to us in his habit of rubbing his face as a child or animal does, in his labor "to obey his own rhythm and not the city's." One need not press the point, for whether Nin intended it or not she has got not a vast image of Romantic love but a vast image of the sources of our time's illnesses. Nin means us, I suppose, to take Djuna seriously. Yet if one looks at the evidence given in the novel, and at Djuna's responses, one sees that Djuna is a remarkably stupid woman who only pretends herself wise, "liberated" in the best modern way. The screws keep turning, for Rango the child also represents Spain, the 16th century, and a memory of the race; and he "recreated for Djuna a natural blood and flesh paradise so different from the artificial paradises created in art by city children." Djuna, in turn, comes to represent not just the Wise Woman, but the American Innocent, a city child whose adventures came out of books "until there was no more distinction between outward and inward at all." (The narrator of the novel gives that description without irony; but the reader is free to supply his own.) There is no easy allegorical scheme. Rango who seems to be an image of civilization is also the forest creature, the color of clay, rough and natural in his acts; Djuna is the city creature who pretends wisdom but who prefers dreams and analysis, and is in matters of the heart, an Innocent. Her political notions body forth American political naiveté. Her wisdom is really innocence; Rango's animality is really experience.

But these formulas do not work, for the fiction is richer than formula. In one scene Djuna allows Rango to "destroy" the past by burning her books. That is a part of the violence in Rango, the Old World man from the New World (Spain to Guatemala to Paris), part of the irrational, the primitive basis for decadence; but it is also part of the evil in the heart of man. Djuna discovers that "none of these maladies of the soul are curable by love or devotion." She finds that the heart has four chambers, and that "a wall separates the chambers of the left from those of the right and no direct communication is possible between them." This, then, is the wisdom of the heart. This is the lesson Djuna learns. But it is her simplistic trust in this "wisdom" that gives irony to the narrative.

With New World insolence, Djuna wonders "Will I break seeking to res-

cue Rango?" But by this time in the novel, there is no possible "rescue."
Djuna has shown us all her inconsistencies: she rejects the "big words" in a
grandly Hemingwayesque manner, except for the big word *love*, whatever
that word may mean to a woman who lives almost exclusively in her fantasies.
Significantly she claims that "everyone says: you must take sides, choose a political party, choose a philosophy, choose a dogma. . . . I choose the dream of
human love." Exactly. She resents having to do the human job of making
choices; but when she does make a choice, she chooses a dream. She worries
about Rango's listless, lazy wife; yet when he gets involved in a revolutionary
scheme to overthrow the government of Guatemala, she is opposed. Djuna
wants not to "help" her man, but to control him, all the while denouncing the
possessiveness of her father and of Rango's wife. She talks, or the narrator
does, quite a lot about freedom, yet it is always Djuna's freedom that is insisted on, and only hers. She denounces Rango's willingness to do battle for
an *idea* of freedom:

> It saddened Djuna that Rango was so eager to go to war, to fight
> for his ideas, to die for them. It seemed to her that he was ready to
> live and die for emotional errors as women did, but that like most
> men he did not call them emotional errors; he called them history,
> philosophy, metaphysics, science. Her feminine self was sad and
> smiled, too, at this game of endowing personal and emotional be-
> liefs with the dignity of impersonal names. She smiled at this as men
> smile at women's enlargement of personal tragedies to a status men
> do not believe applicable to personal lives.

In 1965 this sounds a bit silly; but the time of the novel is between the
wars, and the place is Paris, and there was generally a distrust of "big words"
and causes.

Yet in a complex way Nin has not often achieved, neither character can
be labeled, for Rango is aware that Djuna's notion of "love" is also an abstraction:

> "I love violence, [he said]. I want to serve ideas with my body."
> "Men die every day [Djuna said] for ideas which betray them, for
> leaders who betray them, for false ideals."
> "But love betrays too," said Rango.

In this struggle of one man and one woman are two sides of the heart, and
two sets of values. And while these lovers quarrel in their houseboat on the
river, Europe goes on. Nin has dealt, in delicate prose which stays just this
side of the clichés of popular fiction, with an ancient theme: for why did
Achilles leave the war, and why did he return? And why did Antigone act? It
is the old theme of private values in opposition to public values; the old

theme of love and honor: Djuna would gladly lose the world for love, and call that love gain.

Now, Rango commits a curious blunder, for he wants his mistress and his wife to be friends. Thus the relationship which controls the second half of the novel is willed, not accidental as in *Ethan Frome*. Djuna thinks of this as an "error," but Rango takes a commonsensical view: he needs a nurse for his invalid wife. Djuna, although she enters Rango's house "as his accomplice," still is obsessed with her parents' teaching:

> You must be good. You must keep your dress clean. You must be kind, thank the lady, hide your pain if you fall, do not reach for anything you want, do not attract attention to yourself, do not be vain about the ribbon in your hair, efface yourself be silent and modest . . . *be good or else you will not be loved.*

Laboring under the flawed character produced by this ethic, Djuna enters the household of a neurotic woman who has all the while not been ill, but has pretended illness to keep her husband. Yet once we have come this far, we are confronted with Zora who says she "prayed desperately that someone would save us, and now your are here." The themes twist: the American Innocent, bearer of an ethic of "be good or else you will not be loved," having become the "accomplice" of Primitive Experience, must now be the instrument of Salvation for an invalid European. The "wise" Djuna, so often insistent on her superiority, can only mutter to Zora: "It's a difficult situation." All her pretensions collapse in that speech, again whether Nin intended them to or not, and one suspects not. Beneath the posture of clear-sighted goodness, Djuna seems driven by a desire, as fierce as Hedda Gabler's, to shape and control a human life. In the complex of her motives though, her passion for control over Rango and for her own freedom, she is captive of the household. Zora steals from her, makes impossible demands, fakes a heart attack to keep Djuna in service. Each time Djuna tries to flee, she must return. All the while she is unable to evaluate the two great cant terms which support her and much of contemporary American popular thought: Love and Understanding. The narrator tells us how pitiful Rango and Zora are; but we are allowed to discover for ourselves Djuna's delusions. She says to Rango near the end of the novel: since "the world today is rootless, . . . the only remedy is to begin a world for two; in two there is hope for perfection, and that in turn may spread to all." Since the revolution had failed, since he had nothing else to do, Rango returns to the barge; and after an action which clearly showed the folly of Djuna's notion that "the only remedy is to begin a world for two," the lovers lie in their Noah's ark, until Djuna in a final attempt to control their lives by bringing their deaths, tries to sink the barge. She changes her mind, however, rouses Rango who saves the ark of love; and the novel ends with that barge, "sailing nowhere, moored to the port of despair." Only the reader knows that the despair is not the product of "the world today" but is the product of the characters, their actions, and their notions about the world.

I am not prepared to argue that this is a great novel; but it is a fine achievement by a minor, flawed novelist. The virtue of Miss Nin's writing has always been her intense, feminine insights (as in some short stories, such as "Birth"); and in this book I think she comes as close as she ever did to a balance of intensity and control, of insight and art. I wish Swallow had reissued only *The Four-Chambered Heart*, for now this best of Nin's fictions is buried in the 700 pages of the repetitious, incoherently structured *Cities of the Interior*.

From *Critique: Studies in Modern Fiction* 7.3 (Spring-Summer 1965): 68-74.

Sexuality and the Opposite Sex: Variations on a Theme by Théophile Gautier and Anais Nin

Paul Brians

Much contemporary fiction deals with the changing roles of the sexes, and in particular with the ways in which the emancipation of women affects their sexuality (see, for instance, Erica Jong's *Fear of Flying* and Gail Parent's *David Meyer Is a Mother*.) It can be useful to consider how the problems of women breaking out of traditional roles were treated in novels written in the past, when the stimulus and support of the contemporary feminist movement did not exist. In earlier periods, there tends to be a strong polarity between male and female roles, and the personal emancipation of women is naturally portrayed as the taking on of characteristics associated with the other sex.

Théophile Gautier, in *Mademoiselle de Maupin* (1836), and Anais Nin, writing a century later in *A Spy in the House of Love* (1954), chose similar techniques to allow restless young women to explore the foreign territory of the opposite sex.[1] Gautier's heroine, Madeleine de Maupin, disguises herself as a young man ("Théodore de Sérannes") in order to discover what men are really like, rebelling at the idea of being married to one of these strange masculine creatures without really knowing them as they are, behind the airs they assume to please women. She succeeds, but in the process transforms herself into a new kind of woman, combining qualities of both sexes. In the end she loves and leaves the hero, d'Albert, and rides off to further adventures. Nin's heroine, Sabina, calls herself "a spy in the house of love" and envisions herself as the female counterpart of Don Juan, playing one role after another, taking one lover after another, admiring and achieving the ability to experience intense sex without love, like a man.

The technique of exploring the nature and limits of sex roles by creating characters who take on certain emancipating characteristics of the opposite sex proves fruitful in both novels In very different ways, the tales of the two heroines illuminate such related topics as bisexuality and homosexuality, the fragmenting nature of sex roles and their theatrical character, the tendency of such roles to limit the individual's comprehension of others, and the beneficial or harmful results which derive from efforts to break out of traditional patterns. This paper discusses the use of sexual adventure by Gautier and Nin to explore all of these aspects of male-female relationships.[2]

There is no suggestion that Gautier influenced Nin or that both derived their plots from a common source. (A private communication from Miss Nin's office has assured me that she had not read *Mademoiselle de Maupin* when she wrote *A Spy in the House of Love*.) What is instructive about the comparison is the way in which two different sensibilities explore a number of strikingly similar themes. In addition, comparing and contrasting these two novels brings out the remarkable variety and complexity in each. Finally, together they may tell us more about the nature of the traditional gap between the sexes than either could do separately.

Let us admit at the outset that there are a number of important differences between the two books which it would be foolish to ignore. Though both authors, while believing in differences between the sexes, are interested in exploring the areas in which the sexes overlap and blend, one is a man who approaches the subject from a masculine point of view and the other is a woman with a feminine point of view. It is no coincidence that the character through whose eyes we view the action of most of Gautier's novel is a male, and in Nin's novel, a female. Madeleine is single and a virgin; Sabina is married and highly experienced. *Mademoiselle de Maupin* is largely a novel of theory, including its long and notorious *Préface*, with a minimum of action, most of it concentrated in the last few chapters; *A Spy in the House of Love* is filled with actions, many of them mysterious and unexplained.

Another difference is striking, and more important to our theme: Madeleine de Maupin disguises herself as a man; all of Sabina's roles are aspects of her feminine self. Yet Nin had been thinking about the kind of psychology which inspires Gautier's Madeleine, for in her *Ladders to Fire*, part of the same *roman-fleuve (Cities of the Interior)* to which *Spy* belongs, she demonstrates her understanding of the appeal male clothing may have for a young girl:

> "The first time a boy hurt me," said Lillian to Djuna, "it was in school. I don't remember what he did. But I wept. And he laughed at me. Do you know what I did? I went home and dressed in my brother's suit. I tried to feel as a boy felt. Naturally as I put on the suit I felt I was putting on the costume of strength. It made me feel sure, as the boy was, confident, impudent. The mere fact of putting my hands in the pockets made me feel arrogant. I thought that to be a boy meant one did not suffer. That it was being a girl that was responsible for the suffering."[3]

Despite her extraordinarily adventurous nature, Madeleine's motives in donning men's clothing are not dissimilar. She seeks not only protection from the assaults which would be inevitable if she were known to be an unprotected young woman traveling alone, but also the psychological protection of studying men's nature while disguised, so that she may arm herself against their lies and deceptions.[4] The conventional protection provided by the usual proper upbringing of a young lady actually creates grave dangers for Madeleine. (See *Maupin*, pp. 211-212.) It is experience, not innocence, that will bring her to safety.

Thus, even though Sabina never disguises herself as a man, her assuming of various roles serves a very similar function: providing freedom from the vulnerability of conventional women who give their all to the man they love. Nin herself, in *The Novel of the Future*, has discussed Sabina's motivations:

> She does not want to fall under the domination of man (as her mother submitted to her father). She saw her mother trapped in devotion and pain, and she decided to avoid all similarities to her mother, which in her child's concept meant to be like her father. Her dichotomy was that she felt herself to be either the slave or the enslaved, the seduced or the seductress. She could not bear to be the wife. She lived for seduction.[5]

Not all of this is as apparent to the reader of the novel as Nin intended, but the theme which identifies women with vulnerability and men with safety is clear. Like Madeleine, Sabina does not become a Don Juan out of a simple sense of adventure, but at least partly in self-defense.

Other apparent differences between the two works dissolve when they are more closely examined. Gautier is famous primarily as an early and outspoken proponent of art for art's sake. The preface, taken together with several passages from d'Albert's letters, makes *Maupin* his manifesto, and Madeleine herself is often considered to be primarily the incarnation of this esthetic ideal (a subject to which we will return below). Nin, however, is known as a fictional psychologist, trained and for a time employed as an assistant by psychoanalyst Otto Rank, frequently using psychoanalytical language to describe the motivations of her characters. Yet, though they begin from different world views, they achieve remarkably similar results. In *Maupin* (and in *Maupin* alone of all his works) Gautier's estheticism is informed with a passionate attention to motivation, to the complexities of psychology; while in all of Nin's fiction artistic concerns totally transform the psychological material, making it into something quite different from a series of mere case histories. Her roots are in symbolism and surrealism, and her fiction is even more highly wrought than Gautier's, for all his love of *"l'art pour l'art."* Gautier thought of himself as essentially a poet, and so does Nin – her poems merely happen to be written in prose. For both, art informs, transforms, and explains life, and life itself is often a form of art. Their works are thus ideal subjects for our inquiry into the fictional treatment of social roles.

Here we must explore momentarily a problematic area: the area in which life and fiction overlap. Nin's work, more than that of most writers, invites biographical criticism. She has been publishing for several years now volumes from the famous *Diary* which contains not only the elements of an autobiography, but also sketches for her novels and short stories. Incidents are sometimes lifted out of the diary and inserted into her fiction with hardly a change. The diary has frequently been hailed as her finest work, and though that opinion may be partly the result of a reluctance to take seriously her fascinating but very difficult fiction, Nin herself speaks of it on occasion in similar terms. Perhaps the most useful point of view would be to regard all her writing as one: the diary and the fiction as theme and variations comprising a grand literary symphony.

At times, Nin speaks of her fiction as if it were mere autobiography; at other times, she stresses the element of artifice in the fiction and takes pains to distance herself from the characters she has created. Her intent in regard to the present novel seems to have been to divorce Sabina sharply from herself. In *The Novel of the Future*, she writes:

> The genesis of *A Spy in the House of Love* was more complex. The interpretations of Don Juan always seemed oversimplified to me until I read Dr. Otto Rank's book *Don Juan*. I always felt there were more complex motivations behind sensual restlessness. A story from real life concretized the design. It was the story of a friend who believed her father employed detectives to watch her life in New York among the artists. When her father became seriously ill and near death, she questioned him. He was entirely innocent. Then she realized that she had constantly imagined this, and that whenever anyone looked at her in the subway or in a bar or a restaurant she had fantasied it was a detective. Why? The emotional detective story of this psychological drama began with the question why.[6]

But we must raise a rather difficult problem here. Sabina appears in some of her characteristics to reflect Nin herself. The descriptions of Sabina's motivations quoted earlier sounds very much like a description of Nin's own childhood dilemma, for she was torn between her dutiful, long-suffering mother and her philandering father. Yet the passage from *The Novel of the Future* tells us more about Nin's intentions in creating Sabina than it does about Sabina as she actually exists in the novel. In addition, however, there is a further, even more difficult question to be raised: Sabina's lovers are for the most part easily identified as friends of Nin's from the diary. In fact in her fiction in general we are frequently startled to find men – who are presented as friends in the diary – having sex with female characters who talk, act, and think like Nin in the diary. Even more strangely, although all of her fiction is infused with sexuality, and often presents sex acts directly and elegantly, the Nin of the diary seems to have hardly any sex life at all. She becomes pregnant and miscarries in the first volume, but we hardly know how. This disciple of D. H. Lawrence (her first published book was a highly sympathetic study of his work) and friend of Henry Miller has rigidly excluded her sex life from the diary and endowed her characters with the kind of sexuality that the "I" of the edited diary conceals. The latter is friendly, kind, generous, warm, loving, understanding, and even sensuous, but she almost never seems to have any sex.

The fact is understandable, perhaps stemming from a desire for privacy in this one area, but it does present complications if we want to view the diary and the fiction as a whole. For instance, who is Sabina? She is based on a woman Nin knew. She has Nin's friends as lovers. Sabina's relationship with the narrator of *House of Incest* resembles that between Djuna and Lillian in *Ladders to Fire*, which clearly recalls Nin's relationship with June Miller in the diary, though – in these earlier incarnations – Sabina is modelled on June rather than on herself.[7]

And who is Djuna? In Nin's other novels she often has adventures described as the author's in the diary. Her name would seem to be borrowed from a friend, Djuna Barnes, author of *Nightwood*, a novel with a theme in many ways similar to *Spy*. (Djuna Barnes is mentioned in *Spy*, p. 62, but she is probably not the Djuna of the rest of the novel – perhaps this brief mention is merely a tribute to an author Nin admits has much influence on her).

There are even more difficult questions. For instance, does the fact that her husband plays a somewhat peripheral role in Sabina's life have any connection with the fact that the diary lets us know only very briefly that Nin is married, and excludes the husband almost entirely from the published volumes? The diary enlightens, but it also distracts. At any rate, Nin has never pretended to create her characters and situations *ex nihilo*, and it is clear that she is highly skilled at transmuting experience into art.

But what about Gautier? This lover of artifice who throughout the preface to *Maupin* expresses his preference for art over life would hardly be suspected of using autobiographical elements in his fiction. Biography there is, to be sure: Madeleine de Maupin was a real historical character. She dressed as a man, fought men in duels, loved women, burned down a convent when she abducted from it one woman she loved, and was a great success on the stage; her biography is a major source for the novel. Gautier toned her down, omitting the more sensational aspects of her career, primarily by the devise of focussing on the early years of her life. (The assumption that Gautier's heroine must be distinct from the historical figure is unnecessary; who knows whether or not he imagined her going on to accomplish the rest of her original's feats after riding off at the end of *Mademoiselle de Maupin*?)

All of this is quite conventional use of source material. But René Jasinski points out in his exhaustive study, *Les Années romantiques de Théophile Gautier*, that the character Rosette, who has an affair with d'Albert and loves the disguised Madeleine, is clearly inspired by a woman with whom Gautier was having a tempestuous affair and whom he called "Victorine."[8] Was d'Albert's detachment from Rosette Gautier's attempt to deal with his own infatuation? In addition, Jasinksi details a number of other autobiographical elements in *Maupin*.[9]

These biographical speculations do not explain the formal aspects of the two novels, but they may help to explain why both works are so rich in psychological insights. Nin's fictional psychology has always gained its power from the fact that it is grounded in life, but Gautier's fiction is usually sterile and lifeless. The passion which informs *Mademoiselle de Maupin* and makes it his only living prose masterpiece is psychological as well as artistic, and the power of the psychology is almost certainly derived from its roots in Gautier's own life. One has only to compare the preface with d'Albert's musings to see that Gautier himself has entered into his own fictional world. They speak with the same voice.

In another direction, however, biography may be unhelpful, misleading. Nin has a reputation in some circles for being bisexual, though she has made clear in the diary that her one romantic involvement with a woman was never consummated and that she considers it illusory. Nevertheless the power of the attraction between woman and woman informs much of her fiction. Sabina and the narrator in *House of Incest*, Djuna and Lillian in *Ladders to Fire* experience passions which are described with such intensity that Nin evidently felt the need to correct readers who had misunderstood her intentions in *Seduction of the Minotaur*: "Both Sabina and Lillian, faced with a woman, realized they felt closeness but not desire. They had kissed, and that was all."[10] (It is striking that some of the most passionate and vividly described lesbian passages in literature are Nin's – and she thus deliberately denies the reality of the emotion underlying them.)

Separate *Spy* from the other novels in *Cities of the Interior*, however, and not even a hint of bisexuality remains. Only the most strained interpretation could make anything of the fact that Djuna bears the same name as Djuna Barnes, author of a novel about lesbian love observed by a transvestite doctor who in some ways resembles the Lie Detector of *Spy*. Sabina in this novel, in this phase of her fictional career, is almost fanatically heterosexual. She lives by and through men. They obsess her. Women hardly exist. The role of her friend Djuna, at the end of the novel, is as a confessor, hoping to heal Sabina of her internal divisions and enable her to lead a happy life with her husband, Alan. One of Sabina's lovers, Donald, is a familiar gay type who turns her into a mother, but that is the extent of the bisexuality in the novel.

In *Maupin*, however, bisexuality is a major theme. . . .*

* * *

Whereas Nin shies away from lesbianism, male homosexuality is frequent in her fiction; on the other hand, Gautier hints briefly at male homosexuality and revels in lesbianism. The homosexuality of the opposite sex is both more exotically interesting and more comfortable to deal with for these essentially heterosexual writers. Each creates a character who enters into the territory of the opposite sex without challenging the essence of male-female polarity. Their violations of the stereotypes in fact end by reinforcing those very stereotypes.

Both Gautier and Nin experiment with the structure of the novel, and their experiments are directly related to our theme. Nin is noted for her experimentalism, of course. *Spy* is like a cubist painting, fragments of Sabina's life taken out of temporal context and laid down side by side so that their significance is revealed by the artificial order imposed on them. The scene in the bar at the opening (pp. 7-10) is the same scene in the bar at the end (pp. 126-38), but in between the two we have learned a great deal about Sabina, and the second account of the scene takes on much greater significance. The Lie Detector is clearly a symbol of Sabina's conscience, yet he is given surrealistic concreteness, particularly in his first appearance (p. 5), so that one could hardly be blamed for taking him to be a real person, rather than a projection created by Sabina's neurosis.

Gautier's experimentalism is less radical. He breaks up the temporal flow, as does Nin, but he uses the familiar device of the flashback by way of Madeleine's letters recounting past adventures. More interesting is the way in which Gautier shifts from epistolary style to third-person narrative, to dialogue, and back again, making a point of his absolute freedom to tell the story in whatever mode he likes (see his comments in this connection at the opening of Chapter VI). The story is related in fragments, sharp-edged shards of experience told from radically different points of view. The technique is not mere whimsy, as has often been supposed; it has a profound effect on the presentation of the characters. The conflict between the various narrators' sharply different views of events makes a major contribution toward defining their relationships. These novels filled with disguises, deception, and misunderstanding naturally are written in fragmented forms.

An intriguing touch is the appearance of Madeleine's name twice before she is actually introduced into the story (*Maupin*, pp. 61, 64). It is as if her influence were seeping through some strange time-warp to infiltrate d'Albert's mind before he is consciously aware of her existence. The effect is only noticeable to the reader who has already read the novel at least once, of course; but it has interesting affinities with Nin's use of repeated motifs, particularly the anticipatory glimpse of the bar scene mentioned above.

The fragmented form taken by each narrative reflects the fragmented reality it contains. Sabina, the spy, lives multiple lives, desperately trying to hold the pieces together without letting them actually interpenetrate and fuse. D'Albert patronizes Rosette (see, for instance, p. 105) who in her turn patronizes him (p. 156), and the triumphant Madeleine − who appears at first to be the least experienced, the most in need of protection of them all − seduces, outgrows, and deserts them both. Similarly, Alan, Sabina's husband, her father figure, who provides her with what little stability she has, is constantly deceived and must be protected from the awful truth by Sabina herself (pp. 21-22). The protector is protected in Nin's novel; in Gautier's, the seducer is seduced, the superior cynic made a devoted slave. (In a further irony, d'Albert is proud to be Madeleine's first lover, but she herself was the first, unconsummated love of his mistress Rosette. He sees himself as a source of experience, but in a way Madeleine is far ahead of him. He never catches up.)

But such formulas hardly do justice to the complexity and irony and richness of the personal relationships in these works. Let us begin with the obvious: each uses the symbol of the theater as a vehicle for the shifting roles of the characters. Sabina is a would-be actress, occasionally playing a role such as Cinderella in a children's play; but her real performance is her daily life. She uses her thespian career as an excuse for her frequent absences from home, but she is never more of an actress than when she is spinning elaborate tales about her dramatic triumphs to Alan, when she has actually been making love with another man in a hotel two blocks from their home. Early in the novel she tells him she has been performing in Provincetown, which we know to be false (p. 25); but then we learn she had had an affair in Provincetown at some unspecified time (p. 27). She claims to have been playing there the role of Madame Bovary, whose adulteries were entangled with fiction. She tells Alan how she had begun to really identify with her role, as well she might (p. 19). Her life is a nonstop performance, a quick-change act that only begins to break down in the bar scene at the end of the novel as various roles begin clashing, interpenetrating, revealing the lies, revealing the truth, precipitating the crisis.

Madeleine too lives a role, performing her part as a young man so convincingly that only d'Albert suspects the truth. In addition, she reveals her true sexual identity when she plays the role of Rosalind in an amateur performance of *As You Like It*, with d'Albert playing Orlando (Chapter XI). A woman is disguised as a man playing the role of a woman disguised as a man, a part – by the way – which in Shakespeare's time would have been played by a boy: what dizzying layers of deception! Yet that is not all. D'Albert puts his whole heart into Orlando's speeches, using them to declare his love, and he believes Madeleine is doing the same, but her comments later make it clear that she feels no such passion for him.[20] As in Nin's novel, the assuming of a certain character does not ultimately solve the problem of connection between the sexes: Madeleine must leave, and Sabina weeps for wholeness.

But Madeleine is not the only actor in this comedy.[21] D'Albert, though he professes himself not an actor by nature (*Maupin*), p. 259, delights in erotic games with Rosette. . . . He disguises himself as Triton and Rosette as a nereid, they make love in a gondola; he sneaks into her room like a thief, and finally he has her dress in her finest ball gown and, himself in a bear costume, tears it to shreds and mates with her.

* * *

Roles, disguises, masks: all are designed to conceal the true self, or to reveal only carefully selected aspects of it. Yet the fragmentary and limited way in which people perceive each other in these novels is hardly limited to the results of such deliberate deceptions, and each carries its treatment of the theme beyond the theatrical aspect.

Sabina's role-playing naturally results in the fact that others only perceive carefully selected aspects of her: to Alan she is a dutiful wife and diligent actress, to Philip she is the ideal mistress who makes no claims, and to Donald she is a mother. Yet she does not perceive others any more fully than they perceive her. Mambo, the black nightclub entertainer, resents the fact that it is his exoticism which attracts her, not himself as he sees himself (pp. 60, 60-67). Djuna tells Sabina at the end of the novel that the father she perceives in Alan is her own creation, only a partial perception of him (p. 135).

Her own fragmentation, the pretty compartments she has constructed, not only preclude her own wholeness; they prevent her perceiving the wholeness of others. As Djuna explains to her:

> "You're a danger to other human beings. First of all you dress them in the costume of the myth: poor Philip, he is Siegfried, he must always sing in tune, and be everlastingly handsome. Do you know where he is now? In a hospital with a broken ankle. Due to immobility he has gained a great deal of weight. You turn your face away, Sabina? That was not the myth you made love to, is it? If Mambo stopped drumming to go home and nurse his sick mother, would you go with him and boil injection needles? Would you, if another woman loved Alan, would you relinquish your child's claims upon his protectiveness? Will you go and make of yourself a competent actress and not continue to play Cinderella for amateur theatres only, keeping the artificial snow drop which fell on your nose during the snow storm long after the play is over as if to say, 'For me there is no difference at all between stage snow and the one falling now over Fifth Avenue?' Oh, Sabina, how you juggled the facts in your games of desire, so that you might always win. The one intent on winning has not loved yet!" (pp. 136-37)

D'Albert suffers from a similar inability to perceive people whole. He cares only about the beauty of women. He understands very little about either Rosette or Madeleine as people. He too would be "a danger to other human beings" if he had the power to attract others in as powerful a degree as does Sabina. As it is, his relatively slight hold on Rosette wounds her and does him no good.

* * *

D'Albert sees in women only what he wants to see in them. This tendency is a major theme in Nin's work. Sabina, when Philip looks at her, shrinks from his gaze:

> He turned his eyes fully upon her, now a glacial blue; they were impersonal and seemed to gaze beyond her at all women who had dissolved into one, but who might, at any moment, again become

dissolved in all. This was the gaze Sabina had always encountered in Don Juan, everywhere, it was the gaze she mistrusted. It was the alchemy of desire fixing itself upon the incarnation of all women into Sabina for a moment but as easily by a second process able to alchemize Sabina into many others. (p. 30)

To regard someone else as the fulfillment of a private fantasy is to do worse than view them imperfectly; it is to ignore their individuality. Sabina, as a female Don Juan, turns this same distorting gaze on others, and naturally they resent it. D'Albert does the same to Madeleine. Both d'Albert and Sabina want life to be a succession of perfect moments with idealised partners; but their tunnel vision prevents them from really knowing the actual people who exist behind their fantasies. Just as for d'Albert beauty is all-important in women, so Sabina fears that all she loves of Philip is his looks, his glamor as an opera singer (p. 48). Further, her idealization of Alan as the wise, protective father is flawed by her lies to him, which render him foolish and oddly irrelevant to her real life, but through no fault of his own. Nin sums up this problem and her presentation of it very well:

> The classics were content to describe the romantic (neurotic) illusion which had to be conquered to win love. I highlighted the obstacles which made an enduring relationship impossible (being a masquerade between two personas) or a duel between two people miscast by each other, each insisting on the other's playing the role assigned to him by the lover's need.[22]

It is important to insist on Madeleine's independence, her existence as a real person outside of d'Albert's image of her. It is well to remember that she literally has the last word in the novel. All too often she is perceived merely as an art object, the incarnation of d'Albert's ideal of beauty.[23] She is that to him, of course, and in one passage, she speaks of herself as part of a work of art, but the voice she speaks in seems oddly like d'Albert's, as if Gautier had arbitrarily leant her his hero's point of view. When she brings water for Rosette to drink from her hands, she observes that they made a very pretty group: ". . . il eût été à désirer qu'un sculpteur se fût trouvé là pur en tirer le crayon" (*Maupin*, p. 293). [". . . it is much to be regretted that a sculptor was not there to make a sketch of it" (II, 188).]** But this is a momentary aberration. She is both a sex object and an *objet d'art*, but she is much more, possessing her own motives, ideals, and plans; and she does not allow herself to be confined by d'Albert's narrow estheticism.

Gautier, like his friend Baudelaire, was very interested in relationships between the arts. D'Albert sometimes views the world as a vast sculpture garden. Nin shares this interest and has written extensively on the subject. Her favorite extraliterary art is music (for which Gautier notoriously had no taste whatever). Sabina identifies herself with Stravinsky's firebird, a splendid artistic symbol of the fire images persistently connected with her (p. 69). She also identifies herself with another, more ominous image in art, which symbolizes her fragmentation: Duchamps' *Nude Descending a Staircase* (p. 127) – a comparison which Nin had applied to Djuna in *The Four-Chambered Heart*.[24]

Albouy suggests that art brings freedom as Madeleine is liberated from her sexual ambiguity by acting the part of Rosalind in *As You Like It*; yet it is d'Albert upon whom her performance has a liberating effect.[25] She delays revealing herself to him and gladly reassumes her male guise at the end of the novel, evidently finding it liberating rather than confining.

Music, however, does seem to have healing powers in Nin's world when, at the end of *Spy*, Sabina weeps while listening to a Beethoven quartet (p. 139). She is not yet healed, nor is there any certainty she ever will be, but her tears are clearly cleansing tears, a purifying outburst of honest emotion following upon the catastrophic collapse of her house of mirrors in the preceding scenes.

There are other, really significant differences in the reports our spies bring back from the territory of the opposite sex. One of them is simple enough: it is a matter of time. For d'Albert, frustration is almost preferable to enjoyment. His approach to Madeleine is long and indirect. Madeleine in her turn makes him wait, reawakening his doubts about her sex and nearly driving him mad before she offers herself to him. It is a libertine version of the Protestant work ethic: sweets to easily obtained are hardly worth the having.

This point of view is absent in *Spy*. The archetypal sexual encounter finds Sabina lying naked on the beach, Philip striding up to meet her. This theme is connected with one we have mentioned before: Sabina's need to experience sex without love, without the bonds she so fears:

> Then the absurdity of her expectation amazed her: seeking another kind of fusion because she had failed to achieve the sensual one, when what she wanted was only the sensual one, to reach man's freedom in adventure, to arrive at enjoyment without dependence which might liberate her from all her anxieties connected with love. (p. 40)

> She opened her eyes to contemplate the piercing joy of her liberation: she was free, free as man was, to enjoy without hope.
> Without any warmth of heart, as a man could, she had enjoyed a stranger.
> And then she remembered what she has heard men say: "Then I wanted to leave." (pp. 49-50)

Madeleine, like Sabina, is eager to enjoy a man for the mere experience of it, and she also feels no love:

To prevent my body from posing proudly before my soul, I mean to soil it to the same extent, if – which I doubt – it is any more soiling than eating and drinking. In a word, I mean to know what a man is and the pleasure he can give. Since d'Albert has recognised my sex under my disguise, it is only right that he should be recompensed for his penetration. He was the first to guess that I am a woman, and I shall do my best to prove to him that his supposition was well founded. (II, 291)

One might question whether Madeleine's abrupt departure after her perfect night of love is not really just a peculiar way of fulfilling d'Albert's fantasies. He had earlier let us know that pleasure seldom reaches perfection, and when it does, it is best that it end swiftly and abruptly, without either exploding into excess or falling into decline (*Maupin*, pp. 47-48, 98-99). In her letter to him which forms the ending of the novel, she seems eager to effect a timely departure according to this ideal:

"You think, perhaps, that I leave you because I do not love you. By and by you will find this to be true – I would have stayed if I had thought less highly of you, and I would have made you drink the tasteless draught to the dregs. (II, 312-13)

Yet d'Albert is not the same bored esthete he was before he met Madeleine. One may well doubt whether he would actually agree with her now that his dream has become a reality.

Her action is, at any rate, clearly her own. She warns him in advance it may well be an affair of a single night (p. 363); and the letter quoted above and her visit to Rosette's bedroom both make it clear that she is only seeking to soften the blow by telling d'Albert she is leaving to spare him. It is for herself she leaves. She may have provided the high point of d'Albert's life, the end of his quest, but she is just beginning to live.

Which brings us to perhaps the most significant difference of all between the two heroines: Sabina always moves on, not because she fears to spoil perfection or is seeking new worlds to conquer, but because she is unsatisfied and afraid. At first sight, it would seem that Madeleine is the freer of the two. Having achieved a successful synthesis of elements from the conventional male and female roles, she is emancipated, able to ride off to new adventures, leaving the rather pathetic figures of Rosette and d'Albert behind, consoled, she hopes, by their mutual memories of her. In *Spy*, it is Sabina who is pathetic. She suffers. Her play-acting does not seem to be liberating; it is confining. It is not a lark; it is an oppressive neurosis. Her desire for independence and adventure is only one pole of her personality; the other pole is very different:

. . . she puzzled the mystery of her desperate need of kindness. As

other girls prayed for handsomeness in a lover, or for wealth, or for
power, or for poetry, she had prayed fervently: let him be kind. (p.
25)

Nin herself is as kind as an author as she appears to be in life. She is very
reluctant to present any of her characters in an absolutely unsympathetic way.
In *Spy* she enters Sabina's neurosis sympathetically and sometimes portrays it
in a very positive light indeed (pp. 42-44). Yet the ending of the novel bears
out the impression that Sabina has suffered from her shattered self throughout and is now on the brink of new synthesis. Nin comments on this sort of
suspended ending: ". . . my characters did seem to go through a breakdown
of their false synthesis in an effort to find a more authentic one, a new
one."[26]

How shall we characterize, then, the reports that these two spies in the
house of love bring back? Gautier's heroine not only penetrates the barriers
between the sexes, she demonstrates their conventional nature and forges a
new self free of the confining limits prescribed for a proper young girl. But in
the end, however charming she may be – and she is undeniably charming –
Madeleine de Maupin is a fantasy figure, and a male fantasy figure at that. It
would have been almost impossible to have created a model emancipated
woman in Gautier's time, and she is not one. She is clearly meant to be an
exception, an object of delight to d'Albert's perverse imagination. In more
than one passage her voice echoes his so clearly that it is all too apparent that
Gautier has not bothered to create a new point of view for her (this is true
only occasionally, of course; she is usually very much her own woman). She is
not offered as a model for other women; indeed, she agrees with many of the
male criticisms of women in general (pp. 276-77). Her story is an entertaining
fantasy, though it incidentally makes some acute points about the confining
nature of sex roles, especially for women.

Sabina's story is much more serious, much more authentic. The difficulties involved in exploring the territory of the other sex and becoming ac-
quainted with the natives are not to be solved simply by a change of costume;
and – in the long run – it is probably not a matter of gender at all. Nin's
women are, by and large, as unsuccessful in their relationships with other
women as they are in their relationships with men. Sabina is the type of person who cannot love completely because she denies her own wholeness. Her
goal of sex without love turns out to be neurotic: a sign of weakness rather
than of strength. Djuna makes it clear that Sabina will never be able to love
and fully accept others in the deepest sense until she has accepted and integrated the various facets of her own many-sided self.

In a world in which people are more than sexual stereotypes, loving is
more complicated, more difficult than Gautier's fantasy allows. It is to Anais
Nin's credit that she has explored the complexities and profundities of sexuality and love with a skill and an insight that few authors can match.

NOTES

[1]Anais Nin, *A Spy in the House of Love* (Chicago, Swallow Press, 1959) and Théophile Gautier, *Mademoiselle de Maupin* (Paris: Garnier, 1966). References to these two works will be given in the text.

[2]In preparing this paper, I have benefited greatly from two studies of Nin's work not otherwise cited below: Evelyn J. Hinz *The Mirror and the Garden: Realism and Reality in the Writings of Anais Nin* (n.p.: Publications Committee, The Ohio State University Libraries, 1971) and Oliver Evans, *Anais Nin* (Carbondale: Southern Illinois University Press, 1968).

[3]Anais Nin, *Ladders to Fire* (Chicago, Swallow Press, 1959), p. 47. See also *Seduction of the Minotaur* (Chicago: Swallow Press, 1969), pp. 124-25, where Lillian's fondness for dressing up in her brother's clothes is further analyzed.

[4]She explains her motives in *Maupin*, p. 207.

[5]Anais Nin, *The Novel of the Future* (New York: Macmillan, 1968), pp. 69-70.

[6]Ibid., p. 137.

[7]In *Seduction of the Minotaur* the two fictional cases are compared, p. 126.

[8]*Les Années romantiques de Théophile Gautier* (Paris, Vuibert, 1929), pp. 295-98.

[9]Ibid., pp. 298-301.

[10]*Seduction of the Minotaur*, p. 126. Nin understates here the actual degree of physical intimacy which occurs in these incidents, but this is essentially accurate.*

[20]She ordinarily adopts an ironic, slightly mocking tone with regard to d'Albert, and her final decision to make love with him is clearly made as an erotic experiment and not as an act of romantic passion. See her comments on pp. 356-57.

[21]Anne Bouchard thoroughly explores the disguises and masks in *Maupin* in her article, "Le Masque et le miroir dans 'Mademoiselle de Maupin,' " *Revue d'histoire littéraire de la France*, 72 (1972), pp. 583-99.

[22]*The Novel of the Future*, p. 69

[23]See, for instance, Michel Crouzet, "Gautier et le problème de créer," *Revue d'histoire littéraire de la France*, p. 164.

[[24]Brians reference to *The Four-Chambered Heart* has no corresponding note in the original.]

[25]Pierre Albouy, "Le Mythe de l'androgyne dans 'Mademoiselle de Maupin.' " *Revue d'histoire littéraire de la France*, 72 (1972), pp. 605-06.

[26]*The Novel of the Future*, p. 65.

EDITOR'S NOTES

*I have here excised a lengthy discussion of bisexuality in Gautier's novel while preserving the original footnote numbering in what follows.

**Throughout, Brians provides Gautier's French original followed by an English translation by F. C. DeSumichrast (London: Postlethwaite, Taylor and Knowles, 1909) in two parts. After this quotation, I have provided only the English. The translated quotations are cited by part (roman numeral) and page (arabic numeral).

From *Essays in Literature* 4 (Spring 1977): 122-37.

Lillian Beye's Labyrinth: A Freudian Exploration of *Cities of the Interior*

Suzette A. Henke

Anais Nin's *Cities of the Interior* is a unique work of fiction. It is an experimental *roman fleuve* – an avant-garde novel that makes use of dream sequences, symbols, lyrical metaphors, and many of the techniques we associate with the symbolist prose-poem. The principal focus of this five-volume work is the "multiplication of selves" which Nin found so desirable in fiction, where in the landscape of the imagination one could act out potential dimensions of identity unrealized in actual life. As Nin explains in the first volume of her *Diary*: "I have always been tormented by the image of multiplicity of selves. Some days I call it richness, and other days I see it as a disease."[1].

Trained as a psychoanalyst by Dr. Otto Rank, Nin was fully conversant with Freudian theory. She saw the imagination as a psychoanalytic instrument for healing, a way to identify and come to terms with the separate selves "split" off from the complex, multifaceted ego recognized by the creative artist. Nin apparently agreed with Sigmund Freud's theory, expressed in "Creative Writers and Day-Dreaming," that "His Majesty the Ego" is "the hero alike of every day-dream and of every story."[2] *Cities of the Interior* corroborates the hypothesis that the "psychological novel . . . owes its special nature to the inclination of the modern writer to split up his ego, by self-observation, into many part-egos, and, in consequence, to personify the conflicting currents of his own mental life in several heroes" (*SE* IX, 150).

It might be argued that Nin, consciously or unconsciously, structured her fictional representation of woman in *Cities of the Interior* around the three principal Freudian categories of the self – ego, id, and super-ego.[3] Lillian Beye, the protagonist of the first and last volumes of the novel, clearly serves as a fictional alter-ego for Nin, a "second self" whose life is closely modeled on the author's own experience. In Freudian terms, Lillian embodies the developing ego in its quest for independent self-realization. A female artist in search of creativity and self-expression, Lillian embarks on an extended journey into the recesses of the psyche. Through a series of dreams, memories, and free associations, she explores the labyrinth of the unconscious. In a process analogous to psychoanalytic therapy, Lillian is able to identify the "minotaur" at the heart of masochistic behavior patterns which dominate her life.

Sabina, the fascinating and volatile protagonist of *A Spy in the House of Love*, seems closely to correspond to Freud's description of the id, allied with Eros and the pleasure principle. In touch with the world of primary process, Sabina is a primitive and chaotic personality driven by libidinous instincts. Supposedly "liberated" in her pursuit of hedonistic pleasure, Sabina is actually a tormented spirit who lives dangerously on the edge of schizophrenic breakdown.

In contrast, Djuna, the protagonist of *Children of the Albatross* and *The Four-Chambered Heart*, presents a model of altruism and rational control. She symbolizes the feminine equivalent of the Freudian "superego," or "ego-ideal," that "becomes a representative of the real external world . . . and . . . a model for the endeavors of the ego" (*SE* IX, 167).

In accordance with Freud's theory of creativity, Nin models much of her character development "on childhood memories in the writer's life" (*SE* IX, 152). Analyzing the pathology of "moral masochism," she reveals in *Cities of the Interior* that "the battle with the obstacle of an unconscious sense of guilt is not . . . easy. . . . Nothing can be done . . . but the slow procedure of unmasking its unconscious repressed roots" (*SE* XIX, 50n).

In *Ladders to Fire*, Lillian Beye emerges as the central protagonist of Nin's continuous novel. A highly introspective jazz pianist, and a woman in search of both artistic and emotional fulfillment, Lillian suffers contradictory feelings of altruism and isolation, child-like dependence and aggressive self-assertion. She abandons the refuge of a stable marriage to taste the pleasure of bohemian Paris, only to find herself trapped in the self-effacing role of mother-confessor to a narcissistic lover.

Lillian becomes virtually engulfed by the egotistical personality of Jay, a surrogate father figure whom she serves in a desperate quest for erotic approval. Like the classic neurotic, she is doomed to repeat the past rather than remember it. Having successfully repressed an earlier masochistic attachment to her father, Lillian acts out an Oedipal pathology that tyrannizes her life. She searches compulsively for selfish and brutal lovers who demand subservience and diminish her self-image. Lillian is painfully bound in a sado-masochistic relationship to Jay, an irresponsible painter who requires protection and nurturing, but who never reciprocates on the level of adult affection. This childish and irascible figure becomes a father-judge who wields such power over Lillian's fragile psyche that he is capable of affirming or destroying her unstable ego.

Lillian prostitutes her musical talent for the sake of Jay's painting but never murmurs about his selfish exploitation of her own creative potential. When Jay carelessly leaves a neighbor's piano out in the rain, he finds the destructive consequences of his negligence wonderfully amusing. Lillian realizes that his callousness is paradigmatic: she, like the piano, is being sacrificed to her lover's boyish, bohemian whims.

Jay appears to have remained fixed in a posture of infantile narcissism, never relinquishing the pleasure principle for the reality principle appropriate to adult life. He paints wild, primitive, murderous portraits expressive of a sociopathic desire for "infant omnipotence." Described as a giant mouth, he seems fixated at the oral-narcissistic phase of childhood pleasure. As Freud reminds us, eating is a prototype of identification, as mastication is of destruction. Untroubled by ambivalence, Jay wants to devour everything and everyone, to bring the whole of sensuous life into the orbit of his own voracious ego. His stance of brutality and irresponsibility, though ostensibly claiming allegiance to a Buddhist philosophy of willessness, is actually a Nietzschean assertion of a masculine "will to power" over a dreaded, hostile environment.

Jay is at war with the universe, and Lillian is his hostage. In the nurturing circle of Lillian's affection, he can regress to the oral phase of development, when a "child sucking at his mother's breast has become the prototype of every relation of love" (*SE* VI, 222). In the role of son-lover, he captures the illusion of prelapsarian bliss and sinks down into a fantasy of infant attachment. Riding in a taxi, Jay curls up into the embryonic warmth of Lillian's fur coat and basks in the shelter of her maternal solicitude. Like a protected fetus or a nursing infant, he demands sustenance from his beloved in a symbiotic relationship that drains her of talent, confidence, energy, and passion. A child himself, Jay becomes furious when he learns of Lillian's pregnancy. The threat of "another child" claiming her attention sends him into paroxysms of anger and sibling rivalry.

Psychologically, Jay is both father and lover, son and husband to the vulnerable Lillian. He repeatedly deserts her to seek pleasure with other women, then returns home to the mother-confessor who must heal and forgive her prodigal son. By assuming the role of non-judgmental parent, Lillian conquers her jealousy and suppresses her pain. She dares not judge her insensitive and unfaithful lover, lest she be judged, in turn, by the patriarchal figure who dominates her life. Lillian courts male approval at any cost. Bound in a sado-masochistic relationship to Jay, she is unaware that her life is dominated by obsessive patterns of guilt and self-punishment.

Not until *Seduction of the Minotaur* will Lillian journey through the labyrinth of her psyche and confront the minotaur, a beast of her own making, buried deep within the unconscious. It is she who has introjected the parental superego, an image of the implacable father constantly judging and punishing, and capable of becoming "harsh, cruel, and inexorable against the ego" (*SE* XIX, 167). "The superego arises . . . from an identification with the father taken as model. Every such identification is in the nature of a de-sexualization or even of a sublimation" (*SE* XIX, 54).

Out of "dread of the superego," Lillian turns her destructive instincts inward against the ego and masochistically repeats patters of self-punishment. At the end of *Ladders to Fire*, she commits her "daily act of destruction," a hara-kiri of the spirit:

> *In this invisible hara-kiri she tore off her dress, her jewels, tore off*
> *every word she uttered, every smile, every act of the evening. . . .*
> *And now it was done. A complete house-wrecking service. Every*
> *word, smile, act, silver jewel, lying on the floor, with the emerald green*
> *dress. . . . Nothing to salvage. A mere pile of flaws. A little pile of ash-*
> *es from a bonfire of self-criticism.*[4]

Lillian suffers from extreme masochism, precipitated by a primordial loss of self-confidence during childhood. The inability to conform to the demands of an introjected ego-ideal causes continual anxiety and laceration of the spirit. Self-doubt and depression prompt her to commit quotidian acts of spiritual suicide, erupting from nightly bouts with the syndrome Freud described as "melancholia." As Freud explains, "the ego gives itself up because it feels itself hated and persecuted, instead of loved. To the ego, therefore, living means the same as being loved by the superego" (*SE* XIX, 58). Psychologically, the ego "sees itself deserted by all protecting forces and lets itself die" (*SE* XIX, 58).

In *Seduction of the Minotaur*, the last volume of *Cities*, Lillian journeys to Mexico, the land of her childhood, in quest of self-knowledge and of a recognition of the patterns that emerge from her past. "Some voyages have their inception in the blueprint of a dream," we are told. "Lillian's recurrent dream of a ship that could not reach the water, that sailed laboriously, pushed by her with great effort, through city streets, had determined her course toward the sea" (*Cities*, 465). The Freudian image of an embattled ship "that could not reach water" arises out of a world of primary process as a symbol of spiritual, emotional and sexual paralysis. Lillian feels psychologically blocked and inhibited, cut off by neurosis from participation in the fluid stream of life.

She seeks Golconda, the golden city, a prelapsarian paradise offering the "gold of pleasure" that may, in fact, be "fool's gold." Lillian has entered a transcendent world of mythical possibility, a landscape of tropical "conversion." "Tropic, from the Greek, signified change and turning. So she changed and turned, and was metamorphosed by the light and caressing heat into a spool of silk" (*Cities*, 466). Her personality melts into luxuriant pliability: it has become a "spool" to be unwound, a mystery to be revealed. It is, furthermore, the thread that will lead her to the center of the labyrinth.

In *Seduction of the Minotaur*, Lillian plays the role of the epic hero described by Freud. On a psychological level, she acts out the primordial heroic myth of a quest to "slay the father," to conquer the introjected parental *imago* that takes the form of a monster in her imagination. This totemic beast, half man, half animal, evokes a symbol suggestive of an irascible superego. The judgmental eyes of both father and mother have been internalized in the shape of a monster. As Freud explains, the "superego is as much a represen-

tative of the id as of the external world. It came into being through the intro-
jection into the ego of the first objects of the id's libidinal impulses – namely,
the two parents" (*SE* XIX, 167). The superego, furthermore, "retained essential features of the introjected persons – their strength, their severity, their
inclination to supervise and to punish" (*SE* XIX, 167). A product of the
Oedipal complex, this spectre of parental authority inspires a masochistic
sense of guilt in the adult who can never conform to the exorbitant demands
of an embedded "ego-ideal."

Dr. Hernandez, Lillian's closest friend in Mexico, urges her to explore
the cities of the interior that harbor the minotaur in her dreams. He warns
her that "we live by a series of repetitions until the experience is solved, understood, liquidated" (*Cities*, 479). Like a Freudian analyst, Hernandez believes that the neurotic is doomed "to repeat rather than remember." "Forgetting" may simply obscure a process of psychic repression: "We may seem
to forget a person, a place, a state of being, a past life, but meanwhile what
we are doing is selecting a new cast for the reproduction of the same
drama. . . . The design comes from within. It is internal" (*Cities*, 478).

When Lillian and the doctor take a canoe trip into the jungles of Mexico,
they make a corresponding psychological voyage into an ancient landscape.
The canoe, like a legendary barque, is painted in colors of Mayan blue; it
seems to transport its passengers into a timeless, transcendent realm. Together, Lillian and the doctor explore a communal consciousness, a "rooted"
mythic heritage that will reveal archetypal patterns.

Open to the "presence" of being, Lillian can accept life as a continual
process, a Heraclitean movement that encompasses growth, maturation, and
death. "In Golconda she attained a flowing life, a flowing journey" (*Cities*,
482).

> *She had read that certain Egyptian rulers had believed that after*
> *death they would join a celestial caravan. . . . Scientists had found*
> *two solar barques, . . . one for the night's journey toward the moon,*
> *one for the day's journey toward the sun.*
>
> *In dreams one perpetuated these journeys in solar barques. And in*
> *dreams, too, there were always two: one buried in limestone and una-*
> *ble to float on the waterless routes of anxiety, the other flowing con-*
> *tinuously with life. The static one made the voyage of memories, and*
> *the floating one proceeded into endless discoveries.* (*Cities*, 482-3)

At this point in the novel, Lillian still feels imprisoned in the "lunar
barque" of her imagination, the static world of memory where inhibiting patterns "arrest the flow of life."[5]

In the city of ancient ruins where Michael Lomax dwells, Lillian recognizes a symbolic landscape emblematic of a consciousness imprisoned in an
ossified past. Like a ghost arising from a town embedded in volcanic ash,
Lomax refuses to transcend his burnt-out memories of loss and disappointment. He inhabits a former convent where church bells toll continuously. His

world is "rendered into poetry by its recession into the past." "A city in ruins . . . had to be constructed anew by each person, therefore enhanced into illimitable beauty" (*Cities*, 518). But the morbid silence of the city depresses Lillian and makes her feel a "constriction of the heart" (520).

In the austere environment of these sun-bleached ruins, Lillian begins to comprehend the Indian view of life in the context of historical forces that diminish the individual. The evidence of a once-vital civilization buried in volcanic ash inspires an attitude of "serenity, passivity, a transmutation into resignation. . . . Time, powerless to love one man, promptly effaces him. His sorrows, torments, and death recede into impersonal history" (519). The historical purview is revealing yet invidious: it implicitly obliterates the need for personal regeneration.

Confronted with existential absurdity, Lillian turns away from the threat of nihilism. She flees the homophiliac environment of Lomax's ancient city. In this morbid, funereal setting, she, too, is haunted by ghosts from the past. Her dream of a vulture swooping down and marking her shoulder recalls a similar incident described by Freud in his essay "Leonardo da Vinci and a Memory of His Childhood." Lillian's dream and Freud's analysis are united by a common theme of homosexuality. If the vulture symbolizes an unconscious image of the phallic mother, then Lillian, like Leonardo, must confront the authoritarian parent whose "imago" has invaded adult experience.

All of Lillian's major revelations or epiphanies are evoked by journeys, movement, travel, and change of perspective. The boat trip with Hernandez awakens her to the need for a fluid consciousness sufficiently porous to dwell in the frightening irresolution of the present. On a bus trip to visit Hatcher, an American engineer who resembles her father, Lillian begins to resurrect the repressed memories of her Mexican childhood. As the coach passes through a tunnel, she remembers playing in a half-finished subway system, an underground chamber whose darkness and secrecy enhanced its attraction. Forbidden to explore this mysterious "city of the interior," Lillian disobeyed parental orders and got lost in the terrifying labyrinth. Convinced that she was facing imminent death, she felt traumatized by the sensation of being buried alive in wet clay and engulfed by the womb/tomb of mother earth. Lillian was finally rescued by her own mother, who arrived carrying a candle in the ambivalent guise of savior and avenging angel.

The irate parent impressed a life-long lesson on her timorous daughter: if one disobeys authority to seek dangerous pleasures, the penalty will be severe. If one dares embark on a journey toward self-discovery, the tremendous risks of such a quest will outweigh the possible rewards. *"When you choose to play in a realm far away from the eyes of parents, you court death."*

The woman who rejects the call of duty and obedience, who chooses artistic creativity over traditional roles prescribed by society, invites personal catastrophe. The search for autonomy is perilous indeed. And it becomes all the more dangerous when it involves a conscious rejection of the superego and a psychological rite of passage into unchartered territory of self-actualization.

Lillian's memory of the buried city erupts from her unconscious as a dominant symbol of awakening. It marks the dividing line between the prelapsarian "dream of the transparent child" and the inauguration of guilt and sexual repression. Exploring the abandoned subway, the ingenuous child felt secure in a latent conviction of "infant omnipotence." Symbolically, she remained in touch with the subterranean world of the unconscious and sought a realm of sensuous pleasure forbidden by adult society.

In this dream-memory, the underground maze provides a pictorial image of the psychological labyrinth that the mature Lillian will attempt to explore. The child's traumatic experience serves as a paradigm for the frustration of instinctual need and imaginative pleasure. It suggests the adult prohibition of early sexual researches on the part of the child. At the genital stage of development, Lillian was forbidden to explore either the earthen tunnels of a deserted fantasy world or the hidden mysteries of her own libidinal tendencies. The physical labyrinth functions as a screen image for the female genitalia – convoluted recesses which the mother defines as secret and forbidden. The daughter is forced to perceive her own sexuality as unknowable and her body as untouchable. Her interiority is usurped by the female parent, whose admonitions deny access to autoerotic pleasure. The genitals constitute a mysterious and inviolable labyrinth, a secret realm whose private sensations are inadmissible to the puritanical conscience.

Lillian's mother is stoic and reserved, a woman who inhabits a "house of no-smile" and wages a constant battle against the "savagery" of Mexico. Threatened by the uninhibited atmosphere of the tropics, she takes pains to educate her children in "civilized" codes of European behavior. In the scene that Lillian recalls, the mother functions as an authority figure who destroys her daughter's "infantile" illusions of power and autonomy. She forces the child to relinquish the delights of instinctual gratification and accede to the harsher "reality principle" of adult life.

The minotaur hidden in Lillian's psyche is the child-created totem of an angry parent, a superego that reproves and punishes. Lillian's fragile self-image is contingent on an introjected figure of parental wrath. She still sees herself as a helpless child, rescued and admonished by her mother in a volatile scene of indignant rage. Dwarfed by the matriarchal spectre, Lillian cannot emerge as an independent person. She is perpetually haunted by the voice as conscience, an implacable judge that she can neither conquer nor appease. As Freud explains in "The Economic Problem of Masochism," "the ego reacts with feelings of anxiety . . . to the perception that it has not come up to the demands made by its ideal, the superego" (*SE* XIX, 167).

Because the process of individuation was inhibited at an early stage of development, Lillian feels threatened by unconscious fears of "engulfment" by the mother. She thinks of the female parent as a kind of deity, omnipercipient and all-powerful, and realizes that she has constructed her own self-image through her mother's critical gaze: "She had first seen the world through her mother's eyes, and seen herself through her mother's eyes. Children were like kittens, at first they did not have vision, they did not see themselves except as reflected in the eyes of the parents" (*Cities*, 539).

Lillian remembers her mother as a "great lady," a model of female decorum: "She wore immaculate dresses, was always pulling on her gloves. She had tidy hair which the wind could not disarrange, she wore veils, perfume.... If this is a woman, thought Lillian, I do not want to be one" (539). Obsessed with control and cleanliness, the mother is surrounded by fetishes that suggest phallic power. She is ensconced in a fortress of gloves, veils, hair, perfume – sexual totems that give her an aura of inaccessibility.

The mother's critical blue eyes have become Lillian's "mirror," an introjected screen of judgment and reproval onto which the daughter projects her adult self-image. "You retained as upon a delicate retina, your mother's image of you, as the first and the only authentic one" (540). A stern matriarch has invaded the most intimate spaces of perceptual consciousness. Lillian's eyes "were not her own when she looked at herself" (542).

On New Year's Eve, Lillian begins to acknowledge that she has been psychologically imprisoned in the "underground city of her childhood" and trapped in a nightmare of her own making. But, she assures herself, "you can awaken, and when you awaken you know the monsters were self-created.... The size of each world we live in is individual and relative, and the objects and people vary in each EYE" (543).

Lillian realizes that parents impose on their children a diminutive vision of the self. They continue to "see one *small*" throughout the process of maturation. What psychologists call the "merger" self so desires to belong to a larger, protective family unit that it voluntarily accedes to the diminutive roles prescribed by domestic configurations. At the same time, however, the "seeker" self is motivated by a pressing need for independence. It moves in the direction of self-actualization, until the adult can at last see his/her parents as equals and peers rather than as omnipotent judges. In the eyes of the helpless child, both mother and father assume the exaggerated aspect of mythic, god-like figures. Only after the adult has reached maturity can he/she begin to envision the parents reduced to their "natural size."

In the process of clarifying her own self-image, Lillian realizes that she has always inflated the memory of her mother and father and made them into god-like figures. Now, for the first time, she begins to understand that they, too, must have been frightened, vulnerable, insecure people: "I see my parents small, they have assumed a natural size" (542). "Lillian remembered when she had believed that her mother was the tallest woman on earth, and her father the heaviest man.... But she was regaining her own eyes, and with these eyes, with her own vision, she would return home" (543-44).

On the morning of the new year, Lillian awakens to life "above ground." The hotel's cracked mirror reveals a "schizoid" reflection of "her face in two pieces which could be made to fit together again" (544). Lillian senses that her personality has been fragmented and dissolved in preparation for an experience of renewal. She has succeeded, finally, in shattering an image of the self as "other" – an alienated personality contingent on childhood trauma and molded by the gaze of judgmental parents.

When Dr. Hernandez is shot by drug dealers, Lillian interprets his demise as a ritual sacrifice releasing her from bond-age to a paralyzing past. The doctor emerges as a Christ-figure, a symbolic "scapegoat" for the Mexican community. He is figuratively described as the wise and innocent man-god sacrificed for the sins of the people he loves. His death constitutes a baptism of blood for Lillian, who celebrates the heroism and sphinx-like secrecy of this contemporary priest, a charitable healer incapable of healing himself.[6]

Like Virginia Woolf's Mrs. Dalloway, Lillian psychologically identifies with Hernandez and vicariously experiences the horror of his assassination: "she felt in her body the sound of the car hitting the pole, she knew the moment of death, as if all of them had happened to her" (549). The doctor had died like a deaf-mute signaling in distress, "taking with him his secrets" (550).

Through his martyrdom, Hernandez bequeaths on Lillian the seeds of psychic liberation. "Sudden death had exposed the preciousness of human love and human life" (557). The doctor has given Lillian the material she needs to construct new images of her husband and children. Traumatic loss frees her to discover that she has been searching, all along, for the loved ones she earlier deserted.

On the airplane journey home to New York, Lillian begins to contemplate the "multiple selves" that Dr. Hernandez had hidden from public view, "and with them the invisible areas of life, his and hers, and others" (552-53). For the first time, she recognizes her husband Larry as a multifaceted individual, "an immense new personality."

Bound by her own fears and neuroses, Lillian fashioned Larry in the guise of a surrogate father "who dispensed care and gifts and tenderness." "He had answered her needs!" (554). By consigning her husband to a traditional male stereotype, Lillian refused to nurture the "child" in the man. Now "she could see at least two Larrys, one bearing an expression of hunger and longing, . . . the other as the kind father and husband" (553).

Lillian begins to realize that she and Larry have been "married to parts of themselves only." She wonders "if both of them had not accepted roles handed to them by others' needs as conditions of the marriage" (556). Like the doctor who refused to relinquish the rotting corpse of his deceased wife, each has harbored a static image, a corpse-like "photograph" of the other as an unchanging and immutable love object. By closing the doors to experience and refusing to recognize mutual growth, they have been imprisoned in a stultified past. Each has begun to "crystallize. . . . They were like twins with one set of lungs" (554).

For Lillian, the experiences of Mexico offer hope of radical transformation. Exploring the innermost recesses of consciousness, she is finally able to identify the "Minotaur" as a self-created monster, "the hidden masked part of herself unknown to her, who had ruled her acts," but who now can "no longer harm her" (565). At the heart of the labyrinth, buried deep within the psyche, is Lillian's traumatic memory of the sado-masochistic patterns engendered by her father's ritual spankings. Lillian responded to these beatings with a vivid mixture of pleasure and pain. They aroused "two distinct emotions: one of humiliation, the other of the pleasure of intimacy" (565-66).

Spurned as a child by a harshly critical mother, Lillian sought, in classic Oedipal fashion, to win the affections of her father – a frustrated, irascible and unresponsive male. If she could not win daddy's love, the young girl could at least force him to acknowledge her existence through naughty and rebellious behavior. Corporal punishment was the "only rite shared with her father" and offered a unique experience of sensuous contact with a cold, aloof patriarch. The ignominious ceremony became associated with masochistic pleasure. As Freud explains, "the wish to be beaten by the father comes from the sadistic-anal phase" (*SE* XIX, 165). But if sadistic tendencies are turned inward against the self, then "erotogenic masochism accompanies the libido through all its developmental phases" (*SE* XIX, 164). In "The Economic Problem of Masochism," Freud observes that "moral masochism" is characterized by an unconscious sense of guilt and a need for punishment. "The masochist wants to be treated like a small and helpless child, but, particularly, like a naughty child" (*SE* XIX, 162). If these tendencies are reinforced at an early age, the adult will continue to act out an embedded conviction of guilt or "naughtiness" for which the ego must perpetually be punished.

Lillian remembers watching a titillating "spanking scene" in a pornographic Parisian film and responding with a flood of "sensual excitement. As if the spankings, while hurting her, had been at the same time the only caress she had known from her father. Pain had become inextricably mixed with joy at his presence, the distorted closeness had alchemized into pleasure. The rite, intended as punishment, had become the only intimacy she had known" (*Cities*, 566-67). Astonished by her identification with the little girl in the film, Lillian begins to acknowledge the masochistic patterns that have shaped her psychological life. The minotaur constructed from an internalized image of a stern and sadistic father reinforces in Lillian an intense conviction of guilt and subsequent need to suffer at the hands of an angry patriarch. The beatings satisfied the child's unconscious urge to be punished for the "sin" of erotically desiring the father, as well as for the conviction of worthlessness embedded by a tyrannical superego. As Freud explains, "a sense of guilt, too, finds expression in the manifest content of masochistic phantasies; the subject assumes that he has committed some crime (the nature of which is left indefinite) which is to be expiated by all these painful and tormenting procedures" (*SE* XIX, 162). We "now know that the wish, which so frequently appears in phantasies, to be beaten by the father stands very close to the other wish, to have a passive . . . sexual relation with him" (*SE* XIX, 169).

Attempting an emotional seduction of the father, Lillian was seduced into a web of sado-masochistic responses. She now understands that "the real dictator, the organizer and director of her life had been this quest for a chemical compound – so many ounces of pain mixed with so many ounces of pleasure in a formula known only to the unconscious. The failure lay in the enormous difference between the relationship she had needed, and the one she had, on a deeper level, . . . wanted" (*Cities*, 567).

Oblivious of the masochistic patterns residual in her psyche, Lillian matured into an insecure woman with a negative self-image. Desperately searching for a man who could provide the love denied by her father, she was nevertheless doomed to seek out males who would reinforce early masochistic patterns. "Not enough of the measure of pain had existed in her marriage to Larry." In all her sexual relationships, Lillian has courted "the familiar groove of pain and pleasure, of closeness at the cost of pain" (567). Hence her obsessive attraction to the narcissistic Jay, who offered affection, then punished Lillian through love affairs with other women.

Lillian realizes that each individual is in some way trapped in a self-created myth. We are ineluctably tied to the "grooves etched by the past," and only the shock of psychic upheaval can release us from the deeply-worn patterns that seem to determine the shape of our adult lives. Masochism has imprinted Lillian's psyche and molded her adult relationships. But she recognizes that the "tracks" of obsessive-compulsive behavior are mutable. Once Lillian has successfully identified the obsessions that haunt her, she can begin to "erase the grooves" etched by a lifetime of pathological behavior.

Lillian appears to have been suffering from the syndrome Freud diagnoses as "moral masochism," a neurosis erupting from an "unconscious guilt" and a corresponding "need for punishment at the hands of a parental power" (*SE* XIX, 169). The minotaur that torments her is a monster of her own creation, a superego constructed from the introjected images of her two judgmental parents. She has matured into a fragmented personality, torn between the desire for egoic independence and the need to conform to an "ego-ideal" fashioned by a critical conscience.

In the landscape of Mexico, Lillian is able to flush out the psychic "beast" that has caused so much mental torment. Confronting the sado-masochistic patterns engendered by her parents, she at last breaks free of their psychological authority and embarks on a journey toward creative self-discovery. As the Talmud reminds us, "We do not see things as they are, we see them as we are" (578). Only after we have destroyed the sedimentation of the past can we begin to see things "in themselves," as they really are.

What Lillian sees from the heights of her airplane journey is Larry – not the Larry of memory, but a husband released from the static frame of projected stereotypes. She realizes that Larry absorbed her emotional pain and neurotic turbulence at the expense of his own growth. Like the moon, he had turned only one face toward Lillian and had revealed a strong, changeless, altruistic aspect. "What she has seen of Larry during their marriage was only what he allowed her to see, giant albatross wings, the wings of his goodness" (583). Larry adopted a selfless, "almost anonymous" mask of paternal strength in order to protect and nurture his insecure spouse. On the periphery of life and emotion, he took refuge in silence and a facade of invulnerability.

Acknowledging Larry as a separate, complex individual, a man "thrust into outer space" by childhood trauma, Lillian becomes aware of her husband's vulnerability and prepares to meet him on a new plain of emotional openness. She has the power to draw him back from solitude – to introduce him to a passionate, vivid, heightened life and to give him "intimacy with the world."

Lillian has journeyed in the "lunar barque" of memory to discover the chimera at the heart of her psychic imagination. She now voyages in the "solar barque" of present experience, with a consciousness open to the future. The ego is at last integrated and whole, self-creating and self-delighting. At the end of *Cities of the Interior*, Lillian emerges as a healthy individual who has confronted the "minotaur" of the unconscious and exorcised the masochistic pathology it represents. In the course of the novel, Lillian has successfully analyzed the various stages of parental-identification and male-identification that have tyrannized her life. She is now liberated from the "grooves" of the past behavior and feels free to develop as an independent person capable of love and creativity.[7]

NOTES

[1]Anais Nin, *The Diary of Anais Nin*, ed. Gunther Stuhlmann. 7 vols. (New York: Swallow and Harcourt Brace Jovanovich, 1966-1980), I, 47. Hereafter cited in the text as *Diary*.

[2]Sigmund Freud, *Standard Edition of the Complete Psychological Works*, ed. James Strachey. 24 vols. (London: Hogarth Press, 1953), IX, 150. Hereafter cited in the text as *SE*.

[3]I am considering Lillian, Sabina, and Djuna as the three protagonists of the novel. Evelyn Hinz, who adds Stella to the list of major characters, presents a convincing argument for an association of the four women with the medieval theory of humors. The fiery Sabina is a "modern choleric character"; Stella "is the cook dreamer, a twentieth-century phlegmatic"; Lillian represents "the sanguine temperament"; and Djuna evokes "the melancholic temperament." Hinz judiciously warns us against interpreting Nin's characterizations as psychoanalytic "case histories" and suggests the analogy of modern *psychomachia* in which "Nin personifications of the basic passions battle for supremacy in the female psyche" (*The Mirror and the Garden* [New York: Harcourt Brace Jovanovich, 1973], pp. 63-64). Both Evelyn Hinz and Bettina Knapp point out the mythic resonances of Nin's portraits. As Knapp observes, Nin's characterizations transcend the "personal field of vision. . . . *Ci-*

ties of the Interior dramatizes the conflicts involved in the 'destruction of women' and 'woman's struggle to understand her own nature' " (*Anais Nin* [New York: Frederick Ungar, 1978], p. 96).

[4]Anais Nin, *Cities of the Interior* (Chicago: Swallow Press, 1959, 1974), p. 124. Hereafter cited in the text as *Cities*.

[5]As Oliver Evans explains, "here the land-locked ship is Lillian's own inhibited self, which has sought unsuccessfully for liberation, for the stream it was destined for and on which it could float effortlessly. . . . The nocturnal voyage . . . is the voyage of memory, and is associated with stasis and death – and therefore with land – while the daylight voyage is the voyage of discovery, and is associated with freedom and life – and therefore with water" (*Anais Nin* [Carbondale: Southern Illinois University Press, 1968], pp. 166-67). Benjamin Franklin V and Duane Schneider identify as "one of Nin's most consistent themes" the belief "that escape into the dream or into one's inner self is not only acceptable but necessary, but to reside there exclusively is fatal" (*Anais Nin: An Introduction* [Athens: Ohio University Press, 1979], p. 140).

[6]In commenting on the fifth volume of Nin's *Diary* as the "raw material" for *Seduction of the Minotaur*, Sharon Spencer declares: "Intermingled with the joyous mood of Diary V is quiet sadness in the form of a new recognition; it is death that Nin admits to her writing at this time: the death of Dr. Hernandez in *Seduction of the Minotaur*; in her *Diary* the deaths, first, of her father, then of her mother." Spencer suggests a further correspondence between the novel and the *Diary* insofar as both describe the "success story" of a woman artist "who is determined to seek her own evolution" (*Collage of Dreams* [Chicago: Swallow Press, 1977], pp. 134-35).

[7]As Franklin and Schneider remark, Lillian "has learned that one of life's most difficult tasks is to know oneself, and that after one does that, one may assist another in a similar quest. . . . Knowledge and acceptance of oneself is the key to Nin's perception of mature life" (*Anais Nin: An Introduction*, p. 146).

From *Anais: An International Journal* 2 (1984): 113-26.

Nin's Diary

Un Etre Etoilique

Henry Miller

As I write these lines Anais Nin has begun the fiftieth volume of her diary, the record of a twenty year struggle towards self-realization. Still a young woman she has produced on the side, in the midst of an intensely active life, a monumental confession which when given to the world will take its place beside the revelations of St. Augustine, Petronius, Abélard, Rousseau, Proust, and others.

Of the twenty years recorded half the time was spent in America, half in Europe. The diary is full of voyages; in fact, like life itself it might be regarded as nothing but voyage. The epic quality of it, however, is eclipsed by the metaphysical. The diary is not a journey towards the heart of darkness, in the stern Conradian sense of destiny, not a *voyage au bout de la nuit*, as with Céline, nor even a voyage to the moon in the psychological sense of escape. It is more like a mythological voyage towards the source and fountain head of life — I might say an *astrologic* voyage of metamorphosis.

The importance of such a work for our time hardly needs to be stressed. More and more, as our era draws to a close, are we made aware of the tremendous significance of the human document. Our literature, unable any longer to express itself through dying forms, has become almost exclusively biographical. The artist is retreating behind the dead forms to rediscover in himself the eternal source of creation. Our age, intensely productive, yet thoroughly un-vital, un-creative, is obsessed with a lust for investigating the mysteries of personality. We turn instinctively towards those documents — fragments, notes, autobiographies, diaries — which appease our hunger for more life because, avoiding the circuitous expression of art, they seem to put us directly in contact with that which we are seeking. I say they "seem to," because there are no short cuts such as we imagine, because the most direct expression, the most permanent and the most effective is always that of art. Even in the most naked confessions there exists the same ellipsis of art. The diary is an art form just as much as the novel or the play. The diary simply requires a greater canvas; it is a chronological tapestry which, in its ensemble, or at whatever point it is abandoned, reveals a form and language as exacting as other literary forms. A work like *Faust*, indeed, reveals more discrepancies, irrelevancies and enigmatic stumbling blocks than a diary such as Amiel's, for example. The former represents an artificial mode of synchronization; the latter has an organic integration which even the interruption of death does not disturb.

The chief concern of the diarist is not with truth, though it may seem to be, any more than the chief concern of the conscious artist is with beauty. Beauty and truth are the by-products in a quest for something beyond either of these. But just as we are impressed by the beauty of a work of art, so we are impressed by the truth and sincerity of a diary. We have the illusion, in reading the pages of an intimate journal, that we are face to face with the soul of its author. This is the illusory quality of the diary, its art quality, so to speak, just as beauty is the illusory element in the accepted work of art. The diary has to be read differently from the novel, but the goal is the same: self-realization. The diary, by its very nature, is quotidian and organic, whereas the novel is timeless and conventional. We know more, or seem to know more, immediately about the author of a diary than we do about the author of a novel. But as to what we *really* know of either it is hard to say. For the diary is not a transcript of life itself any more than the novel is. It is a medium of expression in which truth rather than art predominates. But it is not *truth*. It is not for the simple reason that the very problem, the obsession, so to say, is truth. We should look to the diary, therefore, not for the truth about things but as an expression of this struggle to be free of the obsession for truth.

It is this factor, so important to grasp, which explains the tortuous, repetitive quality of every diary. Each day the battle is begun afresh; as we read we seem to be treading a mystic maze in which the author becomes more and more deeply lost. The mirror of the author's own experiences becomes the well of truth in which oftimes he is drowned. In every diary we assist at the birth of Narcissus, and sometimes the death too. This death, when it occurs, is of two kinds, as in life. In the one case it may lead to dissolution, in the other to rebirth. In the last volume of Proust's great work the nature of this rebirth is magnificently elaborated in the author's disquisitions on the metaphysical nature of art. For it is in *Le Temps Retrouvé* that the great fresco wheels into another dimension and thus acquires its true significance. The analysis which had been going on throughout the preceding volumes reaches its climax finally in a vision of the whole; it is almost like the sewing up of a wound. It emphasizes what Nietzsche pointed out long ago as "the healing quality of art." The purely personal, Narcissistic element is resolved into the universal; the seemingly interminable confession restores the narrator to the stream of human activity through the realization that life itself is an art. This realization is brought about, as Proust so well points out, through obeying the still small voice within. It is the opposite of the Socratic method, the absurdity of which Nietzsche exposed so witheringly. The mania for analysis leads finally to its opposite, and the sufferer passes on beyond his problems into a new realm of reality. The therapeutic aspect of art is then, in this higher state of consciousness, seen to be the religious or metaphysical element. The work which was begun as a refuge and escape from the terrors of reality leads the author back to life, not *adapted* to the reality about, but *superior* to it, as one capable of recreating it in accordance with his own needs. He sees that it was not life but himself from which he had been fleeing, and that the life which had heretofore been insupportable was merely the projection of his own phantasies. It is true that the new life is also a projection of the individual's own phantasies but they are invested now with the sense of real power; they spring not from dissociation but from integration. The whole past life resumes its place in the balance and creates a vital, stable equilibrium which would never have resulted without the pain and the suffering. It is in this sense that the endless turning about in a cage which characterized the author's thinking, the endless fresco which seems never to be brought to a conclusion, the ceaseless fragmentation and analysis which goes on night and day, is like a gyration which through sheer centrifugal force lifts the sufferer out of his obsessions and frees him for the rhythm and movement of life by joining him to the great universal stream in which all of us have our being.

A book is a part of life, a manifestation of life, just as much as a tree or a horse or a star. It obeys its own rhythms, its own laws, whether it be a novel, a play, or a diary. The deep, hidden rhythm of life is always there – that of the pulse, the heart beat. Even in the seemingly stagnant waters of the journal this flux and reflux is evident. It is there in the whole of the work as much as in each fragment. Looked at in its entirety, especially for example in such a work as that of Anais Nin's, this cosmic pulsation corresponds to the death and rebirth of the individual. Life assumes the aspect of a labyrinth into which the seeker is plunged. She goes in unconsciously to slay her old self. One might say, as in this case, that the disintegration of the self had come about through a shock. It would not matter much what had produced the disintegration; the important thing is that at a given moment she passed into a state of two-ness. The old self, which had been attached to the father who abandoned her and the loss of whom created an insoluble conflict in her, found itself confronted with a nascent other self which seems to lead her further and further into darkness and confusion. The diary, which is the story of her retreat from the world into the chaos of regeneration, pictures the labyrinthine struggle waged by these conflicting selves. Sinking into the obscure regions of her soul, she seems to draw the world down over her head and with it the people she meets and the relationships engendered by her meetings. The illusion of submergence, of darkness and stagnation, is brought about by the ceaseless observation and analysis which goes on in the pages of the diary. The hatches are down, the sky shut out. Everything – nature, human beings, events, relationships – is brought below to be dissected and digested. It is a devouring process in which the ego becomes a stupendous red maw. The language itself is clear, painfully clear. It is the scorching light of the intellect locked away in a cave. Nothing which this mind comes in contact with is allowed to go undigested. The result is harrowing and hallucinating. We move with the author through her labyrinthine world like a knife making an incision into the flesh. It is a surgical operation upon a world of flesh and blood, a Caesarian operation performed by the embryo with its own private scissors and cleaver.

* * *

She speaks of herself mockingly at times as *"une étoilique"* – a word which she has invented, and why not, since as she says, we have the word *lunatique*. Why not *"étoilique"*? "To-day," she writes, "I described very poorly *le pays des merveilles où mon esprit était*. Je volais dans ce pays lointain où rien n'est impossible. Hier je suis revenue, à la réalité, à la tristesse. Il me semble que je tombais d'une grande splendeur à une triste misère."

One thinks inevitably of the manifestoes of the Surrealists, of their unquenchable thirst for the marvellous, and that phrase of Breton's, so significant of the dreamer, the visionary: "we should conduct ourselves as though we were really *in the world!*" It may seem absurd to couple the utterances of the Surrealists with the writings of a child of thirteen, but there is a great deal which they have in common and there is also a point of departure which is even more important. The pursuit of the marvellous is at bottom nothing but the sure instinct of the poet speaking and it manifests itself everywhere in all epochs, in all conditions of life, in all forms of expression. But this marvellous pursuit of the marvellous, if not understood, can also act as a thwarting force, can become a thing of evil, crushing the individual in the toils of the Absolute. It can become as negative and destructive a force as the yearning for God. When I said a while back that the child had begun her great work in the spirit of an artist I was trying to emphasize the fact that, like the artist, the problem which beset her was to conquer the world. In the process of making herself fit to meet her father again (because to her the world was personified in the Father) she was unwittingly making herself an artist, that is, a self-dependent creature for whom a father would no longer be necessary. When she does encounter him again, after a lapse of almost twenty years, she is a full-fledged being, a creature fashioned after her own image. The meeting serves to make her realize that she has emancipated herself; more indeed, for to her amazement and dismay she also realizes that she has no more need of the one she was seeking. The significance of her heroic struggle with herself now reveals itself symbolically. That which was beyond her, which had dominated and tortured her, which *possessed* her, one might say, no longer exists. She is de-possessed and free at last to live her own life.

Throughout the diary the amazing thing is this intuitive awareness of the symbolic nature of her role. It is this which illuminates the most trivial remarks, the most trivial incidents she records. In reality there is nothing trivial throughout the whole record; everything is saturated with a purpose and significance which gradually becomes clear as the confession progresses. Similarly there is nothing chaotic about the work, although at first glance it may give that impression. The fifty volumes are crammed with human fires, incidents, voyages, books read and commented upon, reveries, metaphysical speculations, the dramas in which she is enveloped, her daily work, her preoccupation with the welfare of others, in short with a thousand and one things which go to make up her life. It is a great pageant of the times patiently and humbly delineated by one who considered herself as nothing, by one who had almost completely effaced herself in the effort to arrive at a true understanding of life. It is in this sense again that the human document rivals the work of art, or in times such as ours, *replaces* the work of art. For, in a profound sense, this *is* the work of art which never gets written – because the artist whose task it is to create it never gets born. We have here, instead of the consciously or technically finished work (which to-day seems to us more than ever empty and illusory), the unfinished symphony which achieves consummation because each line is pregnant with a soul struggle. The conflict with the world takes place within. It matters little, for the artist's purpose, whether the world be the size of a pinhead or an incommensurable universe. *But there must be a world!* And this world, whether real or imaginary, can only be created out of despair and anguish. For the artist there is no other world. Even if it be unrecognizable, this world which is created out of sorrow and deprivation is true and vital, and eventually it expropriates the "other" world in which the ordinary mortal lives and dies. It is the world in which the artist has his being, and it is in the revelation of his undying self that art takes its stance. Once this is apprehended there can be no question of monotony or fatigue, of chaos or irrelevance. We move amidst boundless horizons in a perpetual state of awe and humility. We enter, with the author, into unknown worlds and we share with the latter all the pain, beauty, terror and illumination which exploration entails.

Of the truly great authors no one has ever complained that they over-elaborated. On the contrary, we usually bemoan the fact that there is nothing further left us to read. And so we turn back to what we have and we re-read, and as we re-read we discover marvels which previously we had ignored. We go back to them again and again, as to inexhaustible wells of wisdom and delight. Almost invariably, it is curious to note, these authors of whom I speak are observed to be precisely those who have given us *more* than the others. They claim us precisely because we sense in them an unquenchable flame. Nothing they wrote seems to us insignificant – not even their notes, their jottings, not even the designs which they scribbled unconsciously in the margins of their copy books. Whereas with the meagre spirits everything seems superfluous, themselves as well as the works they have given us.

* * *

In the later volumes of the diary we note the appearance of titles. For instance, and I give them in chronological order, the following: "The Definite Disappearance of the Demon"; "Death and Disintegration"; "The Triumph of White Magic"; "The Birth of Humor in the Whale"; "Playing at Being God"; "Fire"; "Audace"; "Vive la dynamite"; "A God who Laughs". The use of titles to indicate the nature of a volume is an indication of the gradual emergence from the labyrinth. It means that the diary itself has undergone a radical transformation. No longer a fleeting panorama of impressions, but a consolidation of experience into little bundles of fibre and muscle which go to make up the new body. The new being is definitely born and travelling upward towards the light of the every-day world. In the previous volumes we had the record of the struggle to penetrate to the very sanctum of the self; it is a description of a shadowy world in which the outline of people, things and events becomes more and more blurred by the involutional inquisition. The further we penetrate into the darkness and confusion, however, the greater becomes the illumination. The whole personality seems to become a devouring eye turned pitilessly on the self. Finally there comes the moment when this individual who has been constantly gazing into a mirror sees with such blinding clarity that the mirror fades away and the image rejoins the body from which it had been separated. It is at this point that normal vision is restored and that the one who had died is restored to the living world. It is at this moment that the prophecy which has been written twenty years earlier comes true – *"Un de ces jours je pourrais dire: mon journal, je suis arrivée au fond!"*

Whereas in the earlier volumes the accent was one of sadness, of disillusionment, of being *de trop*, now the accent becomes one of joy and fulfillment. Fire, audacity, dynamite, laughter – the very choice of words is sufficient to indicate the changed condition. The world spreads out before her like a banquet table: something to *enjoy*. But the appetite, seemingly insatiable, is controlled. The old obsessional desire to devour everything in sight in order that it be preserved in her own private tomb is gone. She eats now only what nourishes her. The once ubiquitous digestive tract, the great whale into which she had made herself, is replaced by other organs with other functions. The exaggerated sympathy for others which had dogged her every step diminishes. The birth of a sense of humor denotes the achievement of an objectivity which alone the one who has realized himself attains. It is not indifference, but toleration. The totality of vision brings about a new kind of sympathy, a free, non-compulsive sort. The very pace of the diary changes. There are now long lapses, intervals of complete silence in which the great digestive apparatus, once all, slows up to permit the development of complementary organs. The eye too seems to close, content to let the body *feel* the presence of the world about, rather than pierce it with a devastating vision. It is not longer a world of black and white, of good and evil, or harmony and dissonance; no, now the world has at last become an orchestra in which there are innumerable instruments capable of rendering every tone and color, an orchestra in which even the most shattering dissonances are resolved into meaningful expression. It is the ultimate poetic world of *As Is*. The inquisition is over, the trial and torture finished. A state of absolution is reached. This is the true catholic world of which the Catholics know nothing. This is the eternally abiding world which those in search of it never find.

* * *

There are some volumes, in which attention is focussed almost entirely on one or two individuals, which are like the raw pith of some post-Dostoievskian novel; they bring to the surface a lunar plasm which is the logical fruit of that drive towards the dead slag of the ego which Dostoievski heralded and which D. H. Lawrence was the first to have pointed out in precise language. There are three successive volumes, of this sort, which are made of nothing but this raw material of a drama which takes place entirely within the confines of the female world. It is the first female writing I have ever seen: it rearranges the world in terms of female honesty. The result is a language which is ultra-modern and yet which bears no resemblance to any of the masculine experimental processes with which we are familiar. It is precise, abstract, cloudy and unseizable. There are larval thoughts not yet divorced from their dream content, thoughts which seem to slowly crystallize before your eyes, always precise but never tangible, never once arrested so as to be grasped by the mind. It is the opium world of woman's physiological being, a sort of cinematic show put on inside the genito-urinary tract. There is not an ounce of man-made culture in it; everything related to the head is cut off. Time passes, but it is not clock time; nor is it poetic time such as men create in their passion. It is more like that aeonic time required for the creation of gems and precious metals; an embowelled sidereal time in which the female knows that she is superior to the male and will eventually swallow him up again. The effect is that of starlight carried over into day-time.

The contrast between this language and that of man's is forcible; the whole of man's art begins to appear like a frozen edelweiss under a glass bell reposing on a mantelpiece in the deserted home of a lunatic. In this extraordinary unicellular language of the female we have a blinding, gem-like consciousness which disperses the ego like star-dust. The great female corpus rises up from its sleepy marine depths in a naked push towards the sun. The sun is at zenith – permanently at zenith. Space broadens out like a cold Norwegian lake choked with ice-floes. The sun and moon are fixed, the one at zenith, the other at nadir. The tension is perfect, the polarity absolute. The voices of the earth mingle in an eternal resonance with issues from the delta of the fecundating river of death. It is the voice of creation which is constantly being drowned in the daylight frenzy of a man-made world. It comes like the light breeze which sets the ocean swaying; it comes with a calm, quiet force which is irresistible, like the movement of the great Will gathered up by the instincts and rippling out in long silky flashes of enigmatic dynamism. Then a lull in which the mysterious centralized forces roll back to the matrix, gather up again in a sublime all-sufficiency. Nothing is lost, nothing used up, nothing relinquished. The great mystery of conservation in which creation and destruction are but the antipodal symbols of a single constant energy which is inscrutable.

It is at this point in the still unfinished symphony of the dairy that the whole pattern wheels miraculously into another dimension; at this point that it takes its cosmic stance. Adopting the universal language, the human being in her speaks straight out from under the skin to Hindu, Chinaman, Jap, Abyssinian, Malay, Turk, Arab, Tibetan, Eskimo, Pawnee, Hottentot, Bushman, Kaffir, Persian, Assyrian. The fixed polar language known to all races: a serpentine, sybilline, sibilant susurrus that comes up out of the astral marshes: a sort of cold tinkling, lunar laughter which comes from under the soles of the feet: a laughter made of alluvial deposit, of mythological excrement and the sweat of epileptics. This is the language which seeps through the frontiers of race, color, religion, sex; a language which soaks through the litmus paper of the mind and saturates the quintessential human spores. The language of bells without clappers, heard incessantly throughout the nine months in which every one is identical and yet mysteriously different. In this first tinkling melody of immortality lapping against the snug and cosy walls of the womb we have the music of the still-born sons of men opening their lovely dead eyes one upon the other.

From *The Criterion* 17 (October 1937): 35-52. Collected in *The Cosmological Eye*, New Directions, 1939, pp. 269-91.

The Charmed Circle of Anais Nin

Karl Shapiro

[On *The Diary of Anais Nin, 1931-1934.*]

For a generation the literary world on both sides of the Atlantic has lived with the rumor of an extraordinary diary. Early readers of the manuscript discussed it in breathtaking superlatives as a work that would take its place with the great revelations of literature. A significant section of this diary is at last in print and it appears that the great claims made for it are justified.

Two sorts of claims were advanced by the original admirers: one, that the diaries ranked among the best examples of the form in literature. A more important claim was that the Nin diaries represent a breakthrough in literary form, a form that transcends both the art of the "confessions" and the art of the novel itself. The defense of the diary as a major form develops into one of the primary themes of the book.

To give literary structure to one's life is usually the task of the poet, not necessarily that of the diarest or the novelist. The diarist records; the novelist objectifies. Most diaries, in fact, are "creative" only by chance, for there is never enough esthetic distance between the diariest and the diary to allow a perspective. The Nin *Diary* is a striking exception, having the full dimensions of the novel (character, "plot," exposition, dialogue, causal action, and so on) as well as the normal characteristics of the *journal intime*. But in addition the quality of perception, the precision of imagery, the intricate organization, and the exquisite feminine sensibility mark the *Diary* as the work of the poet. Her sympathetic analyses of her chief dramatis personae (Henry Miller, Antonin Artaud, Otto Rank and her father) suggest the hand of the dramatist. Nevertheless, all these elements are fused into a single lucid personal style which is tonally consistent throughout. One makes allowances for the "spontaneity" and scrappiness of even the most famous journals. In this case the writing stands the test of the most formal writing without surrendering the charm of authenticity which is usually the sole appeal of autobiographical literature.

In his introduction, Gunther Stuhlmann points up the central question of the *Diary* vis-a-vis the Nin novels, short stories and criticism. These works are, even on the authority of Anais Nin, distillations from the 150 volumes or so of the *Diary*. They are, so to speak, the *Diary* writing poems. Undoubtedly, one of the reasons why her novels have not been properly valued is the unavailability of the main work. Without the masterpiece of the journal the novels remain shadowy, obscure, beautiful fragments.

The *Diary* had its inception in the desertion of her father, a Spanish composer-pianist Joaquin Nin, from his family. Anais was about 11 years old and accompanied her mother and two brothers to America. The diary is really a letter to the father which her mother never sent. To the child it became "an island, in which I could find refuge in an alien land, write French, think my thoughts, hold on to my soul, to myself." The quest for her father, another major theme of the journal, develops into a full-fledged Jamesian-Proustian "affair" when she rejoins him as a young beauty, accomplished, worldly, and remote.

The *Diary* begins in the winter of 1931 with the remaking of the author's 200-year-old house in Louveciennes on the outskirts of Paris. The village suggests a setting for Madame Bovary but, says the author, "unlike Madame Bovary, I am not going to take poison." She has just finished her first book, *D. H. Lawrence: An Unprofessional Study*, which remains one of the primary studies of Lawrence. The house is equally important: she has the premonition of a world of love and must first create the setting in which to house it. Ordinary life does not interest her, she says: she seeks only the high moments. But when the actors appear on her stage it becomes the ordinary which reveals to her the marvelous. It is Henry Miller who first opens the doors of the quotidian to her:

"When I saw Henry Miller walking toward the door where I stood waiting, I closed my eyes for an instant to see him by some other inner eye. He was warm, joyous, relaxed, natural. . . ."

"He was so different from his brutal, violent, vital writing, his caricatures, his Rabelaisian farces, his exaggerations . . ."

This begins a full-scale portrait of Miller, gradually assembled as her knowledge of him grows. The Miller portrait dovetails with the portrait of June, Miller's second wife who occupies such a prominent place in the Miller canon. June is first seen through Miller's representation of her as she had revealed herself to him. But June had revealed nothing except illusions. Miller "hates poetry and he hates illusion" and is seeking to expose his wife. This woman without identity infuriates Miller; she is a night creature and Anais Nin recognizes the core of the conflict between Henry Miller and June, for Miller has "an eagerness to catch everything without make-up" and expose all objects to the crude light of day. Miller frightens like a voyeur.

When June arrives at Louveciennes the conflict between her and her husband transfers to Anais Nin. For even though "everything Henry has said about her is true" Anais falls under the spell of her beauty and her heavy sensuality. The diarist vacillates between the attraction to Miller the artist and man and June the actress and lover of men and women. Dreams enter the journal and are subsequently acted out. Miller produces in her a rebellion against poetry and illusion. But this would be a kind of suicide. Whereas "June eats and drinks symbols. Henry has no use for symbols. He eats bread, not wafers. June never liked Madeira wine before, but because I serve it at home she drinks it, and asks for it at a café. The taste of me." In the long run, of course, Miller initiates the diarist into open-eyed experience at the expense of "poetry." Each writer modifies the sensibility of the other, to the advantage of each.

Anais Nin's encounter with psychoanalysis begins with her acquaintance with Dr. René Allendy's lectures at the Sorbonne. Allendy had advanced a theory of behavior motivated by unconscious tropisms which run deeper than Freudian environmentalism. Psychoanalysis could help man recognize these unknown impulses and equip him to cope with bad luck, tragedy, and fatality. She becomes his patient (a fairly complete outline of the analysis is presented, ending with her acceptance of Miller's world of poverty and expediency over the luxurious aristocratic world of her father). But this is accomplished at the expense of Allendy who wishes her to repudiate Miller. She is torn between them. The analyst is "a kindly man, an intrepid scientist, a scholar, a man who is seeking to relate science and mysticism . . . and Henry is his opposite. Henry is a sensualist, an anarchist, an adventurer, a pimp, a crazy genius." Allendy and everyone else is suspicious of the diary and would like Anais Nin to return to more recognizable forms of literature.

"Everyone has always stood in the way of the journal. My mother always urged me to go out and play. My brothers teased me, stole it, and made fun of it. It was a secret from my girl friends in school: Everyone said I would outgrow it. In Havana my aunt said it would spoil my eyes, frighten the boys away." Even Henry Miller would say at one point: "Lock up the journal, and swim."

Allendy's failure to convert Anais to his world of sensibility and esthetic failure is too negative for her, and she gives him up, but through him she encounters Antonin Artaud. Artaud, "now weary, now fiery and malicious," is the prototype of the poet damned, as Miller is the *romancier maudit*. For Artaud the theater is "a place to shout pain, anger, hatred, to enact the violence in us." Artaud wishes to enact the rituals of blood in the midst of the audience. He is a drug addict and everyone thinks him mad. But at Louveciennes he feels at home and responds to the feminine order which the diarist has created around her. Like all the men who present their art or their magic to her, he falls in love. She misses Allendy, who was "God, conscience, absolver, priest, sage." But when he became human, "he used his power to separate me from my artist life, to thrust me again into the stifling, narrow bourgeois life." He has tried to separate her from Artaud also and she has no guide. Her father is on the scene but there is also Otto Rank, one of the few psychoanalysts who puts faith in the artist.

She finds her father again when she is a grown woman. She had imagined him cruel, strong, a hero, the famous musician loved of women, triumphant, but she finds him "soft, feminine, vulnerable, imperfect." There is no longer a meeting of father and daughter but of man and woman.

Rank returns her to the role of the woman. He tells her that we know very little about woman. "In the first place, it was man who invented 'the soul'. . . . The women who played important roles thought like men, and wrote like men." But Rank also begins to fight against the diary, to force her back into the role of "artist." Eventually, she decides to become an analyst herself, and Rank, to test her, asks her to his lectures at the *Cité Universitaire*. While she begins to feel deep guilt about the diary Rank is making plans to move to America. The French are not neurotic ("they have accepted the separation between love and passion") and their interest in psychoanalysis is mild.

Rank becomes only another lost father.

The *Diary*, or this section of it, closes with a novelesque, neo-Zolaesque horror of an aborted birth which nearly destroys its author. And the fathers are nowhere to be seen.

For lack of terminology, this *Diary* is what the University of Chicago would call a great book. It is great because of its inherent qualities of style, perspicuity, and natural organization, but more because it is unclassifiable as a book at all. If it is a book it is a new and beautiful kind, shining a strange light on literature itself.

From *Book Week* May 1, 1966: 3.

Free Women

Patricia Meyer Spacks

At the opposite extreme from Lillian Hellman, Anais Nin appears to take pride in "losing." The published volumes of her diary emphasize her unfailing self-sacrifice, her willingness to live without so much as a pen while supplying her writer-friends with typewriters, her eager yielding to others' demands. It is true that this pattern was directly responsible, Miss Nin declares, for a psychic breakdown, but her commitment to the values of orthodox "femininity" remained unchanging. Yet she is also committed to an ideal of personal freedom, which she explicitly associates with the life of the imagination – with "escape," the "illusory," "dream."

The counterpart to the story about Lillian Hellman's *"cojones"* is an episode centered on Anais Nin's breasts. She complains to her analyst, Dr. René Allendy, that her breasts are too small, asking for appropriate medicine. "Are they absolutely undeveloped?" the doctor inquires. She replies no, then: "As I founder in my descriptions, I say: 'To you, a doctor, the simplest thing is to show them to you.' And I do." The doctor begins, she reports, to rhapsodize: "Perfectly feminine, small but well shaped, well outlined in proportion to the rest of your figure, such a lovely figure, all you need is a few more pounds of it. You are really lovely, so much grace of movement, charm, so much breeding and finesse of line." Shortly thereafter, we discover that he has "lost his objectivity"; he can no longer help her. She reflects, "I asked Dr. Allendy to help me as a doctor of medicine. Was this quite a sincere action? Did I have to show him my breasts? Wasn't I pleased that he reacted so admiringly?"

Instead of Lillian Hellman's vocabulary of battle and endurance, Anais Nin uses the language of self-deprecation and self-doubt. She avoids talk of "winning" as she modestly records her victories over a succession of people who fell in love with her: Henry Miller, Henry Miller's wife, her father (he reappears after having deserted the family years before, and soon begins to fantasize that everyone will think her his mistress, then loudly to regret that she is in fact his daughter), Dr. Allendy, Dr. Otto Rank, who succeeded Allendy as her analyst, an Indian revolutionary, a French astrologer. Yet the need to triumph as well as the intermittent compulsion to "lose" is the same as Miss Hellman's, although the arena is different.

Unlike Miss Hellman, who claims realism as one of her virtues and berates herself even for introspection, Miss Nin commits herself explicitly to the value of imaginative reconstruction of reality and to the centrality of writing in her life. Suffering from the twentieth-century problem of fragmentation, she solves it as a diarist, and defines her freedom as the product of her writing: "Because writing, for me, is an expanded world, a limitless world, containing all." But her real "work" appears to be self-contemplation and self-display, of which writing is only one mode. The source of her artistic energy, she believes, is her femininity. Love, service to others, those traditional forms of feminine expression, are other aspects of her self-presentation. "Yes, I see myself always softening blows, dissolving acids, neutralizing poisons, every moment of the day. I try to fulfill the wishes of others, to perform miracles." Despite her obsessive introspection, she conveys a view of herself in some ways as external as Lillian Hellman's self-portrait, because her concern is so much with the creation of effects. Her sense of freedom depends on her ability to manipulate those effects, to control her environment (different rooms painted different colors to encourage different moods), her clothing ("original"), and her companions, in order to show herself to advantage. When she gives birth, in agony, to a six-month fetus, dead at birth, she reports, "Toward eight o'clock I had several spasms of pain. . . . I combed my hair, I powdered and perfumed myself, painted my eyelashes. At eight o'clock I was taken to the operating room." Using all the paraphernalia of feminine attractiveness, she insists on loving and being loved, on working and having her work valued, on her symbolic position, as Woman, at the center of the universe. Demanding freedom, she declares herself to have achieved it.

Much more openly than Miss Hellman, Anais Nin admits the great importance in her life of writing, publication, and relation with others. She seems willing, in fact, to admit just about anything. One does not feel that she is trying to form herself in any particular mold; she quite simply loves and displays whatever she happens to be at any given moment. Yet the sense of limitation is as strong in her lengthy account of a "free" life as in Lillian Hellman's. The Hellman memoir suggests that the cost of freedom from relationship is emotional impoverishment and restriction, but the cost of relationship, for such a woman as the author, is likely to be submission, emotional limitation. Miss Nin's diaries emphasize her resort to frequent bouts of psychoanalysis to rescue her from the desperate restrictions of an untrammeled life. Absorbed in narcissism, she flounders among the multitude of selves she perceives. Committed to fantasies of feminine power, she involves herself therefore in endless responsibilities to others. Her self-display requires an audience, her audience makes demands, her freedom eludes her. Her relationships lead her back only to herself. It seems a strangely symbolic fact that her husband has disappeared, apparently by his request, from her published diaries. The stillborn fetus might, for all we are told, be a virgin birth: the figure of Anais Nin, surrounded by others, exists nonetheless in terrifying isolation and self-concern.

All autobiography must rest on a foundation of self-absorption; men as well as women indulge in self-manufacture and self-display. What is perhaps peculiarly feminine about the autobiographical writing of Lillian Hellman and Anais Nin is the obsessiveness of its implicit or explicit concern with the question of freedom, psychic and social, and the nature of its revelations about freedom's limitations for women. But one may also speculate about the essential femininity of what may be called "defensive narcissism." For Ernest Hemingway or Norman Mailer, writing about themselves, narcissism is a mode of aggression, a way of forcing the world to attend. In woman writers, even writers so assertive as Lillian Hellman, so exhibitionistic as Anais Nin, the characteristic note suggests some- thing close to desperation: it is as though they were writing to convince themselves. The ordering of experience in memoir or diary, the implicit assertion that this life makes sense, seems in these cases a way for the author to remind herself of the value of her own experience, to hold on to the meaning of her life.

From *The Hudson Review* 24.4 (Winter 1971-72): 562-64.

"Excuse Me, It Was All a Dream":

The Diary of Anais Nin, 1944-1947

Evelyn J. Hinz

For almost sixty years, Anais Nin has relentlessly asked a single, but frequently misunderstood question: "Does anyone know who I am?"[1] Today, there are very few readers who could not provide some reply to her questions, and there are many critics who have supplied answers. To some she is "A Mirror For Us All," the inventor of a new "type" of imaginative writing, "a sensitive and percipient twentieth-century Eve" commenting upon "the inadequacies of the eternal Adam"; to others she is "a troubled preadolescent pursuing a dream of reuniting her parents and recovering her father," an "exclusively coterie figure," an escapist who "shuns the real world as if it had a bad reputation."[2] The last answer best provides a clue as to why Nin is not content with such definitions; for her question is an expression of concern not with her public image but with the perennial problem – *what is real?* In a very philosophical sense, therefore, but in an extremely personal manner, the issue to which Anais Nin has addressed her life, is the cause and consequences of the two conflicting definitions of reality. And it is in this unusual combination of subject and method that the uniqueness and value of Nin's work – the most voluminous of which is *The Diary* – resides.[3]

The rationale that governs the writing of *The Diary* and distinguishes it in method and scope from the typical private journal or the philosophical notebook consists of two complementary principles. The first is the one Nin felt to be the secret of Lawrence's writing and first expressed in her "unprofessional study" of his work: "an experience, provided it is lived with intensity and sincerity, often leads out of itself and into its opposite."[4] Nin feels that truth, to deserve the name, must have objective validity; but unlike the "scientist" she does not believe that objective goals can be achieved only through objective means, or that the subjective approach is by definition inimical to universally valid conclusions. To argue that personal experience has only personal relevance is to fall into the modern trap, the fallacy of the objective, a fallacy born of a mechanical rather than a humanistic concept of life. As her *proviso* makes clear, Nin realizes that subjectivity can be a *cul de sac*, but to believe that human beings can be purely objective is to begin with a dead end. Her method in *The Diary* is to avoid the romantic *impasse* not by trying to be objective in her reactions or her records but by subjecting her intuitions and impressions to a rigorous final analysis. This is the inner dialectic of *The Diary* – the continued effort to discover the objective significance of a subjective response. Thus unlike the typical diarist, while at times she records incidents without being able to explain their meaning, she never records things simply because they have happened. And for this reason, the *Diary* itself is never trivial. *The Diary* is not a philosophical work in the sense that it attempts to demonstrate a general system; but in the sense that it is a serious attempt to order personal experience, it is.

The second principle that orders Nin's writing, specifically editing, of *The Diary* explains why, although each volume records new experiences and faces, the work, again unlike that of the simple personal chronicle, has a definite thematic unity and yet also unlike the thesis work is totally organic. "It is always the same story one is telling. But from a different angle" (III, 251). All of our actions are governed by or reveal our orientations to reality; and to the serious writer or thinker, everything that happens serves to confirm or challenge this particular position. The "story" that Nin finds herself telling over and over again, therefore, is the difference between the two basic attitudes about what is real and the conflicts that result when they are manifested in social life, literature, and intimate relationships. Her own conception of reality, which she has come to call "psychological reality" and repeatedly symbolizes through "garden" imagery, is poetic and intuitive and could be described as the psychic (in the old as well as new sense) significance of the phenomenal world; in opposition to it she sees an intellectually and empirically ordered idea of what is real, which she calls "realism" and symbolizes through variants of "mirror" imagery.[5] This conflict between realism and reality functions as the surface dialectic of *The Diary*.

In the first volume of *The Diary*, the story takes its peculiar coloration from Nin's relationships to Henry Miller and the two psychoanalysts, René Allendy and Otto Rank during her Paris years, 1931-34. With Miller, Nin explores the way the reality issue is reflected in conflicts concerning the proper subject and techniques for literature: "My belief in wonder against his crude, realistic details" (I, 57). But at the same time that she asserts her mode of perception, she also recognizes that part of the reason she objects to Miller's approach is that she has never lived in his world. Henry offers to show it to her and she accepts:

Henry said, "Would you like me to take you to 32 Rue Blondel?"
"What will we see there?"
"Whores." (I, 58)

This experience, and others like it, enables her better to understand the realist mind but also confirms her convictions: "He wants to touch bottom. I want to preserve my illusion" (124). René Allendy is pictured similarly, as the realist in the field of psychoanalysis. His psychoanalytic methods consist of his attempt to classify her problems and to return her to "normalcy" – the respectable, statistical average. In opposition to him, Nin finds Otto Rank, a philosopher rather than a scientist of the soul. Originally a Freudian, Rank has come to feel that the nature of the unconscious cannot be reduced to bio-sexual terms; in him, therefore, Nin finds support for her belief that the de-sire to "dream" is indicative of the sensitive and creative personality and not the symptom of a sick psyche.

The Spanish Civil War provides the thematic setting for the second vo-lume of *The Diary: 1934-39*. The "angle of vision" this time is the question of responsibility of the artist to his time and country. The antagonist here is a character named Gonzalo, who believes that the evils of the day can and must be corrected through violent political revolution, and that the individual who is not actively and physically involved is shunning his responsibility. But such an attitude, she learns through her association with him, is a defense mechan-ism: "Rebellions of all kinds attract to their activities weaklings who rebel be-cause they cannot master, destroy because they cannot create" (II, 272). The so-called altruist most frequently is not a person who sacrifices his self for a cause, but one who needs to relate to a cause because he has no self, because he has been taught to equate reality with what are only its political and social manifestations. The artist's role, she argues, is to change the world by chang-ing the thinking that produced it, to free man not from slavish work but from servile commitments.

Finally, in the third volume of *The Diary*, Nin explores the reality issue in terms of the Jamesian "international theme." Believing that " 'Europe is decadent' " (III, 14), Americans have attempted to cut themselves off from their past, but in doing so they have cut themselves off at the waist. The result is a monstrous intellectual giant and the consequence, the modern rootless and alienated figure: the tough male who can only respond to violence, intel-lectual or physical; the frustrated woman who tries to find herself by becom-ing masculine; and their progeny, the anemic youth who cling to virginity or turn to homosexuality to protect themselves against life. The paradox of America, as she sees it, is that here is the land among lands dedicated to "liberty," and yet Americans, as their defenses and role-playing indicate, are extremely insecure and unhappy. The explanation? "Too much social con-sciousness, and not a bit of insight into human beings" (III, 44). In short, too much concern with externals, because of allegiance to a realistic concept of reality.

In the recently published fourth volume of *The Diary*, the main setting is the "village" life of New York; the time, the last years of World War II and its aftermath. The years 1944-49 are also the time Nin's fictional work first begins to attract public attention, and thus in this volume the "angle" from which she continues the old "story" is the situation of the "poet" in a rigidly critical culture. For to a large extent, her success in finding a publisher and an audience means only that the battles she fought privately, as recorded in the first three volumes, must now be waged again in public. Instead of arguing with her friend Henry Miller about the best way to write a story, she is now called upon to defend her writing against the big dean of critics; instead of explaining to the compatriot, Gonzalo, why she does not believe in political involvement, she must now face critics who ridicule her work as irrelevant. As a result, the fourth volume is more public in tone and more documentary in style that the earlier volumes; the focus is less upon her attempts to extract the significance of her private experiences and more upon her attempts to explore the meaning behind the literary conflict. This may mean that volume four of *The Diary* will have less popular appeal; it should mean that it is particular importance to artists and critics.

When someone attacks your work, Nin advises a fellow writer, the first thing to do is to ask three questions: "Who is the person who made the statement? Why? Is it someone whose opinion is valuable?" (123). As her own reactions to criticism indicate, to Nin, the first question is merely preliminary; the third, relative; it is the second question that is crucial. Because to her there is no such thing as an objective critic. Like any other person, a critic has a point of view, and it is according to his *own* standards, wheresoever he has obtained them, that he pronounces his judgment. Therefore before accepting an evaluation, the writer should attempt to discover the point of view from which the criticism is made, the personal commitment behind the seemingly objective statement.

To her American reviewers, Nin's writing is unrealistic and irresponsible:

> "Stella is not real. We never see her going to the icebox for a snack."
>
> "How can you dwell on such neurotic characters at a time like this when only war and politics really matter?" (82)

Nin's first "why" concerns the relationship between the critic and the work in question: "The best way I can describe this criticism is that they only see what I have left out, but not what I have put in" (82). What makes her answer different from the typical defensive reply is that for Nin it forms the basis for the second question. What she has tried to do in her fiction is depict "the pure essence of the personality, stripped of national characteristics, time, and place, the better to penetrate the innermost being, the deepest self" (141). Why, she now asks, do her reviewers criticize her for leaving out social and historical aspects and ignore her presentation of the psychic aspects of character? The answer is as simple as it is basic: because they are operating according to a different concept of reality than she is. To them, reality is "sweat, the present surroundings, politics, ugliness of war, belligerent relationships" (90); to her "Reality was how we felt and saw events, not events as they appeared objectively, because we are not objective" (91). The very concept she is attacking, therefore, is the one according to which they criticize her work. And it is her awareness of this philosophical deadlock that makes her ultimate reply different from that of the average injured artist: her conclusion is not that her critics do not understand what she was trying to do but that they do not understand what she has done – do not understand the reality she has depicted.

Furthermore, like the D. H. Lawrence of *Fantasia of the Unconscious*, Nin realizes that, with respect to her opponents, her position cannot be defended. "It *is* visionary writing. How do you argue about that" (91). Psychic reality is by definition undemonstrable; to define it by means of scientific analysis, like Freud, is to reduce it to the material, and therefore not to prove its true nature at all. To accept the validity of intuition, one must have experienced this type of perception. The poetic writer cannot make his readers understand; his only appeal is to a sensitive audience. Unlike Lawrence, however, Nin does not dismiss the philistines with a brusque "you either believe or you don't";[6] "The best attack," she tells a friend who urges her to fight, "is to continue work. To do better and better work, that is where to put my energy" (123). That, and to address one's work to those who have not surrendered their illusions for the security of the system – to those whom she calls "The Transparent Children" (101).

It is this that accounts for the predominate presence of youthful characters in this volume of *The Diary*, and at the same time for the difference in her relationship to them from the standard situation of a mature woman seeking companionship from young men. The physical aspect is not absent, but its basis is emotional rather than sexual; the "mother" element is not missing, but it is psychologically oriented. The attraction, as she explains, is based upon the similarity between the creative and the adolescent personalities: "The analogy between the artist and the child is that both live in a world of their own making. . . . Both the artist and the child create an inner world ruled by their fantasies and dreams. They do not understand the world of money, or the pursuit of power. They create without commercial intent. They rebel against existing conditions. They cannot be deceived. The realistic world for them is ruled by conscious compromises, self-betrayals, selling out" (99). There are two types of children in *The Diary*, and paradoxically, in either case, the very quality that initially attracts Nin to them is the one that most frequently contributes to her alienation from them ultimately.

"This quality, the quality of renewal, perpetual youthfulness, which I liked in the artist, I find in the homosexuals" (188). While she believes that healthy heterosexuality is the ideal – "What is this world without vital relationships between men and women?" (136) – Nin does not accept the common societal view of homosexuality as sexual perversion. As in all situations, she does make assumptions based on appearances, but attempts to discover the psychological implications of the practice. And what she discovers is that homosexuality is largely a-sexual. What the homosexual is seeking is not physical pleasure in members of the same sex, but a relationship devoid of sex. Homosexual love is narcissistic; the other is loved not for himself but as a projection of the self. The motivation, therefore, is to have unlimited possibilities to create "a joyous, facile, promiscuous world, natural and without permanence" (126), a world of innocence. It is this "child-like" spontaneity and playfulness that is the positive and attractive aspect of the homosexual. But according to Nin, there is a great difference between the European and the American homosexual, and it is the peculiar nature of the latter that makes him a negative figure. "The Spanish homosexual or the French homosexual loved men but did not hate women" (126); the American homosexual is largely characterized by this hatred. The reason is "always some traumatic event which caused a fear of women." Why such events are so peculiar to American males, Nin does not state explicitly, although to judge from the types of women portrayed in *The Diary*, her answer would probably be, specifically, that American women are very different from European women, and generally, that the puritanical aspects of American culture have created a fear of the sexual nature of woman. In any case, "In the American homosexual it was the hatred of woman which was a perversity, for it distorted reality, and made expansion impossible. . . ." In the American, the childlike quality becomes a childishness, a refusal to grow up motivated not by a creative impulse but by fear of "totality, the absolute in love" (125). Thus to her, the American homosexual is not a *gay* person but the opposite: "There is a furtive quality to it all. Or else it comes out in irony, satire, or mockery of itself" (188). As a result, Leslie Fiedler to the contrary, according to Nin American literature contains no novels about homosexual "love," although many about "whoring"; "It is always treated with shame, like men's quest for prostitutes" (188).

If the psychologically young, then, make up one class of children in *The Diary*, the chronologically young constitute the other. It is similarly their gaiety and mobility that appeal to her; in this case, however, the destructive force comes from without rather than from within; their vulnerability is the reason for their corruption. For in America, to "grow up" means to become realistic; because of a confusion of strength with callousness, "The shell is America's most active contribution to the formation of character. A tough hide. Grow it early" (144). Sensitivity must either be surrendered or persecuted; this is the dilemma facing the poet in the modern world. And for this reason, Nin sees the case of the mysterious Caspar Hauser as the prototype for the second set of children (to which she emotionally belongs), and employs the tale as the central motif of the fourth volume. According to her, "The story of Caspar Hauser is a story far more beautiful than that of Christ. It is the story of innocence, of a dreamer destroyed by the world. . . . Power, intrigue, evil cynicism join to murder him" (64).

In the coming of age of a young man named Leonard W., Nin witnesses a symbolic reenactment of Caspar Hauser's destruction – a sensitive youth brutalized into the world's concept of a man, the soldier. "The bell rang unexpectedly. At the door stands a most beautiful man of seventeen, tall, slender, blond, with deep-blue eyes, long lashes, a transparent skin like a *jeune fille en fleur*, a great seriousness in his bearing, a shyness, an innocence, a pu-

rity. It all radiates from him as he stands there and says: 'I am Leonard W.' "
(42). He has come to her by way of her book of stories, *Under a Glass Bell*,
and after discovering that her mode of life is as honest and spontaneous as
her manner of writing, he decides to leave his father – and his father's oil
company – and to join her circle instead. And thus "the dream began" (46).
In her company he feels free to "play" – in all the connotations of the word
– and to live his dreams. He remind her of Caspar Hauser "because of his
innocence and sudden insights. He has intuitions about people which are
those of an old soul" (47). But then the dream ends. Leonard is a "man" and
the world is at war; the mature world dictates, "Go to war. Earn your living"
(82). It is not the demand that is wrong, but the implications and the consequences; "Accept our attitude toward life," is what the order means; and to
obey this dictate is to laugh at one's earlier "weaknesses." Thus when he
writes to her from the army it is "No more Caspar Hauser. That was a romantic concept of his vulnerability!" (91). When she sees him again, it is a
"Leonard who has lost his dewiness, opalescence, transparence, by his life in
the army. With rougher hands and skin, and now a lieutenant. A Leonard less
shy, with a richer voice. he had chosen to go to Japan" (143).

In the literary world, Nin sees her own situation as a variation of the
Caspar plot, but herself as an undefeated Hauser. For as she explains, ironically in an early letter to Leonard, Caspar died because he "was no poet"; "in
the poet, the child, the adolescent never dies" (74). Like Hemingway's
heroes, she realizes she will be beaten but she knows she cannot be destroyed: "I will die a poet killed by nonpoets [but] will renounce no dream,
resign myself to no ugliness, accept nothing of the world but the one I made
myself" (177). In the fourth volume of *The Diary* two critics in particular represent the types of nonpoets who either deliberately or unwittingly are the
enemies of the creative writer. But just as she sees Leonard as typical of the
sensitive person destroyed by a political reality, so she views herself and her
opponents as exemplary of the modern literary situation rather than as specific individuals. "The theme of the dairy is always personal, but it does not
mean only a personal story" (153). In terms of the issues involved, therefore,
the names of many writers could be interchanged with hers; the names of any
number of critics could be substituted for the two who are mentioned. For
this reason, this portion of *The Diary* belongs to literary criticism.

Diana Trilling, whose review she prints in full, is to Nin representative of
the mentality that refuses to grant the artist the power to transcend the facts
of his life, and who consequently reduces art to autobiography and the artist
to the sum of his experiences. Source studies and psychological interpretations are the typical products of such an attitude; a *vicious* circle usually characterizes the criticism. First, the work of fiction is read in the light of the critic's knowledge of the author; for example, according to Nin, "Diana Trilling
assumed because I had studied psychology I was writing case histories" (82).
But second, and perhaps worse, is the reverse practice, to read from the
characters to the author, whereby the author is condemned for the failings of

his characters. "Trilling complains that Lillian and her husband and children are unreal" (121), implying that both Nin's point of view and her writing are unrealistic. But Nin's very purpose in *Ladders to Fire*, as she explains, is to create Lillian's sense of the unreality of her life; "How can one spend the length of a novel making something real which appears unreal to the central character?" (121-22). The problem, in short, is that the literalist is incapable of appreciating the point of view and accepting the validity of psychological reality. To such critics, realism is reality, and anything unrealistic, therefore, is unreal. Instead of requesting from art an expanded consciousness, such critics demand confirmation of their own point of view; instead of an organic literature, they want a mirror of the times. But to Nin, "The most important problem for the novelist is that each generation must create its own reality and its own language; its own images" (154). By insisting upon their standards of reality, the old generation strangles their young.

Whereas Diana Trilling, then, represents the philosophical force antagonistic to the creative writer, Edmund Wilson typifies the academic powers of destruction. A Cronus figure also, he is however the type of critic who hates " 'young writers. I hate them' " (88), not because he is incapable of understanding their work, or is insecure, but because he is too settled and secure. "To me," Nin writes, "he seems to have this hardening of the arteries I find in men of achievement. The florid skin, the satiated flesh, the solidity of the earth and its heaviness. He is didactic; he has conventional ideas about form and style; he has scholarship. He is all brown: brown earth, brown thought, brown writing" (93). The threat that such a critic presents is an indirect rather than a direct one – authority and the tyranny of tradition. Unlike the Trilling type he does not become defensive and vindicative; he simply either ignores what he does not agree with, thereby damning it through indifference, or makes prescriptions for work he likes in order to bring it into line with the established données of literary craft. For example, he praises her work for its " 'amazing insights! Marvelous insights!' " but then explains that he " 'must be severe.' " " *This Hunger* has no form. It is not concrete enough' " (83). He patronizes her by presenting her with a set of Jane Austen: "He was hoping I would learn to write a novel from reading her!" (88). If the Trilling type begins with a definition of reality, the Wilson type begins with a definition of literature. In either case an injunction is laid upon the artist to be an imitator of the past rather than the explicator of the present; and in either case the result is the destruction of creativity, which is renewal rather than repetition.

To Nin, therefore, the critic who cannot accept literary change is simply another example of fixation, and for this reason, although she realizes that such nonpoets will destroy her, she is not disturbed by their criticism of her work. Instead of spending her energies in self-defense, she devotes herself to exploring and revealing the neurotic basis of such pre-determined behavior – not through public pronouncements or caustic comments, but quietly with sympathy in *The Diary*. "The unreality we are suffering from is what I want to make clear, to dispel. Who knows what shadows from the past dictated to

Edmund Wilson his next attraction? The hero of this book is the malady which makes our lives a drama of compulsion instead of freedom" (143). This, consequently, is the answer to the question of how she is able "to dwell on such neurotic characters at a time like this." It is not because she thinks "war and politics" do not matter, but because she believes that the human being matters more. As she puts it, it is because she, like Cocteau, is interested in civilization rather than history (78). An obsession with politics "is as narrow an obsession as any other" (190); further, "The politics they talk about are not humanistic. They are abstract and theoretical" (196). Humanistic politics require that the individual perfect himself before he prescribes for others, because "The range of your vision depends on the extent of the personal development" (157).[7] A politician cannot feel the poverty or hunger of others when he himself is "neurotic, self-centered, or self-contained" (122). To give oneself to the cause is for many a good bargain.

"Why does everyone here believe that by all of us thinking of nothing else but the mechanics of living, of history, we will solve all problems?" Nin asks toward the end of the fourth volume of her *Diary*; "Sometimes one has to be away to think properly" (190). Circumstances make the impulse a necessity; the war is over and her status as a temporary resident can no longer continue. She must leave the United States and re-enter – it is in America that she wishes to live. While she is considering the alternative, she meets a young American from the West, who, hearing that her decision is being based upon her life in New York, wisely expostulates: "You mean that is all you know of America? New York is not America" (197).

Her journey to the South and West confirms the young man's words and her own faith in her ideals. Her trip delivers her of "the toxics of New York," by introducing her to nature and to people "who were natural and gracious," to "bigger artists, unconcerned with ambition" (222). Among the bigger artists, the two who figure in prominence are Lloyd Wright, son of the famous Frank Lloyd Wright, and Jean Varda, the collage artist. Wright, according to Nin, is "the poet of architecture. For him a building, a home, a stone, a roof, every inch of architecture has meaning and was formed from an inner concept" (210). Like her own work, Wright's buildings are designed to "create a more beautiful and satisfying environment" (211). Like hers, his "struggle is against uniformity and wholesale design" (212). But also like her, he is continually opposed by the forces of commercialism: "The transient, the meretricious, the imitation, the pseudo rule the day" (212). In "Janko" Varda, Nin finds another ally, but of a rather different temperament; Wright is the type of poet who employs natural materials to give perfect form to a vision of beauty; Varda is the poet who transforms the ugly into the beautiful. For Wright, architecture is an expression of aspiration; for Varda, "art is an expression of joy" (218). Like the cultists of ugliness, he visits the scrap heaps for his materials; unlike them, his purpose is to transform the ugliness, not to propagate it. Whereas they are motivated by a commitment to realism, he is inspired with a love of life and a sense of its magic. " 'Nothing endures,' said

Varda, 'unless it has first been transposed into myth' " (219). To Nin, he is the only modern artist who creates fairy tales – "not the sickly-sweet fairy tales of childhood but the sturdy fairy tale of the artist" (216).

"If I had not traveled West," concludes Nin after her introduction to these two artists and the America beyond New York, "I might not have wanted to become a permanent resident" (222). As it is, she decides to continue on to Mexico in order to make her re-entry. But instead of legal necessity, her stay in Acapulco promises to become a psychological rebirth. Not because this village is the opposite of the one in New York or a primitivist's paradise, although that is part of it; but rather because among the natives she begins to understand the meaning of tropism: "I remembered that the definition of *tropic* was 'turning,' 'changing,' and I felt a new woman would be born here" (225).

When a friend asked Nin for a short autobiography, presumably for *Harper's Bazaar*, she replied with a letter which began: "That was one question I was hoping you would not ask me but answer for me. . . . My real self is unknown. My work is merely an essence of this vast and deep adventure." But later in the letter, she does attempt to project a death-bed summary: "I wrote, lived, loved like Don Quixote, and on the day of my death I will say: 'Excuse me, it was all a dream,' and by that time I may have found one who will say: 'Not at all, it was true, absolutely true' " (176-77). Though written with a smile ("All of which is not for *Harper's Bazaar*"), the reply does provide an index to the significance of the life recorded in *The Diary*. Her determination to accept no definition of reality that is not born of personal experience, presents a challenge to those who live unexamined lives; her joy in "illusion" makes one question the value of disillusionment; her literary integrity puts a question mark behind the success of writers who have turned "Panza" for popularity.[8]

NOTES

[1]The question appears so emphasized in Nin's *House of Incest* (New York, 1959), p. 20 (first published in 1936). Implicitly, however, the question prompted the keeping of a diary by the eleven year old child Nin: "There was a complex genesis. I was shy of speaking, I was full of feelings and ideas I could not express to anyone." See Nin, *The Novel of the Future* (New York and London, 1968), p. 142 ff.

[2]Respectively: Nancy Williamson, Evelyn Clark, Barbara Reyes, "A Mirror for Us All," *the second wave: a magazine of the new feminism* I (Summer, 1971), 8-9; Harry T. Moore, "Preface" to *Anais Nin* by Oliver Evans (Carbondale and Edwardsville, 1968); Lloyd Morris, "Anais Nin's Special Art," *New York Herald Tribune Book Review* (March 12, 1950), p. 17; and Leon Edel, "Life Without Father," *Saturday Review* (May 7, 1966), p. 91; Frank

Baldanza, "Anais Nin," *Minnesota Review* II (Winter, 1962),263-71; Elizabeth Hardwick, "Fiction Chronicle," *Partisan Review*, XV (June, 1948), 706.

[3]The *Diary* is being published as a series of volumes. Pagination refers to the following editions: *The Diary of Anais Nin: 1931-1934*, edited with an Introduction by Gunther Stuhlmann (New York, 1966), Vol. I; *The Diary of Anais Nin: 1934-1939*, edited with a Preface by Gunther Stuhlmann (New York, 1967), Vol. II; *The Diary of Anais Nin: 1939-1944*, edited with a Preface by Gunther Stuhlmann (New York, 1969), Vol. III; and the recently published *Diary of Anais Nin: 1944-1947*, edited with a Preface by Gunther Stuhlmann (New York, 1971), Vol. IV.

[4]Nin. *D. H. Lawrence: An Unprofessional Study*, with an Introduction by Harry T. Moore (Chicago, 1964), p. 107. (First published in Paris, 1932.)

[5]For an extensive discussion of this conflict as it relates to all of Nin's writing see my *The Mirror and the Garden: Realism and Reality in the Writings of Anais Nin* (Columbus, 1971).

[6]D. H. Lawrence, *Fantasia of the Unconscious* in D. H. Lawrence, *Psychoanalysis and the Unconscious* and *Fantasia of the Unconscious*, Introduction by Philip Rieff (New York, 1960), p. 53. In another article I questions Rieff's contention that Lawrence's statement is "peevishness" occasioned by the failure of *Psychoanalysis*.

[7]In conversation with Nin, she suggested that it was this belief in the need for interior development that made her feel uneasy about The Women's Liberation Movement.

[8]I wish to express my indebtedness to The Canada Council for continued financial assistance and to John J. Teunissen for his critical and moral encouragement.

From *Journal of the Otto Rank Association* 7.2 (December 1972): 21-36.

The *Diaries* of Anais Nin

Lynn Luria-Sukenick

Autobiographical forms raise critical questions which are different from the questions raised by novels and poetry. Because novels and poetry do not purport to be records of fact they do not move us to check veracity: they stand or fall by their convincingness, which need not be a matter of strict mimesis but of truth of feeling, rightness of form, and richness of language. A serious work of autobiography also bases much of its success on these elements but inevitably forces the reader to consider additional criteria, the most prominent of which is – is it true?

Perhaps it would be more accurate to say, does it *seem* true, for we infrequently turn to other accounts for verification of a diary or memoir unless we are scholars: we rely on the veracious tone, the probability, common sense, and proportion of a work for our satisfaction. In certain instances scholarship or common knowledge confirms an author's reputation as a liar, as in the case of Cellini, whose autobiography we enjoy as the brilliant self-revelation of a braggart, as vivid and undeceptive as a braggart in the flesh.

The diaries of Anais Nin, although revised and intensely compressed, and revised – as Nin has said – by the novelist, are, by their nature, a species of autobiography. Although their excellence has caused them to be ranked with works of the imagination, a rank accorded few autobiographies in spite of the current popularity of the genre, they are not novels – one has only to put them next to her novels to feel that – and to ignore that fact is to miss out on the special reading experience which they seem to inspire. Nin's diaries are books of wisdom which have elevated their author to the status of a sage and have had a healing effect on many of her readers, an effect which would be altered if the books were semi-fiction, although, clearly, works of fiction can function as books of wisdom. It is unlikely that anyone has bent to kiss her hem as did one adoring reader of George Eliot, but Nin has evoked in her readers a response similar to the tenacious adulation that surrounded Eliot in her later years, and has joined the company of those great teachers – Eliot, Wordsworth, and the savage but salutary D. H. Lawrence – who had a visionary sense of the healing power of feeling. "The effect of her being on those around her was incalculably diffusive," says George Eliot of Dorothea Brooke, and it is not less true of the Nin who emerges in these diaries, a woman who teaches not through precept but through influence. The diaries, depicting Nin's influence on those around her, also teach us, as readers, how to be influenced, how to be susceptible.

Nin's power to stir us and change our lives is not in direct proportion to the quantity of information in the diaries, not a direct function of how much she tells us. Although Nin places her deepest expectations in the personal and private sphere, the diaries are not confessional works. Nin was a practicing Catholic until her teens and therefore familiar with the ritual of confession; she was a student of psychoanalysis and herself an analyst, accustomed to the recuperative monologues of the analysand, but her diaries are not confessional in the most common sense of the word. She does not seek to unburden herself of material as if the material is an impediment to her freedom, nor does she pay guilty attention to the more ignoble details of her life as if to absolve herself by virtue of her typicality or detestability. If anything, she is herself the priest or lay confessor, confessing to herself by means of the diary, but also, by means of the diary, absolving herself from raw experience by transmuting it into form – not just any form, but conscious and lucid writing which expresses control even when she is discussing her weaknesses.

In certain respects the diaries are as elusive as the father they are written to – the absence of Nin's husband in these pages, for instance, necessarily leaves a fissure which would make all other relationships undergo a geological shift – and Nin's omissions have been a focus for criticism of her work, some readers asserting that she appears to have led a life less conditioned by circumstance than the diaries reveal, thus giving us a falsely reassuring picture of human abilities (insofar as she comes to stand for human abilities). This is a criticism that becomes more important as her diaries tend to become more and more models of life and books of wisdom, for if we look to Peter Pan to teach us to fly but do not see the hook and wire holding him to the ceiling we are in trouble, though he may temporarily increase our optimism.

If Nin does omit crucial elements which would change the tone and nature of the diaries as they now stand she is also persuasive in making us comprehend that these elements are not as crucial as the principles of realism have led us to think. For our idea of what a "life" is, based on only relative tenets of Western perception, economy, and chronology, does not necessarily match the shape or proportion with which Nin lives hers, and it is her great strength that she has resisted habituating sets that conquer and form most of us, her vision changing our notions of the plausible and possible. Just as certain yogis dispel our assumption that we need continuous breath to stay alive, so Nin persuades us that it is not impractical to be guided by dreams, not impossible to defy gravity for a few minutes longer than we think. It is important to note that the characters in Nin's novels also have lives which are, in ordinary terms, unconditioned, possessing an anonymity and inconsistency at odds with the crystallized characterization handed down from the nineteenth-century novel, lives which are not Nin's own but which she sees in a similar way.

For Nin, realism is a form of defeat. She craves the idyllic, the supreme version, and her drive toward the perfect, the harmonized, the Utopian, and her impulse to make things as intense, prolific, and beautiful as possible, is a central feature of the diaries. Transforming her optimism into an esthetic, she believes that the role of the artist is to transform ugliness into beauty, in life as well as in writing. Taking her father's desire to be thought perfect and generously inverting it, she wants others to think they are perfect. And if she makes myth of herself and writes herself large, it is not as a narcissist but out of desire to transform her life by means of discipline and optimism into the most lovely and elevated existence possible.

The supreme version can be a fiction, however, and we do not want diaries to be fiction, nor, for that matter, do we want novels to be fairy-tale. Nin's passion for harmony expresses itself in her distaste for harsh contradiction or polemic. She does not hold the belief that exigence and contradiction are necessary for genuine selfhood. For Nin, logic and argument, all the voices of the head as opposed to the heart, are only translations from an original emotional reality. Feeling and intellect are not different ends of a continuum but exist on separate planes, and she rejects the quality of negation in modernist literature which comes from the hegemony of intellect, for it is the intellect that doubts; the body, the feelings, are usually sure. "The highest goodness is like water," says Lao Tzu. "Water is beneficent to all things but does not contend." Just so with Nin: in both diaries and fiction she emphasizes synthesis over antithesis, maintaining a tone that holds everything in the same plane, neutralizing the distinction between figure and ground, muting conflicts in interpretation. Her style determines that people tend to read her either very loyally – moving by faith to relate, unite, and connect rather than to dispute – or not at all.

Nin's occasional neglect of sincerity and candor in the diaries – the lies she tells to others to make improvements or not to hurt, to maintain harmony and dissolve disruption – is directly related to her desire for perfection. She realizes it as a weakness – this tendency to invent or conceal – and she presents her weakness openly, not only in her own person but in figures who reflect and enlarge the problem, living it out to an extreme degree. Lying – her father's, June's – is a deep concern of Diary I, and is a theme that develops richness in *Spy in the House of Love*, where Nin attempts to find relief from it once and for all, creating a final punctuation in the person of the Lie Detector.

Nin's belief in transmutation and alchemy inspires her to alter the surface and style of things and to take adornment seriously, embracing as a pleasure what many people use only as a strategy of defense. She alters her costume to transform the occasion, dressing like a warrior to resist Artaud, acknowledging the power of the material realm and putting it to magical use.

This passion for adornment is intimately linked to the possibilities of impersonation, for though Nin shows us how impersonation may whittle away selfhood she also makes clear that it can be a temporary but releasing expression of unlived life, truer than rigidly held consistency. If young Werther expressed sincerity by an unchanging mode of dress, mistakenly clinging to romantic simplicity, Nin (who associates romanticism with neurosis perhaps because of this pretense of divided consciousness to innocent unity) dons masks and costumes in order to celebrate the complexity of identity, the unlimited truths of personality. She has a sane longing to be whole but does not pretend, sentimentally, to a wholeness she hasn't earned or an innocence that would simplify her life without being true to it.

"Give a man a mask and he will tell you the truth." Oscar Wilde's dictum suggests that protected by a mask we are more willing, unwittingly perhaps, to be and reveal ourselves. The artist creating his/her own environment goes even further, including the mask as part of the revelation rather than hiding behind it, aware that the creation of a compelling mask expresses degrees of inventiveness and levels of aspiration which are as much a part of the self as ordinary guise. Although Nin escapes the mechanical and hypocritical impersonations of social existence in the diary, her pursuit of "transmutation" continues there, and the diary itself becomes both an active force in transforming her life (as when she draws portraits of people and shows them their portraits) as well as a distilled account of her experience. Notable for a grace and certainty of style, Nin's diary is utterly distinct from the current outpourings of confessional journalism, undigested notation encouraged by the general abolition of etiquette and the preeminence of therapies which encourage and value public revelation of personal material. She does not give herself away in her writings but serves us by remaining intact even after we have devoured her work.

Perfection of, attention to style is suspect in autobiography, for we tend to feel, almost superstitiously – Romantically – that the genuine self – naked, chaotic – cannot be contained by language, and that inadequacy of language or stress of expression pays homage to the large undefinable self. Kerouac's rough work clothes and associative prose seem more authentic at first glance than Henry Adams' balanced and dressed up coat and tie sentences. Yet Adams' prim, if profound, accuracy is as revealing of personality as Kerouac's often evasive casualness. Nin's distilled style is a part of the personality being revealed by it. She has a sense of style – in dress, in personal relations, in her self-discipline – which makes transmutation of the raw into the fine a natural and constant process in her life. Stylization is not only a task of the social self, as it is for most people; it is, for Nin, instinctive and intimate. The diary is edited to make it a manageable length and to prevent injury to the living; it is also highly appropriate to Nin's stance that the diary emerges first as a distilled version of the original, for her life is a highly distilled version of what, with less will and vision, is might have been.

The advocates of spontaneity, from Rousseau on, have regarded artifice as an offense against sincerity and the spirit of democracy (for a doctrine of equality gives value to and an opportunity for candor). A sisterly relation with the reader is desired, a certain obligation to be no better than the reader. But Nin, by aiming high and extracting noble qualities from her experience, improves herself and shows others the way. Nin's distilled style allows us more space for ourselves than the confessional outpourings which make accomplices of us. Her diary, perfected and sometimes reticent, becomes a mirror into which we can look and, often, find ourselves clearly expressed. Her polished surface reflects the reader.

Nin's relation to the reader is not unlike her relationships to real people in the diaries, where her personal allure is clearly an overpowering factor in her experience. Her diaries are seductive rather than confessional, extending to the reader a subliminal invitation to fall in love – with her, *and* the world – and she instinctively knows, having been traditionally feminine in many respects, the importance of concealment to the arousal of desire. Yet she is fascinated by veils actual and symbolic not out of coquetry, or modesty, but out of an appreciation of tact, subtlety, and the more enduring connections these approaches inspire.

Nin's tact, discretion, gentleness and sympathy are crucial to all of her relationships as they are portrayed in the diary, at times, in her own opinion, to excess. Virginia Woolf has stated that sympathy was a concern of laggards and losers, and certainly in the era of modernism it has seemed minor, mediocre, and peripheral. But Nin insists on it – "What makes us human is empathy, sympathy," she says – and she is willing to cry out "This hurts people!" the kind of objection ordinarily made only by unpublished mothers. The most remarkable thing about Nin is how she revives the wisdom of sympathy in an age which tends to be embarrassed by it.

The spareness and omissions of Nin's diaries result partly from her wanting to ignore – in Virginia Woolf's phrase – the "appalling narrative business of the realist," just as her strategy as a novelist is to wean us from simple curiosity and a hunger for ordinary narrative. But it is more than likely that sympathy and discretion are as responsible as formal considerations for the withholding of information in the diaries. Nin's unwillingness to injure coincides with her doctrine of omission and extends the portrait of her as a woman of sympathy. There is in fact a substitution of sympathy for confessional sincerity in the diaries. Nin relates how she sometimes conceals things from others in order not to hurt them, offering warm comfort instead of cold fact. She writes in the diary to compose herself, literally, to offset her empathic merging with others. Yet even this private act, now made public, offers comfort, now to her readers, who receive insights into and a blueprint for the opening of the heart, solicitude and creative energy. The apex of Nin's tact is that she creates an atmosphere of intimacy at the same time that she refrains from a policy of open disclosure. We feel, somehow, that the diaries reach into our lives, that they are intimate about *us*, intimating to us our own latent potential, the latent life force in us.

Nin's wisdom fits nicely into the American credo of "Make thyself" and many of her readers have saved and changed themselves through the inspiration of her work. There is a certain innocence and pragmatism about this reception of her diaries which should be distinguished from the character of Nin herself. She is sophisticated, European, not an innocent, though some skeptics might see her sympathetic nature as innocent. Her naturalness is real but hard won against the cold artifice of her father and her warmer inclinations to masks and perfections. She is not broad and candid by nature but tactful, oblique, delicate. It is this complexity – this chord – her given nature and her growth out of it – that makes her diaries interesting. Her openness is earned and the self she discovers and enriches is all the more authentic for being complex and struggled for.

Only an honest person should tell the truth. Candor does not guarantee integrity of spirit or freedom from self-deception. The indirect autobiographer, humbly aware of this, may have a greater respect for the integrity of the self than the most ardent confessor. The mode or attitude of sincerity does not insure honesty; to behave as if you are telling everything does not mean that you are, and may indeed be a way of disarming reader (and writer) from probing deeper. Discretion is, in effect, an open refusal of information less misleading at times than the confession which accidentally or deliberately conceals.

These are important issues, for there are readers who depend on Nin's diaries to be sincere, straightforward exposition and are then disappointed (or elated) to discover a more complex mix of modes and motives. Others relinquish all the claims and expectations we bring to autobiography and call these novels. But the diaries, however, unconfessional, contain a wisdom in their obliquity and omissions. Nin teaches us to get rid of the dross of our lives, to pursue essence and ignore the masses of ordinary detail we have been trained to think of as necessary or authenticating. She compels us to believe that the supreme version is worth having, and she revives without apology and with panache the importance of sympathy and aspiration.

From *Shenandoah* 17.3 (Spring 1976): 96-103.

Anais Nin in the *Diary*:
The Creation and Development of a Persona

Duane Schneider

The intriguing and engaging narrator of Anais Nin's *Diary* has surely earned for herself a place among the great literary creations to appear in this century. Purporting to reveal aspects of her life (and the growth of her sensibilities) in selections from an autobiographical journal, the narrator knows and relates the truth about herself. In a series of volumes covering the years 1931-1966, the reader is allowed to trace the progress of this narrator/persona (called "Anais Nin") through a set of experiences that simulates the depth and variety of human life and achievement. The creation and development of this narrator unquestionably attest to the power and skill of Nin, the author, and it is therefore unfortunate that many readers have failed to appreciate the difference between the two.[1]

Such confusion is also difficult to understand, as there seem to be ample directions in the prefatory material of the six volumes to deter us from assuming that Nin the author and Nin the narrator are uniform; since we are told that the published *Diary* represents only a fraction of the original, and since both the processes of selection and organization have taken place, we would seem led to conclude that the published versions (having been revised at least once) are carefully wrought works of literature, regardless of the apparent autobiographical nature of their origin.

In any case, Nin never forgot, even if some readers occasionally do, that it "was the fiction writer who edited the diary" (*Novel*, p. 85), and it ought to come as no surprise to find that the values and techniques she employed in her fiction are finely honed for use in the *Diary*. Psychological authenticity, which lies at the heart of all of Nin's work, is effected in the *Diary* as in the fiction through the manipulation of symbolism, dreams, and other dramatic devices which generate a sense of immediacy. Similarly, the *Diary* reveals a fine sense of timing, character development and selection, which Nin initiated and Gunther Stuhlmann aided; as in her fiction, but frequently with sustained concreteness, characters appear and reappear in multiple contexts, while typical of both the fiction and the *Diary* is the presence of a chief female character who is omnipresent – as participant or observer – and whose development is presented through multiple exposures in a variety of contexts, through her own self-analysis, or through the responses she evokes from the satellite characters around her.

There is, however, one important difference between the material as it is presented in the fiction and as it is presented in the *Diary*; namely, the presence within the latter of a central consciousness – that of the persona – through whose mind all the characters and incidents are filtered, interpreted, and colored. Every detail she affords us tells us perhaps as much about herself as it does about the person or incident described. In contrast to the situation in Nin's fiction, therefore, narration in the *Diary* becomes simultaneously self-characterization. Under the appearance of a journal that records real-life situations and individuals, there have, in fact, been gathered a set of compelling "actors" in accordance with the literary principle of point of view. The result is neither fiction in the traditional sense nor diary in the convention sense but rather something of a new art form – the journal-novel.

It is not difficult to describe the characteristics of the persona in each volume of the *Diary*; accounting for the narrator's development and the changes in her characterization, however, may be more problematic. For even if one grants that the "Nin" of the *Diary* is distinct from Nin, the real person, one must still, to a certain extent, take into consideration the way in which her own experiences influenced the editing of the original diary and her creation of a persona. Even if key questions cannot be answered they need to be posed. To what extent, for example, were the frustration and disappointment of her initial fiction-writing years factors in determining the kind of persona Nin chose to construct in the first volumes of the *Diary*? Did she perhaps need to compensate for rejection and disappointment by creating a narrator who, as we shall see, is helpful, attractive, perceptive and observant, one whom a number of colorful characters – Henry Miller, June, Dr. Allendy, Dr. Rank, Artaud, and others – turn toward for emotional nourishment? And did Nin's success in publishing the earlier volumes of the *Diary* and their enthusiastic reception in turn influence the conception of the narrator in the later volumes, where we find (finally) one who is more human, more relaxed, one who can admit errors and mistakes, and who allows for flaws in her characterization? Finally, in this context, one should also notice that while the narrator is characterized as one who consistently trusts the truth of her own emotions and intuitions and who exhibits the kind of faith in herself that only a modernist could,[2] she nevertheless seldom appears to be hermetically sealed or incapable and uninterested in learning more about the human condition; rather she is characterized as one who benefits from insights which allow her and others to live more freely and honestly than before, and with less pain. The thematic truth that lies at the heart of the *Diary*, then, is inextricably connected with Nin's conception of the narrator who is compelled to tell her tale, and who in so doing becomes both the subject (teller) and the object (told about).

The narrator of Volume I (1931-1934) encounters a few special problems, and yet, interestingly enough, the problems of exposition that we might expect to be dealt with are largely left untouched. We are introduced to the protagonist, Anais Nin, fully developed in the Paris of 1931, with house and friends, but virtually no past. That it is an exciting time in the life of the narrator, the tone makes clear. The emotional intensity is reflected in her diction and descriptions: "Ordinary life does not interest me. I seek only the high moments. I am in accord with the surrealists, searching for the marvelous" (I, 5). Infinity becomes an important dimension in the persona's life, as it tends to in many Romantics.

And yet the persona is distinctly different in practice from what she claims to be in theory: there are no surrealistic passages here, but rather a carefully-planned, lucid, detailed description of the narrator's encounters with Henry Miller, a Bohemian writer who revels in earthy living, and his wife June, a magnificent and attractive puzzle who tantalizes the narrator from the beginning. The discussions of June characterize her and introduce her to the reader long before she makes an appearance in these pages. And from the outset she serves as an effective contrast to the narrator, whose role at this time is characterized by fragility and vulnerability. Both the power of June's beauty and the attractiveness of Miller's spirit, awaken and kindle new life – life that was not known to exist – in the persona's psyche. The stage is set for high personal and emotional drama, the richest of all drama: that of self-revelation and penetration. And the simulation of reality gained through the first person narration gives the narrative added immediacy and interest for the reader.

The tale is told with artistry and efficiency, alternating between dialogue and observation. New characters appear, new situations arise, as the narrator makes her course along the three-year span covered in Volume I. With something very much like a plot, the narrator moves from the Miller/June encounter into the psychoanalytic episodes with Dr. René Allendy. With Miller and his circle, the narrator is able to witness at first hand a life of ugliness, violence and shabbiness; full of considerable ambivalence, she travels outward from her lacquered suburban home, with curiosity and trepidation, to experience this other side of life.

But is the narrator really participating in it all? Or is it all safely observed – the violence, the drunkenness, the sexuality? Actually, we are not told. And one of the great irritations to some is that the *Diary* leaves out, it seems, as much as it contains. As in some of Nin's novels, a portion of the context is missing or is deleted. But the enjoyment, the wonder, the pleasure, and the surprise of the persona all seem to be present, and the richness of her life is felt even if it is not described in detail. The scenes between the narrator and June are masterpieces of literary control; Nin's sensitivity to diction here is at its most delicate and discerning. None of Nin's works of fiction has a greater unity than this progress of the *Diary*'s heroine in her first public appearance: not seeking fortune, but looking for friendship, self-esteem and worthy productivity. It is an impressive character delineation that Nin sketches in Volume I: the persona moving from Miller to June to Dr. Allendy and Antonin Artaud (a fine set of characters), while in the background there is the painful contrast of the father's world, a world lost to the narrator both literally and figuratively. The persona is figured as a questor who moves steadily toward levels of self-realization, and in Volume I it is as though each character she encounters somehow contributes to this quest.

However, the strength of Volume I is also its weakness. The character of the persona seems incomplete, unrounded – perhaps unreal. Certainly the narrator is relatively flawless. We soon realize, in fact, that she is depicted as the one who is needed, a kind of savior, and not merely one who needs. Those with whom she comes into contact – Miller, June, Dr. Allendy, Dr. Rank – eventually need her, as does her father. The roles are reversed time and time again. The inversion from being the helped to becoming the helper is made explicit; the persona becomes the Great Mother upon whom her many children depend. This motif, which is developed even more clearly in Volume II, begins to emerge when the diarist observes that she always loses her "guide halfway up the mountain, and he becomes [her] child" (I, 261). The persona who said that she wanted to live only for ecstasy and extravagance may have been speaking more openly than she knew, and for this narrator, at least, the description seems to be most appropriate in her urgent wish to appear heroic and needed. The new life – with many people needing her – is fittingly capped by the ending of Volume I, in which Otto Rank is portrayed as sending the narrator desperate letters to come and rescue him in the United States. "I may not be a saint," she notes, "but I am very full and very rich" (I, 360). And, we might add, very stylized and very incomplete.

The narrator of Volume II shares a great deal with that of Volume I, and the time of composition (editing, organizing and selecting) was probably close to that of the first volume, since Volume II appeared only a year later. Many motifs, themes and characters reappear in this volume, which covers the years 1934-1939. But because the advent of war dominates the scene here, this volume has both a political and social context that is lacking in Volume I. During these years the narrator develops significantly as a writer and forms close and important literary associations with a group made up of Henry Miller, Alfred Perlès, Lawrence Durrell, and others. Of the new characters in the volume, the most remarkable are Gonzalo, a Peruvian Marxist, and Helba, his wife. The narrator's political initiation, and to some extent her portrayal as a person with a social conscience, is managed by Gonzalo. Again, however, the persona is incomplete, only partially revealed. The narrator does travel to the United States to help Otto Rank, but when she realizes the sacrifices she would need to make – chiefly sacrifices that would require her to give up her writing – she breaks with psychoanalysis in favor of art. Her opiate, the diary she keeps, continues to provide her with a direct connection to the world of writing, however, and when she returns to Europe and her friends, they determine to publish their own works and found a press, Siana

Editions (Anais spelled backwards).

These two themes – writing and politics – dominate Volume II, and just as psychoanalysis is given up by the narrator (not, of course, without having heightened her awareness), so does the narrator find herself forced to deal with political realities. She would prefer to ignore politics altogether and explore only her artistic inclinations, but faced with the reality of war and destruction, she finds that art cannot act as a substitute for life, and also finds her own sense of life and its preciousness considerably heightened.

Simultaneously, the narrator cultivates her image as nurturer and protectress – a pattern of self-characterization that echoes Volume I. She continues to be introspective. She recognizes that the constant need for "a mother, or a father, or a god (the same thing) is really immaturity" (II, 21); she also recognizes the need to provide love for those who seek it. And so the portrayal of the narrator as a benefactress emerges more and more, and indeed dominates the larger portion of the volume. Of her friends in Paris, 1935, she writes: "I am the young mother of the group in the sense that I am giving nourishment and creating life. All of them now in motion. When I look at the changes, the transformations, the expansions I created, I grow afraid, afraid to be left alone, as all mothers are ultimately left alone. To each I gave the strength to fly out of my world, and at times my world looks empty. But they come back" (II, 51). Born under the wings of Pisces, the giver, she continues to give at the same time that she pursues her literary career. Reflecting on the austere pasts of each of her friends, she feels more able to cope with her few possessions. She enjoys giving up self-indulgence, luxury, and travel: "I have to pay for Henry's rent, Gonzalo's rent, and to feed them all. No rest. No seashore, no travel, no vacation. Voilà. No Heine's beach costume, no mountain air, no sun on the body. But I get pleasure from seeing how my children live" (II, 201). With her literary companions, the narrator lives an exciting life of the mind, unmasking each other (she says), defending their varied approaches to literature.

And yet, the narrator herself seems more incomplete than ever, and Anais Nin, the author, is not unmasked, nor we feel, was meant to be. The persona is busily engaged with the rites of more self-analysis. Her self-esteem is nurtured by testimonies of her friends, which the narrator reproduces, as though to convince herself of her own value. Her convictions, however, remain unaltered, and much that is the best of Anais Nin's liberality and humaneness is revealed, in spite of the author's preoccupation with creating a persona who will appear to be flawless. When Gonzalo, for example, tries to impose Marxism upon the narrator, she resists, refusing to pass from one narrowminded concept to another, chiefly because she has fought for a spiritually honest and free life (II, 274). She allows, however, that social and political awareness may be necessary to improve the lives of many; yet even on that basis, she has reservations: "I have built a rich private world, but I fear I cannot help build the world outside. Deep down, I feel, nothing changes the nature of man. I know too well that man can only change himself psychologically, and that fear and greed make him inhuman, and it is only a change of roles we attain with each revolution, just a change of men in power, that is all. The evil remains. It is guilt, fear, impotence which makes men cruel, and no system will eliminate that" (II, 154-55).

The narrator's vision of the artist transforming the world constructively is a view that she clings to. On the personal level as well as on the cosmic scale, the function of the artist is a beneficial one, and above all, the persona is characterized as one who maintains these values in her personal relationships as well as in her own ideology, which she is forced to create. It may seem like a role that attracts too much self-aggrandizement, and some find it obnoxious because of the unreal consistent nobility with which the narrator characterizes herself or allows others to do for her.

Given the scope of Volume III – the years 1939-1944 – one might assume that the selection dwells upon the Second World War. Not so. The war exists as a kind of backdrop, but it does not dominate nearly so much as it does in Volume II when the narrator must deal with Gonzalo, the Spanish Civil War, and the preparations for the greater war. With Volume III, the narrator is cast back into America and must cope with her artistic endeavors on American terms, a task that turns out to be difficult. Unable to find a suitable market for her works, she and Gonzalo turn to printing her stories and short novels themselves, tasteful works issued by Gemor Press, largely unnoticed except amidst a coterie of friends and admirers, until one influential friend gives one book a good review in an important magazine: Edmund Wilson's review of *Under a Glass Bell* in *The New Yorker*, 1944.

With an agreeable symmetry, not unlike its predecessors, Volume III begins with difficulty and dislocation (also true of Volumes I and II), but ends with success and acceptance – true in Volume I but only generally so in Volume II. The dovetailing and interweaving of character and motif continue: in time, part of the Paris circle that Nin regrets leaving – Miller, Gonzalo, Helba – appear on American shores. The persona progresses in a logical fashion: the literary initiate of the first volume, who chooses art in the second, becomes the maverick and determined devotee of her own vision in the third volume. The problem she faces is: how does an avant garde writer establish contact with an American audience in 1940? Answer: with extreme difficulty, and never successfully. The persona's consciousness is almost entirely directed toward this problem, and the war lies far in the background. How the persona deals with the problem – another success story, so far as we can tell – perpetuates the pattern of the quest: the goal is established, the obstacles arise and are overcome in the face of great odds, the prize is won and the heroine is acknowledged. The triumphs continue to be kept steadily before the reader, and are made all the more significant by the kinds of difficulties that the narrator needs to overcome (irresponsible friends, impossible demands made by others, the poor taste and insensitivity of the American publishing world). The stamina of the narrator is admirable; the cost of pain is not related in detail until later, in Volume VI.

The contrast between Paris and New York is made explicit in this volume. In Europe, the writer was comfortable among friends with whom she shared a number of values, and the cultured continent reflected these civilized values; in America she finds no intimacy, no café life, but rather opulence and decadence. The narrator's coming to terms with this new world gives a good deal of order – if not unity – to her quest for literary acceptance and recognition. The entire volume, in a sense, reflects the very kind of communication and relationship with readers that the narrator was seeking from the beginning of her career in Paris. To some extent, in the description of the quest, the narrator's quest is close to being achieved.

In view of the principles of literary value espoused in Volumes I and II (to some degree the values of D. H. Lawrence), the rejection by the American literati in the 1940's was predictable. But there is no pretense on the part of the persona that she could change her approach, or ought to. The idea of writing something like *The Good Earth* is to her simply odious; her work, she implies, like herself, is "free and beyond nationalism" (III, 247). Miller's intolerance for American glitter reinforces the narrator's distaste for the country; so far as she can see, Americans are busy rejecting European values, while the isolationism Americans feel is being projected upon her work. The narrator whose value has in the past been unquestioned, now seems dispensable. And so, to save herself, and to triumph, she defies the publishers by printing and publishing her own works, *Winter of Artifice* and *Under a Glass Bell*. The publication of these modest volumes is apparently enough to hearten the narrator and her friends. But to survive financially, they write erotica.

Volume III, however, lacks a continuity that the first two volumes contain. Most of the characters introduced in this volume hold interest for the reader, but seem superfluous. The narration seems for the first time broken at times, slightly desperate if not shrill. The narrator's problems and friendships are not always so engaging as the nature of her literary achievement. She feels abused because her spontaneity and Lawrencean values are not respected (by publishers, who ought to know better). The reward, of course, comes to the narrator in the end, when Edmund Wilson's review brings all sort of benefits and attention, so long sought after. The writer is vindicated, and from this time on she knows that she will have a number of loyal supporters.

Although the details and emphases have changed, basically Anais Nin's depiction of the persona does not shift significantly in the first three volumes: generous, industrious, ambitious, respected by a core of admirers, the narrator pursues her vision of the feminine perception in her own unique kind of fiction. She does not reject psychoanalysis, but subordinates it to her art and vision. But the fully developed, human narrator, portrayed in her weaknesses and vulnerability, has yet to appear. The narrator in Volume III remains a literary creation, not a live human being. The author's defenses, it would seem, are still up.

The fourth volume, covering the years 1944-1947, represents to some degree the legacy earned from the years of the early 1940's. More fragmented than any earlier volume, it is not, however, weak or uninteresting, and contains some of Nin's finest and most poignant observations about life and literature. A number of familiar themes appear: the narrator continues to be concerned about her own artistic and psychological development, conscious of the restrictions imposed by guilt and neurosis, sensitive to those aspects of her existence which seem healthy and life-giving. Her literary life – printing, writing fiction – receives some fascinating attention here; her gravitation toward the young and her disappointment with the "mature" is dealt with in some detail. A strong sense of humanism emerges in this volume, a clear articulation – through the persona – of a vision of how life may be lived in an integrated fashion.

The sense or need of a persona – shall we say the author's? – also seems less urgent in Volume IV. For the first time the narrator does not have to succeed: she has succeeded. She is not fully rounded yet, but the heroics lie further in the background than ever before. The articulation of values is more explicit as well, and there is no compelling feeling that the narrator needs to be victorious. Her life is presented as one with a high degree of integration, and she sees herself as evolving and changing. Fusing her fiction with psychology, she understands the usefulness of focusing on the inner life, even if certain friends are trying to develop the "realist" in her. And with some pleasure, she notes that one of the great satisfactions of her life is that she lives "out what others only dream about, talk about, analyze. I want to go on living the uncensored dream, the free unconscious" (IV, 62). The attempt to free herself and others from the restrictions of neurosis means risk-taking for the narrator on the one hand, and her rejection of the dull, down-to-earth and prosaic on the other hand. Increasingly she sees her life and her writing as inseparable, and the importance of sympathy, movement, and humaneness is made explicit time and time again in the fourth volume, perhaps with a bit of repetition in the tone. The authenticity and deep sincerity of key passages are impressive, and signify the increased development of a persona who seems human and alive.

It thus seems that the further Nin carried her open-ended *Diary*, the more comfortable she became in allowing for a free and open narrator, in place of the narrower persona who seemed to be created with specific roles and images in mind. Expansion, fulfillment and evolution become a manifestation of the narrator's success and acceptance as a fiction writer and lecturer; the dream has become reality. For Nin, the dream, if lived out, provided for more abundant life; but the dream could also become a tragic trap, for to live within the dream and not to bring it into reality could lead to disaster. "You discard realism," Frances Brown tells her, "but not reality" (IV, 70). The persona is thus chiefly an accomplished fiction writer in this volume, no longer an apprentice, no longer needing to publish her work. Her depiction of emotional reality finally finds a greater outlet than ever before through

New York publishers, and the harmony – the diminution of frustration – is totally reflected in the *Diary*'s pages.

Nin organized and edited the materials for the fourth volume from the vantage point of 1970-1971; she had been able to see the immense success of the first three volumes, and in the text of Volume IV, she is less insistent on the value of the diary in the narrator's life. When we are told, however, that "the real Anais is in the diary" (IV, 105), we have no more concrete reflection of that complex author than we had in the earlier versions with their less developed persona. Nevertheless, the narrator is characterized as moving toward her dream of literary success and acceptance in a culture that she had deemed hostile, superficial, and under-developed in those qualities she valued most. The consistency of the narrator is kept steadily before us, sympathetic, humane, but controlled.

The fifth volume, which covers the years 1947-1955, is far different from the first four, and is more fragmented and less sustained even than Volume IV. Although familiar themes appear – sympathy, analysis, fiction writing, travel – no clear focus emerges and no clear theme is developed. It contrasts most strikingly with a work like Volume I, with its dramatic and engaging characterizations that are developed in great detail. The incoherence of Volume V in fact mirrors the incoherence of the narrator's life at this time; more than in any other volume, the persona here is less stylized and artificial. Suffering from depression and attendant emotional problems, as well as physical illness, the narrator encounters difficulties of considerable proportions, not the least of which are the deaths of her parents and a strange kind of hostility on the part of critics and reviewers. For the first time the narrator is depicted as beginning seriously to turn to the diary as her major work, with an eye toward eventual publication. In all its fragmentation, it may well be that Volume V, edited carefully, stands as a masterpiece of organic form, imaging in its structure (with short, undeveloped passages) the disconnected nature of the narrator's life. It may have been at this time that Nin chose to redirect her characterization of the persona toward something less glamorous, less dramatic than she appeared in earlier volumes.

Travel, descriptive passages, the shift from fiction toward the diary, all give Volume V a new and different tone. In fact, however, the kind of literary success the narrator seeks continues to elude her. Her bitterness and sense of estrangement are verbalized with more despair than ever. She sees herself in the traditional artist's role, articulating what all people know and feel, but are unable to speak. And gradually she recognizes that the diary can serve her better, not as a secret retreat or opiate, but rather as her artistic *magnum opus*. The fiction writer begins to try to find a way of providing a flow in the diary "so that it may not seem like a diary but an inner monologue, a series of free associations accompanying the life of several characters" (V, 38). As the persona finds herself continually frustrated in her attempt to be an accepted fiction writer, the idea of capitalizing on the diary seems increasingly attractive. She writes to Maxwell Geismar, a critic with whom she maintained a most ambivalent friendship, asserting her commitment to the diary.

> I don't need to be published. I only need to continue my personal
> life, so beautiful and in full bloom, and to do my major work, which
> is the diary. I merely forgot for a few years what I had set out to
> do.... I have settled down to fill out, round out the diary. I am at
> work now on what I call the volume of superimpositions, which
> means that while I copy out volume 60, I write about the develop-
> ments and conclusions which took place twenty years later. It all
> falls into place. It is a valuable contribution to the faith in the Freu-
> dian system. It can wait for publication.   (V, 217)

The tension evident here, between her quiet commitment and faith on the
one hand, and her urge to press the diary into publication on the other hand,
seems to resolve itself in the narrator's mind, however, when she declares: "I
think what I should do is devote the rest of my time to preparing diaries for
publication, no more novels" (V, 237); but even in the life of the narrator it
was to be eleven years and two novels later before the *Diary* came to be published.

To suggest that the writing of the diary – or the preparation of the diary
for publication – emerges as the narrator's chief preoccupation in Volume V
would be untrue, but one can see the shift in direction clearly enough, from
novel writing and publishing toward diary writing, editing, and success. The
intensity of the pain that the persona (and Nin, the author) felt at the hands
of the critics was considerable, particularly in retrospect. The reader's knowledge that the venture to publish the *Diary* – the very book the reader is
reading – would turn out to be a huge success helps to give this fragmentary
volume a unity of concept and emotion. It does all fall into place, just as does
a drama that we have seen performed before, knowing the pain and pleasure
which will develop the plot.

The sixth volume of the *Diary*, covering the years 1955-1966, contains
more pages, deals with more years, and has far more balance and structure
than earlier volumes. Some will say that it cannot rival the first two contributions to the series, which detail Nin's relations with her literary associates in
Paris; and yet Volume VI brings to the reader a narrator who is more open
and relaxed than before. "I have decided to retire as the major character of
this diary," she writes (VI, 319), and from that point on it was to be called
Journal des Autres (Diary of Others). That the narrator had been the central character in the first five volumes will be readily acknowledged; that the
persona herself can admit this fact openly in Volume VI is something new.
The openness of the disclosure, however, is characteristic of the tone of the
volume; the persona retires quietly in the background and the mood is at
times relaxed. The narrator does not have to center the attention on herself,
and when she speaks she seems to be candid and confident. The tensions and
conflicts of the past have been resolved, she notes, and she now turns to the

editing and copying of the diary, preparing it for publication. It might be said, in fact, that the diary itself now acquires the centrality and focus which the narrator is willing to abdicate.

Again, it is not that these years are totally dominated by the diary; it is a time when the narrator continues in psychoanalysis and assiduously pursues the composition, publication, and distribution of her fiction. The earlier defensiveness and bitterness have virtually vanished. "My connection with the world broke twice: the first time when my father left me. The second time when America slammed the door on my writing. What I have been busy reconstructing is my bridge to the world" (VI, 121). In 1966, finally, the narrative comes full circle, and the narrator is able to witness her triumph and acceptance in the United States as evidenced by the publication of the first volume of the *Diary*.

To summarize briefly, then, the *Diary*, in all its six volumes, details the movement of its narrator, from her first entrances into serious literary composition, through various successes and failures (of virtually every variety), until she finds the true voice that a readership in the United States wants to hear. The persona, created in many ways as a conventional literary heroine, increases in human qualities approximately midway through the narrative and in the final volume is most humanely realized and most fully human of all; narcissism and self-aggrandizement give way to a more balanced self-portrait, one that admits weaknesses along with strengths. As a character in this drama, the narrator becomes more and more unmasked; but we are never certain whether in the process the author also does or not, and we must not assume that the narrator is ever identical with Nin or an accurate representation of her, were such a representation possible.

The legendary *Diary* has, of course, become famous partly because – ironically as the result of the excellence of Nin's art – the narrator seems so "real": she develops; the complexities and nuances of her feelings are explored, and she finally succeeds in her attempt to arrive at a point in her life where she is both accepted and accepting. But the protagonist of the *Diary* is a literary creation, and our awareness of this fact, far from detracting from the quality, value, and interest of the *Diary*, should serve only to enhance our appreciation of Nin's – the author's – humanism and her powers of articulation.

NOTES

[1]The persona's self-understanding, presented in the guise of self-revelation, is the one technique Nin never quite discovered – or rather, perfected – in her fiction. But in the *Diary* she managed it so skillfully that Leon Edel was lured into describing the work as Nin's way "of giving herself concrete proof of her own existence." See "Life Without Father," *Saturday Review*, 7 May 1966, p. 91.

[2]Compare, for example, an ancient historian such as Thucydides who was unwilling to document an event at which he was eye-witness without corroborating his information with other eye-witnesses.

From *The World of Anais Nin: Critical and Cultural Perspectives*, ed. Evelyn J. Hinz. A Special Issue of *Mosaic* 11.2 (Winter 1978): 9-19.

Truth and Artistry in the
Diary of Anais Nin
Joan Bobbitt (McLaughlin)

Since I urge spontaneity, improvisation, free association, it would be a contradiction to say I have a plan, a conscious structure. (IV, 150)[1]

I never generalize, intellectualize. I see, I hear, I feel. These are my primitive instruments of discovery. (IV, 153)

Beginning with the publication of Volume One in 1966, the *Diary of Anais Nin* has inspired both popular and critical effusion. Nin offers the story of her life as a celebration of subjectivity and feeling, a self-proclaimed paean to unfettered emotion. From all indications, she has been accepted at her word. Critics have called the multi-volume work "a continuous moment of intimacy,"[2] as well as "an attempt to give a visible shape and embodiment to human love."[3] The author herself has been heralded as "the closest thing we have to Venus"[4] and "a high priestess in the House of Erotica."[5] Upon close examination, however, the *Diary* reveals a determined and self-conscious design and content, a calculated artistry which is in direct opposition to Nin's espoused ideal of naturalness and spontaneity.

Superficially, the world of the *Diary* meets the requirements which Nin sets for herself. Within its confines may be found a Lawrentian haven where the phoenix is constantly born anew. Instinct and intuition are properly lauded, and a premium is placed on love and relationships. Individuals are judged by whether they are alive or dead-in-life, and the word "fecund" and its various forms sound through the volumes like a battle cry. Indeed these ideas emerge in the *Diary* as literary themes, recurring and developing with a consistency and predictability ungovernable by mere chance.

Several critics have observed this literary quality in Nin's diaries, noting in particular the similarity between her fiction and nonfiction. Anna Balakian's remark that "at times one has the feeling that the diary has literary structure as much and even more than the novel"[6] is a typical response to this similarity. Such recognition, however, rarely moves beyond the presence of these literary devices to explore their reason for being. Though critics acknowledge that they are remarkable, they generally credit these techniques to coincidence rather than conscious plan. When Diane Wakoski comments facetiously that "there are times reading Anais Nin's diaries when I think she invented them and her whole life,"[7] she is actually closer to the truth. For in fact, the world of the diaries is a carefully contrived and beautifully synchronized artistic creation, a world fashioned and executed by Anais Nin.

At the center of this world is the self Nin devises as persona, the divine artificer who determines its laws. Duane Schneider argues persuasively that we must recognize the character of Anais Nin "as the artist's conception of herself."[8] Though the diaries are ostensibly about the evolution of the personality, its development through flux, the character which emerges is remarkably static. While the first six diaries cover thirty-five years of her life, Nin never ages. The description of the young woman of twenty-eight who lives at Louveciennes is virtually indistinguishable from the mature woman of sixty-three who rejoices over the publication of the very diary which chronicles the earlier period. As Ellen P. Killoh observes in her article, "The Woman Writer and the Element of Destruction," "there is much talk about demons and destructiveness but one never really hears them."[9] Robert Zaller points out that "one is almost tempted to think that something told so well could never have been so difficult to live."[10] Indeed, the presence of Nin's personality and the life she leads is perfectly attuned to the ideals she has taken as her maxim. As Nin appears alternately as woman, friend, muse, and artist, she plays her parts flawlessly and predictably. Killoh points out the "emotional distance of the voice which seems to be putting the *Diary* persona through its paces," a voice always "calm, in control."[11] What that voice reveals is Anais Nin as she exists in her own imagination, a woman of many dimensions which fuse to form a completeness of character rarely achieved in reality.

Such observations raise some interesting questions about the exact nature of Nin's work. The facts concerning its inception are well-known. Begun when she was thirteen years old as a personal letter to the father who deserted her, the diary became a necessary part of Nin's existence, eventually growing to more than fifteen thousand pages. The six volumes published during Nin's lifetime contain more than nineteen hundred pages and span the years from 1931 to 1966. As such, it rivals the scope – and complexity – of the most famous diaries in the English language. But is it truly a diary? Critics have searched for an appropriate description of this unusual work. Lynn Bloom and Orlee Holder contend that the work is "actually a hybrid form, alternately functioning as diary, writer's notebook, and autobiography."[12] Pointing to the fictional elements that characterize it, Duane Schneider argues that Nin's diary represents the birth of a new literary form which he calls the journal-novel.[13] Stephanie A. Demetrakopoulas, recognizing the critical difficulty of dealing with "edited versions of original entries," places the diary "in a category of its own."[14]

Granting the difficulty of finding an accurate label, the real question seems to be one of artistic truthfulness, whether the substance of the *Diary* is compatible with the ideal which Nin espouses. Is her work in fact what she presents it as being? In *Design and Truth in Autobiography*, Roy Pascal observes that "when these most private forms (the diary and the journal) are consciously composed as art, which means as something to be communicated, they undergo a somewhat disconcerting metamorphosis."[15] If they are true to their nature, they cannot be "systematically retrospective" or, in Nin's case, viewed as publishable material even as they are being written. The published diaries clearly reveal that quite early Nin conceived of them as something other than ordinary records. In Volume One, she mentions employing a typist to help with the seemingly overwhelming task of making copies of the diaries which she stores in an iron box. By the second volume, the originals have been transferred to a bank vault, and Nin is already working at editing and rewriting earlier diaries, even as she is writing new ones. It is at this point that she first considers showing them to a literary agent and refers to the possibility of having the diaries published. Volume Four contains a letter from Henry Miller describing his efforts to get her diary "launched," and despite her ostensible doubts, Nin has obviously come to regard public acceptance as a desirable end. Clearly, the diaries are not the "untransformed, untransposed, untransmuted material" (VI, 299) which Nin claims them to be. The question of whether they served a therapeutic function, indeed whether she came to accept them as truth, is not within the realm of this study. The "significant fact," as Henry Miller points out, is that the *Diary* was begun in artistic fashion, "as something to influence some one else."[16] In Nin's hands, the diary becomes an art form, with a structure and language "as exacting as other literary forms."[17] Not only does it resemble fiction, it *is* fiction.

That Nin consciously contrived the *Diary* as art should be beyond question. By her own admission, the *Diary* is a country over which she alone reigns. When she is writing in it, she feels "joy at the realization that this is not a sketchbook but a tapestry, a fresco being completed" (III, 173). She is not content to record, but wants "to fill in, transform, project, expand, deepen. . . ." Nothing less than "the ultimate flowering that comes of creation" (II, 110) will satisfy her. Yet the *Diary* presents artistic problems as well. The mechanics for converting the work into "a Joycean flow of inner consciousness" (V, 38) elude her. Though Oliver Evans sees the *Diary* as a "vast and rather formless accumulation"[18] and Lynn Z. Bloom and Orlee Holder deny that she imposes "any artificial structure on the material,"[19] the *Diary* itself reveals Nin's struggle to affect naturalness as she gives artistic shape. She writes of "the conflict of making a riverbed for the flow of the diary so that it may not seem like a diary but an inner monologue, a series of free associations accompanying the life of several characters" (V, 38). Among these characters are Henry Miller and Gonzalo More, not just Lawrentian figures, but subjects for Nin's art. In Volume One, she discusses her habit of recording their words in the *Diary* "almost while people are talking" (I, 155), and later "fill[ing] in, round[ing] out the portraits" (VI, 36). By Volume Six, she acknowledges that she views "the personages in the diary as 'characters,' " and in an interview confesses that her concern over completeness of characterization led to gentle ribbing by her friends that she was writing fiction.[20] She consistently uses "characters" and scenes from the diaries in her fiction and at one point actually considers converting the diary "into a long novel" (IV, 25). Though she abandons the idea, she nonetheless feels the need "to wind up with some sort of climax" (VI, 30) at the end of each volume. She still assigns titles which correspond to the main theme of each manuscript. By imposing the standards of art on life, however, Nin sacrifices her credibility as a diarist.

In *Autobiographical Acts*, Elizabeth W. Bruss argues that the autobiographical writer has certain responsibilities to his or her readers. The author determines the game, sets up the ground rules, but in doing so, raises specific expectations in the reader, and is committed to fulfilling them. The audience must be convinced of the integrity and sincerity of the author or the necessary bond between writer and reader is broken.[21] It is here that the differences between Nin's stated artistic intentions and the reality of her creation prove irreconcilable. The truth of art is not always the same as the truth of life, and Nin promises the truth of life. She professes that sincerity is the very essence of her diary: "I had put my most natural, most truthful writing in it" (VI, 379). Commenting on her method, she insisted that spontaneity and the preservation of authenticity were her chief concerns.[22] To achieve these ends, she found it necessary to record her impressions at the moment. Memory itself was suspect because it "interfered and intercepted and distorted experience," rearranging and reordering in terms of the present.[23] In several personal interviews, Nin goes so far as to deny having rewritten or polished, though evidence from the diaries themselves clearly proves the opposite.[24] Only the recently published *Linotte: The Early Diary of Anais Nin* escapes her systematic rewriting and editing. Needing to ensure the illusion of spontaneity even for herself, Nin steadfastly contends that her *Diary* is not in any sense an "artificial creation."[25]

Nonetheless, the reader is left with more questions than answers. Schneider observes that "the *Diary* leaves out, it seems, as much as it contains."[26] Though Nin assures us that she is "more interested in human beings than in writing, more interested in lovemaking than in writing, more interested in living than in writing" (IV, 177), we actually learn very little about the things which are a basic part of any human life, much less a life based on openness and naturalness. Although she talks about psychological changes, nowhere does she tell her own feelings. Though she lauds physicality, the *Diary* is strangely devoid of sexuality. Harriet Zinnes contends that Nin "knows no taboos, yet there is nothing unlovely in her relation of the crudest moments."[27] Actually, there are no crude moments in the work, and the few references to sex which do occur are so generalized as to be totally impersonal. (Such omissions are particularly curious, given the fact that the *Diary*

contains a number of the erotic stories which are included in *Delta of Venus*.)
While Paul Grimley Kuntz argues that Nin "makes public the most private
aspects of her consciousness,"[28] she nevertheless refuses to acknowledge
personally the very subjectivity and sensuality which she celebrates in theory.
Considering the nature of these omissions, Nin's insistence that the diary is
edited "only in leaving *out* certain things but not in *changing* anything"[29]
seems little more than semantic equivocation.

This fact is immediately evident in *Diary I* where Nin appears as a
grown woman without a past except for stories which embellish the myth of
her abandonment by a prodigal father. Near the end of the volume, Nin announces that she is pregnant, only several days before she is delivered of a
stillborn daughter. The conception appears to have been miraculous for there
is no mention of a husband or lover. Neither the physical nor psychological
effects of the pregnancy are discussed, an equally inexplicable omission. Regardless of a woman's attitude toward her pregnancy, it is hardly a condition
which can be overlooked. Given Nin's pretensions to the role of earth mother, this omission is particularly startling and incongruous. Yet Nin chooses to
ignore this very powerful feminine experience at the same time that she presents herself as an archetypal woman. The birth itself is described in the diary
and later becomes the subject of a short story. However, its significance is
mythological, stripped of ordinary human connotations, and Nin's true feelings about the death of her daughter are never revealed. Shortly after, she is
receiving friends and worrying about her appearance. The entry one month
later details her activities in Paris, and Nin's "illness" quickly becomes a part
of the past.

The father of the child remains a mystery. Whether he is among the
friends who visit Nin in the hospital the reader is not told. Nin claims exclusive rights to the baby, and the loss is hers alone. Early in Volume Two, however, she refers casually to a trip which she and her husband took with Rebecca West. The reference is brief, and he is not mentioned again until the
end of the volume. At that point, World War II threatens, and the husband is
ordered back to the United States. Volume Two concludes with their departure, and Nin's husband disappears permanently from the diaries.

The true nature of their relationship is never made clear, and Nin's feelings about her marriage, indeed the marriage itself, is excised from the *Diary*. The identity of Nin's husband, though obviously known to her friends, is
not revealed, nor is that information included in most standard biographical
sources. Scholarly criticism of the *Diary* generally fails to broach this subject,
though several critics have registered either irritation or amazement at the
exclusion of such vital facts.

Yet such information is essential to any thorough critical evaluation of
the *Diary*. The fact of Nin's marriage to Ian Hugo, also known as Hugh P.
Guiler, a New York stockbroker, necessitates a different view of the work.[30]
In effect, the life contained there is not honestly presented. That Nin married
at twenty and remained so throughout her life is a clear indication that hers

was a life shared, not a life alone, as the volumes suggest. The trips taken, the parties given, the places lived in, were not Nin's exclusive possessions or creations. Though the name Ian Hugo is mentioned in the *Diary*, he is not actively present. No exchanges take place between them, although Hugo does the engravings for several of Nin's books, and she offers purportedly unbiased critical praise for a number of his films. At least one of these films she herself stars in, though that fact is not mentioned either. Ultimately, Ian Hugo is indistinguishable from anyone else in her artistic coterie, and nowhere does Nin identify him as her husband.

Though she has chosen not to play the part of the wife in the *Diary*, Nin does present herself as a self-sacrificing friend and savior, and here too her credibility is called into question. The reader can only guess what part Hugo played in Nin's dealings with others. The presence of a supportive, supporting husband would help to explain how Nin, amid her alleged poverty, managed to travel extensively, discard clothes at will, live in romantic surroundings, and still play the bountiful giver. With some reluctance, Nin later admitted to an interviewer that she was indeed financially dependent during the time she spent in Paris, the period of her greatest generosity.[31] Though she takes credit for it in the *Diary*, obviously the generosity was not hers alone. Yet the existence of Ian Hugo does little to clarify the exact nature of Nin's many relationships, already a critical puzzle. The response of the *Times Literary Supplement* reviewer in his appraisal of *Diary IV* is most apt: "What on earth, one cannot help wondering, was going on behind the scenes of intimate little dramas which she presents to us?"[32] Finally, such questions remain unanswered. If anything, they are further obfuscated by the fact of Nin's marriage.

The explanation of these omissions is that they are necessary to ensure the privacy of the individuals involved, including Nin's husband. Yet Nin's consistent refusal to discuss personal matters, indeed her suggestion that such concern is nothing more than jaded curiosity, would be understandable if she published any other kind of work. But she chose to publish her diary, a work which she celebrates for its frankness. In doing so, she tacitly consented to make her private life public. Consequently, critical interest in that life does not constitute a violation of privacy nor should it be construed as disrespect for those involved. That she should want to publish her personal diary itself raises some interesting psychological questions, but the primary consideration here is whether in doing so Nin is a poseur, offering fabrication and evasion in the name of truth.

According to the symbolic nightmare which she describes in Volume Six, Nin agonized over the question of publication and its effect on the people closest to her. Purportedly, she solved the dilemma by allowing each individual to decide whether he or she wished to be included in the *Diary*. In Volume Six, she writes of her efforts to obtain permissions from "the main personages," noting that no one quarreled with "the essence of the portraits" (VI, 365). Yet her fear of public exposure is belied by her obvious grooming of the work for just that purpose. Similarly, her stated concern for others is hardly evident in the portraits which finally appear in the *Diary*. It is doubtful that many of those depicted, among them notable figures such as Edmund Wilson and Gore Vidal, would have willingly chosen to appear in such an unflattering light. It is not possible to know how much was left out in the final versions which were edited by both Gunther Stuhlmann and Nin, but it seems likely that certain portraits were retained because they enhanced the artistic flavor and hence the commercial appeal of each volume. Admittedly, Nin's friends included some of the most notable names of the time, but it is design, not chance, that their stories, rather than those of lesser figures, should appear in the *Diary*. *Diary VI*, published in 1976, covers the period to 1966, shortly after the appearance of *Diary I* in print. Thus all of the following volumes were revised, rewritten, and edited with the successful publication of *Diary I* an established fact. At the time of her death in 1977, Nin had begun editing Volume Seven, then scheduled for publication in the fall of 1978. This means that the initial entries for those years since 1966 were made with the knowledge that eventual publication was virtually guaranteed. If artistic control was a basic element of preceding volumes, how much more would this be true of any impending diary? Each of Nin's friends and acquaintances during that time would truly become actors in her ongoing drama. More than ever before, Nin would have the power to direct, even to live, her life as she would wish to see it in print.

Nin recognized the problem of continuing to present the *Diary* as a spontaneous, unpremeditated piece of writing. Indeed Volume Seven, as she conceived of it, would concern itself primarily with "the exchange of letters and diaries with other women."[33] In a sense, the *Diary* does end with publication, with the very exposure which she purportedly feared. Even expanded versions of earlier diaries, should they appear, could not alter, even if they challenge, the picture which Nin has chosen to present as truth. As the story of a life, Nin's *Diary* is essentially complete in six volumes, and it is on this basis that it must be judged.

Volume Seven, published in 1980 and edited by Gunther Stuhlmann, must be viewed in the light of this fact. In their recent work, *Anais Nin: An Introduction*, Benjamin Franklin V and Duane Schneider point to the critical necessity of knowing the editorial method of the first six volumes. What principles of selection were used? Which materials were rearranged?[34] Such information is even more important to our understanding of Volume Seven. In general, the final published diary follows the same format as earlier ones. Nin again affirms her basic honesty and openness as an autobiographer: " 'I am a camera.' You, the reader, have the right to know the brand, range, quality of the diarist-camera" (VII, 108). Interestingly, Stuhlmann tries to confront some of the critical objections to previous diaries by including sections where Nin defends the omissions and endeavors to dispel what she sees as damaging "myths" about her. However, much of what she says is repetition, and her evasive attempts at explanation merely call attention to the still problematic nature of the work. Indeed Nin's life in the present is consumed by diaries past and future. The diary itself becomes the subject of the *Diary*: "I file interviews, a box for each country. I have various states of edited Diary, first version, second version, fan letters. I bind the 1970 Diary. File photographs and notes for future diaries" (VII, 169). Appropriately, she likens herself to a seamstress saving bits of textiles (VII, 308). However, the fabric which she has woven (and rewoven) is nearing completion. Volume Seven only extends through 1974 and concludes with a description of her fairytale trip to Bali, an ending which she specifically selected and tailored for that purpose. At Nin's own request, the diaries which chronicle the final two years of her life and her bout with terminal cancer will not be published.[35]

Yet what do we finally know of that life? Elizabeth W. Bruss points out that by definition any autobiographical writing must coalesce in the shape of "a personality, a self, an identity; it must have, as Blake might say, 'a human face.' "[36] At the end of the diaries, however, the real Anais Nin remains elusive. Though she exalts openness, she excises from her work everything humanly important, everything that does not affirm her masks and personal fictions. While she offers her self, she presents only a metaphor of self. Ultimately, emotion is reduced to a mere artifact, and reality becomes indistinguishable from artistic creation.

NOTES

[1]Anais Nin, *The Diary of Anais Nin, 1944-1947*, IV (Harcourt Brace Jovanovich, 1971. Subsequent references to *Diary* volumes are included in the text.

[2]Deena Metzger, "The *Diary* and the Ceremony of Knowing" in Robert Zaller, ed., *A Casebook on Anais Nin* (New American Library, 1974), p. 133.

[3]Orville Clark, "Anais Nin: Studies in the New Erotology," in Zaller, p. 110.

[4]Diane Wakoski, "A Tribute to Anais Nin," in Zaller, p. 152.

[5]Clark, p. 111.

[6]Anna Balakian, "The Poetic Reality of Anais Nin," in Zaller, p. 116.

[7]Wakoski, p. 148.

[8]Duane Schneider, "The Art of Anais Nin," in Zaller, p. 50.

[9]Ellen P. Killoh, "The Woman Writer and the Element of Destruction," *College English* 34(1972): 37.

[10]Robert Zaller, "Anais Nin and the Truth of Feeling," in Zaller, p. 182.

[11]Killoh, p. 37.

[12]Lynn Z. Bloom and Orlee Holder, "Anais Nin's *Diary* in Context," *Mosaic* 11.2 (1978): 197.

[13]Duane Schneider, "Anais Nin in the *Diary*: The Creation and Development of a Persona," *Mosaic* 11.2 (1978): 10.

[14]Stephanie A. Demetrakopoulas, "Archetypal Constellations of Feminine Consciousness in Nin's Diary," *Mosaic* 11.2 (1978): 122.

[15]Roy Pascal, *Design and Truth in Autobiography* (Harvard University Press, 1960), p. 3.

[16]Henry Miller, "Un Etre Etoilique," in Zaller, p. 9.

[17]Miller, p. 6.

[18]Oliver Evans, *Anais Nin* (Southern Illinois University Press, 1968), p. 3.

[19]Bloom and Holder, p. 202.

[20]Barbara Freeman, "A Dialogue with Anais Nin," *Chicago Review* 24 (1972): 33.

[21]Elizabeth W. Bruss, *Autobiographical Acts: The Changing Situation of a Literary Genre* (Johns Hopkins University Press, 1976), p. 11.

[22]Anais Nin, *A Woman Speaks: The Lectures, Seminars, and Interviews of Anais Nin*, ed. Evelyn J. Hinz (Swallow Press, 1975), p. 171.

[23]Nin, *A Woman Speaks*, p. 153.

[24]Nin, *A Woman Speaks*, p. 171.

[25]Nin, *A Woman Speaks*, p. 179.

[26]Schneider, "Anais Nin in the *Diary*," p. 12.

[27]Harriet Zinnes, "The Fiction of Anais Nin," in Zaller, p. 36.

[28]Paul Grimley Kuntz, "Art as Public Dream: The Practice and Theory of Anais Nin," in Zaller, p. 95.

[29]Nin, *A Woman Speaks*, p. 179.

[30]*New York Times*, 16 January 1977, Sec. 1, p. 28, col. 1.

[31]Nin, *A Woman Speaks*, p. 104.

[32]Review of *The Diary of Anais Nin, 1944-1947*, IV, by Anais Nin, *Times Literary Supplement*, 12 May 1971, p. 553.

[33]Anais Nin, *In Favor of the Sensitive Man and Other Essays* (Harcourt Brace Jovanovich, 1976), p. 82.

[34]Benjamin Franklin, V, and Duane Schneider, *Anais Nin: An Introduction* (Ohio University Press), 1979), p. 170.

[35]Gunther Stuhlmann, Preface to *The Diary of Anais Nin, 1966-1974*, VII, p. vi.

[36]Bruss, p. 12.

From *The Journal of Modern Literature* 9.2 (May 1982): 267-76.

Dropping Another Veil:
Anais Nin's *Henry and June*

Philip K. Jason

With the appearance of *Henry and June* (New York: Harcourt Brace Jovanovich, 1986), the students of Anais Nin's life and work are forced to make serious readjustments. This volume brings the sequence of publications drawn from Nin's diaries into what we might call its "second series," the new title dealing with approximately half of the time period covered in the first volume: *The Diary of Anais Nin: 1931-1934* (New York: HBJ, 1966). In the intervening years, there appeared six more volumes of *Diary*, tracing Nin's life into 1974, and then four volumes of *The Early Diary of Anais Nin* which reached back to 1914 and left us once again in 1931.

Though the cycle was complete, the *Early Diary* volumes had begun to change our way of looking at Nin, in part because they were edited differently from the volumes that had been published earlier about her later life. The *Early Diary* seemed more deeply textured, more spontaneous, and more artistically innocent. People not treated or named in the 1931-1974 coverage were now put center stage, including Nin's cousin, Eduardo, and her husband, Hugh Guiler.

A number of things happened to account for the differences between these subsets of the first cycle. First of all, Nin's death early in 1977, and perhaps the period of illness leading up to it, removed the author's own hand from the editorial process. Secondly, the *Diary* volumes for 1955-1966 (no. 6, published in 1976) and 1966-1974 (no. 7, published in 1980) no longer were the product of the same dedicated diarist who had written the material on which the earlier diaries were based. In fact, beginning with *Diary* 5, we see a shift in Nin's attention so that the published diaries following the mid-forties, the period during which she is most successfully engrossed as a published writer of fiction and as a public personality, can cover eight, eleven, and eight years in single volumes – much greater gulps of time than in volumes drawn from earlier periods in Nin's life. Even so, a reticence about personal relationships continued through these volumes, a reticence refreshingly absent from the four volumes of the *Early Diary*.

In an "editor's note" to *Linotte: The Early Diary of Anais Nin, 1914-1920* (1980, but seemingly prepared by 1978), John Ferrone writes, "This is the first volume of Anais Nin's diary to be published essentially in the form in which it was written." There is some qualification to that claim, but any reader can sense the difference. As we follow the maturing young woman from this volume through the next three of the *Early Diary*, all of these with prefaces by Nin's brother, Joaquin Nin-Culmell, we can only wish that Nin's often stated aversion to mere facts had not been so severe. The fullness and candor of these volumes underscored the questions that had been nagging at readers of the *Diary* volumes from the beginning: (1) what is being left out, and (2) how do these omissions falsify portraits of the self and the others?

Readers were told, from the beginning, about omissions in deference to those who wished to guard their privacy. Perhaps, too, potential legal problems were avoided by bringing only carefully selected material to press. Still, the images of Nin and her world that were created in the published *Diary* volumes were taken as truthful, reliable images in which incidentals had been stripped out. Why should anyone quibble over the fact that Nin could present the truth of her life without mentioning her husband? In fact, few did quibble, charmed by what *was* given and revealed . . . for all autobiographical writings come to us as revelations.

Henry and June, billed as "from the Unexpurgated Diary," is definitely a revelation. In it, Nin's complex emotional and sexual life is presented vividly, insistently, and almost exclusively. Her grand passion for Henry Miller, a passion returned by Miller and fulfilled over and over again, is set against the more tender and more steady affections she felt for her husband. A complicating attraction to June Miller makes Anais both Henry's rival and his lover, and June's instinctive eroticism becomes a willed ideal for the formerly repressed Anais who, in her late twenties, awakens to the force of her own sexual appetites and energy.

The story is kept in narrow focus: Anais, Henry, June, and Hugh – who is kept in the dark about what's going on. Nin's feeling of compartmentalization, of multiple selves – a theme in all of her writings – is here given an almost clinical elaboration. How different is *this* Anais Nin from the one we met twenty years earlier in *Diary* volume one? To judge by behavior, quite different. Is one more authentic? Well, that depends. Here are some impressions.

The Anais Nin of *Diary 1* comes across as a rather cautious explorer of relationships. She is always trying to size people up, testing the waters of potential involvements to guard against getting in over her head. Indeed, the famous portraits in this diary are as much judgments as anything else, as the budding writer is at pains to measure herself against her new acquaintances. This tendency toward being judgmental is one of Nin's least attractive traits, though she seems unaware of it. She remains demure, somehow reserved, even as she adventures into the more bohemian aspects of Paris life. Her treatment of her relationship with Miller is, of course, what must be examined in order to make comparisons with the new revelations of *Henry and June*.

In *Diary 1*, Miller is a diamond in the rough . . . a coarse genius to be nurtured and possibly refined. He is presented as an artistic type more than as a masculine force. Henry's painful relationship with June is examined from a caring but still relatively detached perspective: Nin seems, in the sections of the diary prepared for print, to be exercising control, seeing things clinically. Though there are signs of her discomfort and instability, she more often comes across as a woman who laments about insecurity while all the time directing the well-diagrammed traffic of her own life and the lives of those around her. We are let in on the magnitude of passion driving Henry and June, often destructively, but Nin's own passions are treated more abstractly.

Henry and June turns all this upside down. Now Nin is swept away in tides of passion, hardly able to comprehend the nature and dimensions of her newly-released sexual self. She is a woman cheating on her gentle, attentive husband – and working hard to find convincing rationalizations for her behavior. Henry's complexity is more richly presented now, though his artistic self takes second place to his Priapic self: he, while often acting like an unworthy pilgrim at some kind of aristocratic shrine, initiates Nin into the truths of her own body. The moments of guilt recorded in *H & J* seem genuine, as do the ongoing betrayals and self-justifications. Nin is attractively smudged, roughed up, in this newly released material. No longer uniquely the giver, she is taking from Henry even while she works to please him. And she is taking from Hugh, too, even while she worries herself over homemaking duties.

H & J enriches our understanding of the personal dynamics underlying Nin's fiction. From the material presented in *Diary 1*, it was always easy to identify the fictional Djuna as Nin's main surrogate, the female personality closest to herself. Djuna had mind: understanding, cool judgment, maturity. The Anais of *H & J* is more like the fiery Sabina: uncentered, lusty, and imprudent. Earlier readings of the fiction and diaries together invariably concluded that Sabina was, in large part, a portrait of June. Given the additional material on June in *H & J*, this identification still makes sense; however, the new portrait of Nin's own restlessness suggests that Sabina is more of a composite. *H & J* opens up new possibilities for exploring the relationship between the diaries and the fiction. More important for the present are the new opportunities for finding the elusive Anais Nin.

In that quest, neither volume is satisfactory. One does not balance or sufficiently complicate the other when they are read as separate entities. The present volume, with its narrow focus and somewhat surprising revelations, can be enjoyed as a "work" in itself, but it is difficult to say whose work it is or what it represents. And, because it collects and orchestrates *content* omissions from *Diary 1*, *Henry and June* renders that volume incomplete and – more important – distorted. Appearing twenty years apart, these treatments of 1931-32 will find different readers, as well as readers who have lived with one set of impressions for two decades and now have different ones to contend with. Some of these readers will feel cheated. Are these volumes only publishing enterprises, business deals, with little concern for communicating the essential pattern of Nin's manuscript diaries?

A more generous response is that we are getting now what only now it is possible to get, and the same was true when *Diary 1* appeared. Still, reading the volumes consecutively or even side-by-side, weaving back and forth between entries written about the same time, does not give readers the texture of the source or of the evolving Anais we are always seeking. There is no way to put the pieces together again. The game of hide and seek, a psychic pattern always present in either volume (and anywhere else we might look in Nin's work) has been magnified by the way in which the diary material has reached the public.

Which is all to say that we have to take these carvings from Nin's diaries on their own terms and not confuse them with either the manuscript material or the life that is being, somehow, given a testimony. We have been offered a startling instance of the distance between art and life, even when the art is the art of the diarist. The Anais who is randy for Henry and June, remorseful and defiant, troubled and ecstatic, is an Anais who had been obscured by the cool, powdered shell of delicacy and decorum – the *tonal* Nin of *Diary 1*. And didn't Nin's readers always know that something was being held back – that the restraint of the published diary volumes didn't reveal the sources of feeling released in the fiction? Many can now say, "I knew it all the time."

It is much clearer now why psychoanalysis became important to Nin. The ways in which she was pulled apart by conflicting needs and desires – the extremes and intensities of those conflicts – are more understandable now that we have *Henry and June*. The polarities of Nin's early *House of Incest*, as well as Miller's particular interest in that work, are "explained" by revelations in *H & J*. What few readers know is that much of this story had been told long ago, although only a handful of Nin scholars are familiar with the long abandoned fiction drawn from the same material that we are now able to explore.

In 1939, when Nin published the first (Paris) version of *Winter of Artifice*, the collection included a story entitled "Djuna" that thinly disguised the relationship between Henry, June and Anais given in part in *Diary 1* and more fully in *H & J*. Never reprinted, the story shows the impact of this triangular relationship on Nin at a time when she was making the transition from diarist to fiction writer.[*] It is one of many examples of how diary materials that had been suppressed in the published versions found their way into Nin's fictions. Elsewhere, I have written about how Nin's relationship with Otto Rank is more intimately revealed in her story "The Voice" than it is in the published account of *Diary 1* and *Diary 2* (see "The Princess and the Frog" in *Anais, Art, and Arts*, ed. Sharon Spencer, Penkevill Press, 1986). In addition, the portrait of Hugh that appears in *H & J* as well as in the volumes 3 and 4 of *Early Diary* confirms everyone's suspicion that the betrayed "Alan" of *A Spy in the House of Love* gave us glimpses of the Hugh

Guiler (or Ian Hugo) missing from the diary volumes published in the 1960s and 1970s.

Ironically, the most intimate parts of Nin's life were, until now, more fully revealed in her fiction than in the published diaries. Of course, it is impossible to make air-tight cases for turning all of her fictions into *romans a clef*; still, Nin's tendency to protect people in her diary volumes and exploit them for artistic purposes is a bit bewildering. Certainly those people knew who they were, and anyone with imagination and curiosity could make safe guesses. Hugh Guiler is only now, after his death, embarrassed by name, but what did he make of his earlier portrait as "Alan"?

The tension between revealing and veiling is one of the most powerful factors in Nin's work. Not only is it a theme or motif in many diary passages and many stories and novels, but it is the theme of her career as a woman relating to others through words: the theme of her public self, then, as well as her private self. The Anais of *Henry and June* was revealed, no doubt, to privileged readers long ago. Now, the wider world that knows her through her writings has, through Rupert Pole's selection of these formerly suppressed diary materials, an erotically unveiled Anais to contend with. For those who will make *Henry and June* the first of Nin's writings that they experience, the impression will be powerful and seemingly cohesive and total. They will be seduced into taking the part for the whole. From them, as from the rest of us, much still remains veiled. Much will always remain veiled.

Nevertheless, between its own covers *Henry and June* is a remarkable book: fresh, gripping, and pulsing with life. It has none of the studied quality that too often dulls the impact of some of the previously published diary materials. And, because it tells such a sharply focused story, *H & J* has a unity lacking even in Nin's best long fiction. In fact, it could easily be passed off as a work of fiction.

It's a great story, unveiling an Anais at the peak of her adventurousness, her creativity, and her sense of freedom. Her relationship with Henry, though not idyllic, was thoroughgoing in scope and intensity. And Anais, so shaken by what she felt and did, was as *out of herself* as she would ever be. This was her grandest passion, and this record of it is among her grandest achievements – if not for style than for sheer immediacy and power. Her unwillingness to abandon Hugo at this time changed the direction of her life and Miller's. The heat of their constrained, furtive affair was incendiary; the art of each begun during this period was rarely surpassed in their later careers. They were under each other's spell: soulmates, fleshmates, unique contributors to one another's very different paths as writers. They were almost collaborators in art, as they were in life.

Nin's meditations on types of love and types of faithfulness respond to her feelings for a large cast of characters. Her cousin Eduardo is still a player in Nin's complex emotional life. Her analyst, Dr. Allendy, is an adventure waiting to happen. Memories of John Erskine bubble up. The tempestuous, destructive June and the passive, supportive Hugo – both of whom undergo significant changes in the course of the year – are layered into the complex equation of Nin's and Miller's expanding identities. But in this torrid year, Anais and Henry recreated themselves and one another. Because he had the courage to treat Anais as a strong woman rather than as a childlike, frail decoration, Henry liberated the woman who was there and exiled the adolescent. Because he took her seriously as a fellow artist, Henry won her as no one had before or would again.

Though it took Nin a while to be sure of it, her diary writing was her major literary achievement. *Henry and June* confirms this, even while it further complicates those questions of the "whole truth" and of literary genre. Until quite recently, we have had very little of this kind of writing: an intelligent, articulate woman's record of her sexual liberation. And this record of a wild affair of the early 1930s, a record almost totally lacking in references to Paris during the Depression, has an eerie, timeless quality. Lacking the sense of time and place conveyed by details published in *Diary 1*, *Henry and June* has at its core the concreteness of the bodily self. In such a fashion, the second series of Nin's diaries has begun. What's next?

*Editor's Note: This story became once again available in *Anais: An International Journal* 7 (1989): 3-22.

From *Anais: An International Journal* 6 (1988): 27-32.

A Story Never Told Before — Reading the New, Unexpurgated Diaries of Anais Nin

Erica Jong

Anais Nin: the very name conjures exoticism and eroticism. There should be a specific word for this heady combination. In fact there is: her own name, Anais, which has become a perfume, a vast library of books, an almost museum-sized collection of photographs, and of course the archetype of the contemporary writer as woman.

Like any archetype, she is loved and hated – with the *same* evidence being used for each canonization, each attack.

Kate Millet saw Anais Nin as the first portraitist "of the artist as a woman." Millet suggests that "our form is autobiography," and she dubs Nin "A Mother to Us All."

Why are there so few positions in between adoration and detestation? Because Nin is seen as a representative of woman's psychological and sexual freedom. The response to her depends on the reader's degree of liberation. For women who seek freedom – artistically and sexually – she is the pioneer, validating our quest. For women who fear freedom, she becomes the target, evoking a furious response which may be only anger at oneself for being unfree.

To men she is an enigma – seductive to some for her sexual and literary sorcery (which have the same roots and in fact become one). but repellent to others for her manipulativeness, her old-fashioned, nineteenth-century sexual romanticism, and the highfalutin' tone her writing sometimes takes. Since few men have a visceral understanding of the problems women writers face, they may consider Anais Nin's strategies duplicitous, deceptive, seven-veiled.

What *are* the problems a woman writer faces? Let's get this straight, once and for all. Virginia Woolf described them brilliantly in *A Room of One's Own* (1928), but half the world, apparently, hasn't heard.

First, there is the need for privacy and silence – which a woman's life often lacks. If she is a wife or a mother, even the caretaker of a brother, father, mother, aunt or lover, she is assumed to *need* no private time or space. Writing cannot happen in a crowd.

Next, she lacks money to support her for *fulfilling herself* – those few guineas a year Woolf's hypothetical woman writer needed. The guineas are more now, but they are usually earned by giving up time to write. Woolf's hypothetical woman writer had a private income – albeit small. As for husbands, they *used* to support wives, but they supported them on condition of certain services being performed – social, sexual, maternal, culinary. It is the rare husband, even today, who can free his wife from social appointments, family duties, child care, and let her mind fly free. The wife who says "I'm writing. I won't be home for dinner," is often the wife who is about to lose her job. Since men still have a preponderance of the world's money, and women (except for a tiny elite) are dependent on men's attitudes, they must either change their men, tiptoe around them, lie to them, or get divorced and live alone.

These options are more than ever possible today. But a sense of family is hard to lose. Family warmth grounds the dreamer. Men who dream surely need this warmth, and their getting it is not always antithetical to their family affections. Women who dream often have to give it up.

These are only the domestic problems. What if a woman solves them somehow and goes out into the world to present her creative work? She finds that her sex is a built-in bias, that men rule the definitions of prestige, that her gender goes in and out of style every decade or so. In the 70s – in. In the 80s – out. In the 90s – in, for a while, but who knows for how long?

She also faces the Whore/Madonna dichotomy. Women who write about sex are presumed to be whores. (*Good* women write domestic novels, sweeping historical potboilers, romances that make no literary claims, or biographies of historical figures. Good women do not shake the status quo.)

There is, of course, a little room for rebels and renegades – especially if they are dead. Virginia Woolf is safely dead, safely modernist, safely categorized as "Bloomsbury." Gertrude Stein is safely dead, safely modernist, safely categorized as "lesbian." She doesn't shake men up because she's clearly *out* of their domestic and sexual spheres. She need not be judged by the prejudices of heterosexual love. Woolf and Stein are both *sui generis* at last.

But for women who live *in* the world, sleep with men, like their children, and enter into the sexual debate through their books, the reception is much chillier, much more contentious.

Anais Nin knew all these things long before my generation discovered them. She knew she had to survive, find time to write, have money to live, and somehow fulfill her sexual and literary potential. Even though she'd married very young to a man who did not stir her sexually, she loved and needed him. Though she idealized him recklessly, she also knew that unless she was to live only half a life, she would have to perfect deceit. The same holds true for many women today.

Nin had been seduced and abandoned by her father in childhood, then strictly brought up by her all-suffering Catholic mother. She was at first so afraid of sexual love that she married a man who shared her fear, and the marriage, it is said, remained unconsummated for at least two years. He patiently waited for her to blossom, worshipping her as an angel-artist. She also began to write in a melange of languages none of which was wholly hers at first. (Spanish, French, and English warred for hegemony on her tongue.)

So Nin developed various strategies essential to her as a writer/wife. To learn about sexuality without sacrificing her stabilizing marriage, she learned to deceive. It came easily to her because she was expert at deceiving herself. She had blocked all her terrifying sexual memories from childhood.

To write her journals, she fictionalized them, even to herself. To publish her journals, she expurgated them. To be honest to history, she left manuscripts of these secret journals to literary executors who shared her vision; they saw that the journals were published after her death.

Two have so far appeared: *Henry & June* and *Incest*.

I suspect that no married woman writer has ever succeeded as well in sacrificing none of her work. Sylvia Plath's journals and literary remains were partly destroyed. Laura Riding repudiated her early art and hid by changing her name. Virginia Woolf committed suicide in her prime. Jean Rhys stopped writing for decades, sunk in alcoholism. Marina Tsvetayeva, Anna Wickham, Sara Teasdale ended their own lives. Only Anais Nin and Colette went on writing as they ripened and left us all they wished to leave.

But French women don't count. Even in the eighteenth century, they were allowed to be intellectuals while the rest of us were still hiding manuscripts under the embroidery hoop. Colette had a whole tradition to draw upon. Few of us can count on this. Nin presented her expurgated journals to the public in the 1960s and 70s but she left the most stirring stories for after her death. The first, *Henry & June*, appeared in 1986. It stunned with its sharpness, frankness, vividness. Decades after *Tropic of Cancer*, in an age when sex was all but discredited, *Henry & June* still seemed electrifying. It told the story of Anais Nin's love-affair with Henry Miller, beginning with their meeting in October 1931 and ending with Henry Miller's wife June's return to Paris in October 1932.

It chronicles an extraordinary love-triangle between a seductive Miller, his seductive June, and a seductive Nin – a triangle that really becomes a quadrangle if you count Nin's husband Hugo's quiet and half-knowing part in it.

The story *itself* would be seductive, even if the principals were not known:

A beautiful young writer, not yet thirty, is ensconced in the lush suburbs of Paris a few years after the crash of '29. Her banker-husband, who was much richer when she married him, travels a lot leaving her in the fantasy world of her villa, keeping her journal, dreaming of being a member of the bohemian artistic set in Paris. Her father was a celebrated musician who left the family when she was a girl. Her mother, an artist turned drudge. Her husband is her loving protector, but sexually they are incompatible. He longs to be an artist himself, but works at the bank to support her and her whole family, including her disapproving Catholic mother. He is a WASP who went to Columbia and was disinherited for marrying her. Her loves her madly, but he is confused about what he wants to be when he grows up. He is also both sexually repressed and sexually hungry.

One day at lunch with a lawyer she knows through her husband, our heroine meets a bohemian guttersnipe from Brooklyn who is writing the book to end all books, the book to tell what is left out of books. This "Brooklyn boy" is already nearly forty, and he talks as wildly and brilliantly as he writes. He's as much in love with literature, philosophy and D.H. Lawrence as she is. He's vital, animal, fierce, drunk with life. His sexuality is powerful, but, unlike his writing, he is courtly in pursuit.

She finds herself drawn to him, and becomes entangled. Then, suddenly, his wife appears from America.

She is equally fascinating – a vamp, a flapper, a magic talker, a blonde bisexual from Greenwich Village. She also dreams of becoming an artist of some sort.

She and the young writer-wife fall in love, or lust, or sisterhood – or all three at once. The three weave their webs around each other, and around the writer's husband, who comes back to pay the bills and take everyone out to dinner.

The young writer and the Brooklyn wildman analyze both the vamp and the husband, and become passionate lovers in the process. They make love to the vamp (and challenge the husband) through each other. The husband is aroused by all the frenzy in the air, but he doesn't really want to discover why. Even when he comes home to find the Brooklyn wildman in his bed, he is jollied out of seeing what he saw by his magical muse of a wife. As the quadrangle grows hotter, the young writer discovers how to write more vividly, how to make love with her whole self, how to surrender to a man and also to the muse. The Brooklyn guttersnipe is equally inspired. He finishes his fearless book and shows it to his inamorata. It is indeed "the last book" by "the last man alive." With her encouragement he goes in search of a publisher. Then the vamp comes back for the final confrontation.

In this story, who is the muse and who is the creator? The two women vie for the role of muse, and the two men vie for the role of lover. The young writer is sure she has created everyone. The Brooklyn guttersnipe believes that he is the lifeforce. The vamp believes that both writers are stealing her soul. The husband believes he is getting a soul out of all this pain.

It's a hell of a story and Anais Nin tells it fiercely. Her good-girl *pudeur* stripped away, she writes with a burning pen. Her sexuality open, she seduces her husband, her analyst, her lover, her muse, her lover's wife. The story is told with sure, searing strokes, with no flowery prologues or codas.

But *this* story, in *this* form, will go unpublished until after the author's death at seventy-four. She will not publicly humiliate her husband (or else she fears to expose herself), so the version of it that first appears depicts pillow-conversation occurring instead in cafés. No wonder something seems to be missing! No wonder the prose seems vague.

The year after the mad triumph of having written *Henry & June* into her secret Journal, Anais Nin begins to tell another story, the story of her discovery of love, from October 1932 to November 1934. This is released sixty years later as: *Incest, From "A Journal of Love."*

The love in this case is still for Henry Miller (with whom her life and loins are still entwined); with her husband Hugo who has become more sexual; with her first analyst, Dr. René Allendy (whom she once loved but now abandons); her second analyst, Dr. Otto Rank (with whom she is currently entranced); with Antonin Artaud, the actor/poet; and Joaquin Nin, her father, the musician, whom she seduces for revenge for his having seduced and abandoned her in childhood. She triumphs over his Don Juanism with her far stronger impersonation of Donna Juana.

It's a "Journal of Love" unlike any ever published before. It dares to describe the ultimate act of incest. What does she feel? What does he feel? No other writer has dared this much. If Henry Miller wanted to write what was left out of men's books, Anais Nin has succeeded in writing all that has been left out of women's books for centuries.

The central incident in *Incest* (at least in the present retelling of the story) is Anais Nin's seduction of her father (or her father's seduction of her). I notice that our language contains no word for mutual seduction – but it was really that. After much letter-writing, foreplay, many regrets about not having truly known each other as child and parent, the two came together at Valescure-St. Raphael, at the now defunct Coirier's Grand Hotel, each of them temporarily fleeing another life.

They discover how alike they are in their sexual selves. Joaquin Nin y Castellanos discovers his daughter, his double. Anais discovers her father, the myth, as a mere man – a rather rigid, fussy, controlling man, almost fifty-four, who suffers from lumbago and regrets.

Like any father-figure, he seduces her by telling her how his wife failed to understand him – but in this case his wife is her mother!

Like any daughter-figure, she confesses her past, her hurts in childhood, her love-affairs. She is seeking absolution – but in this case he is the *author* of her primal hurts. All the love-affairs have sought in vain to assuage them, but now she has the real thing in her snare.

She confesses that all her journal-writing was for him, that her craft has always been an attempt to bring him back.

He in turn confesses that his whole life has been tainted by his abandonment of her, that he has been seeking her everywhere, in other women, but now he has "found [his] match."

They discover that they both love to go to the same hotel room with other lovers, delighting in duplicity, aroused by the secret knowledge of betrayal. They discover that they are mirrors of each other, the perfect narcissistic love. They are both picaresque heroes, both afraid of intimacy, both flirts and illusionists, who flee. But they cannot flee each other.

Nin's father teaches her her own faults, her own defects of character. She is both attracted and repelled by him.

He confesses: "I don't feel toward you as if you were my daughter."

She confesses: "I don't feel as if you were my father."

And with that (and a little more psychologizing), he kisses her mouth. And then comes "a wave of desire." And then, though she is both "terrified and desirous," she "melts," and he "emptied all of himself in me . . . and my yielding was immense, with my whole being, with only that core of fear which arrested the supreme spasm in me."

She holds back her own orgasm and retreats at once to her room to be alone, feeling "poisoned by this union" She is guilty, but suddenly in possession of some primal mystery. The mistral blows so hard it cracks the windows. She feels humbled and defiled. "The sperm was a poison," she writes in her journal, feeling she has succumbed to "a love that was a poison."

She longs to run away but must know the end of the mystery. So she stays on, succumbing again and again to her father's passion, never having an orgasm, yet being filled with his sperm, so "overabundant" that she walks down the hall to her room "with a handkerchief between [her] legs."

He claims he wants to replace her other lovers, but despite his orgies of repeated penetration, he fears the loss of his *"riquette,"* his virility. He fears that she is young and will abandon him for younger men. He admits jealousy of Hugo, of Henry, of all the letters she receives from them daily. But for all his supposed twinship with Anais, he fails to have an inkling of *her* feelings – her utter confusion and bewilderment, her embodiment of the incest taboo in her failure to find orgasm, her sadness, her remorse. She is *tormented* about lying to everyone to achieve this gloomy union; he fails to understand that, too.

What is remarkable about Anais Nin's telling of the tale is not only the description of physical incest, but the willingness to record all her feelings about it, even before she fully understands them. The taboo is so strong that most women writers have mythicized and disguised these feelings not only in fiction and poetry but also in autobiography. I felt that I was reading a story never told before. Not only is the father dissected, but the daughter's feelings are anatomized.

Only once have I confronted such material in my own writing and it took me by surprise. In *Fanny, being the True History of the Adventures of Fanny Hackabout-Jones*, I was unwittingly drawn into an incest-myth. Nor was the incest intentional on my heroine's part. She was raped by a stepfather who turned out to be her father. Several would-be adapters of the book for stage or screen have warned me that this is the one part of the book that *must* be changed. The incest taboo is that strong.

Nin not only broke this primal taboo, she also had the audacity to write about it. It's true that the prose in this episode becomes filled with "unreality" – a word Nin used often when she is confused by emotional contradictions.

Henry is real; Hugo is real; Rank is real; even the elusive Antonin Artaud is (almost) real. But her father dissolves in a poisonous mist and when he cries and says he cannot let her go, she is all the more determined to leave. She rationalizes away his bad character, embellishes his sensitivity, tries in every way to idealize him. But he comes across as a weak and selfish man who knows neither his own heart nor his daughter's, a man incapable of either filial or genital love.

The *"padre-amour"* (note that Anais uses Spanish and French in describing it) is the shortest section of the book, though it provokes the title. (All Nin's actual diaries had titles like *"La Folle Lucide," "Equilibre," "Uranus," "Schizoidie & Paranoia,"* "The Triumph of Magic," "Flagellation" . . . *"Audace,"* "The Definite Appearance of the Demon," or "Flow – Childhood – Rebirth."

Nin's own titles were specific and revealing. *Incest* is faintly commercial (though whether it will sell books in an era when The Anti-Sex League has won in America is impossible to say). The title may actually be a liability. Nevertheless, it is psychologically true to the book. Anais Nin's multitudinous seductions were all incestuous at heart. She was forever wooing and winning her mythic father by mimicking his behavior. He was the Zeus who ruled her mental universe.

The first part of *Incest* tells of Nin's waning ability to idealize Henry Miller (though their affair continues), of her starting to see Henry as "a perverse, irresponsible child" whose fierce honesty can be "another way of hurting."

But *Henry & June,* or rather a fictionalized version of it, for which she is seeking publication while writing *Incest* (through William Aspenwall Bradley, the agent she found for Henry), is seen as too soft on Miller, too idealizing. This response thwarts publication, but only makes Nin more determined than ever to continue writing her unsparing daily journal.

In fact, it is just the *dailiness* of the journal that makes it revolutionary. *Incest* goes on to explore Hugo's discovery of his wife's affair (through reading her Journal), and Anais's Scheherazade-like ability to talk him out of what he has read (and seen), claiming her Journal to be erotic fiction based on fantasy. She swears to Hugo that there is another, still *more secret,* journal which reveals her innocence. Wanting to believe, Hugo believes and forgives. Anais is left with her husband's quiet kindness and her own ravening guilt. She is both elated and depressed by her ability to be so many women at once – playing each part with utter conviction.

In *Incest,* she complains that Henry stops reading her writing, that he has thousands of faults. Yet she still sometimes dreams of "finding Hugo a woman who can make him happy" and departing for life with Henry.

Six months after the first meeting, her father comes to her house in Louveciennes, and makes love to her again. He pleads for utter fidelity between them, knowing it is impossible for them both. This time she feels nothing but compassion for him (which disguises her need for revenge).

She becomes involved with Otto Rank, her second psychoanalyst, who demands that she give up her diary, her "opium," and leave it in his hands. This ultimate surrender propels their love-affair. Father-commands are always aphrodisiac to Nin. Through Rank, Nin is able to dismiss her father as a lover. She finally tells him what a narcissist he is and hardens her heart to all the men in her life. She feels herself becoming a "primitive woman" who loves at least four men at once. With her new power she persuades Jack Kahane to publish *Tropic of Cancer*, after a vacillating two-year wait. She underwrites the publication with money borrowed from Rank. But still her own journals remain unpublished.

In London, she meets Rebecca West and finds herself more admired than Henry. This is a special kind of validation.

In May 1934, she discovers herself pregnant with Miller's child. A heroic struggle begins in her mind between Henry the child-man and little Henry, the fetus. She knows that Henry wants no rival in a child; and she knows that she cannot present Henry's child to Hugo. She imagines a war between the child and her artist-self. Over Hugo's objections, she goes to the *sage-femme* to abort the child.

It is a sacrifice she is making, and she is well aware of the cost. She describes the labor and the stillbirth with a vividness which still makes me cringe and weep on the tenth re-reading. The unborn fetus becomes an abandoned child like herself:

> So full of energy my half-created child that I will thrust back into the *néant* again. Back into obscurity and unconsciousness, and the paradise of non-being. I have known you; I have lived with you. You are only the future. You are the abdication.

Then comes the battle of birth, the futility of pushing out a dead baby. Anais stops pushing and the doctor rages at her and causes her deliberate pain. "The pain makes [her] howl."

Finally, the little sacrifice is pushed into the light. It is a girl baby, perfectly formed, perfectly dead.

With this act, Anais feels she has delivered herself as an artist. She has killed the woman in herself, committed female infanticide, both on her child and on herself.

With one act she has repudiated her mother, her father, Henry, Hugo, Rank, and all the men who want to possess her. She will never face abandonment again.

Tropic of Cancer, that other baby, bursts into the world. Henry is launched and accordingly she loses interest in him (though he does not in her). She sails for America to become a psychoanalyst, with Rank.

What Anais Nin has created here is nothing less than a mirror of life. The fluctuations of moods, the flip-flops from hate to love that mark our frail humanity, are seen in *process*, as never before.

Nin was doing what Marcel Proust, James Joyce, and Henry Miller were doing, but she was proceeding from within a *wo-man's* consciousness. Where Miller is often impossible to follow because of his plotlessness and stubbornly non-linear time, Nin is always lucid. She reflects the change of mind and mood by an accretion of precise descriptions, not by the loopy repetition we often find in Miller.

Nor does she veil her story in ancient mythology and clever coinages like Joyce. But she has the same modernist urge to explode time and abolish space. The space inside the mind is all that interests her.

If Nin was such a pivotal and important figure in the history of modern literature, why has she been so maligned?

The first reason is obvious: sexism. The second is also obvious: our unique cultural fear of sexuality. The third reason is equally obvious: what she has created is new (a kind of writing which hybridizes autobiography and fiction). Since we belong to a species that fears the new for no other reason than because it is not old, Nin's creation of a new form is troubling.

But Nin has also been deeply misunderstood because of the *sequence* in which her work appeared.

For years she was the great unpublished author, whispered and gossiped about, known for her literary love affairs, and her vast artistic and psychoanalytic acquaintanceship. The few novels that appeared under her name were written in an obfuscating experimental style, and issued from precious avant-garde publishers. Even her book on D. H. Lawrence was known only to a coterie.

In the early 70s, with the rebirth of feminism, the so-called "Second Wave," Nin was published to a large, hungering audience, but published in ways that obscured the immensity of her achievement. The books were expurgated to spare the feelings of Hugo and countless others who were still alive. Nin's reputation rose with feminism and fell with its repudiation. It rose with the movement for sexual liberation and fell when that movement retreated in the Reagan-Thatcher-Bush years.

Now, in the age of AIDS-panic, unexpurgated Nin journals are gradually reappearing. But Nin is out of fashion as a contemporary feminist because the political winds have shifted. She is a seductress in a time when all seduction is presumed to be rape, a sensitive chronicler of inner emotion and psychoanalytic transformation when all that is wanted from women writers is angry agitprop which repudiates Freud and all "dead white males."

But the largeness of her contribution will remain for other times, other politics. Like Colette, she told the inner story of a woman's life from girlhood to old age. She neither committed physical nor creative suicide. She was indefatigable (as every artist must be), and she left a body of work that other women writers can build upon. We can love her or hate her. Either emotion will be useful for our future writing. But she is there like a mountain. She must be climbed.

There are signs that, as this century ends, she is about to be recognized.

A number of books about her have recently been published or are about to be published. And the unexpurgated journals will keep on coming. They will continue to be attacked by women who are afraid of freedom and by men who like women that way. But for our daughters and granddaughters, they will be there. When tomorrow's women are ready, they will read Anais Nin and be transformed.

Future generations will discover her with the excitement we felt when we discovered Virginia Woolf, Colette, Simone de Beauvoir, Edna St. Vincent Millay, Jean Rhys, Zora Neale Hurston, Angela Carter, Sylvia Plath, Anne Sexton.

She will give confidence to women writers who need to validate their own subject matter.

Perhaps that's the greatest influence a writer can have on the future: To inspire new practitioners of the craft. They will adore her, detest her, debate her, rewrite her, interpret her. And why not? She is mother. And mother is the earth from which we spring.

From *Anais: An International Journal* 12 (1994): 15-25.

Nin Herself

Looking Again at Anais Nin

Maxine Molyneux and Julia Casterton

Introduction (Julia Casterton)

In 1970 Maxine Molyneux interviewed Anais Nin; they talked about the third volume of Journals, which had just been published in England. The transcript of the discussion went the way of all print that is not quickly presented to a reading public: it disappeared into a drawer and lay, often considered but never finally used, for ten years. Last summer Maxine and I began to talk about Nin's work. I had just read the erotica and also taught some of her fiction in a women's writing class. We remarked on how uneasily her work sits in the history of women's writing in this century, and the problems she presents to feminist analysis because of this. Although she died in 1977, her work presented itself to us as a prodigious spread: a temporal spread in that her writing began early this century and continued until her death, and a cultural spread also, spanning arid uneasily moving back and forth between Europe arid America. The very history of tier writing, then, assailed us as formidable, a perhaps undigestible chunk. So many other women writers had made their marks during that time and subsequently disappeared, perhaps to he rediscovered by our generation. Nin had, on the other hand, quite simply but quite unaccountably (in the light of the tragedies in store for others, notably Woolf and Plath, who made writing their choice) *carried on writing*. The persistence of Anais Nin was a question in itself.

We did not want to reject or ignore her work because it doesn't fit into any predictable pattern, because it cannot be cited in the same breath as that of contemporaries as diverse as Jean Rhys, Simone de Beauvoir, and Virginia Woolf, who can be far more unproblematically "claimed" as the literary grandmothers of present day feminist writers. On the contrary, her writing presented itself to us as perhaps more engaging and challenging because of the questions it raises about writing and femininity. She seemed to be a living exception to the notion of "the totality of women" that has bugged feminist theory for so long[1]. While her highly-regarded contemporaries are involved in writing which indicates a general oppression of women, and are amenable to a theory of patriarchy that is now (perhaps wrongly) widely accepted, the importance of the father and the celebration of sexual difference that we find in Nin's work sets her apart; she stands as *another* voice, making different meanings and representations of women. She is a dissonant element that asks to be heard in a long line of women writers who can sometimes, perhaps mistakenly, be registered as a fully-constituted orchestra playing in harmony. She seems to be one of those stereotypes (mother/witch/child/whore) we thought we had cast off and as such, she is a clanging cymbal to us.

Nin was always aware of the unacceptability and heterogeneity of her writing, but for quite different reasons from the ones we were thinking about. An emigré, an American in spite of herself, she recognized and acknowledged the problems of a writer trying to use forms (familiar and acceptable in Europe) in a country whose literary traditions were quite alien to her own history as a writer. She was a problem in her lifetime, and accepted herself as such; and now, when the importance of surrealist writing is fully recognized in America, she presents problems of a different nature for feminists. We wanted to examine her *as* a problem, not dismissively or condemningly, but in a way which would perhaps reveal to us the inefficacy and unhelpfulness, of blanket statements that feminists often make about women writers. So we looked again at the "self-revelation" of the 1970 interview, and now, these ten years later, offer it along with Julia Casterton's commentary as an example of a possible exercise, a possible interrogation that can be made of a "difficult" woman writer.

Interview

(conducted by Maxine Molyneux on the publication of Anais Nin's third volume of Journals, on May 27th, 1970)

MM: You are, of course, best known for your fictional work, yet from reading the Journals/Diaries one can see that these are extremely important for you, and are by no means just an adjunct to the fictional writings. Are your Journals/Diaries in fact more important to you than your other writings?

AN: Yes. I think they are because they are fuller. Yet that feeling was not there at the beginning. I used to think that my novels were my best writing but the novels were the formal work and I rind that people like the spontaneous, natural work better. Also, I think that probably in the Journals I unknowingly and unconsciously produced more complete portraits of people and went deeper than in the novels, and gave more. That may have been due to a natural shyness in the formal work, but the formal work, you know is fiction and I wasn't satisfied with that, I am more satisfied with the Journals.

MM: The first volume of the Journals/Diaries was published in 1931. The second one in 1934. The present volume carries the account of your life up to 1944. Are you planning to publish further volumes? [Editor's note: Molyneux means to refer to years covered, not publication dates, but is inaccurate in any case.]

AN: Yes I am working on volume 4 and I think it will go as far as a volume 5. I have to keep a few months ahead of what is being published to keep my feeling of honesty. The only way I can get this feeling of honesty is to convince myself that I was able to keep a secret, and since I was able to keep a secret for so long I suppose I believe that I will continue to keep it and that no-one will see what I wrote last month. Otherwise I would lose that thing that the diary has, which is that it is being written without the feeling that anyone is going to read it.

MM: How do you think your next Journal will compare with this one?

AN: The themes change mostly, and the atm sphere. Volume 4, which I am covering now, still deals with New York but there will be a change when I begin to leave New York to travel and to go to other countries.

MM: Does your style and approach change from one Journal to another?

AN: Yes, my style changes as I change. It's living and changing with me. At first it's tentative and not so sure when you are in your twenties, and then you become a little more firm when you are in your thirties, and as you mature the style of course changes again. You become more incisive. You have a better knowledge of what is important. When you are twenty you think everything is important. In editing now, I try to take out repetitions and minor subjects, minor themes. When a person isn't described in full it's not very interesting and becomes name dropping, something people tend to do in diaries – you know – there's the joke about the person who writes "Andre Gide came to dinner" and doesn't say anything more about him. So where I have done that I take that out. When I just mention a name and don't give the person, I take it out.

MM: Do you see the Journals as being primarily about yourself or about the people and society you know?

AN: I think it's both. By exploring yourself you begin to understand others better, by knowing yourself you also make a better friend to others. I think that my portraits of other people are more important than my self portrait. And they are full length portraits. It's the relationship between people that really wins out in the Diary. The way the friendships developed and the relationships to people. That's why I never understood some of the reviews talking about the self portrait because the important thing in the Diary is the relationships between people. And I have a thousand characters in the diaries, so I wouldn't call it exactly a self portrait.

MM: Yet one of the criticisms that has been leveled at you is that you did not sufficiently develop the personalities of those you write about. Was that because you didn't know them well enough?

AN: The portraits that remain undeveloped are simply because I didn't know them more than that. I said all I knew about them at the time. For instance I met people like Tanguey only a few evenings; he went to live somewhere else and I never saw him again. When I have known someone over a long period of time there are almost continuous portraits in the diary. It would be phony in a diary to say I knew more about Tanguey secondhand. If I had written in what I found out about him in books or what I heard about from others. You see, I wanted to have everything like journalism that could be checked by me. So it's more authentic sometimes to make a small portrait of a person you have only seen a few times than pretend to make a full portrait. I do make a full portrait of Miller, I have now in the later volumes Miller 20 years later, Miller 30 years later because there was a continued knowledge of his life. But I never cheated in that way. I don't want secondhand knowledge, you see.

MM: What about the influences on your early work? You discuss your involvement with the surrealist movement in your journals. How important was this to you and also how did its sudden collapse affect you?

AN: You know, surrealism really didn't die. Dogma always dies. The very severe laws of a movement die, but the influence of surrealism seeped in and came out in American pop art. It just becomes a little more denuded. Some of the writers that I wrote about in a book called the *Novel of the Future*, are still using surrealistic methods but they are not as dogmatic. There's John Hawkes (they are very little known in England I think), there is William Goyen published by Owen, and Daniel Stern. In other words we have some writers who at a certain moment in the novel, I don't mean all the way through, use a surrealistic way of taking flights, just as Miller did when he went off the ground in some surrealist passages. So it really hasn't died, it can't die, we need that.

MM: But you did yourself identify with the literary surrealists?

AN: I wasn't identified with the *dogma* and I don't think they would have accepted me, because I didn't obey all the rules. But I did use surrealism when it was suitable in a novel. When you are trying to deal with many layers of life simultaneously there is no other way to deal with it. If you are telling a very simple thing of external reality you can be very naturalistic and realistic but a moment comes when as the surrealists said our lives become past, present and future on three lines, as it were, musically, and you need the surrealist way of writing. Symbolic. And in a way a lot of the symbolism that the young use came out of that acting out, like burning their draft cards, covering themselves with blood. They did a lot of theatrical things that could have been inspired by Artaud. They try to present you with history.

MM: What about the earlier generation? Were people like Gertrude Stein important to you?

AN: We had a very strange attitude in the thirties. Everything that happened in the 20s was very, very ancient. We were beginning everything anew. A feeling everybody has. Gertrude Stein, Hemingway and Scott Fitzgerald are three people I never met. They belong to the 20s. We thought of them as the 20s. Of course surrealism was born in the 20s, but it became really full blown in the 30s. So those things we were not interested in. I wasn't really very attracted to Gertrude Stein.

MM: In your 3rd Journal you write of the conflict you experienced between leaving Europe and accepting life in America. After a period of 30 years or so, do you still feel this regret, or have you come to terms with it?

AN: I think I do regret leaving Europe. I think I remain fairly European although more than half my life has been spent in America. I feel more at home in Europe. I mean my link in America is with the young. The people I am in harmony with and think the same way and feel the same way are the students and the young. The young are my readers. The older America which I first went to, which I describe in Diary Three, I never did have a very close link with. I have a very close bond with the New America.

MM: Is it the idealism of the youth movement with which you identify?

AN: Yes. That is why someone described the third Diary as the volume of prophesy because in the '40s the criticisms I made were the same ones that the young make now. That the commercial world was not humanistic, that there was great concern with politics but not with relationships: all these things were the things that the young decided that they could no longer tolerate. So, at a certain point we met. The things I prophesied, that America would pay a high price for all its toughness, all these things came true. Now the new generation is entirely different.

MM: What prophesies will you be making in the fourth Journal?

AN: In the fourth Journal there is again the conflict between the older generation and the young. In America I took the side of the young in the very beginning because they were the future. In a way I foresaw the romantic period they are going through, this idealistic period. They work on ecology, they work to save nature, they work to stop war – all these things we were in sympathy with and they are really the themes of the two diaries in America. That is why I allowed them to be published. Not because, well you know, they were just reminiscences of the past and all that, but because they seem so relevant to the present, and the people I described are influences in the present. Miller, you know, was part of a revolution and caused a great deal of the things we see now. And Artaud is a great influence in the theatre now in America, I don't know if he is as much here. Then Rank, you know they have rediscovered Rank because he had a school for social workers. So these people who seemed out of the past have a strong influence on the present.

MM: This raises the question of what you think the role of the artist and the writer is today?

AN: The role of the writer is not always a very conscious one. Some people say he reflects his period. Sometimes he's against it. Sometimes you seem to be against the trend as I was in the 40s, I seem to be not in the trend of American thinking. Sometimes you represent the future. So it's very difficult to know where a writer is going to be, how useful he is going to be. In the 40s I was thought to be outside American culture but this was a useful thing, and now I'm inside it, a vital part of it. In fact I lecture and my books are taught in American universities. So we can't predict very much what is the role of the writer. If he has any integrity he either represents his period or the conflict against it which represents the future. I think I represented the conflict and therefore became prophetic of the future. I didn't accept America as it was in the 40s.

MM: Although you are now accepted into American literary culture do you still see yourself as playing a critical and even prophetic role?

AN: Now I'm in my time. But you can't tell. I couldn't tell even at this time. I was treated as a foreigner then; and now, as you know, the American young have taken up Eastern religions and they read Hesse and read me and they have become terribly interested in the 30s. In other words, they are making all the connecting links which give them strength to make a new world. I have accepted the world that is to come, that I hope is to come. I have accepted the world of the young, and that means anywhere between twenty and thirty years old. You see, the people who are now, for example, professors at college were students ten years ago and they were reading me. Now they're teaching me. So I have a lot of hope that a lot of other people don't have about the future. And the young lawyers who are graduating, the very young ones in their thirties are the ones who are trying to work within the system, discovering laws by which they could stop war – and I'm in sympathy with all that.

MM: Do you feel you have contributed to helping this cause?

AN: I'm sure I have.

MM: How do you feel about contemporary cultural developments?

AN: The artists I find a little more difficult to go along with. Pop art for example, folklore, folk art, I don't feel so close to it. I feel very close to their films, the underground films, which I understand a little better. I'm not so fond of pop art. But it must have some connection for them. But I am very fond of their folk singing.

MM: Perhaps you are a romantic.

AN: Yes, but so many of them are, so many of the young are. They're trying to make much tenderer relationships between men and women, much less belligerent. I am not speaking of course of the radical students, the violent radical students. I am speaking of the hippies who want peace. Their motto is peace and love (laughs).

MM: And you go along with that.

AN: Yes. I don't even go along with women's emancipation movement because they are declaring war on men (laugh). I don't think men are responsible for our not growing or our liberation, because so many men have helped me to become liberated. I think that's something women have to do from within, and within their own frame. I consider myself liberated, but I was helped by men; so I'm not going to declare war on men. Professional things I am in sympathy with. They would like to have women directors in films; I would like that too. Especially in America the culture is very masculine orientated, in a tough pseudo-masculine way. Europe doesn't have that, I don't think. Europe has a better balance between feminine and masculine. In America you don't make your own way, you push your own way, there is a real cult of aggressivity, but they are paying a terrible price for that. They're paying the price of violence.

MM: One of your observations in the diary is that to ignore the individual is destructive, and by knowing yourself as an individual you are helping "this cause" along.

AN: Yes. Especially in America. You see I can't speak for Europe because really I haven't lived here for the last few years. But in America they had a period when all the writers were writing about alienation, the strange, being alienated from everybody, not caring, not being able to make a relationship. And all the time, women and I, not only I but women writers are writing about relationships. But they didn't want to read that, you know this was romantic, this was love. But today the young are fully aware of that and the reason they felt the alienation was that they wouldn't have any relation to themselves. So that is why I always deny when people say that the diary is self-concerned and self-engrossed; I say you have to begin with the self, you have to exist. Because otherwise you don't reflect others, you don't understand, you don't relate to others if you are selfish and if you are nothing. The young understand precisely that it begins by having your own integrity; then you are like a mirror or recorded. You are able to see others, understand them and relate to them.

MM: Is it not difficult to launch this particular battle in America?

AN: Yes, it is difficult for the students and for the young today; they are in great danger, but they are courageous. My battle was different. It was a subterranean battle, and for many years I was considered what is called an underground writer, which meant that I never came to the establishment surface publicity thing, but today it's all harder. They have to endure greater physical dangers but at least they're heard; they have the press and they are being listened to. But what they did for me was to give me the silent treatment, that is for twenty years the work was ignored, my existence was ignored – except in colleges. You see that was a different way of dealing with me. That was . . . Today, different things are brought to the surface and there is a bigger battle going on but they are at least heard. Their poetry is published, Negro poetry is published, the Negro is heard. There is much what they call "visibility."

MM: But is the situation getting better? The Americans are still in Vietnam.

AN: No, I think in America it is getting worse. The conflict is greater. The War is part of it, is a cause of the conflict. There are three things causing conflict. Too much oppression, very inadequate leaders, and. the revolt of the young, who are concerned with many things. First they want to stop war; and then, as you know, they are interested in ecology. Nature is being destroyed and these are concerns which are very genuine. Some of the battles they have won. There was a very dramatic battle in Santa Barbara, when they were going to drill for oil and ruined the entire sea coast, destroying the birds and animal life. The students and the people of the town won their battle – they are not drilling any more. So occasionally there is a battle that is won. And with the writers too. I thinks the writers are much more . . . are not silenced as I was before.

MM: What are those writers writing now? What is their project, what are your friends doing now?

AN: Well for one thing we had the Negro literature, which was previously ignored and which came out very strongly. Then there was that of all the oppressed people of America – Mexicans, the Indians, the Negroes – these people and their work have suddenly become very clear to everyone. You see, they do symbolic things. They act. I think in our days revolution was perhaps literary – was made in cafes and talked about; but this is very active. The Indians took over an island, as you know, near San Francisco, and that dramatized the fact that they needed the land that had been taken away from them. And they wanted to be proud of their ancestry, proud of their history. Now the Negroes have done the same thing. So you now see books around about what the Negro has contributed to American culture. I loved them very much and was very close to them and had many friendships. Though I realized at the time that opening my home to Negro writers was not enough and much more had to be done, I didn't know at the time how. People were not as organized. There was only the Left if you wanted to do anything, and they didn't seem to be very effective. Even Richard Wright would leave that after a while. So I think that that was probably not the right time. It came later. Then there was effective action.

MM: Which way do you think things are going to go now? We seem to have got to a certain stage of "liberation," we are much freer from a lot of things, and if we are not free we are at least aware of what is wrong. How will the 70's and 80's develop?

AN: Freedom is a dangerous thing. In America they had a great deal of freedom, for example, because they didn't have much tradition, and they didn't have the power of the parent. If you have a great deal of freedom given to you from the outside and you have no inner discipline or inner integrity, then you just go to pieces. A lot of Americans had done that, young Americans, because they didn't have anything to fight even against, because the parents were not there at all. They left them to do whatever they wanted. We didn't have tradition without throwing it all overboard. For example, they [Americans] don't learn how to write, they won't learn how to paint, they won't learn how to make films. They won't read the classics. In one way it made them more courageous about the future because they had nothing to respect in the past. Everything was to be destroyed, as they say. But on the other hand it's more important to know yourself, to have some kind of structure already, so that you can withstand experience. They can't withstand experience. They take drugs and they break down and they end up in asylums. They haven't anything. This is the point about my struggle for the inner life. I see the image – it's like going to the bottom of the sea to have oxygen; you have to withstand the pressure of the outside by having an equal inner life, clam up enough to withstand the outside and the freedom so that you can know your-self. You see, I feel free but I am directing myself; that's freedom. But I'm not free to destroy myself or to destroy other people's experiences. I think freedom means getting rid of dogma – dogmatic religion, dogmatic educa-tion, dogmatic parenthood, dogmatic everything – and [finding] the genuine-ly religious feeling. This is not particularly a dogma or a humanistic feeling, and is not particularly a system of politics. To find political attitudes, wisdom and understanding of what is happening is not necessarily belonging to a group.

MM: How do you find this genuine religious feeling?

AN: Well you have to have your own, your own world, the thing that was condemned in the Diaries. This is the very thing from which, because I was uprooted and because I lost a father, I had to create an inner world to sustain me. If the young had that, they could cope with the whole world. I think that what it is, is that I accepted need for a personal world, and that this personal world was going to help me not get desperate about the world situation but to act in it, and to survive in it. I carried on a revolt against conventional pub-lishers in the U.S. Finally they had to accept me.

I had a printing press until Edward Wilson discovered me, which I tell in this diary, and then the commercial publishers came along – which shows how sincere they are. So then they took up the books but were so annoyed that each book didn't sell millions of copies that they dropped me one after another. So I was back again at zero and I found that I didn't come up to the standards of sales. Then I found a marvelous independent romantic publisher called Allen Swallow, who was printing things in his garage and grew from that, and who was not greedy and who was not commercial and didn't have a big house. He took on all the books and kept them all in print and it was to him that I owe everything. If it hadn't been for Swallow, I don't even think the diaries would have been taken up by Harcourt Brace. Harcourt Brace took up the diaries thinking they would sell about a thousand copies. So the commercial people never had the face to do it but Swallow did. And today, unfortunately he died prematurely before he had the reward; today I would be his best seller.

Commentary   (Julia Casterton)

To write about the "work" of Anais Nin would seem perverse. It is surely rather her life that shines out, not eclipsing but apparently transcending the delicately-built scriptural artifice through which she presents herself to us. Like others who have made the confession their mode, we imagine it is she we are reaching through her narratives (as though the narratives themselves

were webs, enticing yet distorting vision), she who presents herself to us finally, wordlessly, the whole woman. And she encourages this fond delusion, for
she is so very silent in the Journals. It is she who writes, yes, but rarely she
who speaks in them ("I think that my portraits of other people are more important than my self-portrait"). Henry Miller, Antonin Artaud, Otto Rank,
and what they say of her, "give" us this woman of seemingly endless tenderness, generosity, altruism, whose only self-affirming activity appears to be the
writing of the diary, the diary that asserts her self-abnegation.

These are perhaps observations that become self-evident to all addicted
diary readers, but they nonetheless appear to be obscure to Anais Nin in the
act of her writing. On the contrary, she emphasizes the immediacy, honesty,
accuracy of her confessional skills ("Unknowingly in the journals I produce
more complete portraits of people and went deeper than in the novels arid
gave more"), ingenuously denying the artifice of the diary, its simultaneous
secrecy and exposure, its power of creating a world that, before it is written,
remains inchoate and inarticulate. There is a subtle treachery about a diary:
even after it has rendered a particular *milieu* articulate, its inhabitants have
little power of appeal or redress: they have been written; the diary has fleshed
them with words already. Anais Nin would protest that one writes a diary to
preserve the things one loves, but it is as well to remember also that in the
recreation of one's world through writing, there resides the need to master
that world, to exert power over it. While the diary may seem to be, and be
claimed by Nin to be, all accurate representation of a particular reality, it also
contains a desire to control that reality.

In asserting the difference between the diary and the fiction, Anais Nin
claims: "The Journals supply the key to the mythical figures and assert the
reality of what once may have seemed to be purely fantasy. Such a marriage
of illusion and reality – or illusion as the key to reality – is a contemporary
theme.[2] Are the Journals, then, the truth behind the fictions, the clue which
facilitates one's escape from the fictional labyrinth? Or do the fictions represent realities lying behind the "truthful" observances of the Journals, realities
which the veils of control and discretion have shrouded? I think both questions can be adduced, and that in the tensions between the two lie both the
problems and potencies of Anais Nin's work: the fictionality of fiction and the
truthfulness of "an honest record" are both placed under interrogation.
Such rude observations would seem to bear a totally disjunctive relation to
the reflections on femininity, made by Julia Kristeva in *About Chinese Wom-
en*, in whose opening sections she discourses on the marginality of the feminine under patriarchy:

> ... witch, child, underdeveloped, not even a poet, at best a poet's
> accomplice... woman is a specialist in the unconscious, a witch, a
> bacchanalian, taking her *jouissance* in anti-Apollonian, Dionysian
> orgy ... A Marginal speech ... a pregnancy: escape from the bonds
> of daily social temporality ... woman deserts the surfaces – skin,

eyes – so that she may descend to the depths of the body, to hear, taste, smell the infinitesimal life of the cells.[3]

And yet the disjunction would seem to be an actual one: Anais Nin appears as all the creatures on Kristeva's list at different moments in her diary, even while she is refusing the part of *simply* the poet's accomplice, simply the witch, simply the specialist in the unconscious, by her activity of writing herself as all these things, controlling her representations, naming others so she will not be wholly enthralled by their naming of her. Furthermore, she questions the whole notion of the marginality of the feminine by centralizing the marginal. She asserts that the artist must go *under*, below the surface of the narrative sequence (where events are told one after the other, in measured time), and so reach the heart of an experience. Such an experience is often, for Nin, marginal or outside the city: a barge rocking below the pavements, a tent in an astrologer's studio, the half-lights of the *demi-monde*. Anais Nin seems to define herself as Kristeva claims femininity is defined under patriarchy: witch-enchantress, perfumed, with kohl on her eyes; tiny, bird-like woman, too small to bear children; all-giving mother who buys spectacles for Henry Miller and so cannot afford stockings for herself; martyr, writing erotica against her will, for money, to keep her "children." She presents herself as a problem because she *uses* these labels, rather than refuses them, to assemble herself as an artist. What is so difficult about her is that although most women writers have struggled painfully against such debilitating labels, she seems to rejoice in them, to turn them to her own advantage in a way we have come to regard perhaps as manipulative, wheedling, underhand – just like a woman. In the Journals these definitions of femininity, which we now reject as constricting, are the means by which she writes about herself, the means by which she effaces herself. It is as though she were posing before them, playing with them, seeing if they fit.

And the Journals, although they begin as a letter to her father, from whom she is separated (and so, presumably, a means of feeling close to him, as if to say "See father, I am making my own life, as you do"), become a means of claiming her difference, refusing the identification with him. In a curious way, because of their intrinsic form, they become a testament of herself as a woman, alien to the father. They bespeak their writer despite Nin's repeated assertions of her self-effacement. But perhaps one should think in terms of the complex archeology of the self, rather than self-effacement, when considering Nin's work. In the Journals she does not, indeed, present herself as a consistent, logical personality holding certain formed, firm opinions which can be expressed in a similar form to any interlocutor. Quite the reverse: she writes herself as a sort of conspirator in the self-revelation of others. With Caresse Crosby she is a fellow-adventurer, a sympathetic intriguer who encourages her flights, wild projects and fantasies; with Kenneth Patchen she is a force of discipline, refusing his continual demands of money as a strong mother would refuse the regressive demands of a child. This complex multiplicity of selves, layers of contradictory formations which do not immediately suggest any kind of unity, presents huge problems for the interviewer whose task must be to reach her subject and render her in a fashion accessible to her readers. Moreover, there is an incongruity between the exposition of a self composed of many traces and fragments which hang together in a questionable integrity and the self Nin presents in the interview, remarkable, in the light of her writings, for its consistency, homogeneity, the sureness of her response and the rationality of her arguments. Perhaps this clash could be explained by saying that in the interview Nin is looking back on her past life from the vantage point of the wisdom of age, but somehow one suspects this not to be the full explanation. Could it be that the interview is yet another conspiracy, this time with Maxine, and that far from offering an explanation, a key to the self of Anais Nin which reveals the unity behind the contradictions, it stands on the contrary as yet another contradiction, yet another facet of the self to be taken into consideration along with all the others?

I have selected several short passages from *A Spy in the House of Love* which seem to indicate the problem of selfhood as it presents itself in Nin's writing. At one point I interject a quotation from the interview which I feel illustrates the closeness of the Journals to the fictions, their common preoccupation with similar questions and problems. The pointed drawing-attention to this similarity is also partly by way of explaining my desire to speak of both the Journals and the fictions in the same breath.

> It was a woman's voice; but it could have been an adolescent imitating a woman, or a woman imitating an adolescent.

> One half of the self wants to atone, to be freed of torments of guilt. The other half of man wants to continue to be free.

> . . . the only way I can get this feeling of honesty is to convince myself that no one will see the one I wrote last month. (the interview)

> She was compelled by a confessional fever which forced her into lifting a corner of the veil, and then frightened when anyone listened too attentively. She repeatedly took a giant sponge and erased all she had said by absolute denial, as if this confusion were in itself a mantle of protection.

> Also the cape held within its folds something of what she imagined was a quality possessed exclusively by man: some dash, some audacity, some swagger of freedom denied to woman.[4]

The compulsive desire to confess, to display one's guilts, and the simultaneous need to cover up the confession, to confuse the confessor: these fragments from *A Spy in the House of Love* seem to suggest the dilemma posed by the Journals, and also the delusive transparency of the self presented to Maxine in the interview, the self which claims to be all "there," available for the interviewer and the reader, and yet somehow seems to dodge and evade, to elude the questioner.

The act of confession implies a confessor, an eye that sees, an intelligence that approves or condemns – and the "art" of the Journals involves a series of flights towards and away from such a figure. The diary describes a struggle, away from the father, away from the analyst who seeks to force her to cease keeping a diary, away from the consuming demands of close male artist friends. But within this struggle resides a series of appeals to these men (all constellated round the image of "father") to shrive, to forgive, to direct. And perhaps it is in the imitation of the father (the cape swung cavalierly round the shoulders, the pursuit of sexual adventure, the determined taking-up of the pen to "produce" a world) that these guilts are worked through, explored, and on occasion escaped from: ". . . because I had lost a father I had to create an inner world to sustain me . . ." (interview)

But the father returns in many guises, and the writing forms perhaps an index of the permanent necessity of coming to terms with him. In *A Spy in the House of Love* he appears as the lie-detector, who corners Sabina and explains her to herself:

> Some shock shattered you and made you distrustful of a single love. You divided them as a measure of safety . . . There is nothing shameful in seeking safety measures. Your fear was very great.[5]

The good father (the lie-detector/confessor) enables Sabina to confront the source of her divided loves, which is a fear of a repetition of the trauma that occurred in her past. Analogously, Anais Nin works through the divisions in her self throughout the diary, and perhaps by reference to the fictions one can adduce that the source of these divisions lies in her early separation from tier father. One could go further and suggest that the fictional transformations of the father (into, for example, the lie-detector) prevent her ever totally rejecting him. Making him fictionally into a good father, or at least exploring the possibility of a good father, protects him and discreetly, overlays his original betrayal. Could it be that this desire to protect the father (who also connotes the past, familial law, and some kind of regulated relation to the outside world) lies at the root of Nin's refusal to participate in or sympathize with political acts of dismantlement, political strategies that involve a head-on collision with state apparatuses? ("Freedom is a dangerous thing. In America they had a great deal of freedom because they didn't have the tradition, and they didn't have the power of the parent.") This is an interesting utterance in the context of an America riven with the conflicts and contradictions thrown up by the Vietnam war, and one would have wished Nin to be a little more specific. Is Vietnam the destructive game of an undisciplined child who needs the power of the parent to protect and prevent it from its own worst excesses? A piece of Mailer-like mass psychology which leads to the conclusion that the unspent aggressive tendencies of "mankind" should be channeled into harmless war games in some isolated corner of the Pacific? If this is indeed the import, then Nin's reasoning betrays a rather alarming facility for sliding from individual to social or political analysis, and perhaps an alternate refusal to engage with the specific complexities of the public realm. In Volume 3 of her Journals Nin repeatedly berates her friends who stick simply to political analysis, accusing them of disregarding the individual human aspect; her own comments indicate a massive swing in the opposite direction.[6]

What is clear is that Nin reserves her approbation for those who are prepared to work for change from within pre-existent institutions, within a given body of law to discover the statutes which will secure the end of the war. According to her own analysis then, the powers of the father (political and legal apparatuses) are not wrong in themselves, and if one looks hard enough one will find an aspect of state/parental authority which necessitates a cessation of conflict in Southeast Asia. The other view, that Vietnam arose out of the distortions and deformations within the American legal/political system, Nin seems to reject altogether, and she has little time for those she dismisses as "the violent radical students" (interview). It appears from the interview that Nin's approach to political understanding takes her through an individualistic moralism, and that she finally remains in that thoroughfare. It is through transformations in the individual that she understands social and political change to be engendered: "Do you think you have contributed to helping this cause?" "I'm sure I have" (interview). And one does not wish to look askance at such an assertion, particularly in view of the demand for the integration of public and private change that has been made so potently by the women's movement. Nin goes further, however, and opposes the feminism that could have been marshaled in her favour: "I don't even go along with the women's emancipation movement because they are declaring war on men." She asserts that the origins of our oppression lie elsewhere, not in the collective desire of men to subject women. One recalls a similar statement made by Virginia Woolf in *A Room of One's Own*:

> It was absurd to blame any class or any sex, as a whole. Great bodies of people are never responsible for what they do. They are driven by instincts which are not within their control. They too, the patriarchs, the professors, had endless difficulties, terrible drawbacks to contend with. Their education had been in some ways as faulty as my own. It had bred in them defects as great.[7]

Do we find in Anais Nin's work, then, a striving towards an understanding of patriarchy, of her own location within a patriarchal social order? I think that would be too large a claim, and one should perhaps attenuate it by drawing attention to Nin's own consenting implication in the production and consumption of what on the surface appears as a quite conventional brand of erotica.

Nin claims that the writing of this erotica is done reluctantly, because it is so hard to support oneself as a writer. She admits she does it for Henry Miller and other writer friends even more impecunious than she. These are the let-out clauses outside the erotic fiction, the explanations she makes for writing them in Volume 3 of her Journal. They smack of the justifications of a destitute woman, whoring to feed her family. Inside the fiction the let-outs are rather different: they consist of the revenge of the prostitute/passive, sexually-desiring woman on her client/keeper/oppressor. For example: the sailors on board a ship buy a rubber woman who fulfills all their needs. She has perfectly human orifices, is loving, accepting and compliant, and they all adore her. Unfortunately for them, however, she gives them all syphilis. Another example: the women in a disorderly house perform gymnastic sexual acts for affluent voyeurs. One of them wears a false penis, and gyrates in long, rather boring copulation with her partner. This tedious, unsatisfying penetration goes on for a while, and then the "male" partner unhitches her phallus, leans over and licks the clitoris of the other. The "female" partner comes, and one is left with a sense of the inadequacy of the male clients in the eyes of the prostitutes. The clients simply do not produce pleasure, and the women make the voyeurs aware of this. Both examples describe forms of revenge; the oppressive situation is not dismantled or escaped from, but those who play the oppressive role are made to feel wanting and somehow ridiculous.

The erotica are fascinating reading because of the way they manage to inhabit two worlds: the tantalizing, enclosed world of conventional pornographic fiction, an onanistic delight to the male (and perhaps also female) reader, and the world of women's desires, at odds with purely specular pleasure, a world which seeks its own gratification and gently, subtly subverts tile demands made by the anonymous publisher who commissions the writing, Perhaps the most interesting fact about the erotica in connection with Maxine's interview is that Anais Nin does not mention them; they consumed a considerable part of her working life while she was writing the third volume of the Journals, and yet they are missing from her account of these years in the interview.

What can we make of this absence? Perhaps it has something to do with the possibility that the erotica stand as some kind of threat, an invasion of the inner world she has created in the Journals to sustain herself through the loss of her father. The security of the private sphere is threatened by the erotica, for in writing them she is forced to bend to the publisher's desires and pleasure; she is still writing, but within an alien mode, one where she is unable to create and sustain her own private world. During the years described in Volume 3, the writing of the erotica constitutes her only − forced and reluctant − engagement with the public world, until the time when she abandons all hope of being published by anyone other than herself, and gets to work on her own press. At a time when she could not obtain a readership, the publisher who consumes her amorous couplings is the only person with whom she enters into a professional relationship, the only person who gives her money for her writings.

The arrangement with the publisher involves a threat both to Nin's writing and to her closely private and preserved sexuality. And yet I believe the threat proves fruitful, for if she does not mention the erotica in her interview, neither does she mention her desires, her sexuality, in the published Journals. Only in the erotica do we catch glimpses of her understanding of her own and other women's desires and gratifications – and though these desires are represented in the framework of and under the pressure of the demands of a single, rich male reader, they are nevertheless glimpses we would otherwise have been denied. In her preface to *Delta of Venus* she delivers her apologia and attempts to justify offering them finally for open publication:

> Here in the erotica I was writing to entertain, under pressure from a client who wanted me to "leave out the poetry." I believed that my style was derived from reading of men's works. For this reason I long felt that I had compromised my feminine self. I put the erotica aside. Rereading it these many years later, I see that my own voice was not completely suppressed. In numerous passages I was intuitively using a woman's language, seeing sexual experience from a woman's point of view. I finally decided to release the erotica for publication because it shows the beginning efforts of a woman in a world that had been the domain of men.[8]

She goes on to say that until the unexpurgated edition of the diary is published the erotica are the only examples in her work of these "beginning efforts." There is a large irony here: we have moved from Nin's early assertion that the diaries are the key to the fictions to the admission that the erotica – written under conditions that would seem entirely inappropriate to the representation of female desire – provide a clue that, because the diary remains as yet in an expurgated form, is absolutely essential to an understanding of Anais Nin's particular literary strategies.

The erotica stand, I believe, as a salutary warning against the unified self that looms at the reader in the interview. They form a hole, snag, an imperfection, in the external uniform of goodness which the benign public self of Anais Nin presents to our disappointed and disbelieving eyes. An almost audible and tangible silence in her discussion with Maxine of the years 1939 to 1944, the erotica insist upon themselves as an unintegrated part of Nin's public self.

NOTES

[1]The concept of "the totality of women" has formed an underlying bone of contention within the women's movement for the past ten years. Those who unreservedly accept it emphasize women's commonly-held experience of oppression under patriarchy, an experience which, it is claimed, crosses class lines and forms the basis for an exclusively feminist politics. Those who reject the concept lay stress upon the social and cultural differences between women that slice through the so-called commonly experienced patriarchal oppression. The rejectionists necessarily arrive at political consequences that demand alliances beyond feminist separatism. The insights and methodologies of other discourses, notably Marxism and psychoanalysis, have been constantly brought to bear on the debates around the implications of "the totality of women."

[2]Anais Nin, Preface to *Under a Glass Bell* (Athens, Ohio: Swallow Press, 1948).

[3]Julia Kristeva, *About Chinese Women*, trans. Marion Boyars (New York: Urizen Press, 1977): 14. An assertion such as this, emerging with such frequency from left intellectual French culture in the last few years, may well indicate the depth to which the roots of surrealism penetrate certain parts of French society. Anais Nin herself experienced the force of surrealism at her most formative creative period. Kristeva's description of woman under patriarchy bears a striking resemblance to Nin's descriptions of herself in Volume 3 of her Journals.

[4]Anais Nin, *A Spy in the House of Love* (New York: Bantam Books, 1968), pp. 1, 2, 5, 7.

[5]*Ibid.*, p. 117.

[6]A similar orientation is evident in her fictions. In the story about the loss of her barge in *Under a Glass Bell,* the problem of how to save the barge is seen in purely personal terms: if the police inspector sympathizes with her and takes her side, she will magically be able to bypass the instruction issued by the Paris waterways. Here again an appeal to a dominant male figure is being made, an appeal for approval and legitimation.

[7]Virginia Woolf, *A Room of One's Own* (New York: Harcourt, Brace and World, 1929), p. 38.

[8]Anais Nin, Preface to *Delta of Venus* (New York: Bantam Books, 1978), p. xv.

From *The Minnesota Review* 18 (Spring 1982): 86-101.

A Mirror of Her Own: Anais Nin's Autobiographical Performances

Elyse Lamm Pineau

> I step on the stage of the Edison Theatre holding a metal mask be-
> fore my face. . . I say to the audience: "For centuries woman has
> worn a mask and played many roles. Today she is unmasking her-
> self and showing her true face." And I remove the mask and read
> from the *Diaries*. (*Diary* 7: 243)

In the course of her life, Anais Nin performed herself through numerous
masks: the theatricality of her self-presentation, the autobiographical heroine
of her sixty-year *Diary*, and the performance narratives of her fictional
women. In each case her performance of self was masked--embedded in social activity or mediated by literary art. With the demand for personal appearances that followed the publication of her first *Diary* in 1966, however,
Nin ascended a new stage. She was called upon to assume the mantle of her
autobiographical legend, to enact herself on university and professional stages nationwide. From 1966-73, Nin toured college campuses, reading aloud
from the *Diary*, lecturing on the self-creating enterprise, and encouraging
students to pursue a similar agenda in their own lives. The effect was transformative, as Maxwell Geismar recalls in his 1979 retrospective for the *Los
Angeles Times*.

> Suddenly Anais became an object of adulation. a literary spokes-
> man [spokesperson] for the young on college campuses. She be-
> came a cult figure, and the charming, beguiling, mysterious, elusive
> person that I knew so many years before became terribly adept at
> self promotion. I suppose I shouldn't have been very surprised.

Performance marked the culmination of Nin's autobiographical project, for it
provided an ongoing, public, and collective enactment of her *Diary* persona
on college campuses nationwide. Performing the *Diary* reframed the private
document as a public script, transformed its heroine from a textual to a

living presence, and invited a community to share in its autobiographical intimacy. In other words, performance enabled Nin to "remove the mask" in order that the mask could become a shared reality.

It is ironic that Nin's performances remain largely untapped by either performance scholars or Nin enthusiasts. Evelyn Hinz's collage of edited transcriptions in *A Woman Speaks: The Lectures, Seminars and Interviews of Anais Nin* marks the only critical account of "one of the most fluent, engaging and spontaneous speakers of our time . . . a woman who calmly commands audiences of thousands" (vii). Hinz makes several insightful observations about Nin's performance style in her preface, but these introductory remarks are never developed, nor have they been extended by other critics. This essay re-examines Nin's celebrity based on 77 unpublished, unedited audiotapes of Nin's lectures, interviews, seminars and discussions.[1] These tapes, many of which Nin recorded herself on a hand-held machine, are the only existing collection outside of the Nin Foundation and the University of California-Los Angeles Special Collections.[2] The essay focuses on the aesthetic and rhetorical strategies Nin used to successfully negotiate her *Diary* identity through performance. It foregrounds the continuity between her autobiographical and performance personae, identifies some structural and stylistic features that characterized her lectures, and critiques the editorial control she exerted in conversation with the audience. Informed by the assumption that Nin skillfully constructed her audience as *co-performers* of her *Diary* identity, I ask which "scripts" of her persona she enabled and which she excluded. Lastly, I suggest some 'implications we might draw about autobiographical performance and, more specifically, about women's self-identifying practices.

I begin by proposing a distinction between the "performance of autobiography" and "autobiographical performance." I take the "performance of autobiography" to refer to those performance events in which an autobiographer might read aloud from her work, reflect on her creative process or share anecdotes alluded to in her text. She maintains a certain critical distance from her work, in order to talk about it as a product of her experience. While the audience draws connections between the author-as-performer and the author-as-textual-subject, it is understood that these identities are distinct. indeed, one of the pleasures of hearing an author perform is the re-negotiation of identity that her presence activates in the audience "Is this the body I imagined, the voice I intuited, the relationship I experienced while reading?" However fully an author might embody her text in performance, she also "removes the mask" in order to comment upon her own performance within and of the work.

"Autobiographical performance," as I will use the term, is informed by an "aesthetic of incarnation" whereby the performer presents herself as a living text, the embodied presence absent from the literary experience. She speaks from within the text rather than about it, working actively to blur her identities as author and subject. By collapsing the distinction between her textual and lived identities, she offers both as simultaneously present in her performing body. Whatever masking or unmasking occurs in performance serves to create continuity between these identities rather than distinctions. Most importantly, the autobiographical performer frames her text as a continual process, thereby inviting her audience to participate in its ongoing enactment. This collective performance positions the audience to affirm the authenticity of the central persona and her experiences.

Certainly, the distinctions between these two modes of performance are rarely as marked as I have suggested; one might more appropriately describe moments falling along a continuum between one or the other. Anais Nin, however, framed her lectures so completely within the mode of autobiographical performance that these distinctions offer a useful foundation for identifying the characteristics and the consequences of this performance style.

Recall Nin's use of a metal mask to frame her performance at the Edison theatre. By manipulating one of the primary symbols of theatrical experience, Nin situates herself as a skilled participant in a rich tradition of performance rituals. She further situates herself in a rhetorical tradition of women's emancipation by invoking the mask as a metaphor for social roles which need be shed. Significantly, Nin claims authority as a spokesperson for her gender by positioning herself as "Everywoman" struggling to liberate herself from patriarchal constraints. This rhetorical move was predicated upon her claim that "the *Diary* was written by many women" and was prerequisite to the empathic identification upon which she grounded her performances (Marin College). The Everywoman stance, however, evoked conflicting responses from her feminist contemporaries. Kate Millet embraced Nin as "a mother to us all" whose *Diary* was "a basic primer for the triumph of female personhood . . . the voice of woman herself," in the same year that Laurie Stone attacked her as a "superficial Jean Brodie . . . oblivious to the degree to which all of her perceptions, tastes, values and ideas are a function of her social class" (4, 46). Recent feminist theory has taught us to be suspect of Everywoman's seemingly transparent universality. As Kay Capo and Darlene Hantzis point out, any essentialist depiction of Woman decontextualized from her culture, class, and ethnicity is a dangerous anachronism, both theoretically and practically. Moreover, the tension of claiming to perform autobiography and Everywoman simultaneously doubly masks the historical and ideological situation of the autobiographer within the "collective" for whom she claims to speak. While Nin's assumption of the Everywoman role remains a central point of critique in her work, such critique does not negate the rhetorical efficacy of framing her performance in this voice. Shedding the patriarchal mask to speak of "female" experience in a distinctly "feminine" voice enabled Nin to align herself with the rhetoric of "sisterhood" prevalent in early feminism and, by extension, to ground the relational dynamics of her performances.

While these positionings establish Nin's credibility as an aesthetically skilled and rhetorically astute practitioner, they are not, in themselves, indicators of autobiographical performance. Nin engages an incarnational aesthetic when she removes the literal mask only to don the mask of her *Diary* heroine, suggesting that what she now presents is her unmediated, naked, "true face." This framing moment fuses the three layers of Nin's autobiographical experience: her lived reality as the writer of the *Diary*, her inscribed reality as the Diary heroine "Anais," and her performance reality as a celebrity lecturer. Rather than holding these identities in dialectical tension, however, Nin presents them in seamless continuity. Throughout her lectures she will continue to signal the audience through a variety of aesthetic and rhetorical strategies that these personae are not only simultaneously present, they are the same. In doing so, Nin invites the audience's complicity as co-performers of her *Diary* identity. If they authorize the continuity among her personae, they participate in transforming her into her imagined shape.

Assuming with Maxwell Geismar that Nin's transformation was successful, we can examine the dynamics of this incarnation in the themes, style and structure of her performances. The following descriptive analysis identifies the continuity between Nin's *Diary* and stage personae, the rhetoric of her opening remarks, the dialectic between autobiographical and performance contexts negotiated throughout the lecture, the incarnational dimension of the Diary readings and transitions, and the editorial control she exerted in conversation with the audience. The critical stance is not intended as a commentary on Nin's integrity – even her most vitriolic critics grant that her performances were sincere – but rather, it is a means to foreground the meticulous craft of her self-construction.

Nin explained to the students of Skidmore College that it was her awareness of "the painful loss of faith in the reality of the creative will" that motivated her emergence into the public eye. Her lectures urged audiences to explore the imaginative possibilities of their own identities and encouraged them to embrace the selves they could create. At Dartmouth, she charged her audience "to take responsibility for the second birth of the self . . . the self that could be created." To the graduating class at Reed College she offered a gift of faith: "the faith that we must turn to ourselves as a creative piece of work – not only in the arts but in the creation of our lives." Nin had used the *Diary* to document her own development "as a creative piece of work" by relating her experiences in psychoanalysis, her literary and sexual awakenings, and her insistence upon a personal aesthetic informing all aspects of her life. This self-creating aesthetic is echoed consistently in the *Diaries*, from the eleven-year-old child who "wished to turn myself into lots of words, lots of sentences" to the mature artist who claimed that "becoming a work of art interests me more than creating one" *(Linotte* 145; *Diary* 4: 177). Despite the instant popularity of the first published *Diary,* Nin feared that the written text could not carry the burden of proof. The demand for personal appearances, she maintained, was "an expression of the need to be sure there was integrity between the writer and the *Diary,* that the *Diary* was not an invention – that it was not image-making in the false, fraudulent sense" (Skidmore College). "They needed to hear my voice. They needed me to be there," Nin reflected in her last *Diary* (224). She saw performance as a means of "lending my presence because so many need to ascertain that I am real; ascertain that I have the voice of my words, the body of my words, the face of my words" (224). Performance offered the most powerful reassurance that the imagined life was possible because it gave living proof that the imagined self was real.

By her own admission, Nin's performances were motivated by a desire to incarnate her autobiographical heroine. In order to initiate her audience in their own identifying practices, she needed to prove that she was, indeed, the remarkable self-created woman her readers had encountered in the *Diary*. This drive toward incarnation is readily apparent in her promotion. An early publicity photo by Swallow Press captures Nin in her dual role as embodied heroine of the *Diary* and "goddess" of the self-creating process. Nin is shown seated on the floor of a bank vault with the 150 manuscripts of the *Diary* stacked around her. In the background are safety deposit boxes – the "tabernacle" of the *Diaries* against which the photographer's flash frames her face in a halo of light. One side of her face is illuminated, the other cast in shadow as she reads from an open manuscript on her lap. According to Peter Owen's 1968 review for the *New York Times*: "She is seen like a saint, dwarfed beside her own holy relics. . . . She is the Priestess of the *Diary* which is herself, raised to the Divinity of Art . . ." Jill Krementz's 1971 publicity still captures Nin striding across a college campus with her trademark black cape swirling around her; the caption reads "Anais Nin: Scheherezade of the 20th Century." This dramatic, full-length cape had been immortalized in the second and third *Diaries,* and according to Rupert Pole, "by the time of the Anais Nin Celebrations at Berkeley [1972] it had become her trademark and was exhibited in Berkeley dress shops as 'The Nin Cape' " *LA Times,* Oct. 31, 1982). Such promotional strategies underscore the pervasive identification of Nin with her *Diary* persona and confirm the appropriateness of "incarnation" as both the driving force and the shaping aesthetic of her performances.

As Nin's popularity soared, her audiences increasingly were comprised of her *Diary* community. Four volumes had been published when she reached the peak of her celebrity in 1971 and the readers with whom she had maintained a lively correspondence flocked to see her in person. By all accounts, there was a remarkable congruence between the heroine of the *Diary* and the woman who presented herself on stage. Evelyn Hinz describes the moment of Nin's appearance as a kind of mystical materialization.

> As one watches her approach the microphone one never has the feeling that here is the author coming out from *behind* the hard covers of her book, but rather that here is the woman herself stepping out from *between* its pages. It's quite as if one were sitting and

reading the *Diary* and suddenly looked up to see the image one had formed become real (x).

The immediate response to Nin's presence was commonly one of spontaneous affirmation. As she boasts in the final *Diary*: "Even before I speak, they give me standing ovations at Harvard, at Berkeley, so it is the work they respond to and then I speak from the heart of the work" (224). The continuity between her literary and stage personae was so pronounced that some experienced a disorienting *déja vu*. Adele Aldridge, a participant in the Magic Circle Weekend, claimed "a feeling too intense for any words. A fourth dimensional event-time telescoped and expanded all at once" (Harms, 80).

Such affirming responses suggest that Nin's performances were mediated by her audience's familiarity with the *Diary*, whose detailed self-portraits provided an imaginal framework for recognizing her stage persona. The *Diary* offers indelible images of Nin's "heart-shaped face which was over-delicate, fragile, eyes which are deep and sad, hands which are delicate, a walk which is a glide" (1: 51). Beatrice Formentelli, one of several critics to critique Nin's selfportraiture, argues that one might actually caption sections of the *Diary* like an annotated "album of photographs" featuring Nin in various moods, poses and performances (89). In "The Difficulty of the Real" Formentelli cites numerous examples: "Anais posing for a painter in a Watteau costume" (1: 117), "Anais in the hospital after the stillbirth – 'Perfume and powder, the face all well' " (1: 346), "Anais at the beach in Provincetown – 'I wear my sarong dress, sea-shell necklace, the sea-shell comb' " (3: 127), or "Anais as Scheherezade" (5: 140). Evelyn Hinz, on the other hand, favors a more organic justification for the continuity between Nin's autobiographical and performance personae. She argues that it is not "a question of likeness to photographs," but a function of "the perfect correlation between her appearance and gestures and the style and substance of her writing" (ix). Hinz claims that audiences responded to "the same fluidity and grace" in her movements, "the same quality of tenderness and honesty in her smile" and the same "tremulous," "melodious," and French-accented voice one intuits from the way she relates her experiences in the *Diary* (ix). Whether the continuity arose from craft or quintessence, it is clear that audiences approached Nin's performances with little ambiguity about her physical presence. From a performance standpoint, the effect of sudden materialization was not difficult to achieve. As Hinz astutely concludes: "possibly it is the thrill of recognition, rather than simply seeing her in person that sweeps audiences to their feet the moment she walks on stage" (x).

The "thrill of recognition" might have grounded the initial affirmation of Nin's identity, but it could not have been sufficient for sustaining two hours of performance. Rather, Nin's celebrity is indicative of a skilled practitioner, capable of negotiating her identity within the bounds of a shared text-in-effect, the shared script of the *Diary*. One might ask, then, how Nin, as a contemporary Scheherezade, performed her life story so as to ensure its ongoing enactment? More specifically, what were the structural and stylistic features of the lectures that enabled her to construct her audience as co-performers of her *Diary* identity?

The lectures given between 1971-73 are representative of Nin's mature performance style. She was preparing the fifth *Diary* for publication when she embarked on a national tour of more than sixty campuses. A typical "Evening with Anais Nin," as her lectures were sometimes billed, lasted about two hours and was held in large university auditoriums or theatres. There were two structural components: a 45 to 60-minute lecture culminating in a reading from the *Diary* and an hour-long question and answer period, or "furrawn."

The pattern of Nin's opening remarks reveal a deft rhetorical hand. She needed to create a spirit of complicity with her audience, a shared responsibility for the direction and tenor of the evening. Her initial words were often invitations: "I feel like a troubadour, waiting to know what you would like to hear" (Harms 77). She stressed her accountability to audience needs and expectations: "As I was coming to you today I was thinking: what would I like most to be given on a day like today?" (Reed College). Often she would reverse the assumed performer/audience relationship, claiming that it was she who benefited from their interaction: "I know that you think you discovered me when I published the *Diary* but really, I discovered you" (Central Michigan University). To reinforce their common ground, Nin might redefine "artist" as an inclusive category that embraced the diverse activities of her listeners. In her keynote address for Berkeley University's Festival of the Arts, Nin subtly reminded her audience that they were already engaged in a collective creative act.

> I call an artist whoever has created, willed – whoever creates with anything, a garden or a child, or a life, or friendships, or relationships or a weekend such as John Pierson did this time . . . created this fraternity that I have found to be true and genuine and profound.

The Berkeley address – a performance Nin claimed as one of her most skillfully crafted – shows her working very astutely to dissolve the hierarchy implicit in her position as self-created artist and celebrity spokesperson. By renaming, and hence revaluing, any intentional endeavor as "artistic," Nin established a shared foundation from which she could argue the aesthetics of identity construction. More importantly, she cued the audience into their role as "true, genuine and profound" collaborators in constructing her performance identity. In other words, Nin momentarily removed the mask of her celebrity status in order that she and her audience could come together in co-creative intimacy.

Nin's introductory remarks established a tone of intimate dialogue with her audience; she acknowledged their presence, established common ground, encouraged their participation, and began to position them as co-performers of her *Diary* identity. The opening to her 1972 Marin College lecture exemplifies the rhetoric of intimate collaboration evoked by the invitational frame.

> We want to have a "furrawn" – which comes front the beautiful Welsh word meaning the kind of talk that leads to intimacy. It can be a talk with one person, it can be a talk with all of you. It is something that you will participate in.

Yet, even within this spirit of intimate collaboration, Nin did not relinquish her authority as the charismatic, self-created heroine. As one who had completed the self-creating enterprise and stood before them transformed into her imagined shape, Nin would re-instate herself as the guide for the evening's journey. At Berkeley, she concluded her prefatory remarks by reclaiming a measure of authority: "By artist I really mean the magician who has the power to levitate and I have promised to teach you tonight to levitate."

In the body of her lectures, Nin negotiated a skillful dialectic between the world of the *Diary* and the contemporary world of her audience. Her method was to recount an event from her life and then open up the boundaries of interpretation until its relevance to the lives of her audience became evident. As she prefaced one evening at Marin College: "I wanted to read to you a few passages from the *Diary* and then talk from them on, as a beginning." According to Hinz, "the general impression her lectures generate is that of a rhythmic interchange: back from the present to the *Diary* and forward from the Diary to the present" (xi). The effect of these temporal shifts was threefold. First, they underscored the contemporary relevance of issues Nin had addressed in the *Diary*, such as women's social and economic status, racial injustice, technological alienation and cultural colonialism. Second, Nin's braiding of lived, autobiographical and performed texts reinforced the continuity between her *Diary* and stage personae. The incarnational aesthetic is grounded in intertextuality between past and present, literature and performance, or the shared texts of speaker and audience. Nin could move smoothly from the *Diary* to dialogue because she presented herself as the stable anchor – the echoing voice, so to speak – heard consistently within all contexts. The final and most significant effect was to destabilize the *Diary*, to shift its status from completed product to a perpetually open and ongoing process, shared and shaped at every level by her audience. Again, from the Marin College evening:

> And this is what I discovered today, that the *Diary* no longer belongs to me. It was written by many women, it was written for many women and many women have said, "This is my diary." And this is dedicated to the women in the audience.

Nin moves her audience from the margins of the performance to the center of the *Diary* itself by blurring the boundaries of its central subject. The Everywoman stance enables her to redefine the Diary as a shared text, "at once personal and no longer personal." Moreover, it allows her to cast the audience as collaborative partners, both in its writing and its performance. In other words, by blurring the boundaries of the *Diary*, Nin re-activates its identifying power.

Nin would frequently culminate the lecture portion of the evening by reading aloud an extended section from the *Diary*. If she had been exploring the value of theatre and ritual in a technological society, she read of her relationship with Antonin Artaud (Marin College; *Diary* 1: 188). When the topic was professional women, she might relate the story of Frances Steloff, creator of the Gotham Book Mart and publisher of avant-garde fiction (Central Michigan University; *Diary* 3: 178). The obvious purpose of these *Diary* readings was to ground Nin's ideas in her work. The dramatistic purpose, however, was to return Nin to the literary world from which she had materialized. In a sense, the *Diary* transitions provided the transformational moment between Nin as "living document" – the embodiment of her text – and Nin as magician of the creative process who would teach her audience "to levitate." According to Hinz, the effect was almost sacramental.

> Just as she comes out of the Diary to speak in person, having spoken, having reassured her audience that the woman who is speaking to them is the same woman who spoke from the *Diary*, she then withdraws back again into its pages, leaving her audience with the *Diary* in place of her physical presence, leaving them with the place where she may always be found and from which she will always continue to speak. (xi)

How apt that Hinz implicitly invokes a secular analogy to the "Word Incarnate" and the *Diary* as a "living document." In these transitions we see Nin skillfully fuse her literary and living personae by refraining the *Diary* as the site of ongoing conversations with her "disciples." Her identity as the *Diary* heroine will continue to be authenticated as long as her community seeks her in the pages of her "sacred" text.

The "Evening" at Marin College offers a particularly skillful example of the *Diary* transition.[4] Nin concluded her lecture on the "second birth of the self" by reiterating the importance of autobiography as a vehicle of rebirth. She stressed the need for women to trust the integrity of their own voices, to speak of female experience in a distinctively female idiom. The transition proceeded as follows:

> For the women I wanted to read a moment of awareness when I chose my path as a writer to be different from that of man. It was a night in a café in Paris, long time ago in the thirties when we spent the night arguing – Henry Miller, Lawrence Durrell and myself –

about the difference between man and woman's writing. . . . [she opens the *Diary*] "That night they suddenly attacked my personal relation to all things . . ." (*Diary* 2: 231-35)

The *Diary* account of their argument culminates in Nin's assertion that "woman was born to represent union and communion and communication" (235). Closing the *Diary,* Nin deftly connected the *Diary's* model of "women's communication" with the correspondence she had received from readers following its publication.

> Now this concern with woman's role as the life-line, as the connection, as the bringing together . . . is what was fulfilled in the *Diary*. But I didn't know it until you responded and answered in the same tone in which I wrote. That is, the letters I received are like a visit from a friend. You are able to call me by my first name, to write me about intimate things; in other words the level of our communication is never superficial. It always goes to the heart of the matter. And in this I found fulfillment.

She reminded the audience that the intimacy of their letters and the need they expressed for personal contact was the reason she stood before them today. She then invited them to interact with her according to the "feminine" model of intimacy which the Diary had initiated between them.

> I wanted this, tonight, to be a conversation with you. We purposely kept it intimate and small [laughter] – or we wanted to – so that we could talk together as we would perhaps if you just came to see me. I'm sure you have had questions in your mind about the work. . . . So I want you to speak to me and question me and act as you would if you came to visit me.

Transitions such as this worked thematically to link Nin's voice in the *Diary*, the letters and the performance, but they also worked rhetorically to position her audience to respond "in the same tone" in which she had written. Having guided her audience along the permeable boundaries of her life and writing and established the *Diary* as their shared text, Nin released the voices she had been "coaching" implicitly throughout the evening. The conversations which followed these transitions were to be modeled after the relationship the audience already had established with her through the *Diary*.

Nin concluded every performance with an hour of open dialogue or "furrawn." These interactions were certainly "open" in that Nin fielded uncensored questions from the floor, asked students to relate their own writing experiences and frequently continued discussion with individuals as she was being ushered from the auditorium. Hinz recalls that regardless of the size of the audience or of the formality of the performance space, "each individual comes away with the feeling that there has been a personal and intimate conversation with Anais Nin" (xii). In "The Art of Being a Person" James Leo Herlihy attributed this intimacy to Nin's "highly developed sense of the other" wherein "each person her eyes met – even for a second – got this feeling that she was seeing them; that there really was a person there seeing who they were" (68). There is considerable evidence that Nin was genuinely interested in her audience's ideas and experiences. When a student opened the Skidmore Surrey House discussion by asking what she would like to talk about "before we start pinning you down with questions," Nin responded like a gracious hostess.

> I think that should be mutual. I think you ought to tell me what you would like to talk with me about – what things you would like to explore. Because after all you have already read me, you know me, you know the things I'm interested in. . . . So I think it would be better for me to find out what it is like for you to question. . . . I would like to know what is in your minds and what preoccupies you, and you know, what the work made you think about.

Yet, at the heart of the intimate atmosphere, the open invitations and the sincere concern for students that Nin generated, she maintained a subtle but pervasive control over the content and tenor of discussion. To acknowledge the sincerity of the furrawn does not prohibit a critique of its practice, for Nin was no less skilled in framing discussion than she was in framing her performance.

Nin used two strategies during the furrawn which reveal her editorial hand. First, she insisted that audience members be familiar with the Diary before engaging her in conversation. "I want to have a dialogue with somebody who has read the work and has questions about the work," she explained at the San Francisco Esalen Seminar.

> As I saw it, we were getting together in order to discuss some kind of study or growth development of woman. That's the story I'm telling, or that I'm using. I have really nothing to say or to exchange with those who haven't come to the work. I don't understand why they come.

According to Nin, familiarity with the *Diary* directed the audience's energies toward constructive dialogue. They approached her with expectations and questions that she felt a responsibility to address.

> You have entered through the work and you have a right to your expectations. And if I disappoint them, you have a right to say the work and the person don't coincide, don't synchronize, that they don't represent the same thing. That's all right, because you have en-

tered the work and you have made a demand of the person who did
it. (Esalen Seminar)

Of course, Nin's audiences did not always seek a genuine dialogue about
the *Diary*. She frequently encountered what she termed "aggressive curiosity
seekers . . . the curse of those who haven't yet made their individual selection
of reading the work before coming to talk with me" (Esalen Seminar). Nin
had little patience with this kind of audience member. As she told interviewer
Judy Chicago: "facing them was like going into enemy country." If a question
indicated that a student had not read the *Diary*, Nin's response was curt and
cool. Likewise, if someone questioned the authenticity of the *Diary*, Nin
might counter by challenging their familiarity with the work. Once, a California Technical Institute student glibly asked Nin if she had edited the *Diary*
"to make it more trendy and stylish?" Nin retorted by shifting the responsibility back on the student: "That's a question I shouldn't even be asked! If you
had read it, you wouldn't ask that question. It is self-evident." In other words,
if the *Diary* provided a common ground for Nin's interaction with her audience, its absence created a vacuum in which meaningful dialogue with her
was impossible.

Within the parameters of the *Diary* itself, Nin maintained a firm editorial hand on the kinds of questions she considered appropriate. She refused to
discuss aspects of her personal life which had been edited for publication.
Given the sizable biographical gaps in the published *Diary*, however, such
prurient interest was inevitable. In particular, the omission of her marriage to
Hugh Guiler led to many confrontations on this issue, and Nin exercised a
range of strategies for dealing with such questions. Occasionally, she explicitly outlined "taboo" questions as in the following caution to students at the
University of Michigan.

> The only question I won't answer − I know you want to ask me − is
> what is not in the *Diary*. Ultimately you will read the whole thing a
> few years from now. But now you must remember that if I have a
> right to share my life, I don't have the right to impose that on oth-
> ers.

More often, Nin would simply deflect personal questions as they arose in discussion. She kept a "stock answer" for inquiries about her husband: "The
marriage I cannot talk about because the husband asked not to be in the *Diary*. And this was stated in the preface to volume one. I guess nobody reads
prefaces!" (Marin College). If this disclaiming joke did not deflect personal
questions, Nin recast her right to privacy as an artist's ethical obligations to
her subjects. "All that I could give you, I gave you, and if you feel that there is
more left out than I gave, that is something I can't help. . . . What you call the
holes in the *Diary* are there because I did not wish to be destructive of other
human beings" (Chicago Psychological Institute). Occasionally, a student

pressed the issue or became antagonistic and Nin curtly cut off further interaction: "I won't discuss that" (Santa Clara University).

This is not to say that Nin faced uniform affirmation, or that the critical
contingent in her audience remained silent. Both her performances and her
Diaries evoked scathing critique on the grounds of narcissism, aestheticism,
and bourgeois individualism. Laurie Stone's review of the fifth *Diary* for *The
Village Voice* takes Nin to task for participating in women's continuing oppression rather than her liberation. In "Is the Bloom off the Pose?" Stone
writes:

> She seems to have stood for a certain kind of woman writer who, in
> her concern above all with the private, her awareness of clothes, her
> squeamish refusal to look at the unclean and ugly in life, and her
> overwhelming narcissism, was a threat to all women who had cho-
> sen to be intellectual, concrete and political as a way of being new
> and free. (43)

Stone credits this stance – what she calls "the Jean Brodie syndrome" – as
the reason such early feminists as Diana Trilling, Elizabeth Hardwick, and
Frances Keene "penned their reviews in blood" (43).

This line of critique seems to have been played out predominately in
print since Nin's most vocal critics shunned participation in her performances. While the final *Diary* refers to occasional confrontations with "aggressive
radical feminists," there is no record of these confrontations on any of the
performance tapes (7: 182). Instead, Nin uses the *Diary* to surround her critique with affirming testimonials or to present them as "fringe hostilities" silenced by the larger audience.

> At Harvard, three hostile, aggressive women prevented me from
> finishing my talk. Really psychotic! I was ashamed of them. The
> public hissed them out! And half the audience stayed on until
> twelve – long past the lectures (*Diary* 7: 182)[5]

If we accept the *Diary* accounts – and in the absence of complete performance records there is no data to refute them – such challenges rarely became part of the performance discourse. The substance and tenor of the fur-
rawns remain as I have characterized them: skillfully designed to reinforce
Nin's *Diary* persona.

Reflecting on Nin's editorial hand, one cannot refute her right to certain
privacies, nor discount her ethical responsibility to protect those wishing to
remain invisible or anonymous. It would be naive, however, not to recognize
another agenda underlying her responses. By maintaining control over the
conversations, Nin ensured a degree of complicity between the image she had
constructed in the *Diary* and the persona the audience experienced on stage.
One could make the argument – and some leaders may be led to this conclu-

sion – that the ostensibly dialogic furrawn was, in reality, a carefully controlled activity of capitulation in which intimacy and participation actually
meant reinforcement of the *Diary's* central characters. Such an interpretation, however, implies a duplicity in Nin's performances which neither the
tapes nor the *Diaries* bear out. Nor does it give credence to the hours she
spent with individual students after a lecture, the performance commitments
she continued to meet while undergoing cancer treatments, nor the documented evidence of her empowering effect on young writers.[6] I favor a more
generous interpretation, therefore, that recognizes the craft of Nin's self-construction without discounting her sincerity. The performance issue remains
not with the integrity of her identity, but with the structure of its enactment.

Anais Nin's lectures are exemplars of autobiographical performance because they dramatize the dialectical constitution of identity that is the heart
of self-performance. In *Role-Playing and Identity: The Limits of Theatre as
Metaphor,* Bruce Wilshire persuasively articulates the dialogic construction
and performative basis of human identity. "The self's identity," he contends,
"involves a fusion – and at times confusion – of its more direct experience
of itself and its view of other's view of itself" (172). He offers a cogent sche-
ma for synthesizing the features and functions of Nin's autobiographical performances.

Wilshire argues that self-identifying activities are based on collaborative
fictions that – like theatrical personae – mediate the interconnected identities of performer, character and audience. His key concepts, "standing in"
and "reciprocal authorization," describe how actor and audience experience
mutually affirming images of themselves through the shared illusion of a
dramatic character. According to Wilshire, the performer "stands in" for the
audience by "standing in" for a dramatic character who in turn "stands in"
for a possible human experience (24). I have shown how Nin's incarnational
aesthetic enabled her to "stand in" for the autobiographical construct
"Anais," who was already "standing in" for the audience's faith in self-creation. In other words, "Anais" intervened between Nin and her audience as a
mediating fiction, such that Nin's performance gave "concrete presence to an
imagined absence" – an absence of faith in the created self redeemed by the
imagined absence of the *Diary* heroine (31). This dramatic presence is mutually signifying, Wilshire continues, because of the "space of complicity"
between performer and audience wherein each reciprocally authorizes the
other's identity.

> The shimmering fictional character is the locus through which the
> actor is given back to [her]himself through the audience and the
> members of the audience are given back to themselves through the
> actor. . . . The actor is authorized by the audience and the audience
> by the actor. (94)

Similarly, I have argued that the *Diary* functioned both as a shared script for the collective enactment of Nin's identity, and as the basis for empowering her audience to embrace their own self-identifying aesthetic. As her audience was "swept to their feet by the thrill of recognition," they authorized the continuity between her autobiographical and performance identities, and when they flooded her with testimonials they gave witness to the *Diary's* authorization of their own creative selves. Viewed from this perspective, Nin's performances speak eloquently to the fragility of human identities that must be continually reconstructed in the presence of an affirming performance community. In the intimate co-performance of her *Diary* persona Anais Nin assumed her legendary status; in performance, her identity finally found lasting sustenance.

Finally, I wish to extend my observations about Nin's performances into the larger critical context of women's self-identifying practices. Nin's life-text remains engaging because she raises issues specific to women's performance of self and the tensions that surround her autobiographical voice. As Tristine Rainer eulogized at the Nin Memorial Tribute: "she provided a model of a woman who found individual creative solutions to the contradictions of being a woman and an artist." At the same time, Nin is a problematic writer/performer because she assumes a psychological model of the universal feminine – "woman is a mermaid with her fishtail dipped in the unconscious" – whose emancipatory path lies not in political action, but in a "descent into the real womb to discover its secrets, its labyrinths" (*Diary* 1: 235). Nin's Everywoman is grounded in archetypal images of woman as muse, mother, daughter, lover, seductress or Goddess.[7] The fact that "she uses such images rather than refuses them to assemble herself as a woman and an artist" continues to stand out, according to Julia Casterton and Maxine Molyneux, "as a clanging cymbal of stereotypes apparently discarded in the modern age" (86). Moreover, Nin's insistence upon privileging a psychological rather than a socio-political arena for women's emancipation makes her doubly problematic. Interviewer Judy Oringer once accused Nin of having "a romantic vision of the world, searching for the liberation of the individual as if she or he lived in an isolated, contained existence" (44). Nin responded that hers "was not a romantic vision but a psychological one" and she feared that the feminists' political agenda was misguided "blind collective action" designed to further divide the sexes rather than emancipate the individual (45). Such apolitical naiveté is hardly justifiable, but it is understandable in light of Nin's lifelong advocacy of psychotherapy and the personal empowerment she experienced through analysis. To her credit, Nin acknowledged that "the inward journey" was not an alternative but a prelude to socio-political transformation, and that she stressed the psychological path "simply because it was the way that I know" (Central Michigan University). "I'm not a political specialist," she confessed to the graduating class at Dartmouth; "I know exactly in what realm I have some wisdom. . . . I mean I'm just not very skillful in that particular [political] form of expression."

How, then, does the contemporary reader – particularly the feminist reader/critic – respond to the tensions inherent in Nin's writing and performances? Traditionally, critics have either ignored the tensions by unproblematically embracing her as a "goddess of the self-creating process" or they have rejected her work outright as "a monumental cathedral to her ego" (Miller 102; Traba 14). Such blanket statements grossly oversimplify the complexities of Nin's autobiographical project and disallow any rigorous examination of either the *Diaries* or the performances. I have suggested, therefore, an alternative reading of her performances that foregrounds the rhetoric of self-naming over the names themselves, not "Anais" but the process of her construction. Julia Casterton and Maxine Molyneux have modeled a similar strategy in "Looking Again at Anais Nin." Both women were uneasy with Nin's problematic position within the history of twentieth-century women writers, but were reluctant to dismiss her prodigious accomplishments as both author and public figure. Resurrecting an unpublished interview which Molyneux had conducted with Nin in 1970, they noted a curiously subversive rhetoric underlying her irritatingly conventional self-representation. Casterton's commentary concludes:

> By her very activity of writing [performing] herself as all these things, controlling her representations, naming herself and others, she ensures that she will not be wholly enthralled by others' naming of her. (94)

Nin used her *Diary* to claim voice and visibility out of cultural silence and invisibility. She used performance to challenge the marginality of female experience by moving it to the center of public discourse. Furthermore, her insistence upon drawing the parameters of her own subjectivity – however dissonant they may be with contemporary feminist views – marked a significant departure from the patriarchal order within which she wrote and performed. In other words, one need not be enthralled by Nin's legendary beauty to appreciate the beauty – and the ideological power – of her legend. She remains a problematic writer/performer, but one who cannot easily be dismissed without also dismissing the aesthetic and rhetorical skill of her self promotion as well as the documented evidence of her empowering effect on other women artists. Kate Millet has described her as "the beginner, the shaper in the process of becoming" whose legacy is "a procession of women loving women becoming ourselves" (8). My analysis has presented Nin as an accomplished performer who not only successfully negotiated her own identity, but enabled the identity constructions of her performance community. To read her performances without acknowledging these factors would seriously misrepresent her performance achievement. Ultimately, Nin was, as Millet very simply concludes: "imperfect, just as we are, but with greatness" (8).

In the final analysis, Anais Nin is an example of how autobiographical performance can transform the introspective looking glass of personal texts into the more empowering "speaking glass" of communal performance. By activating a kind of doubling mirror such performances reciprocally authorize the identity constructions of both performer and audience. In effect, autobiographical performance's aesthetic of incarnation may become an aesthetic of reincarnation as women performers authorize their female audience to speak of their own female experiences and feminist consciousness. For this reason, Anais Nin's life and work continue to offer a point of entry into the characteristics and the consequences that attend women's self-construction.

NOTES

[1]I gratefully acknowledge Rupert Pole, trustee of the Nin Foundation, for providing me with the complete audio tape collection and access to Nin's personal performance memorabilia. A former actor and companion of Nin's, Pole also offered valuable insight into her performance style in a series of interviews conducted in July, 1987.

[2]The performance tapes are a valuable, but flawed resource. Regrettably, UCLA Special Collections has made little attempt to systematize the archival information on the recordings; several tapes are incomplete, some are incorrectly labeled, and a few lack any identification whatsoever. With one exception, the essay cites only complete tapes which have been accurately identified. Performances are cited in the text by location with additional bibliographic information provided in the Works Cited.

[3]In "Emerging Woman," a 1973 lecture given at Central Michigan University, Nin cites James Joyce as the original source for the term furrawn: "the kind of talk that leads to intimacy." She appropriated it to describe her conversations with the audience, and Evelyn Hinz uses it to title the final chapter of *A Woman Speaks.*

[4]While the UCLA archives labeled this tape as the 1972 "Evening with Anais Nin" given at Marin College, it does not replicate the Marin lecture identified by Rupert Pole and cited elsewhere in this paper. Given that both the introductory and concluding remarks are missing from the tape, attempts to identify it correctly have been unsuccessful.

[5]The tape labeled as this 1971 Harvard lecture is actually in unidentifiable performance piece combining voices and synthesized music. Nin's voice is not recognizable any where on the tape.

[6]Many testimonials appear in the final *Diary*, although the most striking examples were performed in a two-hour Memorial Tribute following Nin's death. This witnessing continues through frequent retrospectives and memoirs published annually in *Anais: An International Journal.*

[7]For a thorough analysis of archetypal images and themes in Nin's, writing see: Bettina Knapp (1978); Deanna Madden (1975); Sharon Spencer (1977); and Dennis Miller (1985).

WORKS CITED

Capo, Kay and Darlene Hantzis. "(En)Gendered (and Endangered) Subjects: Writing, Reading, Performing and Theorizing Feminist Criticism." *Text and Performance Quarterly* 11 (1991): 249-66.
Formentelli, Beatrice. "The Difficulty of the Real." *Anais* 2 (1984): 77-94.
Geismar, Maxwell. "Anais Nin: An Imprecise Spy in the House of Love." *Los Angeles Times* 13 May 1979: 3.
Harms, Valerie, ed. *Celebration with Anais Nin*. Riverside, Conn.: Magic Circle Press, 1973.
Herlihy, James Leo. "The Art of Being a Person." *Anais* 1 (1983): 67-69.
Hinz, Evelyn, ed. *A Woman Speaks: The Lectures, Seminars and Interviews of Anais Nin*. Chicago: Swallow, 1975.
Knapp, Bettina. *Anais Nin*. New York: Ungar, 1978.
Madden, Deanna. "Laboratory of the Soul; The Influence of Psychoanalysis on the Work of Anais Nin." Diss. U of Miami, 1975.
Miller, Dennis. "Glimpsing a Goddess." *Anais* 3 (1985): 102-4.
Millet, Kate. "Anais: A Mother to Us All." *Anais* 9 (1991): 3-8.
Molyneux, Maxine and Julia Casterton. "Looking Again at Anais Nin." *Minnesota Review* 1982: 86-101.
Nin, Anais. *The Diary of Anais Nin. 1966-1974*. 7 vols. New York: Harcourt, 1966-80.
_____. *Linotte: The Early Diary of Anais Nin. 1914-1920*. New York: Harcourt, 1978.
_____. Commencement Address. Reed College, 13 May 1971.
_____. Interview with Judy Chicago. 14 Feb. 1972.
_____. "On Creativity." Women's Committee, Psychoanalytic Institute. Chicago, 5 Oct. 1972.
_____. "Esalen Seminar." San Francisco, 6-8 Oct. 1972.
_____. "An Evening with Anais Nin." Marin College, 13 Oct. 1972.
_____. Conversation. Skidmore Surrey House, 30 Oct. 1972.
_____. Lecture. Dartmouth University, Nov. 1972.
_____. Keynote Address. "Festival of the Arts." Berkeley University, 2 Dec. 1972.
_____. Lecture. Santa Clara University, 10 Feb. 1973.
_____. Lecture. California Technical Institute, 13 Feb. 1973.
_____. Lecture. University of Michigan, 27 Feb. 1973.
_____. "Emerging Woman." Central Michigan University, 21 March 1973.
Oringer, Judy. "Interview with Anais Nin." *Ramparts* 1971: 44-45.
Owen, Peter. "Priestess of the Diary." *New York Times* 11 Jan. 1968: D35.
Pole, Rupert. "The Nin Cape Caper." *Los Angeles Times*, 31 Oct. 1982: B11.
Rainer, Tristine. "A Tribute to Anais Nin." Anais Nin Memorial Tribute. Los Angeles. 21 Feb. 1977.
Spencer, Sharon. *Collage of Dreams: The Writings of Anais Nin*. Chicago: Swallow, 1977.

Stone, Laurie. "Anais Nin: Is the Bloom off the Pose?" *The Village Voice*, 26 July, 1976: 43-44.

Traba, Marta. "The Monumental 'I' of Anais Nin." *Under the Sign of Pisces* Winter, 1976: 8.

Wilshire, Bruce. *Role-Playing and Identity: The Limits of Theatre as Metaphor*. Bloomington: Indiana UP, 1982.

From *Text and Performance Quarterly* 12.2 (April 1992): 97-112.

Bibliography

Alberti, Frank S. "Anais Nin, Reader of Proust: The Creative Affinities." *Under the Sign of Pisces: Anais Nin and Her Circle* 10.2 (Spring 1979): 3-12.

Andersen, Margret. "Critical Approaches to Anais Nin." *Canadian Review of American Studies* 10.2 (Fall 1979): 255-65.

Bair, Deirdre. *Anais Nin: A Biography*. New York: G. P. Putnam's Sons, 1995.

Balakian, Anna. "Anais Nin and Feminism." Spencer 23-33. Rpt. as "A Tale of Two People" in *Anais: An International Journal* 6 (1988): 58-66.

_____. "The Poetic Reality of Anais Nin." Introduction to *Anais Nin Reader*. Ed. Philip K. Jason. Chicago: Swallow Press, 1973. 11-30. Rpt. in Harms's *Celebration with Anais Nin* and in Zaller 113-31.

_____. " '. . . and the pursuit of happiness': *The Scarlet Letter* and *A Spy in the House of Love*." Hinz 163-70.

_____. Rev. of *Anais Nin* by Oliver Evans. *American Literature* 41.1 (Mar. 1969): 130-33.

Baldanza, Frank. "Anais Nin." *Minnesota Review* 2 (Winter 1962): 263-71.

Barnes, Daniel. "Nin and Traditional Erotica." *Seahorse: The Anais Nin/Henry Miller Journal* 1.1 (1982): 1-5.

Barillé, Elisabeth. *Anais Nin: Naked Under the Mask*. Trans. Elfreda Powell. London: Lime Tree, 1992.

Benstock, Benjamin. "The Present Recaptured: D. H. Lawrence and Others." *Southern Review* NS 4 (July 1968): 802-16. Rev. of *Diary* 1.

Benstock, Shari. *Women of the Left Bank: Paris, 1900-1940*. Austin: University of Texas Press, 1986.

Bloom, Lynn Z., and Orlee Holder. "Anais Nin's *Diary* in Context." Hinz 191-202. Rpt. in *Women's Autobiography: Essays in Criticism*. Ed. Estelle C. Jelinek. Bloomington: Indiana University Press, 1980. 206-20.

Bobbitt, Joan. "Truth and Artistry in the *Diary of Anais Nin*." *Journal of Modern Literature* 9.2 (May 1982): 267-76.

Bradbury, Malcolm. "Aesthetic Decadence." *Manchester Guardian* 12 Sept. 1968: 14. On *Bell*.

_____. "New Novels." *Punch* 21 June 1961: 953-54. On *Seduction*.

Bradford, Jean. "The Self: A Mosaic, A Loving Perspective on the Diaries of Anais Nin." *Journal of the Otto Rank Association* 12.1 (Summer 1977): 14-25.

_____. "Venus Rising on the Ful Shell: Anais Nin and the Archetypal." *Anais: An International Journal* 13 (1995): 114-23.

Brandon, Dolores. "Anais Nin: Sister to the Creators of Modern Dance." Spencer 101-24.

Brennan, Karen. "Anais Nin: Author(iz)ing the Erotic Body." *Genders* 14 (Fall 1992): 66-86.

Brians, Paul. "Sexuality and the Opposite Sex: Variations on a Theme by Théophile Gautier and Anais Nin." *Essays in Literature* 4 (Spring 1977): 122-37.

"Briefly Noted – Fiction." *The New Yorker* 12 Dec. 1964: 244. On *Collages*.

Broderick, Catherine. "Anais Nin's *Diary* and the Japanese Literary Diary Tradition." Hinz 177-89.

_____. "The Song of the Womanly Soul: Mask and Revelation in Japanese Literature and in the Fiction of Anais Nin." Spencer 176-91.

Broderick, Catherine, with Masako Karatani. "The Reception of Anais Nin in Japan." *Under the Sign of Pisces: Anais Nin and Her Circle* 5.1 (Winter 1974): 5-11.

Brodin, Pierre. "Anais Nin." *Vingt-Cinq Américains: Littérature et Littératurs Américains Des Années 1960*. Paris: Nouvelles Editions Debresse, 1969.

Burford, William. "The Art of Anais Nin." In *On Writing*, by Anais Nin. Hanover, N.H.: Daniel Oliver Associates, 1947. 5-14. Pamphlet rpt. Yonkers, N.Y.: Alicat Bookshop, 1947, as number 11 in the Outcast Chapbook series. Essay rpt. in *Anais: An International Journal* 8 (1990): 40-44.

Carruth, Hayden. "*The Four-Chambered Heart*." *Providence Sunday Journal* 29 Jan. 1950: 10.

Casey, Florence. "A Bird Does not Need to Study Aviation." *Christian Science Monitor* 14 Jan. 1969, C: 1. On *Novel*.

Célérier, Patricia-Pia. "The Vision of Dr. Allendy: Psychoanalysis and the Quest for an Independent Identity." *Anais: An International Journal* 7 (1989): 78-94.

Centing, Richard R. "Emotional Algebra: The Symbolic Level of *The Diary of Anais Nin, 1944-1947*." Zaller 169-76.

Chase, Gilbert Culmell. "From 'Kew' to Paris: A Personal Memoir." *Anais: An International Journal* 1 (1983): 60-62.

Chase, Kathleen. "Anais Nin and Music: Jazz." *Under the Sign of Pisces: Anais Nin and Her Circle* 11.1 (Winter 1980): 15-22.

_____. "Anais Nin – Rumour and Reality: A Memoir by Kathleen Chase."

Under the Sign of Pisces: Anais Nin and Her Circle 6.4 (Fall 1975): 1-8.

_____. "Being 'Family' in France, 1930-1934." *Anais: An International Journal* 1 (1983): 63-66.

_____. "*Cities of the Interior,* by Anais Nin." *Two Cities: La Revue Bilingue de Paris* 15 May 1960: 100-03. Unsigned.

Clark, Orville. "Anais Nin: Studies in the New Erotology." Zaller 101-11.

Cole, Barry. "Soothsayers." *The Spectator.* 13 Sept. 1968. On *Bell.*

"*Collages* by Anais Nin." *Los Angeles Free Press* 26 Nov. 1964: 8.

Conn, Jeanne. "Anais Nin and the Beats." *Kerouac Connection* 21 (Spring 1991)): 20-21.

Cushman, Keith. "The View from *Under a Glass Bell.*" Hinz 110-19.

Cutting, Rose Marie. *Anais Nin: A Reference Guide.* Boston: G. K. Hall, 1978.

"D. H. Lawrence in Retrospect." *Times Literary Supplement* 5 May 1932: 327.

Davis, Robert Gorham. "Anais Nin's Children of Light and Movement." *New York Times Book Review* 23 Nov. 23 1947: 36. On *Children.*

_____. "The Fantastic World of Anais Nin." *New York Times Book Review* 28 Mar. 1948: 24. On *Bell.*

Dearborn, Mary V. *The Happiest Man Alive: A Biography of Henry Miller.* New York: Simon & Schuster, 1991.

Deduck, Patricia A. *Realism, Reality, and the Fictional Theory of Alain Robbe-Grillet and Anais Nin.* Washington, D.C.: University Press of America, 1982.

Demetrakopoulos, Stephanie A. "Anais Nin and the Feminine Quest for Consciousness: The Quelling of the Devouring Mother and the Ascension of the Sophia." *Women, Literature, Criticism.* Ed. Harry R. Garvin and Catherine F. Smith. Lewisburg, Penn.: Bucknell University Press, 1978. Simultaneously a special issue of *Bucknell Review* 24.1 (Spring 1978): 119-36.

_____. "Archetypal Constellations of Feminine Consciousness in Nin's First *Diary.*" Hinz 121-37.

Dennison, Sally. "Anais Nin: The Book as a Work of Art." *Alternative Literary Publishing: Five Modern Histories.* Iowa City: University of Iowa Press, 1984. 119-55.

Dick, Bernard F. "Anais Nin and Gore Vidal: A Study in Literary Incompatibility." Hinz 153-62.

DuBow, Wendy M. "The Elusive Text: On Reading *Diary I.*" *Anais: An International Journal* 11 (1993): 22-36.

_____. *Conversations with Anais Nin.* Jackson: University Press of Mississippi, 1994.

Durrell, Lawrence. Preface to *Children of the Albatross.* London: Peter Owen, 1959. 9-10. Rpt. in Zaller 2.

Edel, Leon. "Life Without Father." *Saturday Review* 7 May 1966: 91. On *Diary* 1.

Ekberg, Kent. "The Importance of *Under a Glass Bell*." *Under the Sign of Pisces: Anais Nin and Her Circle* 8.2 (Spring 1977): 4-18.

_____. *"Waste of Timelessness and Other Early Stories* by Anais Nin." *Under the Sign of Pisces: Anais Nin and Her Circle* 8.3 (Summer 1977): 12-17.

Ellmann, Mary. *Thinking About Women*. New York: Harcourt Bracc Jovanovich, 1968.

Evans, Oliver. *Anais Nin*. Carbondale: Southern Illinois University Press, 1968.

_____. "Anais Nin and the Discovery of Inner Space." *Prairie Schooner* 36 (Fall 1962): 217-31.

Faas, Ekbert. " 'The Barbaric Friendship with Robert': A Biographical Palimpsest." Hinz 141-52.

_____. *Young Robert Duncan: Portrait of the Poet As Homosexual in Society*. Santa Barbara: Black Sparrow Press, 1983.

Fancher, Edwin. "Anais Nin: Avant-Gardist with a Loyal Underground." *Village Voice* 27 May 1959: 4-5.

Fanchette, Jean. "Notes pour une Préface." *Two Cities: La Revue Bilingue de Paris* 15 Apr. 1959: 56-60.

Fay, Marion. "Selfhood and Social Conscience: On Reading Some Stories in *Under a Glass Bell*." *Anais: An International Journal* 13 (1995): 100-08.

Ferguson, Robert. *Henry Miller: A Life*. New York: W. W. Norton, 1991.

Ferrone, John. "The Making of *Delta of Venus*." Spencer 35-43.

Fitch, Noël Riley. *Anais: The Erotic Life of Anais Nin*. Boston: Little, Brown, 1993.

Ford, Hugh. *Published in Paris: American and British Writers, Printers, and Publishers in Paris, 1920-1939*. New York: Macmillan, 1975.

Fowlie, Wallace. Rev. of *Anais Nin Reader*. *New York Times Book Review* 9 Sept. 1973: 26-27.

_____. "The Girlhood of Anais Nin." *New York Times Book Review*, 13 August 1978: 11. Rev. of *Linotte*.

Franklin, Benjamin, V. "AN and the Rare Book Trade." *Under the Sign of Pisces: Anais Nin and Her Circle* 3.1 (Winter 1972): 11-16.

_____. "AN's Recordings, Editorship of Periodicals, and Films." *Under the Sign of Pisces: Anais Nin and Her Circle* 2.4 (Fall 1971): 7-10.

_____. "Anais Nin." *American Writers in Paris, 1920-1929. Dictionary of Literary Biography 4*. Ed. Karen Lane Rood. Detroit: Gale Research, 1980.

_____. "Anais Nin: A Bibliographical Essay." Zaller 25-33.

_____. *Anais Nin: A Bibliography*. Kent, Ohio: The Kent State University Press, 1973.

_____. "The Textual Evolution of the First Section of 'Houseboat.' " Hinz 95-106.

Franklin, Benjamin, V, and Duane Schneider. *Anais Nin: An Introduction*.

Athens: Ohio University Press, 1979.

Friedman, Ellen G. "Anais Nin." *Modern American Women Writers*. Ed. Lea Baechler, A. Walton Litz, and Elaine Showalter. New York: Charles Scribner's Sons, 1991. 339-51.

_____. "Escaping from the House of Incest: On Anais Nin's Efforts to Overcome Patriarchal Constraints." *Anais: An International Journal* 10 (1992): 39-45.

Friedman, Melvin J. "André Malraux and Anais Nin." *Contemporary Literature* 11.1 (Winter 1970): 104-13. Rev. of Evans.

Friedman, Susan Stanford. "Women's Autobiographical Selves: Theory and Practice." In *The Private Self: Theory and Practice of Women's Autobiographical Writings*. Ed. Shari Benstock. Chapel Hill: University of North Carolina Press, 1988. 34-62.

Fuller, John. "In the Truck." *New Statesman* 1 May 1964: 688. On *Collages*.

Fülop-Miller, René. "Freudian Noah's Ark." *New York Times* 29 Jan. 1950: 4. On *Heart*.

Garoffolo, Vincent. Rev.of *Under the Glass Bell and Other Stories*. *New Mexico Quarterly Review* 18 (Summer 1948): 247-49.

Geismar, Maxwell. "Anais Nin: An Imprecise Spy in the House of Love." *Los Angeles Times* 13 May 1979, sec. 5: 3.

_____. "Temperament vs. Conscience." *The Nation* 24 July 1954: 75-76. On *Spy*.

Gilbert, Sandra M. "Feminism and D. H. Lawrence." *Anais: An International Journal* 9 (1991): 92-100.

Gilbert, Stuart. "Foreword to *House of Incest*." Zaller 1. A portion appears in *Dairy* 2, 146-47.

_____. "Passion in Parenthesis." *Reading and Collecting* 1.12 (Nov. 1937): 23. On *House*.

Gottlieb, Elaine S. "New Fiction of America." New York *Herald Tribune Books* 8 Nov. 1942: 14. On *Winter*.

Goyen, William. "Bits and Images of Life." *New York Times Book Review* 29 Nov. 1964: 5, 24. On *Collages*.

_____. "Portrait of the Artist as Diarist." *New York Times Book Review* 14 Apr. 1974: 4. On *Diary* 5.

Graham, Kenneth. "Ruined Raj." *The Listener* 5 Sept. 1968: 313. On *Bell*.

Griffin, Barbara J. "Two Experimental Writers: Djuna Barnes and Anais Nin." *American Women Writers: Bibliographical Essays*. Ed. Maurice Duke, Jackson R. Bryer, and M. Thomas Inge. Westport, Conn.: Greenwood Press, 1983. 144-66.

Griffith, Paul. "The 'Jewels' of Anais Nin." *Journal of the Otto Rank Association* 5.2 (Dec. 1970): 82-89.

Hahn, Emily. "*Winter of Artifice*." *T'ien Hsia Monthly* Nov. 1939: 435-38.

Haller, Robert A. "Anais Nin and Film: Open Questions." Spencer 135-38.

Hamalian, Leo. "A Spy in the House of Lawrence." *Anais: An International Journal* 13 (1995): 14-26.

Hardwick, Elizabeth. "Fiction Chronicle." *Partisan Review* 15 (June 1948): 705-11. On *Bell*.

Harms, Valerie. "Anais Nin, Witch of Words." *Maria Montessori, Anais Nin, Frances Steloff: Stars in My Sky*. Riverside, Conn.: Magic Circle Press, 1975. 82-118.

_____, ed. *Celebration with Anais Nin*. Riverside, Conn.: Magic Circle Press, 1973.

_____. "The Dream Is the Key – The Drafts That Became *House of Incest*." *Anais: An International Journal* 5 (1987): 102-10.

_____. "Interaction and Cross-Fertilization: Miller and Nin." *Anais: An International Journal* 4 (1986): 109-15.

Hart, William. "Analysis of the Antagonisms Inherent in the Human Struggle." *Houston Post* 16 Nov. 1947, sec. 4: 21. On *Children*.

Hauser, Marianne. "Anais Nin: Myth and Reality." *Studies in the Twentieth Century* 2 (Fall 1968): 45-50.

_____. "Thoughts on *The Diary of Anais Nin*." *Journal of the Otto Rank Association* 5.1 (June 1970): 61-67.

Henke, Suzette A. "Anais Nin: Bread and the Wafer." *Under the Sign of Pisces: Anais Nin and Her Circle* 7.2 (Spring 1976): 7-17.

_____. "Anais Nin: A Freudian Perspective." *Under the Sign of Pisces: Anais Nin and Her Circle* 11.1 (Winter 1980): 6-14.

_____. "Lillian Beye's Labyrinth: A Freudian Exploration of *Cities of the Interior*." *Anais: An International Journal* 2 (1984): 113-26.

"Herself Surprised." *Times Literary Supplement* 24 July 1969: 829. On *Novel*.

Hicks, Granville. Rev. of *The Novel of the Future*. *Saturday Review* 25 Jan. 1969: 25-26.

Hinz, Evelyn J. "Anais Nin." *Contemporary Literature* 13.2 (Spring 1972): 255-257. On *Diary* 4.

_____. "Anais Nin: A Reader and the Writer." *The Canadian Review of American Studies* 6.1 (Spring 1975): 116-27.

_____. "The Creative Critic." Harms 57-65.

_____. " 'Excuse Me, It Was All a Dream': *The Diary of Anais Nin, 1944-1947*." *Journal of the Otto Rank Association* 7.2 (Dec. 1972): 21-36.

_____. *The Mirror and the Garden: Realism and Reality in the Writings of Anais Nin*. [Columbus]: Ohio State University Libraries, 1971. Revised ed. New York: Harcourt Brace Jovanovich, 1973.

_____. "Recent Nin Criticism: Who's on First?" *Canadian Review of American Studies* 13.3 (Winter 1982): 373-88.

_____, ed. *The World of Anais Nin: Critical and Cultural Perspectives*. Winnipeg: University of Manitoba Press, 1978. Simultaneously a special issue of *Mosaic* 11.2 (Winter 1978).

Hodgart, Patricia. "Fire of Exile." *The Spectator* 26 May 1961: 771. On *Seduction*.

"Hothouse Crusader." *Times Literary Supplement* 29 Jan. 1971: 113. On *Spy*.

Hoy, Nancy Jo. "The Poetry of Experience." *Anais: An International Journal*

4 (1986): 52-66.

Hugo, Ian. "The Making of *Bells of Atlantis*." Hinz 77-80.

Irgang, Margret. "Always: 'I Want!' Never: 'I Have.' " *Anais: An International Journal* 13 (1995): 95-99.

Jason, Philip K. "Anais Nin." *Research Guide to Biography and Criticism*. Ed. Walton Beachum. Washington, D.C.: Research Publishing, 1985.

_____. *Anais Nin and Her Critics*. Columbia, S.C.: Camden House, 1993.

_____. "A Delicate Battle Cry – Anais Nin's Pamphlets of the 1940s." *Anais: An International Journal* 8 (1990): 30-34.

_____. *"The Diary of Anais Nin." Masterplots II: Nonfiction Series*. Pasadena: Salem Press, 1989.

_____. "Doubles/Don Juans: Anais Nin and Otto Rank." Hinz 81-94.

_____. "Dropping Another Veil." *Anais: An International Journal* 6 (1988): 27-32. On *H&J*.

_____. Foreword. *Anais Nin Reader*. Ed. Philip K. Jason. Chicago: Swallow Press, 1973. 1-8. Rpt. New York: Avon Books, 1974. 1-8.

_____. "The Future of Nin Criticism, A Review." *Journal of the Otto Rank Association* 7.1 (June 1972): 82-90. On Hinz.

_____. "The Gemor Press." *Anais: An International Journal* 2 (1984): 24-39.

_____. "Oscar Baradinsky's 'Outcasts': Henry Miller, Anais Nin, Maya Deren and The Alicat Book Shop Press." *Anais: An International Journal* 3 (1985): 109-16.

_____. "The Princess and the Frog: Anais Nin and Otto Rank." Spencer 13-22.

_____. "Teaching *A Spy in the House of Love*." *Under the Sign of Pisces: Anais Nin and Her Circle* 2.3 (Summer 1971): 7-15.

_____. "Warring Against Her Partisans." *Anais: An International Journal* 4 (1986): 123-126. On Scholar.

Jelinek, Estelle C. "Anais Nin: A Critical Evaluation." In *Feminist Criticism*. Ed. Cheryl L. Brown and Karen Olson. Metuchen, N.J.: Scarecrow Press, 1978. 312-23.

Jennings, Elizabeth. "New Novels." *Listener* 7 May 1964: 769. On *Collages*.

Johnson, Joyce. "Body and Soul: Anais Nin and Henry Miller," *Book World* 20 December 1987: 1-3. On *A Literate Passion*.

John-Steiner, Vera. "From Life to Diary to Art in the Work of Anais Nin." *Creative People at Work: Twelve Cognitive Case Studies*. Ed. Doris B. Wallace and Howard E. Gruber. New York: Oxford University Press, 1989. 210-25.

Jong, Erica. "A Story Never Told Before: Reading the New, Unexpurgated Diaries of Anais Nin," *Anais: An International Journal* 12 (1994): 15-25.

_____. "Donna Juana's Triumph," *Times Literary Supplement* 25 June 1993: 3-4.

Kamboureli, Smaro. "Discourse and Intercourse, Design and Desire in the Erotica of Anais Nin." *Journal of Modern Literature* 11.1 (March

1984): 143-58.

Karsten, Julie A. "Self-Realization and Intimacy: The Influence of D. H. Lawrence on Anais Nin." *Anais: An International Journal* 4 (1986): 36-42.

Kavaler-Adler. Susan. "Anais Nin and the Developmental Use of the Creative Process." *Psychoanalytic Review* 79.1 (Spring 1992): 73-88.

Keith, Kay. "*Ladders to Fire*." *San Francisco Chronicle* 8 Dec. 1946, "This World" sec.: 11.

Kennedy, J. Gerald. "Place, Self, and Writing." In *Imagining Paris: Exile, Writing, and American Identity*. New Haven: Yale University Press, 1993. See esp. 14-21. Material first appeared in *The Southern Review* 26.3 (Summer 1990): 496-516. Section on Nin 505-11.

Killoh, Ellen Peck. "The Woman Writer and the Element of Destruction." *College English* 34.1 (Oct. 1972): 31-38.

Kingery, Robert E. "New Books Appraised – Fiction." *Library Journal* 1 Jan. 1948: 40. On *Bell*.

Kirsch, Robert. "Anais Nin's Literary Labyrinth." *Los Angeles Times* 27 Apr. 1973, sec. 4: 14. On *Reader*.

Knapp, Bettina L. *Anais Nin*. New York: Ungar, 1978. (Some of the material from Knapp's chapter on *House* also appears as "Anais/Artaud – Alchemy" in Hinz 66-74.

_____. "The Diary as Art: Anais Nin, Thornton Wilder, Edmund Wilson." *World Literature Today* 61.2 (Spring 1987): 223-30.

_____. "*The Novel of the Future*." *The Village Voice* 10 Apr. 1969: 6-7.

_____. " 'To Reach Out Further Mystically...' Anais Nin." *Research Studies* 47.3 (Sept. 1979): 165-80. Rpt. in Spencer 65-85.

Korges, James. "Curiosities: Nin and Miller, Hemingway and Seager." *Critique: Studies in Modern Fiction* 7.3 (Spring-Summer 1965): 66-81.

Kraft, Barbara. "Lux Aeterna Anais: A Memoir." *Seahorse: The Anais Nin/Henry Miller Journal* 2.2, 2.3, and 2.4 (1983): 1-5, 1-7, and 6-16.

Krizan, Kim. "Illusion and the Art of Survival." *Anais: An International Journal* 10 (1992): 18-28.

Kubasak, Sharon. "Doing the Limbo with Woolf and Nin: On Writer's Block." *Centennial Review* 32.4 (Fall 1988): 372-87.

Kuntz, Paul Grimley. "Anais Nin's 'Quest for Order.' " Hinz 203-212.

_____. "Art as Public Dream: The Practice and Theory of Anais Nin." *Journal of Aesthetics and Art Criticism* 32 (Summer 1974): 525-37. Rpt. in Zaller 77-99.

Lang, Violet R. Rev. of *Under a Glass Bell* and *Children of the Albatross*. *Chicago Review* 2.4 (Spring 1948): 162-63.

Lawlor, Patricia. "Beyond Gender and Genre: Writing the Labyrinth of the Selves." *Anais: An International Journal* 7 (1989): 23-31.

Legman, Gershon. "The Erotica of Henry Miller and Anais Nin." *Under the Sign of Pisces: Anais Nin and Her Circle* 12.3-4 (Summer/Fall 1981): 9-18.

_____. Introduction. *The Private Case: An Annotated Bibliography of the Private Case Erotica Collection in the British Library*. Comp. Patrick J. Kearney. London: Jay Landesman Ltd., 1981. 11-59.

Lieberman, E. James. *Acts of Will: The Life and Works of Otto Rank*. New York: Free Press, 1985.

Lyons, Herbert. "Surrealist Soap Opera." *New York Times Book Review* 20 Oct. 1946: 16. On *Ladders*.

Lytle, Andrew. "Impressionism, the Ego, and the First Person." *Daedalus* 92 (Spring 1963): 281-296. On *Cities*, p. 285.

McEvilly, Wayne. "The Two Faces of Death in Anais Nin's *Seduction of the Minotaur*." *New Mexico Quarterly* 38 (Winter-Spring 1969): 179-192. Rpt. as "Afterword" to the fourth and later Swallow printings of the novel and in Zaller 51-64.

_____. "Portrait of Anais Nin as a Bodhisattva: Reflections on the *Diary, 1934-39*." *Studies in the Twentieth Century* 2 (Fall 1968): 51-60.

_____. "The Bread of Tradition: Reflections on the Diary of Anais Nin." *Prairie Schooner* 45 (Summer 1971): 161-67.

_____. "A Map of Music – Strange Dimensions of Politics and War." Spencer 126-33.

McLaughlin, Richard. "Shadow Dance." *Saturday Review* 20 Dec. 1947: 16-17. On *Children*.

MacNiven, Ian S. "Criticism and Personality: Lawrence Durrell – Anais Nin." *Anais: An International Journal* 2 (1984): 95-100.

_____. "A Room in the House of Art: The Friendship of Anais Nin and Lawrence Durrell." Hinz 37-58.

Marcinczyk, Reese. "A Checklist of the Writings of Anais Nin, 1973-1976." *Under the Sign of Pisces: Anais Nin and Her Circle* 8.1 (Winter 1977): 2-14.

Margoshes, Adam. *"Seduction of the Minotaur." Village Voice* 10 May 1962: 5-6.

Martin, Jay. *Always Merry and Bright: The Life of Henry Miller*. Santa Barbara: Capra Press, 1978.

Martin, Jex, Jr. "Modern Version of Old Fable: Woman Loses Femininity When She Enters Man's World." *Chicago Sun Book Week* 17 Nov. 1946: 14. On *Ladders*.

Mathieu, Bertrand. "On the Trail of Euridice." *Anais: An International Journal* 10 (1992): 63-76.

Méral, Jean. "Cities of the Interior." *Paris in American Literature*. Trans. Laurette Long. Chapel Hill: The University Press of North Carolina, 1989.

Merchant, Hoshang. "Out of and into the Labyrinth: Approaching the Aesthetics of Anais Nin." *Anais: An International Journal* 8 (1990): 51-59.

Metzger, Deena. "The *Diary*: The Ceremony of Knowing." Zaller 133-43.

Miller, Dennis R. *"Delta of Venus*: Sex from Female Perspectives." *Seahorse:*

The Anais Nin/Henry Miller Journal 1.4 (1982): 6-11.

———. "Glimpsing a Goddess: Some Thoughts on the Final *Diary*." *Anais: An International Journal* 3 (1985): 102-08.

Miller, Henry. "Letter to William A. Bradley, Literary Agent." *Sunday After the War*. Norfolk, Conn.: New Directions, 1944. 276-84.

———. "On *House of Incest*: A 'Foreword' and a 'Review.' " *Anais: An International Journal* 5 (1987): 111-14.

———. "Scenario." *The Cosmological Eye*. Norfolk, Conn.: New Directions, 1939. 75-106.

———. "To Anais Nin Regarding One of Her Books." *Circle* 1.2 (1944): n. pag. Rpt. in *Sunday After the War*. Norfolk, Conn.: New Directions, 1944. 284-97.

———. "Un Etre Etoilique." *The Criterion* 17 (Oct. 1937): 35-52. Rpt. in *The Phoenix* 1 (June-Aug. 1938): 67-94. First collected in *The Cosmological Eye*. Norfolk, Conn.: New Directions, 1939, 269-91. Also in Zaller 5-23.

Miller, Margaret. "Diary-Keeping and the Young Wife." *Anais: An International Journal* 3 (1985): 39-44.

———. "Seduction and Subversion in *The Diary of Anais Nin*." *Anais: An International Journal* 1 (1983): 86-90.

Millett, Kate. "Anais – A Mother to Us All: The Birth of the Artist as Woman." *Anais: An International Journal* 9 (1991): 3-8.

Molyneux, Maxine, and Julia Casterton. "Looking Again at Anais Nin." *Minnesota Review* 18 (Spring 1982): 86-101.

Moore, Harry T. Introduction. *D. H. Lawrence: An Unprofessional Study*, by Anais Nin. Denver: Alan Swallow, 1964. 7-14.

Mudrick, Marvin. "Humanity is the Principle." *Hudson Review* 7.4 (Winter 1955): 610-19. On *Spy*.

Nalbantian, Suzanne. "Into the House of Myth." *Anais: An International Journal* 11 (1993): 12-15.

———. "The Mythification of Selfhood in Anais Nin." *Aesthetic Autobiography: From Life to Art in Marcel Proust, James Joyce, Virginia Woolf, and Anais Nin*. New York: St. Martin's Press, 1994.

Niemeyer, Doris. "How to Be a Woman and/or an Artist: The Diary as an Instrument of Self-Therapy." Trans. Gunther Stuhlmann. *Anais: An International Journal* 6 (1988): 67-74.

"Nin, Anais." *Current Biography* (Feb. 1944): 493-95. Rpt. in Nin's *Realism and Reality*.

Nin, Anais, and Henry Miller. *A Literate Passion: Letters of Anais Nin and Henry Miller, 1932-1953*. Ed. Gunther Stuhlmann. San Diego: Harcourt Brace Jovanovich, 1987.

Norse, Harold. *Memoirs of a Bastard Angel*. New York: William Morrow, 1989.

"Not to Need, but To Be Needed." *Times Literary Supplement* 12 May 1972: 552. On *Diary* 4.

Oliveira, Ubiratan Paiva de. *"A Spy in the House of Love*: An Introduction to Anais Nin." *Ilha do Desterro* 14.2 (1985): 71-81.

Paine, Sylvia. *Beckett, Nabokov, Nin: Motives and Modernism*. Port Washington, N.Y.: Kennikat Press, 1981.

Papachristou, Sophia. "The Body in the Diary: On Anais Nin's First Erotic Writings." *Anais: An International Journal* 9 (1991): 58-66.

Pétrequin, Marie-Line. "The Magic Spell of June Miller: On the Literary Creation of Female Identity in Anais Nin's *Diary*." Trans. Gunther Stuhlmann. *Anais: An International Journal* 6 (1988): 43-57.

Perlès, Alfred. "Fathers, Daughters and Lovers." *Purpose* 12.1 (Jan.-Mar. 1940): 45-48. On *Winter*.

Pierpont, Claudia Roth. "Anais Nin's 'Journal of Love,' " *The New Yorker*, 1 March 1993, 74-90.

Pineau, Elyse Lamm. "A Mirror of Her Own: Anais Nin's Autobiographical Performances." *Text and Performance Quarterly* 12.1 (Apr. 1992): 98-112.

____. "The Performing Self: An Alternative Reading of *Seduction of the Minotaur*." *Anais: An International Journal* 12 (1994): 65-73.

Podnieks, Elizabeth. "The Theater of 'Incest.' " *Anais: An International Journal* 13 (1995): 39-52.

Pollitt, Katha. "Apologia Ended." *New York Times Book Review*, 13 July 1980: 7. Rev. of *Diary VII*.

Potts, Margaret Lee. "The Genesis and Evolution of the Creative Personality: A Rankian Analysis of *The Diary of Anais Nin*." *Journal of the Otto Rank Association* 9.2 (Winter 1974-75): 1-37.

"Private View." *Times Literary Supplement* 16 Mar. 1962: 186. On *Lawrence*.

Rainer, Tristine. "Anais Nin's *Diary I*: The Birth of the Young Woman as an Artist." Zaller 161-68.

Rank, Otto. "Preface to *House of Incest*." *Anais: An International Journal* 3 (1985): 49-54. First published in *Journal of the Otto Rank Association* 7.2 (Dec. 1972): 68-74.

____. "Reflections on the Diary of a Child." *Journal of the Otto Rank Association* 7.2 (Dec. 1972): 61-67.

____. "Feminine Psychology and Masculine Ideology." *Beyond Psychology*. Philadelphia: E. Hauser, 1941. Rpt. New York: Dover, 1958. 235-70.

Rev. of *Under a Glass Bell and Other Stories*. New York *Herald Tribune Weekly Book Review* 21 Nov. 1948: 33.

Riberia i Goreriz, Nuria. "Proust, Rimbaud, and the Surrealists: On the Development of Anais Nin's Artistic Theories." *Anais: An International Journal* 12 (1994): 44-55.

Richard-Allerdyce, Diane. "Anais Nin's Mothering Metaphor: Toward a Lacanian Theory of Feminine Creativity." *Compromise Formations: Current Directions in Psychoanalytic Criticism*. Ed. Vera J. Camden. Kent, Ohio: Kent State University Press, 1989.

____. "Narrative and Authenticity – The *Diary* Now and Then." *Anais: An*

International Journal 13 (1995): 79-83.

Rock, Joanne. "Her Father's Daughter: Re-Evaluating an Incestuous Relationship." *Anais: An International Journal* 13 (1995): 29-38.

Roditi, Edouard. "On Proust and Pierre-Quint." *Anais: An International Journal* 7 (1989): 95-101.

Rolo, Charles. "The Life of the Heart." *Atlantic* (Feb. 1950): 86-87. On *Heart*.

_____. "Potpourri." *Atlantic* (Aug. 1954): 86. On *Spy*.

Roof, Judith. "The Erotic Travelogue: The Scopophilic Pleasure of Race vs. Gender." *Arizona Quarterly* 47.4 (Winter 1991): 119-35.

Root, Waverley Lewis. "The Femininity of D. H. Lawrence Emphasized by Woman Writer." *Chicago Daily Tribune* (European edition) 28 Mar. 1932: 2. Rpt. as "Literary Sexism in Action" in *Anais: An International Journal* 6 (1988): 75-76.

Rosenblatt, Jon. "Anais Nin's Allegories." *Under the Sign of Pisces: Anais Nin and Her Circle* 10.4 (Fall 1979): 8-12.

Rosenfeld, Isaac. "The Eternal Feminine." *New Republic* 17 Apr. 1944: 541. On *Bell*.

_____. "Psychoanalysis as Literature." *New Republic* 17 Dec. 1945: 844-45. On *This Hunger*.

Rosenfeld, Paul. "Refinements on a Journal: *Winter of Artifice* by Anais Nin." *The Nation* 26 Sept. 1942): 276-77.

Sagulo, Veronica Park. "The Italian Response: How the Critics Dealt with Anais Nin's Work." *Anais: An International Journal* 6 (1988): 111-17.

Salber, Linde. "Two Lives – One Experiment: Lou Andreas-Salomé and Anais Nin." Trans. Gunther Stuhlmann. *Anais: An International Journal* 9 (1991): 78-91.

_____. "Life As Provocation: On Writing a Biography of Anais Nin." Trans. Gunther Stuhlmann. *Anais: An International Journal* 12 (1994): 26-30.

_____. *Anais Nin*. Hamburg: Rowohlt, 1992.

Sayre, Gary. "*House of Incest*: Two Interpretations." Spencer 45-58.

Schneider, Duane. "Anais Nin in the *Diary*: The Creation and Development of a Persona." Hinz 9-19.

_____. "The Art of Anais Nin." *Southern Review* 6.2 new series (Apr. 1970): 506-514. Rpt. in Zaller 43-50.

_____. "The Duane Schneider Press and Anais Nin." *Under the Sign of Pisces: Anais Nin and Her Circle* 4.1 (Winter 1973): 5-9.

Scholar, Nancy. *Anais Nin*. Boston: Twayne, 1984.

_____. "Anais Nin Under a Glass Bell." *Michigan Quarterly Review* 20.3 (Summer 1981): 308-12.

_____. "Anais Nin's *House of Incest* and Ingmar Bergman's *Persona*: Two Variations on a Theme." *Literature/Film Quarterly* 7.1 (1979): 47-59. Rpt. in Spencer.

_____. "A Checklist of Nin Materials at Northwestern University Library."

Under the Sign of Pisces: Anais Nin and Her Circle 3.2 (Spring 1972): 3-11. (As Nancy Scholar Zee).

Schwichtenberg, Cathy. "Erotica: The Semey Side of Semiotics." *Sub-Stance* 32 (1981): 26-38.

Secrest, Meryle. "Economics and the Need for Revenge." *Anais: An International Journal* 6 (1988): 33-35.

Seybert, Gislinde. "Between Love and Passion: Some Notes on the Physical in 'Henry & June.' " Trans. Gunther Stuhlmann. *Anais: An International Journal* 9 (1991): 67-74.

Shapiro, Karl. "The Charmed Circle of Anais Nin." *Book Week* 1 May 1966: 3. On *Diary* 1.

Smith, Harrison. "Ladies in Turmoil." *Saturday Review* 30 Nov. 1946: 13.

Snitow, Ann. "Women's Private Writings: Anais Nin." *Notes from the Third Year*. New York: n.p., 1971. Rpt. in *Radical Feminism*. Ed. Anne Koedt, Ellen Levine, and Anita Rapone. New York: Quadrangle Books, 1973. 413-18.

Snyder, Robert. *Anais Nin Observed*. Chicago: Swallow Press, 1976.

Spacks, Patricia Meyer. "Free Women." *Hudson Review* 24.4 (Winter 1971-72): 559-73.

Spencer, Sharon. "Anais Nin." *Critical Survey of Short Fiction*. Englewood Cliffs, N.J.: Salem Press, 1981.

_____. "Anais Nin." *Critical Survey of Long Fiction*. Englewood Cliffs, N.J.: Salem Press, 1983.

_____. "Anais Nin: A Heroine for Our Time" *Journal of the Otto Rank Association* 12.1 (Summer 1977): 1-13.

_____. "Anais Nin's 'Continuous Novel': *Cities of the Interior*." Zaller 65-76.

_____. "The Art of Collage in Anais Nin's Writings." *Studies in the 20th Century* 16 (Fall 1975): 1-11.

_____. "*Cities of the Interior*: Femininity and Freedom." *Under the Sign of Pisces: Anais Nin and Her Circle*. 7.3 (Summer 1976): 9-16.

_____. *Collage of Dreams*. Chicago: Swallow, 1977. Expanded edition, New York: Harcourt Brace Jovanovich, 1981.

_____. "Delivering the Woman Artist from the Silence of the Womb: Otto Rank's Influence on Anais Nin." *The Psychoanalytic Review* 69.1 (Spring 1982): 111-29.

_____. "The Dream of Twinship in the Writings of Anais Nin." *Journal of the Otto Rank Association* 9.2 (Winter 1974-75): 81-90.

_____. "The Feminine Self: Anais Nin." *American Journal of Psychoanalysis* 50.1 (Mar. 1990): 57-62.

_____. " 'Femininity' and the Woman Writer: Doris Lessing's *The Golden Notebook* and the *Diary* of Anais Nin." *Women's Studies* 1 (1973): 247-57.

_____. Introduction. *Cities of the Interior*, by Anais Nin. Chicago: Swallow Press, 1974. x-xx.

_____. "The Music of the Womb: Anais Nin's 'Feminine' Writing." *Breaking*

the Sequence: Women's Experimental Fiction. Ed. Ellen G. Friedman
and Miriam Fuchs. Princeton, N.J.: Princeton University Press, 1989.
161-73.

_____. "A Novel Triangle: Anais Nin – Henry Miller – Otto Rank." *Journal
of the Otto Rank Association* 14.2 (Winter 1979-80): 7-16

_____. *Space, Time, and Structure in the Modern Novel*. New York: New York
University Press, 1971. Rpt. Chicago: Swallow Press, 1974.

_____, ed. *Anais, Art and Artists, a Collection of Essays*. Greenwood, Fla.:
Penkevil, 1986.

Stern, Daniel. "The Diary of Anais Nin." *Studies in the Twentieth Century* 2
(Fall 1968): 39-43. The material here is almost identical with that in
Stern's review, "Princess of the Underground," printed in *The Na-
tion* 4 Mar. 1968: 311-13.

_____. "The Novel of Her Life: *The Diary of Anais Nin, Volume IV, 1944-
1946*." *The Nation* 29 Nov. 1971: 570-72. Rpt. in Zaller 153-56.

Stimpson, Catharine R. "Authority and Absence: Women Write on Men."
Confrontation 7 (Fall 1973): 81-91.

Stone, Albert E. "Becoming a Woman in Male America: Margaret Mead and
Anais Nin." *Autobiographical Occasions and Original Acts: Versions
of American Identity from Henry Adams to Nate Shaw*. Philadelphia:
University of Pennsylvania Press, 1982. 190-230.

Stone, Jerome. "Fiction Note: The Psyche of the Huntress." *Saturday Review*
15 May 1954: 32. On *Spy*.

Struck, Karin. "Logbook of Liberation." Trans. Gunther Stuhlmann. *Anais:
An International Journal* 6 (1988): 36-42.

"Stuff of Dreams." *Times Literary Supplement* 16 June 1961: 369. On *Seduction*.

Stuhlmann, Gunther. "Edward Titus Et Al." *Anais: An International Journal*
7 (1989): 113-18.

_____. "The Genesis of 'Alraune' – Some notes on the making of *House of
Incest*." *Anais: An International Journal* 5 (1987): 115-23.

_____. "Into Another Language: Some Notes on Anais Nin's Work in Trans-
lation." *Anais: An International Journal* 1 (1983): 120-36.

_____. "Léon Pierre-Quint: Mastering the Art of Marcel Proust." *Anais: An
International Journal* 6 (1988): 123-24.

_____. "What Did They Say? Writings about Anais Nin – An Informal Sur-
vey." *Anais: An International Journal* 1 (1983): 91-105.

_____. "Years of Friendship: Correspondence with Caresse Crosby, 1941-
1970." *Anais: An International Journal* 2 (1984): 40-58.

_____. "Discretion and Revelation: The Difficulties of a Secret Life: Anais
Nin at Ninety." *Anais: An International Journal* 11 (1993): 119-24.

_____. "From 'Jim' to 'Jamie': Tracing a Friendship in Anais Nin's *Diary*."
Anais: An International Journal 12 (1994): 120-24.

Sugisaki, Kazuko. "The Dream and the Stage: A Study of the Dream in Anais
Nin's Fiction and in Japanese Noh Drama." Spencer 87-99. Rpt. in

Anais: An International Journal 6 (1988): 77-85.

Sukenick, Lynn. "Anais Nin: The Novel of Vision." Zaller 157-60.

_____. "The *Diaries* of Anais Nin." *Shenandoah* 17.3 (Spring 1976): 96-103.

Tibbetts, Robert A. "The Text of *On Writing*." *Under the Sign of Pisces: Anais Nin and Her Circle* 4.3 (Summer 1973): 1-7.

_____. "*A Spy in the House of Love*: A Note on the First Printings." *Under the Sign of Pisces: Anais Nin and Her Circle* 8.3 (Summer 1977): 1-4.

Trilling, Diana. "Fiction in Review." *The Nation* 26 Jan. 1946: 105-107. On *This Hunger*. Collected in her *Reviewing the Forties*. New York: Harcourt Brace Jovanovich, 1978. 143-47.

Tytell, John. "Anais Nin and 'The Fall of the House of Usher.'" *Under the Sign of Pisces: Anais Nin and Her Circle* 2.1 (Winter 1971): 5-11.

_____. *Passionate Lives: D. H. Lawrence, F. Scott Fitsgerald, Henry Miller, Dylan Thomas, Sylvia Plath — in Love*. Secaucus, N.J.: Carol Publications, 1991. Rpt. New York: St. Martin's, 1995.

"*Under a Glass Bell and Other Stories*." *Virginia Kirkus Service* 15 Dec. 1947: 678.

Van der Elst, Marie-Claire. "The Birth of a Vocation." Spencer 5-11.

_____. "The Manuscripts of Anais Nin at Northwestern University." Hinz 59-63.

_____. "The Recognition of AN in France: A Selective Bibliography." *Under the Sign of Pisces: Anais Nin and Her Circle* 2.2 (Spring 1971): 10-12.

Vidal, Gore. "Taking a Grand Tour of Anais Nin's High Bohemia Via the Time Machine." *Los Angeles Times Book Review* 26 Sept. 1971: 1+. Rpt. as "The Fourth Diary of Anais Nin" in *Homage to Daniel Shays: Collected Essays 1952-1972*. New York: Random House, 1972. 403-09.

Waddington, Miriam. "Review of Anais Nin's *The Novel of the Future*." *Journal of the Otto Rank Association* 4.1 (June 1969): 54-60.

Wakoski, Diane. "The Craft of Plumbers, Carpenters & Mechanics: A Tribute to Anais Nin." *American Poetry Review* (Jan.-Feb.1973): 46-47. Rpt. as "A Tribute to Anais Nin" in Zaller 145-52.

Watson, Fred. "Allegories in 'Ragtime': Balance, Growth, Disintegration." *Under the Sign of Pisces: Anais Nin and Her Circle* 7.2 (Spring 1976): 1-5.

West, Paul. "D. H. Lawrence: Mystical Critic." *Southern Review* NS 1 (Jan. 1965): 210-28.

Wickes, George. *Americans in Paris, 1903-1939*. New York: Paris Review Editions/Doubleday, 1969.

Williams, William Carlos. " 'Men . . . Have No Tenderness': Anais Nin's 'Winter of Artifice.' " *New Directions No. 7*. Ed. James Laughlin. Norfolk, Conn.: New Directions, 1942. 429-36.

Wilson, Edmund. "Doubts and Dreams: *Dangling Man* and *Under a Glass Bell*." *The New Yorker* 1 Apr. 1944: 70, 73-4. Section on *Bell* rpt. in Zaller 3-4.

_____. "Books – Isherwood – Marquand – Anais Nin." *New Yorker* 10 Nov.
       1945: 97-101. On *This Hunger*.

_____. "Books – A Note on Anais Nin." *New Yorker* 26 Nov. 1946: 114. On
       Ladders.

Wolcott, James. "Life Among the Ninnies." *New York Review of Books* 26
       June 1980: 21. On *Diary 7*.

Wood, Lori A. "Between Creation and Destruction: Toward a New Concept
       of the Female Artist." *Anais: An International Journal* 8 (1990): 15-
       26.

Young, Marguerite. Rev. of *Anais Nin Reader. New York Woman* Sept. 1973:
       12.

Young, Vernon. "Five Novels, Three Sexes, and Death." *Hudson Review* 1.3
       (Fall 1948): 421-32. On *Bell*

Zaller, Robert. "Anais Nin and the Truth of Feeling." *Arts and Society* 10.2
       (Summer 1973): 308-12. Rpt. in Zaller 177-83.

_____, ed. *A Casebook on Anais Nin*. New York: NAL/Meridian, 1974.

Zinnes, Harriet. "Anais Nin's Works Reissued." *Books Abroad* 37.3 (Sum-
       mer 1963): 283-86. Rpt. as "The Fiction of Anais Nin" in Zaller 35-
       41.

_____. "Reading Anais Nin." *Carleton Miscellany* 14 (Fall-Winter 1973): 124-
       26. On *Reader*.

Index

Allendy, René, 31, 32, 157, 158-59, 162, 179, 209
Anaïs: An International Journal, 6
Anais Observed, 46
Artaud, Antonin, 46, 155, 157, 179, 209, 225

Bair, Deirdre, 3, 4
Balakian, Anna, 2, 4, 53, 190
Baldanza, Frank, 2, 4, 9
Barnes, Djuna, 64, 77, 106, 109, 122
Barillé, Elisabeth, 3
Bashkirtseff, Marie, 68
"The Basque and the Bijou," 92, 99
"Birth," 14-15, 76, 77, 79
Bloom, Lynn, 191, 192
Bobbitt (McLaughlin), Joan, 3, 5, 190
Bogner, Inge, 32
Boyle, Kay, 73
Brennan, Karen, 2
Brians, Paul, 5, 118
Broughton, James, 3
Burford, William, 4

Casteron, Julia, 3, 215, 248
Centing, Richard, 6
Children of the Albatross, 21, 22-23, 78, 112, 113, 134
Cities of the Interior (*Cities*), 65, 9, 10, 22, 56, 59-60, 111-12, 117, 119, 123, 133-45

Collages, 63-64, 111
Cutting, Rose Marie, 6

D. H. Lawrence: An Unprofessional Study, 1, 156
Deduck, Patricia A., 4
Demetrakopoulos (Gauper), Stephanie A., 5, 6, 29, 191
Delta of Venus, 2, 90-103, 194, 231
Diaries 68-69, 121, 147-54
The Diary of Anais Nin, 87,121, 161-71, 172-77, 178-90, 190-98, 199, 216-24, 236-47
    Vol. I, 31, 47-49, 58-59, 155-58, 162, 174, 180-81, 190, 194, 200-02
    Vol. II, 31, 34, 40, 48, 55, 58-59, 90, 163, 181-83, 192, 194
    Vol. III, 32, 92-93, 163, 183-84, 192, 219, 230
    Vol. IV, 59, 161-71, 185, 186, 190, 192, 193, 195, 217, 219, 236
    Vol. V, 32-33, 186-87, 192
    Vol. VI, 34, 187-88, 193, 195
    Vol. VII, 196-97, 233
Don Juan, 118, 120, 127
DuBow, Wendy M., 3
Duchamp, Marcel, 26, 36, 128
Durrell, Lawrence, 9, 24, 34, 40, 58, 181

The Early Diary of Anais Nin, 193, 199, 200
Electra complex, 57
"Elena," 94-95, 96-97, 98
erotica, 89-103, 230-31
Evans, Oliver, 2, 3, 4, 17, 192

Fire, 4
Fitch, Noël Riley, 3
The Four-Chambered Heart, 6, 10, 23-24, 26, 33-36, 38, 106-07, 113-17, 128, 134
Franklin, Benjamin, V, 3, 6, 80 96, 241
Freud, Sigmund, 5, 18, 32, 102, 133-43 passim
Fülop-Miller, René, 106

Gauper, (see Demetrakopoulos)
Gautier, Théophile, 118-32
Geismar, Maxwell, 5, 107, 186, 233, 236
Gilbert, Stuart, 4, 67
Great Mother archetype, 29-44 passim
Guiler, Hugh, (see Ian Hugo)

"Hejda," 18-19
Hellman, Lillian, 158-60
Henke, Suzette A., 5, 133
Henry and June, 3, 199-204, 207-09, 211
Hinz, Evelyn J., 2, 3, 5, 161, 237, 240-42
Holder, Orlee, 191, 192
House of Incest, 5, 12-13, 56-57, 64, 67-68, 106, 123
"Houseboat," 14, 80-88
Hugo, Ian, 10, 13, 17, 69, 77, 194, 195, 202-03, 211-13, 244

In Favor of the Sensitive Man and Other Essays, 49
Incest, 3, 209-14

Jason, Philip K., 199
"Je Suis le Plus Malades des Surrea-listes," 77
Jelinek, Estelle C., 5, 45
Jong, Erica, 2, 118, 205
Journal of the Otto Rank Assocation, 6
Joyce, James, 9, 18, 27, 213
Jung, C. G., 5, 29ff, 39, 41

Kamboureli, Smaro, 2, 89
Killoh, Ellen P., 191
Knapp, Bettina L., 3, 5
Korges, James, 5, 111

"The Labyrinth," 79
Ladders to Fire, 10-11, 27, 45, 105-06, 119, 122-23, 134-36
Lang, Violet R., 77
Lawrence, D. H., 1, 12, 19, 46, 77, 94, 102, 108, 121, 153, 165, 172, 184
"Life on the Seine," 81-87 passim
"Linda," 96
Linotte: The Early Diary of Anais Nin, 193, 200, 236
Little Birds, 2, 89-103
Luria-Sukenick, Lynn, 3, 5, 172
Lyons, Herbert, 105

"Mandra," 93-94
"Marcel," 94
"Mathilde," 98, 100
"The Maya," 101
McLaughlin, (see Bobbitt)
Miller, Henry, 3, 4, 9, 12, 13, 15, 16, 19, 34, 40, 46, 58, 77, 91, 99, 106, 112, 121, 147, 155-57, 159, 162, 179-82, 192, 200-04, 207-09, 211-13, 218, 225
"A Model," 94, 98, 101
Molyneux, Maxine, 3, 215, 248
"The Mouse," 14, 76, 79
Mudrick, Marvin, 5, 108
music, 57 ff
The Mystic of Sex and Other Writings,

7n

Nalbantian, Suzanne, 6

Nin, Anais
    works by, see individual titles
    interview with, 6-24

Nin, Joaquin, 9, 155, 209-10

"Notes on Feminism,' 48, 49

The Novel of the Future, 2, 6, 68, 120,
    121, 178, 218

On Writing, 2, 112

Perlès, Alfred, 4, 181

Pierpont, Claudia Roth, 3

"Pierre," 102

Pineau, Elyse Lamm, 3, 233

pornography, see erotica

Potts, Margaret Lee, 5

Proust, Marcel, 18, 27, 147, 148, 213

"The Queen," 95

"Rag Time," 76, 79

Rank, Otto, 5, 7, 19, 32, 40, 46, 121,
    133, 157-58, 159, 202, 209, 212,
    225

Realism and Reality, 2, 18, 112

Robbe-Grillet, Alain, 4

Roof, Judith, 2

Root, Waverley, 1

Rosenfeld, Isaac, 1, 5, 76

Rosenfeld, Paul, 2, 68

Salvatore, Anne, 6

Sartre, Jean Paul, 24

Schneider, Duane, 3, 5, 178, 191

Scholar, Nancy, 3, 5

Schwichtenberg, Cathy, 2

*Seahorse: The Anaïs Nin/Henry
    Miller Journal*, 6

Seduction of the Minotaur, 6, 10-11,
    12, 15, 21-22, 25-26, 27, 60-63,
    123, 136-45

Shapiro, Karl, 154

Snitow, Ann, 52

Snyder, Robert, 46

Solar Barque
    see *Seduction of the Minotaur*

Spacks, Patricia Meyer, 158

Spencer, Sharon, 2, 3, 5, 6, 55

A Spy in the House of Love, 6, 11-12,
    45, 107-10, 118-32, 134, 174, 227

"Stella," 13

Stuhlmann, Gunther, 6, 87, 155, 178,
    196

Sukenick, (see Luria-Sukenick)

Swallow, Alan, 5, 9, 27

This Hunger, 4

Trilling, Diana, 4, 167-68, 245

"Two Sisters," 98

Under a Glass Bell, 14, 17, 18, 76-79,
    80, 113, 167, 183

"Under a Glass Bell," 76

*Under the Sign of Pisces: Anaïs Nin
    and Her Circle*, 6

Varda, Jean, 46, 169

Vidal, Gore, 4, 20, 34, 196

"The Voice," 13-14, 70, 71, 74, 202

Williams, William Carlos, 2, 24, 70,
    77

Wilson, Edmund, 4, 5, 24, 75, 106,
    168-69, 183, 196, 224

Winter of Artifice, 13, 31, 68-69, 70-75

"Winter of Artifice," 13, 31, 56-58,
    68-69, 70, 71-75, 78

A Woman Speaks, 32, 234

Woolf, Virginia, 14, 18, 36, 58, 73,
    76, 141, 176, 205, 206, 214, 215,
    229

Wright, Lloyd, 169

Zaller, Robert, 4, 6, 191

Zinnes, Harriet, 193

About the Editor

PHILIP K. JASON is Professor of English at the United States Naval Academy. His books include the *Anais Nin Reader* (1973), *Nineteenth Century American Poetry* (1989), the *Creative Writer's Handbook* (1990), and *Anais Nin and Her Critics* (1993), while his articles have appeared in such journals as *Critique, College English, South Atlantic Review, Mosaic,* and *Anais: An International Journal.*